Modernizing
the
Mountaineer

Modernizing
the
Mountaineer

People, Power,
and Planning
in Appalachia

David E. Whisnant

THE UNIVERSITY OF TENNESSEE PRESS

KNOXVILLE

Originally published by the Appalachian Consortium Press, 1980.

The paper in this book meets the minimum requirements of the American National Standard for Permanence of Paper for Printed Library Materials. ∞   The binding materials have been chosen for strength and durability.

Library of Congress Cataloging in Publication Data

Whisnant, David E., 1938-
        Modernizing the mountaineer: people, power, and planning
in Appalachia / by David E. Whisnant.—Rev. ed.
                    p.   cm.
        Includes bibliographical references and index.
        ISBN 0-87049-823-1 (pbk: alk. pa.)
        1. Appalachian Region—Economic policy.   I. Title.
HC107.A127W48   1994
338.974—dc20   93-37800
                                                  CIP

Contents

Part III: Reactions and Alternatives

Preface

I SHOULD BEGIN by telling how this book came to be. I was born and raised in the Blue Ridge Mountains of western North Carolina, which have kept their hold on me through my more than twenty years of being away. I felt their hold quite early in life, but have been long years coming to understand it. I began to understand, in fact, only after a period of alienation and exile such as has been experienced by hundreds of thousands of other Appalachian out-migrants. Writing this book has been a major part of my quest for understanding.

At one level, therefore, the book is an artifact of one person's political and cultural education, a record of an attempt to come to terms with the complex history of both self and region, neither of which can be distinguished entirely from the other. The problem of description has at every point proved inseparable from the problem of *relation*. And because relation, as both fact of my birth and continuing process, has shaped my point of view, it is only fair that it also should be described.

I lived in the mountains until I was eighteen—not in a coal camp or a remote hollow but in a well-kept village owned by one of the first large chemical industries to bring what I only gradually came to see as a mixed kind of progress to the region. Thus one of my earliest memories is of seeing a once clear stream near my home run sluggishly with its burden of chemical waste, and of smelling carbon disulfide in the air twenty-four hours a day. But another early awareness was that my father had a better job, and I a more privileged life, than most of my friends in our county grade school. We were lower middle class, but middle class nevertheless, and it would be years before I began to come to terms with the implications of that central fact.

At eighteen I left the mountains for Georgia Tech to learn to be an engineer, paying my way by working alternate terms at the plant that was still fouling the air and water. But I don't recall thinking much about the contradictions. I studied diligently, did well, and ultimately would have joined my classmates in a job at North American Rockwell, Dow Chemical, or Standard Oil but for one almost chance happening. I began to read rather randomly from a list of books an English professor handed me at the end of one term: William James's *The Varieties of Religious Experience*, Alexis de Tocqueville's *Democracy in America*, Thorstein Veblen's *Theory of the Leisure Class*, Wilbur Cash's *The Mind of the South*, Thomas Wolfe, Henry Adams, Alfred North Whitehead, Theodore Dreiser, David Riesman's *The Lonely Crowd*, and many others. That reading, I now recognize, began to call everything into question.

As I hitchhiked from Atlanta to Asheville, North Carolina, every three months to my job, I began to see things I had not seen before: that blacks worked in the plant only as maids and janitors, that women did much of the work for which male executives took credit, that hundreds of workers were breathing dilute sulfuric acid year after year from the open spinning troughs. The relative ease and security of my own childhood had been dearly bought. That both were also elusive I learned one Monday morning when my father lost the job he had had for twenty-seven years. The trauma surrounding that event provided a concrete grounding for the still-abstract critique of the system I was acquiring from my reading.

And yet, so durable is conditioning and so obscure the real alternatives that it was to be about another decade before I was able to act significantly on what I was learning. My life in the meantime was a series of never more than partially successful attempts to resolve the tension between doing what I had been taught to do, and been told was worth doing, and trying to find what my compatriot Thomas Wolfe would have called my lost self—the authentic self that was struggling to be born out of my own resources and meandering self-education. And not only to be born but to find work worth doing. Viewed unsympathetically, the process could be seen as a protracted and merely personal identity crisis. Viewed more broadly, it was a particular manifestation of a dilemma based in the very structure of American life, and felt with special acuteness by Appalachian out-migrants.

As I came to realize that one of the costs of my "privileged" youth was cultural alienation, my belated political education began to be paralleled by a more or less simultaneous exploration of my cultural origins and of the multileveled significance of having been born and raised in an exploited region. One of the many tests of capacity for upward mobility I had passed, after all, besides accepting one of the several relatively indistinguishable life plans offered me, was a willingness to undergo cultural stripping. I had sold newspapers and bagged groceries to earn my city–high school tuition, rejected the late-night country-music programs from WSM in favor of "serious" music, and donned an ill-fitting borrowed tuxedo to usher at the spring performances of the Metropolitan Opera in Atlanta. But there remained always an ambivalence, a vague sense of self-betrayal, and a suspicion that I was buying a mess of pottage.

Nevertheless, between my eighteenth and thirty-fourth years I was out of the region more than I was in it—politically and culturally as well as physically—and continued to be a beneficiary of many of the institutions (especially foundations and universities) that were reinforcing its inequitable political and social system. During that time my entire experience communicated to me that most of the conventional rewards in life were destined to flow to atomistic, mobile people, and that attachment to place or kin or particular cultural traditions was nostalgic or impractical, both of which were implicitly antisocial.

During the conflicted late 1960s, however, when I was a junior faculty member at a large university, I began (partly by watching and reading about the growth of black awareness, the struggle over the war, and the counterculture) to be aware of how essential cultural stripping is to social and political containment, of how similar in many respects the situation of Appalachia was to that of the ghettos and Vietnam, and of how careerism distorts personal growth, dulls social awareness, and constrains the political freedom of middle-class intellectuals. In mid-1970 I worked out some of those perceptions in two tentative articles whose relationship to each other was then only partially apparent to me: one on careerism (*Soundings*, Summer 1970) and another on Appalachia (*New South*, Fall 1970).

A little more than eighteen months later, I came back to North Carolina and began this book. By then it had become clear that although alienation and cultural stripping were only partly reversible, an authentic attempt to make sense of (and work out of) my jumbled history might paradoxically function as a center and reservoir of energy for far better work than I had yet done or would be likely to do otherwise.

The sense of personal clarification and direction was exhilarating, but practical problems remained: how to move beyond a still relatively inchoate sense of identification with the region, how to build upon and use skills I had acquired for other purposes, and especially how to make sense of the conflicted political and cultural situation in the region, which was the legacy of a century of simultaneous exploitation and missionary uplift, a recently concluded decade of federal programs that hadn't worked, and frustration and anger among Appalachian people, a few of whom appeared to have collaborated in their own undoing.

Fortunately, I stumbled upon a few helpful essays by Edgar Friedenberg, Carl Rogers, Robert Coles, and others. More pertinent than any were Frantz Fanon's "The Pitfalls of National Consciousness" and "On National Culture" in *The Wretched of the Earth* (1968). By then I had come (along with many others) to accept the argument that Appalachia was in some respects an internal colony, and I therefore saw myself repeatedly in Fanon's analysis of the role of middle-class intellectuals in a colony seeking or experiencing decolonization. One thing Fanon helped make clear was how my work was to be related to my former training and goals. "In an underdeveloped country," he said, "an authentic national middle class [must] betray the calling fate has marked out for it, and put at the people's disposal the intellectual and technical capital that it has snatched when going through the colonial universities." The skills were not to be a cause for guilt or apology; they were merely to be used in a new way.

Another vexing problem was to establish an equitable and functional relationship between those whose good fortune it had been to acquire the skills and those who had not acquired them. The inequity in skills, buttressed by the natural tendency of human beings (and perhaps especially intellectuals and professionals) to act out of a need for self-esteem, tended to replicate hierarchical relationships among those who otherwise shared a common commitment to regional reconstruction. Again Fanon was to the point. If care is taken, he said,

> . . . to use only a language that is understood by graduates in law and economics, you can easily prove that the masses have to be managed from above. But . . . if you are not obsessed by the perverse desire to spread confusion and rid yourself of the people, then you will realize that the masses are quick to seize every shade of meaning and to learn all the tricks of the trade. . . . Everything can be explained to the people, on the single condition that you really want them to understand.

Thus one functions not as an expert but as a skilled co-worker in a common enterprise.

A final problem was how to understand and accept the implicitly regressive aspects of my return to the region, which were most apparent in my concurrent turning again to the cultural traditions of

Appalachia—especially the music and dance and folkways. Ultimately I learned that those cultural traditions themselves had to be reinterpreted, but for the time being the problem was adequately resolved by Fanon's insistence that one must go back not to what was (or maybe never was) but to what is and what is emerging. Speaking of the role of native writers in decolonization movements, he says:

> The colonized man who writes for his people ought to use the past with the intention of opening the future, as an invitation to action and a basis for hope. But to ensure that hope and give it form, he must take part in action and throw himself body and soul into the national struggle. You may speak about everything under the sun; but when you decide to speak of that unique thing in man's life that is represented by the fact of opening up new horizons . . . and by raising yourself and your people to their feet, then you must collaborate on the physical plane. [It is not enough] to try to get back to the people in the past out of which they have already emerged; rather we must join them in that fluctuating movement which they are just giving shape to, and which, as soon as it has started, will be the signal for everything to be called into question. Let there be no mistake about it; it is to this zone of occult instability where the people dwell that we must come; and it is there that our souls are crystallized and that our perceptions and our lives are transfused with light.

I therefore offer the chapters that follow not as the last or definitive word but as a tentative beginning, and perhaps as part of a base on which others can subsequently erect a more complete political and cultural analysis of the region and its people. My own analysis, besides reflecting my personal experience, is based on an abundance of documentary sources and interviews, which I have marshaled as carefully and handled as responsibly as I know how. But I have also tried not to deceive myself about the complexities and risks involved in the process.

Complete objectivity, if it is ever possible (and I have serious doubts about that), is possible only where one's personal history, feelings, values, and social and political preferences are in no way even peripherally involved. I have observed such cases but rarely, and have encountered none in my own experience. Certainly my encounter with the present subject does not constitute such a case.

The only objectivity to which I pretend is therefore limited, conditional, and even paradoxical. Having made my point of view as clear as possible, I encourage readers to make whatever interpretative allowances they feel are necessary. I know of no other way to write about things that move one deeply, when being moved is so much at variance with the core assumptions, norms of behavior, and styles of argument customarily expected of those of us who were trained as professional scholars and teachers before we knew fully who we were.

To ask me (or in fact anyone) to say what Appalachia is *really* like is roughly equivalent to asking Faulkner or Wolfe what the South was really like: It is both beside the point and impossible to answer. That I am far from being a Faulkner or a Wolfe I freely admit; I am also aware of the differences between writing novels and writing social and cultural analysis. But with respect to the question of objectivity it is a difference of degree; anyone who writes about human society writes of a phenomenon that is inescapably both "in here" and "out there." Like Emerson in his maturity, we can only report what we see; we cannot verify that it exists in any absolute sense.

In Henry James's *The Ambassadors*, the sophisticated European Miss Barrace says that "the light of Paris seems always to show . . . what things resemble." But does it also show them "for what they really are," asks the naive American Lambert Strether. Miss Barrace, wise with the knowledge that we inhabit a world of nuance, shadow, appearance, and insoluble enigma, answers in amusement and perhaps a bit of pity, "Oh, I like your Boston 'reallys'!"

So here is my book. Its subject is limited. I have tried to avoid Lambert Strether's Boston reallys and to make as responsible a statement as my knowledge and relation to the subject allow.

During the years I worked on this book, I received help, useful criticism, and encouragement from so many sources that to acknowledge each here is impossible. Special thanks, however, are due to Robb Burlage, who first took note of my work and encouraged me to continue, and to Archie Green, whose generosity and unwavering confidence and support have been crucial on more than one occasion, and whose personal integrity has been a model.

The splendid staff of the Duke University Library provided me with both a place to work and invaluable materials and assistance on many occasions. I benefited also from the help of many other libraries, including the Harry Lasker Library of the Highlander Research and Educational Center, the Southern Historical Collection of the University of North Carolina, the Weatherford-Hammond Collection of Berea College, the Disciples of Christ Historical Society, and the Wisconsin State Historical Society. Several libraries repeatedly made materials available on loan; especially helpful in this regard were the state university libraries of Kentucky, Tennessee, and West Virginia.

Financial support for the preparation of one chapter came from the Southern Investigative Research Project of the Southern Regional Council. A substantial grant from the Humanities Program of the Rockefeller Foundation enabled me to give full time to writing during my final year of work. Several sections of this book depend heavily on the prior investigative work of a number of people, a substantial portion of which was published in the *Mountain Eagle* of Whitesburg, Kentucky, and the *Louisville Courier-Journal*. Those whose work proved particularly helpful were James Branscome, Keith Dix, Thomas Gish, Anita Parlow, Bill Peterson, Phil Primack, and Ward Sinclair. I am of course solely responsible for all of the interpretations, opinions, and conclusions expressed here.

Special gratitude is due to my daughters, Beverly and Rebecca, who love the mountains as I do and who have understood my work with a maturity far beyond their years. Somewhere in the midst of my work, I discovered a note on my desk, scrawled in Beverly's five-year-old hand. It said, "I have a daddy who is MaKeing a gooD Book." I hope she is right.

Introduction

HOWEVER MUCH recent state and federal Appalachian development efforts may seem to be the legacy of New Deal, New Frontier, and Great Society professional planners, they are above all the intellectual and political progeny of a hundred years of exploitative private development in the mountains, and the condescending middle-class missionary attitudes and activities that accompanied it. A direct line ties many aspects of the Tennessee Valley Authority (TVA), the Area Redevelopment Administration (ARA), the Office of Economic Opportunity (OEO), and the Appalachian Regional Commission (ARC) to the economics and politics of the early coal and land barons and pioneer corporations. A parallel line leads to the social and cultural theories and values of the early churches, settlement schools, and foundations that provided a liberal façade for private development.

For at least a hundred years, individuals, groups, and agencies have tried to "help," to "solve the problem," to "develop the region": the churches with their preaching stations, settlement schools, and hospitals; the United Mine Workers and other unions with their labor-organizing drives and benefit programs; state and local governments with myriad policies and programs stretching back at least a century to the state immigration bureaus of the 1870s; the special programs of private organizations (especially foundations such as the Russell Sage, Ford, and others); and most recently the federal programs of the 1960s. "Appalachia," John Fetterman said in *Stinking Creek* (1970), "is Mecca for those driven—both by demons and by self-guilt—to do unto somebody, somehow."

The symbiotic relationship between missionaries and private developers proved devastating for the region historically. Its intellectual and political legacy is proving no less deadly as it perpetuates itself in contemporary planning documents, purchased with federal funds, and the agencies and programs that issue from them. The first footnote in many such studies leaves no doubt that the study's formulators have drunk deeply at the stream of misinformation that flows perennially from the missionary movement and its recent academic heirs. A perusal of virtually any page of such a document suggests that the wisdom of the early private developers and the missionaries survives in a hardy but profoundly uncritical oral and written tradition among planners and agency administrators.

Unfortunately, most writing about the Appalachian region was long confined primarily to portraying the conditions that produced the "do something" urge. Although recent years have witnessed the appearance of sophisticated critical studies of many aspects of the region's history, analysis of missionary, planning, and development efforts in the region has remained sparse indeed.

The early period of missionary activity at the turn of the century produced a number of official reports from church mission boards, as well as a shelf or two of missionary memoirs. What Robert F. Munn called the "second discovery" of Appalachia in the 1930s led to a great many journalistic articles and several books on volunteer relief efforts in the coalfields and textile towns. And the period of major federal intervention in the 1960s called forth reams of consultants' studies of federal development programs. But thus far there has been no single source one could turn to for an analytical overview of what the church missionaries, the secular "uplift" workers, and the technocratic planners and developers have done in the region.

My object is to provide a tentative initial account of some of the most important of these efforts, and in particular to assess their political and cultural origins and implications. Because of the vastness of the subject, and in some cases the lack of detailed preliminary studies, no single book could treat the topic comprehensively. I have therefore limited myself to discussing selected efforts that were especially important in themselves, that spawned other efforts, that highlighted issues with special clarity, or that were important enough at the national and regional level to make knowledge of them essential for understanding the response to missionaries, planners, and developers in local communities. I see this present study, therefore, as only one piece of a puzzle being assembled by many hands.

In the limited number of case studies I have attempted, I have focused upon one central question: not, Did a missionary or planning or development effort "work" in some limited (usually economic) sense? but, instead, Out of what complex social dynamic did it arise, toward what vision of a desirable social order was it directed, and how did it impinge upon the human lives it touched? Out of that central concern, many related questions have arisen: How have missionaries, planners, and developers formed their notions about the region and its people, and how have those notions both guided their efforts and affected existing power relationships in the region? How has their work affected interaction between the region and mainstream America? Who has actually been served best by the various efforts? What does our experience with the problems of the Appalachian region reveal about our national identity and priorities? Is the mainstream a viable model for regional development, as has been almost universally assumed? How have people in the region responded and reacted to missionaries, planners, and developers? Have any promising alternative strategies emerged out of nearly three-quarters of a century of official programs? And finally, what indigenous human resources remain to shape humane reconstruction of the region?

I have grouped the chapters into three sections. Part I focuses on an organization—the Council of the Southern Mountains (CSM)—that brought a large body of the early missionaries together and eventually projected and tried to carry out something of a regionwide program for Appalachia. Although the Council lacked both the vision and the resources to implement a bold program, it became an important forum in which the region and its problems were discussed for more than sixty years. Its history offers insight into the complexities faced by later planners and developers, as well as by latter-day secular missionaries such as the Appalachian Volunteers.

Part II concentrates on federal programs: the Tennessee Valley Authority (from 1933 on), the Area Redevelopment Administration (1961–63), the Office of Economic Opportunity (1964–68), and the Appalachian Regional Commission (from 1965 on).

Part III surveys activities that have arisen both out of and in opposition to state and state-federal development efforts: the Appalachian Volunteers (AVs), the Congress for Appalachian Development (CAD), and local resistance to state-federal planning in the Kentucky River Area Development District (KRADD). A final chapter probes some relationships between culture and regional development.

Although the chapters have been treated as relatively independent case studies, connections among them are many. Besides the obvious fact that all are concerned with one multistate region, there are other important geographical connections. Letcher County, Kentucky, for example, has been almost constantly in the public eye since Harry Caudill's *Night Comes to the Cumberlands* (1963). The county's two most

effective spokesmen (Caudill and *Mountain Eagle* editor Tom Gish)
figure importantly in the chapters on the Tennessee Valley Authority,
the Office of Economic Opportunity, the Appalachian Regional Commission, and the Congress for Appalachian Development (CAD). The
Cumberlands area of Kentucky and Tennessee, which gave Caudill
his title, was the site of major development efforts by both OEO and
ARA. The Kentucky River Area Development District controversy
was chronicled primarily in the *Mountain Eagle*; Letcher County is
one of the district's eight counties. The tourist-oriented area of western North Carolina figures importantly in Chapters 3 and 6.

Actual organizational connections are perhaps as important as
geographic ones. Indeed a chart representing connections among the
organizations treated in the various chapters might resemble those
frequently used to show interlocking directorates among large banks
and corporations. For example, the Council of the Southern Mountains received major funding in the 1960s from OEO. Part of it went
to start the Appalachian Volunteers, which also received money from
ARA and later directly from OEO. The AVs used some OEO funds
to try to take over or reform OEO's local programs. ARA also gave
money and staff help to the Conference of Appalachian Governors
(CAG) and the President's Appalachian Regional Commission (PARC),
both of which were antecedents of ARC, which was itself in one sense
the inheritor of ARA's "infrastructure" approach to development.
The splitting of mid-1960s Appalachian aid between OEO and ARC
sometimes led to serious conflict at the local level and found (for
example) the ARC-created Kentucky River Area Development District charged in the late 1960s with mismanaging OEO "special impact" funds intended for Letcher County. That conflict contributed
to the more general wrangle over planning and development in the
KRADD counties, treated in Chapter 9. The Congress for Appalachian Development was organized by Gordon Ebersole, who had been
frustrated by the failure of the Interior Department and ARA (for
whom he had worked) to face the challenge of natural-resource development, and by Harry Caudill, a persistent critic of TVA, OEO,
and ARC.

Several specific issues (in addition to those already articulated
above) also weave in and out of the various chapters. Chief among
them are the use of natural resources (especially public versus private
development), the advisability of recreation and tourism development, and local versus state-federal control of planning and development.

In general, I understand the Appalachian region to be one in
which the presence of rich natural resources (coal, oil and gas, water

power, land, labor) has led to systematic extractive exploitation and special-purpose development (such as tourism), controlled initially by individual entrepreneurs and more recently by corporations that are increasingly being assembled into multinational conglomerates. Regional governmental and service institutions and organizations have become for the most part captives of the dominant financial and political interests that both created and, in turn, were reinforced by the dynamic of exploitative development. Hence essential social services such as housing, transportation, communications, health care, and education have deteriorated (or in many cases never been created) as a result of a regressive tax structure, class-biased social policies, and collaborative systems of patronage.

Although these patterns are almost universally present, the geographic, geologic, and historical diversity of the region has caused them to be manifested in a variety of forms. Strip-mining is a critical problem in eastern Kentucky, southwestern Virginia, eastern Tennessee, and West Virginia, but not at all in western North Carolina, where tourist development is a more serious concern. Even the problems associated with industrial development vary greatly within the region. Some previously nonindustrialized areas are beginning to receive their first fugitive garment factories. Elsewhere, a modern chemical complex at Charleston, West Virginia, has long since thoroughly polluted the Kanawha River. Farther north, in the heavily industrialized areas of Pennsylvania, factories using recent technologies have taken over buildings abandoned by older heavy industries.

It is ironic that a region for so long characterized by a single stereotype is actually almost too diverse to generalize about at all. Some tentative generalizations are, nevertheless, possible concerning the histories, policies, and activities of the missionary, planning, and development agencies I have studied. I present them here briefly as a guide to my arguments and conclusions in the case studies that follow:

1. They generally assume that Appalachia is a "deviant subculture" whose problems owe more to physical isolation, depleted gene pools, pathological inbreeding, clan wars, hookworm, moonshining, and welfarism than to the nation's unceasing demands on the region for cheap labor, land, raw materials, and energy.

2. Like the missionaries who insisted that mountain children would be saved only if they learned which side the fork goes on, the plans and programs have insisted that their grandchildren mold themselves to bureaucratic conceptions of middle-class social organization and lifeways.

3. They accept mainstream values and idealized social, economic, and political norms as the natural boundary of feasible approaches to development.

4. They reject any approach to planned, democratic, community-based public development that promises to alter—or fails to rationalize—established patterns of private entrepreneurial development.

One comes away from reading the studies and analyzing the programs suspecting that Al Capp must have been commissioned to write Appalachia's history, Norman Rockwell to paint the dream vision of its future, and the Corps of Engineers to build the Heavenly City.

Even the one development effort that began as something of a noble dream vision—TVA—has proved to be a profoundly mixed blessing. During its early years, its liabilities (for example, a reactionary racial policy and an agriculture program co-opted by the American Farm Bureau) were substantially offset by progressive accomplishments in other areas. In the 1950s, however, TVA converted to coal-fired steam generation and focused narrowly on supplying cheap electricity to an artificially stimulated market. The result was that it turned much of the coal-bearing area of southern Appalachia into a strip-mined wasteland. Recently environmental awareness, energy conservation, and a search for more humane and accountable ways of conducting the public's business have come to the forefront of public attention. But TVA continues to lumber through the valley like a blinded and bewildered bureaucratic anachronism—signing its *n*th long-term contract for nonunion strip-mined coal, building nuclear plants, preparing to flood the valley of the Little Tennessee in violation of the Endangered Species Act, and contemptuously dismissing public demands for accountability and a consideration of alternative policies.

TVA's successors have lacked even the veneer of noble rhetoric that seemed so promising in the early 1930s. The ARA was the first concrete result of John F. Kennedy's promises in his epochal 1960 West Virginia primary campaign. But ARA perceived no "seamless web," projected no vision of democratic planning and development. It was based instead upon a narrowly conceived and poorly funded jobs and job-training strategy that subsidized private industry and was glibly rationalized as "infrastructure" development. All ARA actually delivered were a few scattered jobs and industrial sites; an underwear plant for Norton, Virginia; a couple of highly questionable tourist facilities; and some pamphlets suggesting rather desperately that other Appalachian people might consider growing strawberries, raising feeder pigs, or cultivating mushrooms in caves.

Ironically, public attention was focused on Appalachia during the post-ARA mid-1960s primarily by the War on Poverty. But OEO was designed upon metropolitan ghetto models; it was not addressed to any of the region's structural dislocations or systemic problems. Only Title II (Community Action) held any promise at all. But OEO received only pilot-level funding, and Title II was emasculated by paranoid congressional and administrative constraints. The primary Appalachian legacy of the War on Poverty was frustration and a well-justified cynicism.

The main Appalachian development agency since the mid-1960s has been ARC, a nearly unmitigated disaster in every respect. ARC is conventional, business-oriented, status quo, pork-barrel politics masquerading as "creative federalism." Prohibited by its legislative charter from addressing the critical problem of natural-resource development, ARC settled for a growth-center, trickle-down, infrastructure approach. In practice this amounted to building roads and vocational schools to serve business and industry; hiring consultants to rationalize the importation of fugitive apparel plants; paying doctors to build themselves new hospitals; encouraging socially and culturally destructive, economically marginal tourist development; and cavalierly advising people in its administratively created hinterlands to move to town if they wanted jobs and services—or out of the region if they didn't like it. Lately, ARC has been tinkering with communications satellites and industrial-site development. Pressing problems of strip-mining, black lung and other occupational diseases, secondary and higher education, housing, and community-based primary health care have been dealt with belatedly and gingerly if at all. The energy question has been sidestepped entirely.

The history of development efforts and agencies in Appalachia as I have come to understand it teaches me the nearly surreal durability of bad models and the essential superficiality of analysis that undergirds them. We have not yet seriously entertained the possibility of substantive and structural change—either within the region or in its relationship to the rest of the nation. The business community's economic need for the wealth of the region turns out to be matched by the larger public's manipulated psychic "need" (treated in Henry D. Shapiro's recent *Appalachia on Our Mind*) for Appalachia as a reassuring norm against which to gauge its own well-being and self-esteem. The hallmark of development efforts, public and private, has been their genius for rationalizing each in terms of the other.

By the powerful we mean, of course, those who are able to realize their will, even if others resist it. No one, accordingly, can be truly powerful unless he has access to the command of major institutions, for it is over these institutional means of power that the truly powerful are, in the first instance, powerful.

C. Wright Mills, *The Power Elite*

The History of a Book, the History in a Book, and a Book as History: Reflections on the New Edition

> . . . nunca he vuelto a leer ninguno de mis libros por temor
> de arrepentirme (I have never gone back to read any of my
> books for fear that I would repent [having written them]).
> Gabriel García Marquez, *Doce cuentos peregrinos* (1992)

SINCE FEW OF US have been blessed with even a modicum of the transcendent talent of a García Marquez, no doubt we should be especially mindful of his caution. On the other hand, because the talents of most of the rest of us who write books *are* so comparatively modest, we expect no more, when we look again years later at what we wrote, than that what we reencounter will be workmanlike and serviceable. The necessary limit of those expectations is part of what affords me the courage to revisit a particular moment of my own living and learning that found its way into a written text a long while ago.

In the preface I wrote to this book nearly twenty years ago (six years before the book finally appeared in print—a fact I will return to presently) I said that *Modernizing the Mountaineer* is "at one level . . . an artifact of [my] political and cultural education." Having recently re-read both the book itself and the reams of correspondence about it that remain in my files, that seems even more true now than I felt it to be at the time. But with the passing of the years other things have become true as well, the main one of which is that both this book and those of other scholars and writers that preceded and followed it are now items in other and larger processes—the waning of the 1960s and the coming of Nixon-Reagan-Bushism, the shifting of Appalachia from the center to the edge of the screen of public attention and policy concern, the development of the Appalachian studies enterprise, and the emergence of new paradigms of inquiry and scholarly writing (oral history, the new social history, cultural studies, and postmodern ethnography).

In these brief retrospective comments on *Modernizing the Mountaineer* I want to reflect on the history *of* the book (where it came from in my own process and how—after long delay—it saw the light of day), the history *in* the book (the kind of history I tried to make it, and the kind it seemed to be to others) and the book *as* history (where it is now situated after nearly twenty years).

The History of the Book

In the preface to the original edition I spoke briefly of my early years in the mountains, and of coming to be aware of "Appalachia" as a region. But in a single sentence which elided the more complicated story of where *Modernizing the Mountaineer* came from, I passed over the several years of personal and professional searching and reevaluation that lay between the dawn of that awareness and the appearance of my first tentative article on the region in 1970. At this juncture a slightly fuller account seems called for.

As a graduate student in American literature at Duke University in the early sixties, I had spent many weekends and summer days driving through the North Carolina mountains, using the old (but recently republished) WPA *North Carolina Guide* to ferret out historic sites and craftspeople like the Woody brothers of Spruce Pine, ironworker Bea Hensley, and gem-cutter Roby Buchanan. By my third year in graduate school I was looking rather desperately for a dissertation topic on the mountains or *something* that would connect better with part of what I had lived or felt, that might make more sense to me than yet another dissertation on Hawthorne or Henry James or whomever. But since I had encountered no one at Duke who knew or cared anything about the mountains, I wrote a dissertation on a minor southern historical novelist, loaded a U-Haul truck, hitched a 1960 Volkswagen behind it, and went off to teach in the Midwest.

After two frustrating and (as I now realize) alienating years as a "junior man in American literature" at the University of Illinois, I opted for a year of teaching in a small college. That took me, as it happened, to Memphis, Tennessee, in the year that Martin Luther King, Jr., was assassinated during a garbage workers' strike. I returned to Illinois in the summer impelled (like so many at the time) to reconfigure my work and my life. But how? Toward what end? King's assassination and the marches and demonstrations I participated in thereafter moved me not into the civil rights movement, but back toward the rather vague preoccupation about Appalachia I had had for about five years but had not known how to act on.

As I did not know at the time, but learned slowly over the ensuing years, I was but one of a generation of young Appalachian-born scholars (many of us the first in our families to attend college, to say nothing of graduate school) upon whom the social, political, and cultural turmoil of the Kennedy-Johnson-Nixon years had a profound impact. Even as we labored earnestly to understand what those new experiences and opportunities might mean in terms of the received paradigms, those very paradigms—of identity, of gender, of race, of war and patriotism, of work and career—were shifting and reshaping in ways at once exciting and bewildering. Truly wondrous were the ways in which people responded to both the bewilderment and the excitement.[1]

Among the relatively few generalizations that might be made about those responses is that virtually all of us had to figure out how to reformulate the essentially system-serving skills we had snatched on our way through the universities, in order to place them at the service of surging new political-cultural passion and slowly dawning insight. Not much was clear except that what we did would not be fully congruent with what we had been trained to do, and that much of what we wrote would not look or sound like the things we had been trained to write. The latter proved especially problematic when one applied for grants, came up for promotion, or sent articles and books off to journals and presses. In post-Sputnik parlance, many envelopes were being pushed at once.

The pushing I myself was doing (at least the part of it that issued eventually in *Modernizing the Mountaineer*) happened this way: Sometime after the Ford Foundation-sponsored *The Southern Appalachian Region: A Survey* appeared in 1962, I had bought a copy (perhaps at the Southern Highland Handicraft Guild fair in Asheville, North Carolina, which I had begun attending as a high-school student). At the time, it was the only book about Appalachia I owned, or knew about, and I read and reread it as time permitted while I was in graduate school and later (after 1965) as I taught my courses in the English Department at the University of Illinois. On Christmas Day 1968, sitting at my flush-door-supported-on-filing-cabinets desk looking out over the flush-door-flat plains of Illinois, I filled several pages of notebook paper with ideas for what I wanted to call a Center for Mountain Culture (a library and archive, academic courses, a journal, summer institutes, a grants program). I began to devote all the time I could spare to trying to bring some such institution into being: reading feverishly to remedy my ignorance, writing letters to scores of foundations and anybody else I thought might be able to help, circulating a proposal I wrote and rewrote many times, driving back and forth to the Southeast to meet with anyone and everyone who showed any interest.

By February 1969 I had a full-scale prospectus in hand for a program that looked very much like the Appalachian studies programs and centers that began to spring up several years later, and had received substantial encouragement from several universities and foundations. But during much of the academic year 1969-70 I was away from home working on the Woodrow Wilson Foundation's National Humanities Series (an ill-begotten venture, as it turned out), and when I returned to my own project the news was hardly encouraging. For a few months it looked as if funds might be available at least for a small conference to explore the idea, but that possibility soon evaporated as well.

A growing stack of correspondence made clear that I was enmeshed in a veritable Br'er Rabbit thicket of Catch-22s. The modest amount of credibility I then had with university administrators and foundation officials derived from having recently earned a Ph.D., but the training I had gotten by doing so was in fact only marginally useful for my new purposes, and the disparity between what I was "trained to do" and what I *wanted* to do created the continual problem of having to explain and justify myself to the English Department at one end of the line and to administrators in foundations and regional universities at the other. To continue to work on the project I needed much more time than I could continue to steal from my job as a professor of American literature, and the only way I could see to get it was to create some such program as I had in mind. But it was proving virtually impossible to do that from where I was then situated. Foundations wanted me to be on a faculty inside the region rather than outside it before they were willing to commit any money, but so far as I was able to discover there *were* no jobs of the sort my efforts were directed to creating, and none could be created without the money.

In any case, a series of letters that drifted in during the fall term of 1970 made it clear that the project was doomed; I had done my best, but had not been able to cause it to happen.[2] Fortunately, others were experiencing greater success with their efforts; there were (although I did not yet know it) promising stirrings at various points in the region. The Appalachian Volunteers had already come upon—and passed from— the scene. Highlander Research and Education Center had turned from civil rights to Appalachia. Appalachian Film Workshop was making its first short black-and-white films. The Black Lung Association was growing, and a variety of community organizations were on the horizon.[3]

In any case, some of what I personally had been thinking—about the region, about the university, about what sort of professional self-definition was coming to make sense to me—I put into several very tentative essays.[4] After reading one of those essays, Robb Burlage invited me to a meeting of the Union of Radical Political Economists (of whom I had never heard) in West Virginia, where I met people who were working and thinking in what to me were fresh and exciting ways. Shortly thereafter, Steve Cox of the University of Tennessee Press wrote to ask whether I might develop some of my ideas from the essays into a book. By late June 1971, I had drafted a proposal.[5] Although it was a proposal for a book I was in fact still woefully unprepared to write, during those first six years of teaching I had read a great deal, learned much that I had not known, developed some new ways of thinking about and doing my work, traveled in the mountains much more widely than I ever had before, and met some politically and socially committed people whose knowledge and sophistication surpassed my own by far.

In the meantime, amid the continuing anti-Vietnam, feminist, environmental, and civil rights agitation of the period, I turned my efforts toward trying to help organize the first faculty union at the University of Illinois. Becoming president of that fledgling union proved to mesh but poorly with my concurrent promotion and tenure review, and I lost my job after a harrowing struggle that taught me that the formal values of the university could be rationalized away with great finesse. As it happened, it was *that* event, rather than getting a grant or a job to develop an Institute of Appalachian Studies, that took me back to North Carolina to work on *Modernizing the Mountaineer*. At the end of the academic year in 1972, my wife and I sold our house (the first we had ever owned), loaded another in what was becoming a long series of U-Haul trucks, took our two young daughters, and headed back to North Carolina.

For the next three years I worked steadily, reading in libraries, and traveling as often as I could to the mountains to go to meetings, work in archives (such as they were at the time), and interview people. On July 25, 1975, I sent the completed manuscript to the University of Tennessee Press—about a week before I loaded yet another U-Haul truck and headed for Baltimore to teach again—this time in an American Studies program. In late September I signed a publication contract. The manuscript moved rather expeditiously through the editorial process until it hit a snag: after a long and conflicted negotiation, the press demanded that I remove a chapter that was critical of the Tennessee Valley Authority. I refused, and my contract was canceled.[6]

Although I was unaware of the larger context at the time, the incident situated my book within the complicated politics in which university presses had been enmeshed since Cornell University established

the first one in the United States in 1869. The idea behind their formation was to publish scholarly books too specialized or controversial to
find a popular or mass market.[7] The first southern ones appeared at Trin-
ity College (later Duke) in 1921 and the University of North Carolina in
1922. The University of Tennessee Press was organized in 1940, in
what Roger Shugg calls the "second phase" of university-press publishing (between the world wars); most of the other southern presses joined
the list between the end of World War II and 1970. By as early as
1949, thirty-five university presses had published more than sixteen-
thousand titles, and the list was growing at the rate of seven hundred
per year.[8]

The politics of such a history were more complicated than the rising
curve of production implied, however. Noting with evident pride that
United States-style university presses are not common elsewhere in the
world, Shugg praised them rather unproblematically in the heady late
1960s for being "committed to the publication of free scholarly inquiry
regardless of political implications . . . without fear or favor . . . free
of any dominating influence by church or state, or by race, class, or
political party."[9] But no one familiar with the politics of either publishing or the university in the United States could easily believe that
combining the two would produce such an ideal state of affairs. And
for university presses situated within *public* universities (as most southern ones were), the politics of public funding added another thick layer
of complexity and nearly inevitable conflict.

Despite the structural constraints and political monitoring attendant
upon state funding, some university presses located within public universities did courageous work upon occasion. When he was hired by the University of North Carolina Press in 1925, William T. Couch was cautioned
that the press could not publish books dealing with race, religion, or economics. Nevertheless, Couch was soon publishing scholarly books by African-
American authors as well as such controversial volumes as Arthur Raper's
The Tragedy of Lynching (1933) and his *Sharecroppers All* (1941).[10]

Even Couch's University of North Carolina Press had its limits, however.
Soon after *Sharecroppers All* appeared, Couch encouraged Rayford Logan, an
African-American intellectual, to include some left-wing pieces in a collection he was to edit, to be called *What the Negro Wants*. Couch soon
became uneasy, however, about what some of the contributors (W. E. B.
Du Bois in particular) were saying about interracial marriage and ending segregation. What Negroes appear to want, he concluded, was "far
removed" from what "they ought to want." Hence what the Negro
"needs most urgently," he judged, was "to revise his wants."[11] After
months of contentious negotiation, Couch finally agreed to publish

Logan's book, but only with a publisher's introduction disclaiming responsibility for the views expressed in the articles.[12]

Such controversies and pressures—by no means confined to a single university press—continued through the McCarthy years of the 1950s and into the rise of the civil rights, anti-Vietnam, and feminist struggles in the mid-1960s. *Modernizing the Mountaineer* was simply—as I slowly came to realize—another book caught at a particular historical moment within a delicate but persistent dialectic: formally, public universities are created to seek the truth, however incongruent with received wisdom; practically they must tack a perilous course through the fickle winds and buried shoals of politics. University presses, as creatures of the institutions in which they are situated, cannot escape that dialectic.

Newspaper coverage of the cancellation of my University of Tennessee Press contract provided a bit of comfort, but I had to look for another publisher nevertheless.[13] During the next two years the manuscript made the rounds from one commercial or university press to another. Commercial publishers found it too specialized for a mass market—of merely "regional" rather than "truly national" interest and import, as one editor put it. And other university presses, after inquiring into the book's history with the University of Tennessee Press, reported in letter after letter that they would rather not involve themselves.[14] Finally, in mid-July 1978, I signed a new contract with New York publisher Burt Franklin and began the editorial process again.

Being distant from and essentially ignorant of the regional politics that had led to the prior publication difficulties, Burt Franklin moved into production with the book without questioning its content. Publication was announced, but repeatedly delayed by the company's own financial difficulties and administrative disorganization. Some preview copies went out to reviewers in late 1979, and at least two reviews appeared shortly thereafter, but by mid-1981 purchase copies were still unavailable.[15] Unable to persuade the company after two and a half years to fulfill its contractual obligation, I had hired lawyers earlier that year to help get the book released. At the end of April the rights reverted to me, and I began to look for yet another publisher—six years after I had signed the first publication contract.[16]

Fortunately I was able rather quickly to place the book with the Appalachian Consortium Press, which offset it from the Burt Franklin edition, designed a cover, and placed it immediately into production. Copies were available soon thereafter, and remained fairly reliably so for nearly a decade.[17] It was in the Appalachian Consortium Press edition that *Modernizing the Mountaineer* became known to the several generations of students who have by now passed through Appalachian studies (and other) programs and courses. But the consortium itself—a product of the wave of interest in Appalachia that arose in the mid-1960s—did not prove to be the most stable and healthy of organizations when that wave began to fall during the Reagan and Bush years of cutbacks in social programs, supply-side economics, and the consequent shift in student interest from socially engaged programs of study to MBA degrees and the promise of six-figure incomes. By late 1990 it became necessary to look (again) for a new publisher.

During the years after the University of Tennessee Press canceled my original contract, my relationship with the Press (and especially with its subsequent director, Carol Orr) remained cordial. What had happened was the result of the particular structural and political circumstances of the historic moment, and was, it seemed to me, something from which one could learn a great deal, but about which it was pointless to remain preoccupied and bitter. When I approached the press in late 1991, they were eager to issue a new edition of the book, and untroubled by the issues of content that had led to the cancellation of my original contract.

Things have thus in a sense come full circle with this new edition, but it is also important to remind oneself that the situation in the region (and in the country) has changed dramatically during these eighteen years. From the history *of* the book, I turn to the history *in* the book: to a few brief reflections on what sort of history it is, and what predisposed it to be that sort of history.

The History in the Book

Writing in mid-1975 to tell me my manuscript had been approved for publication, University of Tennessee Press Director Louis Iglehart informed me that the press board accepted it "upon condition that the 'negative' or 'polemical' aspect of the manuscript be toned down." We want the reader, he continued some months later, "to accept you as an objective scholar, albeit a disillusioned one; we can hope that the reader will even be persuaded by your findings. He must not be turned off, his suspicions of your integrity aroused."[18]

In a good-faith effort to meet Iglehart's objections concerning tone, I did try to modulate the rhetoric somewhat. But ultimately, it seemed to me, the history I was trying to relate (of outright exploitation, of manipulation, of collaboration, of shallow symbolic "helping" gestures where structural reforms were called for) *was* an outrageous history, and it was beyond both my abilities and my intentions to render it in a cool, dispassionate, and conventionally "scholarly" way. "I think there is virtually no chance that any reader would ever accept my book as an example of anything like what usually passes for 'objective scholarship,'" I replied to Iglehart. "Indeed," I continued,

> it has never been my wish for it to be accepted as that, and I cannot imagine its becoming that without being rewritten from a completely different point of view. Which is to say, written by somebody else. My intention was . . . to write from my own point of view and to make that point of view clear to the reader. I expected that intelligent . . . readers would make whatever interpretative corrections they felt were necessary. The strength of the book, it seems to me, lies partly in its being not a routine scholarly book, but a serious piece of social criticism written from a somewhat unconventional, but nevertheless coherent and defensible, point of view.

Granting in his reply that "one of the attractions of your manuscript is its reflection of your very personal and intense point of view," Iglehart nevertheless continued to be bothered by the differences between *Modernizing the Mountaineer* and the majority of the books he was used to dealing with. As the weeks dragged by and the issue remained unresolved, I became unsure, as I told him, that "the book you wish to publish is the same book I have written."[19]

Tension over the issue was exacerbated, of course, by concurrent negotiations over whether the chapter critical of the TVA would be retained. Although the matter was formally closed by Iglehart's letter informing me that my refusal to remove the offending chapter "will prevent us from publishing your manuscript," the negotiations had foregrounded at least three issues related to the politics of the writing of revisionist historical narratives: the relationship of universities and their presses to structures of power and vested interest, which I have already commented on briefly above; the dialectic of personal-professional reevaluation and reconstruction experienced by many young scholars in the late 1960s, which I wrote a bit about at the time and which I have expanded upon somewhat here; and the shifting definitions of scholarship from the 1960s onward.

I have briefly described my own process of moving into, through, and thence at least partly outside of the system of academic scholarship as it was constituted in the mid-1960s. That movement was impelled by the particulars of my own personal history, my (lamentably tardy and slow) intellectual growth through college and graduate school, and the intersection of both with larger social, intellectual, and political movements of the late 1960s and beyond. Having had virtually no formal training as a historian which might have at once helped and freighted me with established formulas of historical narration and rhetorical style, I was both free (perilously free, I have always felt) and compelled by circumstance to cobble together my own approach to the task. In the process, I learned most from those activist scholars and journalists who were writing on civil rights, environmentalism, educational reform, feminism, the anti-Vietnam movement, anti-colonialism, and related topics. Most especially I learned from some who were writing new things about Appalachia: Ward Sinclair of the *Louisville Courier-Journal* and Homer Bigart of the *New York Times;* the indefatigable Harry Caudill; Robb Burlage and Jim Ridgeway of the Institute for Policy Studies; Keith Dix of West Virginia University; folklorist and labor historian Archie Green; West Virginia journalist Bill Blizzard and eastern Kentucky editor Tom Gish; West Virginia politicians Ken Hechler and Paul Kaufman; some angry and dazzlingly intelligent scholars such as C. Wright Mills, Staughton Lynd, Michael Harrington, Todd Gitlin, Frances Fox Piven and Richard Cloward; and many another besides.[20]

And what kind of writing was this I was reading and learning from? Upon what presuppositions did it rest, and what sort of rhetoric did it employ? Much of it was written by people who had come to understand that the old paradigm of scholarly objectivity had been invoked so regularly in the service of imperialism, racism, class privilege, male dominance, cultural chauvinism, and other questionable agendas that it was problematic at best, and that new approaches to social, political, and historical analysis were called for. They were people more likely to think (and write) in terms of structures of interest and discourses of power than of unproblematized foundational truths, established institutions, and "scholarly objectivity." These were also people who were writing to new and very mixed audiences slowly forming around issues of race, class, gender, war and peace, and the environment—to concerned academics in both the sciences and the humanities, to progressive legislators and policy makers, to community activists and organizers, to concerned citizens drawn for the first time in their lives into debate over public issues.

Much of the writing this configuration produced was angry (it had every reason to be), issue-focused, intense, and unabashedly confrontational. And although mainstream media and establishment academics and politicians tended to denigrate it as "merely polemical," "radical," or (a favorite dismissive term on the evening news) "hard core," much of it was in fact closely argued and carefully documented as people learned to ground their arguments in the public record and the detailed studies their opponents preferred to ignore (congressional hearings, General Accounting Office studies, corporate annual reports, purloined Pentagon papers, and the like). Those characteristics constituted real gains for progressive politics, but they also ran directly counter to much received wisdom about scholarly inquiry, the norms of scholarly publishing, and the life of an academic (especially a young one) in the university.

Out of such dynamics, as best I can understand it, came *Modernizing the Mountaineer* and much of the other early revisionist work on Appalachia.[21] In a broader frame, those dynamics also interacted symbiotically with larger processes which have continued to shape scholarly inquiry in the ensuing decades: the development of the new social history, reflexive ethnography, oral history, cultural studies, women's studies and ethnic studies, and the breaking down of conventional disciplinary boundaries. Of the early stages of these, then, *Modernizing the Mountaineer* is an artifact: conceptually, politically, rhetorically.

Finally, it may be helpful to consider briefly what has happened within Appalachian studies since I finished writing this book in 1975, and how that subsequent history inevitably changes the role that a new edition will play in the discourse.

The Book as History

Part of my concern in the foregoing has been to clarify that *Modernizing the Mountaineer* was a product of the early and mid-1970s, when revisionist scholarship on the region was in its early stages, rather than the early 1980s (as the Appalachian Consortium publication date would imply), when it was much more fully developed. When I started writing, the corpus of "new" writing on Appalachia was still small. The most prominent were the Ford Foundation survey of 1962, Caudill's *Night Comes to the Cumberlands* (1963), Weller's *Yesterday's People* (1965), Fetterman's *Stinking Creek* (1967), John Stephenson's *Shiloh* (1968), Gitlin and Hollander's *Uptown: Poor Whites in Chicago* (1970), Brit Hume's *Death and the Mines* (1971), and Walls and Stephenson's *Appalachia in the Sixties* and Archie Green's *Only a Miner* (both 1972). From the mid-seventies onward, however, the shelf of Appalachian scholarly books grew steadily. Shapiro's *Appalachia On Our Mind* and Gordon McKinney's *Southern Mountain Republicans* appeared in 1978, Eller's *Miners, Millhands, and Mountaineers* and Gaventa's *Power and Powerlessness: Quiescence and Rebellion in an Appalachian Valley* in 1980, Corbin's *Life, Work and Rebellion in the Coal Fields* the next year, Batteau's *Appalachia and America* and my *All That Is Native and Fine* in 1983, Patricia Beaver's *Rural Community in the Appalachian South* in 1986, Stephen Foster's *The Past Is Another Country* in

1988, Joe Trotter's *Coal, Class and Color* and Altina Waller's *Feud* in 1990, and Stephen Fisher's *Fighting Back in Appalachia* in 1993. Along the way came (besides other books too numerous to mention) the films of Appalshop, stacks of new novels and poetry and short stories, and countless sound recordings. In the process, the earlier broader-scale and necessarily defensive analyses yielded to more detailed and focused ones facilitated by that earlier work, by the formation of new archives and formal programs of study, and by the development of new analytical paradigms. Even now, numerous doctoral dissertations are in the works which will refine our understanding still further.[22]

The existence of this at once passionate and solidly researched body of work means at the first level that no responsible scholar, public official, or journalist can continue with impunity to make the sweepingly denigrating generalizations that were so routinely made during the "Appalachian decade" of the 1960s (although irresponsible ones continue to make them, nevertheless). At another level, however, as the body of work grows, so should interest in the story of its own creation, and the relationship of that story to the social, economic, political, intellectual, and cultural changes of the past thirty years. Each book, article, film, or sound recording is both a contribution to a new analysis and an analyzable constituent document in the growth of that analysis, and each may (and must) be read in both ways by future scholars. They are all, that is, artifacts of their own individual and collective processes of creation.

I hope, of course, that the bits of history I tried to relate in *Modernizing the Mountaineer* will continue to be useful in themselves to a new generation of scholars. Beyond that, I hope that the book's reissue will induce others to add their perspectives to the still only rather sketchily told stories of African Americans, Native Americans, women, and immigrant groups in the region; of such organizations as the Council of the Southern Mountains, the Appalachian Volunteers, Appalachian Film Workshop, the folk and settlement schools, the Commission on Religion in Appalachia; of the myriad local versions of state and federal economic development programs, and the many local efforts to shape or monitor or oppose those programs; and of many other programs and organizations, both public and private. Much has by now been told, and it has been my great pleasure to try to help tell some bits of it. But a vast amount remains yet to be told—both about what has happened historically in the region and about what happened to the tellers of that history in the process of telling.

In any case, the work that has gone before—my own and that of many others—helps make it possible to tell those stories in ever more precise, nuanced, and insightful ways. To say that is—for me, at least—to recall one of the happier ironies of the early years of revisionist scholarship in the mountains: the work that was in many ways so lonely was nevertheless work we were doing together.

Chapel Hill, North Carolina
May 1993

Notes

1. For a brief thoughtful statement by another young Appalachian, see Mike Smathers, "Notes of a Native Son," *Mountain Life and Work* 49 (February 1973): 19-22.

2. Despite the considerable encouragement Appalachian State University had given me earlier, the final (October 12, 1970) letter, from Paul Sanders, vice-president for academic affairs, informed me that the university would not be able to commit resources to what by then I had come to refer to as an Institute for Appalachian Studies. It was to be another two years before Appalachian State launched *Appalachian Journal.*

3. For an excellent survey of some of these efforts as well as later ones, see Stephen L. Fisher (ed.), *Fighting Back in Appalachia: Traditions of Resistance and Change* (Philadelphia: Temple University Press, 1993).

4. "Career and Calling: A Personal Record and Tentative Suggestion," *Soundings* 53 (Summer 1970): 111-23; "Finding New Models for Appalachian Development," *New South* 25 (Fall 1970): 7-77; and "The University as a Space and the Future of the University," *Journal of Higher Education* 42 (February 1971): 85-102.

5. Proposal dated June 21, 1971; author's file. Some years later I reflected briefly on the URPE meeting and related matters in "Developments in the Appalachian Identity Movement: All Is Process," *Appalachian Journal* 8 (Autumn 1980): 41-47.

6. Letter from the press's director, Louis Iglehart, July 27, 1976; author's files.

7. Roger Shugg, *The Two Worlds of University Publishing* (Lawrence: University of Kansas Libraries, 1967), p. 1. Johns Hopkins followed in 1878 (or, by other reckonings, 1890), California and Columbia in 1893, Yale in 1908, and Harvard in 1913.

8. Net sales had nearly quadrupled in ten years; by 1958, total annual titles had grown to nearly thirteen hundred. *Association of American University Presses Directory, 1991-1992* (New York: Association of American University Presses, 1991), passim; Shugg, *Two Worlds,* p. 3; Chester Kerr, *The American University as Publisher: A Digest of a Report on American University Presses* (Norman: University of Oklahoma Press, 1949), pp. 1-10; Helen L. Sears, *American University Presses Come of Age* (Syracuse: Syracuse University Press, 1959), passim. Shugg notes (p. 19) the influence of the $175 million Ford Foundation five-year grant to university presses in 1956, given to subsidize the publication of books in the humanities and social sciences. For a list of university presses and their founding dates through 1947, see Sears, *American University Presses,* pp. 19f.

9. Shugg, *Two Worlds,* pp. 3, 13.

10. On Couch's publishing books by African Americans in the 1930s, and his earlier courageous determination to keep the press above political sycophancy, see Daniel J. Singal, *The War Within: From Victorian to Modernist Thought in the South, 1919-1945* (Chapel Hill: University of North Carolina Press, 1982), pp. 265-72, 297.

11. Kenneth R. Janken, "African-American Intellectuals Confront the 'Silent South': The *What the Negro Wants* Controversy," *North Carolina Historical Review* 70 (Apr. 1993):

153-79 (Couch quoted, p. 167). Couch was backed up by the press's paid scholarly reviewers, including the dean of the University of North Carolina School of Journalism.

12. Ibid., pp. 162-74.

13. See *Knoxville News-Sentinel*, August 16, 1976; Kirk Loggins, "UT Press Refuses to Print Book With TVA Criticism," *Nashville Tennessean*, August 17, 1976; Associated Press piece in *Baltimore Sun*, August 18, 1976, and in *New York Times*, August 24, 1976; and Ward Sinclair, "Appalachian Book Hits Snag on TVA," *Louisville Courier-Journal*, October 24, 1976, p. 4.

14. The necessity not to draw this chronicle out interminably must elide important details of the process, as well as nuances among the responses of the various university presses. Several rejected the manuscript summarily; one editor tried valiantly but unsuccessfully to get it past his press's director. I omit detailed citations because the larger politics of the process, and not personalities, are of interest here.

15. My letter to Tom Franklin, October 10, 1980; Patricia Beaver to Burt Franklin & Co., February 25, 1981; author's files. For the early reviews, see Steve Fisher, "*Modernizing the Mountaineer*: A Review Essay," *Appalachian Journal* 8 (Autumn 1980): 60-66, and Norma Hawes's review in *National Review*, March 6, 1981, p. 238.

16. Magini, Raab & Lidinsky to Burt Franklin Co., February 12, 1981; Brylawski & Cleary letter to Burt Franklin & Co., February 25 and May 1, 1981; my letter to Burt Franklin & Co., April 27, 1981. As late as November 1981, Burt Franklin & Co. was still claiming rights to the book (my letter to Barry Buxton, November 18, 1981) (all letters in author's files).

17. One of my few pieces of good fortune during the long process was that Burt Franklin & Co. had never bothered to register the book for copyright. Brylawski & Cleary registered it in my name on March 20, 1981.

18. Letters from Iglehart, 24 Sept. 1975 and 3 Feb. 1976; author's files.

19. Iglehart letters of September 24, 1975, and February 3, 1976; Whisnant to Iglehart, February 9 and March 29, 1976; author's files.

20. Editors David S. Walls and John B. Stephenson's *Appalachia in the Sixties: Decade of Reawakening* (Lexington: University Press of Kentucky, 1972) preserves a good selection of the sorts of pieces to which I refer here.

21. In "Developments in the Appalachian Identity Movement: All Is Process" and "Mountaineers and Sandinistas: Cultural Politics in Appalachia and Nicaragua," *Southern Changes* 14 (December 1992): 4-15, I reflected on some of the problematic aspects of such revisionist projects.

22. An excellent recent example is Jane S. Becker, "Selling Tradition: The Domestication of Southern Appalachian Culture in 1930s America," Ph.D. diss., Boston University, 1993.

PART I

THE
MISSIONARY
BACKGROUND

CHAPTER 1

Workers in God's Grand Division:
The Council of the Southern Mountains

> The Appalachian mountains might be appropriately called one of
> the grand divisions of the United States. It is one of our oldest
> regions, with the traditions and customs of an honored and revered
> ancestry.
>
> *Mountain Life and Work* (1925)

THE OPENING OF THE Appalachian region to large-scale economic
exploitation during the last third of the nineteenth century coincided,
as the opening of new colonies frequently does, with the coming of
hundreds of missionaries. The first trains to reach many an Appalachian county seat bore not only the advance agents and engineers
employed by the coal barons who had learned of the region's rich
seams but also the preachers and missionary ladies sent by the denominations to harvest the bountiful crop of unchurched souls reputed to have burrowed back into the hollows, and to teach the swarms
of children thought to be growing up in heathen illiteracy. By the
turn of the century (further stimulated by the rapid growth of
women's involvement in home missions work in the 1870s, the WCTU
in the 1880s, and the women's clubs of the 1890s), there were scores
of new churches and "church and independent schools" scattered
throughout the region.[1]

During the decade and a half prior to World War I, innumerable
"uplift" enterprises were added to those of the churches and the
independent and denominational schools as state and federal agencies, private foundations, and such other groups as the Red Cross
sent "mountain workers" to organize clinics, literacy programs, and
agricultural improvement projects. By 1908, when the Russell Sage
Foundation gave John C. Campbell $3,000 to "take a wagon and
spend six months to a year travelling through the mountains" to
survey social and economic conditions, it was evident that two con-
tradictory problems had arisen among mountain missionary workers.[2]
The region was so large and sparsely settled, on the one hand, that
workers were isolated from each other. But on the other hand, the

3

churches' intense quest for converts was producing some quite un-Christian jealousy and competition among them.

Campbell's letters show that as he continued his travels for several years, he sensed the need to put the secular mountain workers in touch with one another, to mediate the jealousy and incipient conflict among the church workers, and to bring both into a working relationship with each other and with the national agencies (such as the National Conference of Charities and Corrections) whose conferences he himself attended regularly to discuss work in the mountains.

In Washington in early 1912, Campbell met a Mrs. Gielow, who wanted her own Southern Industrial Education Association to become "*the* clearinghouse for all mountain work." Mrs. Gielow, Campbell said, had "studied for a career in some dramatic line [but] gave [it] up . . . to take up the work for the mountaineers." Campbell found both the Association and the lady ill-equipped for the job.[3] The various annual conferences of mountain workers being sponsored by single denominational groups seemed no better suited to the task, and the interdenominational Mountain Workers Conference and Bible School that had been held at Maryville College each year since 1900 focused on evangelical religious work.

By mid-1912 Campbell was talking with the Russell Sage Foundation's John Glenn and others, including Katherine Pettit of the WCTU's Pine Mountain Settlement School, about establishing "an interdenominational federation of mountain workers."[4] From his new position as director of the Foundation's regional office (later called the Southern Highlands Division) in Asheville, North Carolina, Campbell worked through the fall of 1912 to encourage recent moves by Southern Baptists and Southern Presbyterians to organize such a federation.[5]

In response to a call from several church boards, an organizational meeting was held at Atlanta's Fourth Avenue Presbyterian Church on April 24, 1913. The intention was to provide, as the call expressed it, an opportunity for discussion and cooperation among "all persons engaged as workers in . . . the mountain schools; . . . trustees of such schools and members of all Mission Boards engaged in the mountains and all active friends of the mountaineers connected with Foundations and Societies for their uplift."[6] After hearing addresses by Campbell and others on education, social conditions, agriculture, and "the Exceptional Mountain boy, his training for the Gospel ministry," the thirty-five participants laid plans for a permanent organization to be called the Southern Mountain Workers Conference. "There were no discordant notes save one," Campbell reported to Glenn, "and that was sounded by a little Congregational man who could not rise above a local disagreement with the Baptists."[7]

A meeting of the group in Knoxville, Tennessee, the next year drew more than eighty people from twelve denominations and independent groups to hear speeches and reports on health, schools, religion, folklore, and related topics. "It seemed almost impossible," Campbell wrote to Glenn, "that we could have an interdenominational conference . . . without some jarring note. Not one was sounded. . . . They know each other now, and I think it is an assured thing for some years to come."[8] Indeed the meetings were to continue uninterrupted for sixty years.

But there was disagreement, actually, from the very beginning. An outspoken public-health nurse from Altapass, North Carolina, complained to Campbell that the 1915 annual meeting was an opportunity for "some so-called Christians [to listen] to gossip of the rankest sort" during "personal conferences" in the hotel lobby. "[No] more conferences for me," she told him. "There are too many preachers for a heathen of my stamp and standing." Such complaints were relatively few, however, and Campbell was convinced by 1917, when more than 150 people attended the annual meeting, that "the Conference is one of the best things—if not the best—that I have brought to pass."[9]

With Campbell's death in the spring of 1919, however, the Conference began a period of drifting under the dedicated but not very effective leadership of the Reverend Isaac Messler. Although the Russell Sage Foundation closed its Asheville office and began to reassess its work in the mountains, Campbell's influence on the Conference continued through his wife for a time after his death. After 1921, however, she became absorbed primarily in her own work on Danish folk schools. The Russell Sage Foundation continued its contributions toward expenses for the annual meetings, but by late 1923 it was clear that more permanent arrangements would have to be made to sustain the organization.[10]

In Campbell's absence, the arrangements took a more conservative turn. Campbell had faced the difficult task of trying both to mediate among the various conservative (but doctrinally opposed) views of the church groups that formed the nucleus of the Conference and to maintain an openness to such unchurchly participants as the public-health nurse from Altapass. His wide learning, strength of character, wit, and breadth of vision had allowed him considerable success in both. At the same time, he had tried to keep the Conference relatively loose and informal, without a position or program of its own, because he feared, as he told Glenn, that "reactionary influences might be set in motion if it were felt that the Conference were tending to become more than a mere conference."[11]

Nevertheless, Campbell had on occasion taken the annual meeting as an opportunity to present views that contrasted strongly with the prevailing orthodoxies of mountain workers. At least twice during the early years, he invited U.S. Commissioner of Education Philander P. Claxton to address the group. Claxton, a native of central Tennessee and former superintendent of schools in Asheville (1888–93), had developed strong notions about problems in the mountains. "There is a good deal of sentiment displayed when people talk about the mountains," he told the Conference in 1915, "and those living in the mountains are called the 'Mountain Whites' or by some other term that sounds like a popular rose. . . . There is a general impression that these are a peculiar people, and I think that you who are engaged in mountain work are largely responsible for it." But mountain people are not all that different, Claxton insisted. "Turn off the sob stuff now; the time for that has gone by forever."[12]

Reminding his listeners that "The gospel that Christ preached was a gospel of discontent," he turned to consider the exploitation of the region's natural resources. "In this section of the country," he said, "there is more opportunity for wealth . . . than anywhere else in the whole United States. . . . The people live in wealth and do not know it." He then told the assembled mountain workers of the thousands of walnut trees that had been shipped out of Haywood County, North Carolina, "to make the inside furnishings for Kaiser Wilhelm's palace in Berlin," and of the region's bountiful reserves of coal and water power.[13] Two years later he gave essentially the same address again and reasserted that there was "no such thing as a breed of 'Mountain Whites.' "

Claxton's 1917 address brought strong complaints from the superintendent of schools of the Presbyterian Women's Board of Home Missions, who said, "It may be that some of our workers are unduly pious, but we shall have to recognize . . . that it is these pious workers who have done the most for mountain people and who are likely to stick the longest."[14]

Although a Congregationalist minister himself, and certainly not radical politically, Campbell had long feared that the organization would be taken over by its most pious and conservative element, represented most prominently in his own mind by what he called the "Berea [College] group."

As an abolitionist and multiracial institution formed in the mid-nineteenth century, Berea College had a radical past. But by the end of the century it had become quite conservative under the leadership of its president William G. Frost. "I am a little bothered about President Frost [as a speaker for the first conference]," Campbell had written to Glenn in March 1913, "for I think it would be unwise to put him forward. He is, however, very prominent in mountain work, but he has said some very disparaging things about Southern white people . . . and in a letter just received he wants to know why Berea was left out in the call issued."[15] Although a motion to move the second annual meeting to Berea had been referred to committee at the Atlanta meeting, Glenn agreed that Frost would be a "difficult subject to handle," and Campbell reported the next year that "Frost has tried for two years to draw the Conference to Berea." His attitude seemed to be, Campbell said, "that he alone understands what needs to be done in the mountain country."[16]

Although Glenn had cautioned Campbell not to become indebted to Berea even to the extent of accepting proffered free food and lodging during his travels, after Campbell's death and the reassessment of the Russell Sage Foundation's priorities Glenn began to advise (partly at the urging of Frost and Berea's new president, William J. Hutchins) that the Conference be moved to Berea.[17] By mid-1924 it was clear that there was no feasible alternative. Thus the opening of an office in Berea in 1925 began an association between the college and the Southern Mountain Workers' Conference that was to remain almost unbroken for nearly the next half century. Most of the controversies that were to mark those close to fifty years were begun during the first decade. The missionary spirit associated with Berea remained by far the dominant strain, but Philander Claxton's analysis lurked always in the background.

The Anglo-Saxon Thesis, the Church, and the Machine Age in the Hills

The strategic significance of the move to Berea may be seen in the ambivalence and confusion of a "Program for the Mountains" statement the Conference adopted shortly thereafter. It attempted to comprehend the relationship between whatever cultural uniqueness the region could be argued to have and the industrial and commercial development that dominated the rest of the country and was moving steadily into the mountains. "Give these people an organization and a program," the statement said, "and you have the means of directing great forward movement."[18] But the approach was paternalistic and the program itself much less tough-minded than what Commissioner Claxton had advocated a decade earlier. It called primarily for "God-fearing homes"; improved health and sanitation; an "agriculture fitted to the . . . mountains"; better roads, schools, and recreational opportunities; and stronger churches. Instead of focusing on the untaxed movement of coal into Northern markets and hardwood into the Kaiser's palace, the statement emphasized self-help and the "cooperation that we can get from other sections of the country."

The dominant motif was symbiosis. "Northern and Eastern artisans and capitalists are our friends and we invite them among us," the program said, "but we must not permit them to crowd us out and take away our . . . birthright. There is no insinuation that this . . . birthright [is] being dishonestly taken from us. [It is] simply slipping from our hands because of our inability to hold it." The program went on to envision the public schools as a mechanism for "coupling national patriotism with local patriotism," and the churches as instruments for electing "God-fearing, country-loving [officials] who will do their duty."

Thus the solutions to problems in the mountains were judged to lie in integrating the region's politics and economy into the mainstream while preserving, if possible, its picturesque and nostalgic folkways and religion. Fundamental structural alterations, both inside the region and in its relationship to the rest of the nation, were not part of the Conference's program for the mountains.

Arguments about cultural uniqueness centered on the Anglo-Saxon thesis that Commissioner Claxton had called "sob stuff." It held essentially that the mountain region had been settled originally by "pure Anglo-Saxon stock," which isolation had kept unmixed generation after generation. On the surface it was a purely ethnographic statement, and it was accepted among both piously nostalgic laymen and trained anthropologists.[19] But underneath it was more than that, and it had several regrettable effects. The most important was that it obscured the actually very mixed ethnographic and cultural character of the region, into which thousands of blacks and immigrants had been brought (sometimes literally by the trainload) to work on the railroads and in the mines, and in which thousands of American Indians who had managed to survive the first wave of colonization still lived.

The Anglo-Saxon thesis also reinforced the conservatism of the church as a powerful determinant of Conference policy and programs. A Presbyterian minister prominent in the work of the Conference told those who attended the 1926 annual meeting that "the work we do has its ends in [the] continuance [of] these rugged, brave, natural people . . . upon these great highlands, a source of white, sturdy, Protestant contributions to our American life."[20] Such arguments encouraged the Conference to remain conservative politically and oriented exclusively toward church, educational, and local community work with white Protestants. It was also on occasion the basis for essentially racist and jingoist posturing. "We have reached the point," a speaker asserted at the 1927 meeting, "where we can . . . tell the whole country about these Anglo-Saxon, mountain-locked, one-hundred percent Americans."[21]

The critical issues facing the Conference during the years after 1925 were neither ethnographic nor ecclesiastical, however, but political and economic: how to deal with the basic forces at work in a resource-rich region that long before 1900 had literally been mapped out for systematic exploitation by the surrounding industrial economy. Within its self-chosen limits, the Conference's options were few, as is clear from the position it took on industrialization in the mountains.

In the first issue of *Mountain Life and Work* in 1925, editor Marshall Vaughn invited future contributors to tell "the story of the coal development of the Appalachian mountains and the real pioneering that was necessary to bring it up to its present situation." "We want to hear the story of the timber and lumber industry," he said, "and what it has meant to the modernizing of our great centers of population and trade." Mountaineers, Vaughn continued, have an "inferiority complex" that has "found expression in . . . humble submission to outside invasion." Nevertheless, Vaughn saw a healthy symbiosis between mountaineers and outside capital: "The mountains [are] a region of vast resources that [has] been blocked out of the wild by a great people and held in trust . . . for the modern capitalist to develop and utilize."[22]

Similar views were expressed year after year at annual meetings. The social service secretary of the Congregational church, speaking in 1925, extolled the capacity of industry to humanize itself. He cited the "vision . . . love [and] latent goodwill" of Swift and Company and the Rockefellers, and warned that "Socialists, Anarchists, and the I.W.W." had to be conquered in the mountains.[23]

Indeed, it seems to have been generally believed that the ills attendant upon industrialization could be reduced only by Christianizing industry. Meeting in the First Presbyterian Church in Knoxville during the 1925 session, an "Industrial Round Table" discussion group noted the negative effects of industry in the mountains and considered the "possibility of obtaining the cooperation of heads of companies" in alleviating them. The consensus was that "the employers have hearts, and they vaguely realize the evils of their industrial system but . . . do not know what to do about it. If approached in the right way they would welcome counteractive influences."[24]

The Conference soon found itself, in fact, in the unenviable position of being alternately beggar and missionary to industry. In 1930 the industrial secretary of the Federal Council of Churches of Christ in America told the Conference the need was for "more Americanism in industry" and suggested that mountain working people "represent American traditions and are impervious to the imported ideas of foreign radicalism." His own experience in the textile industry had convinced him that if unions were needed at all, the American Federation of Labor's United Textile Workers (which had proved relatively weak during strikes at Elizabethton, Tennessee, and Marion and Gastonia, North Carolina, the previous year) would suffice.[25] Two years later, in the midst of the Depression, a consultant on industrial relations of the Protestant Episcopal church said at the annual meeting that 1 percent of the American people owned 33 percent of the wealth, that wage earners controlled only 3.5 percent, and that General Motors and Ford controlled three-quarters of the automotive industry. Nevertheless, he continued, "I am not saying that [such concentrations] are unwise." His solution was to Christianize industry. Although "capitalism carries in itself denials of the principles which underlie Christian living, . . . the redemption of modern industry is its redemption by a group of Christian principles," he concluded.[26]

The reality was, of course, that industrialization (especially the development of the coal, lumber, and textile industries) had brought serious problems to much of the region and that the churches had mostly declined to take note of them. Warnings of trouble to come had been inserted into *Mountain Life and Work* by a few writers beginning about 1929. An article headed "Mountaineers in Mill Villages" during the year of the Gastonia textile strike warned of "the development of [an] industrial caste system in this country—a condition of semi-servitude in which the freedom-loving mountaineer will be caught." The "smoldering fire [that] flames up again in the Harlan coal areas" claimed the attention of a later writer.[27]

Officially, however, the Conference tried to remain above the controversy. A January 1930 editorial in *Mountain Life and Work*, referring to the textile strikes in which many mountain workers were involved, noted merely that the incidents "furnish data that must be weighed by both proponents and denunciators of industrialization." The Conference's effective consensus position on industry in the mountains was that industry was there and even more was needed. Some ills attended its coming, but they could be reduced or eliminated by the application of Christian principles to industrial development. In the meantime, radical and foreign ideas and strategies for coping with the problem had to be resisted, and in that struggle Anglo-Saxon mountaineers could be counted on.

Taking such a position not only prevented the Conference from dealing effectively with the problem itself but also insulated it from

other potentially useful contemporary institutions such as the Southern Summer School for Women Workers in Industry (founded 1927)
and the Highlander Folk School (founded 1932). Both had significant
ties with still other organizations with more direct approaches to labor
and industrial problems. Such groups were mentioned frequently in
Mountain Life and Work, but the Conference seems never to have
sought a working relationship with them.[28] For all practical purposes,
it remained in the free-enterprise camp. As late as 1944, President
Arthur Bannerman, likening the struggle in the mountains to the
struggle against fascism in Europe, said that "we who live in democratic America know that here [in the mountains] too private enterprise and independent institutions may not survive unless we who
believe in them make a united fight for their survival."[29]

The 1930s were, in one sense, a period of growth for the Conference. Led since 1928 by Helen Dingman, a New Yorker who had
left her teaching job at Wellesley to work in Harlan County, Kentucky,
and then at Berea, the Conference initiated some small health programs in 1930 and an "itinerant recreation service" in 1934. The staff
grew to six toward the end of the decade, and there was a move
toward formal incorporation in 1938.[30]

Despite talk of an "expanding program," however, the Conference
was ultimately left without a single important function that its conservative ideology would allow it to undertake. The settlement schools
with which it had worked for several decades had largely been supplanted by the public schools, with which virtually no relationship
appears to have been established. Its early work with agriculture had
been rendered largely irrelevant in many areas by the mining boom,
which moved thousands off the farm and helped convert the region
to a cash economy. The Southern Highland Handicraft Guild, which
the Conference had helped to establish in 1930, was now independent
and in some ways stronger than the Conference itself. The New Deal
seems to have come and gone with relatively little notice.[31] Thus the
"old" work, which (whatever its limitations) had flowed naturally out
of the Conference's original personnel, values, and assumptions, was
complete. Its domain of interest and influence was reduced to dab-
bling with the more picturesque aspects of regional folkways (folk
songs, folk speech, recreation, and crafts), operating bookmobiles,
and distributing used books and clothing.

Some of the most striking evidence that the Conference had difficulty responding both to endemic problems of resource exploitation
and labor strife and to alternative strategies for regional development
lay in its largely ineffectual attempt to become involved in the cooperative movement toward the end of the 1930s.

By 1913, when the first gathering of mountain workers was held, the international cooperative movement was already a functioning reality. Swedish co-ops entered the world commodities market on their own as early as 1918.[32] A cooperative cheese factory was operating in the North Carolina mountains as early as 1915, and the highly successful Farmers Federation was formed in Asheville in 1920. In 1921 John C. Campbell's comprehensive regional survey suggested that co-ops held the best promise for agricultural resource development in the region.[33] The John C. Campbell Folk School's work with co-ops was discussed at annual meetings of the Conference regularly after 1925, as were co-op activities elsewhere in the world: the Rochdale movement in England (begun in 1844); the Irish movement led by Sir Horace Plunkett, Patrick Gallagher, and George Russell; co-ops in Nova Scotia; the Kagawa movement in Japan; the La Laguna project in Mexico; and activities in other regions of the United States.[34] By 1935 the international co-op movement had 120 million members and there were many co-ops in the mountains of Appalachia.

The Appalachian co-op movement was well suited to the geophysical, economic, and social character of the region and had some promise of moving beyond its basically agricultural beginnings (as it had in Sweden) to embrace ownership of natural resources, banking, the generation of power, and most forms of manufacturing and distribution.

Thus from at least 1925 on, the Conference could have taken a major role in co-op development in the region. But until 1930 it had no programs of its own, and it was 1938 before it sought a grant from the Earhart Foundation of Detroit and hired someone to direct its co-op work. Even then, it designed a limited and conservative program, and it ceased to be involved at all when foundation seed money was withdrawn.

The Reverend Ellsworth Smith of the American Baptist Home Mission Society spent one month learning about co-ops in Nova Scotia before becoming director of the Conference's Adult Education Cooperative Project in late 1938.[35] Smith came at a critical time: Both supporters and opponents of co-ops were very active. Efforts had recently been made by oil companies in Knoxville to defeat a gasoline co-op, and local department stores had "exerted pressure on the Knoxville *News-Sentinel . . .* to cease printing articles on cooperation and to force its employees to resign from the cooperative." Arriving at a Cumberland mining community to speak, the president of the Knoxville Cooperative Association was greeted by mine guards who prevented most residents from attending the meeting.[36] Nevertheless, the first Southeastern Conference on Cooperation, held in Greenville, South Carolina, in the summer of 1939, attracted nearly three hundred people from thirteen states. Blacks and whites participated on an equal basis.[37]

But Ellsworth Smith apparently was unable to accept the full social and political implications of the movement. He shared the views of Nova Scotia's Father J. J. Tompkins, a parish priest who turned to co-ops as a hedge against both poverty and "atheistic Communism."[38] The divided desire both to end poverty and to avoid drastic structural changes in the system that created it was apparently widely shared by other Conference members interested in co-ops. In October 1936 one of the most influential of them, President Hutchins of Berea, reported on his recent tour of Denmark and Sweden, where he had heard lectures on "cooperatives, the Welsh mining situation [and] Mr. Gandhi and his program" and visited a "community of forty-five farmsteads created out of the breaking up of one estate." At a small, well-managed farm, Hutchins said, he was served "coffee . . . with good plates and cups, and spoons that looked to me like silver."

On the whole, Hutchins's impression of the "middle way" was positive. The Danes "are a happy people," he said, "working . . . toward a time when none shall have too little and none too much." Nevertheless, he was bothered by what he considered to be the communistic inclinations of the movement. Thus, during his visit to a trade-union school in Denmark in which "a practical Socialism was being taught," he was relieved to find "no evidence of Communist teaching."[39] The problem, as he and others in the Conference saw it, was to gain the material benefits of the middle way without accepting its political implications.

The Conference's actual work with co-ops was limited to setting up several dozen "study clubs" in a three-county area in Tennessee, distributing literature, holding conferences at Berea, and reporting on co-ops in *Mountain Life and Work*. By the end of the project's first year, nine co-ops had been formed, but Smith cautioned against expecting more dramatic results. The temptation, he said, was "to conclude that the system must be changed before we can achieve more significant results, and so relieve ourselves of immediate responsibility."[40] By the fall of 1940 Smith had resigned to become pastor of a Presbyterian church and been replaced by C. C. Haun, director of the Rural Life Department at Vanderbilt University.

Haun's desire to "repeat the Nova Scotia transformation in the Southern Appalachian Mountains" was not to be fulfilled. By early 1942, though of the opinion that cooperation "is more of a necessity for us than for the people of any other region," Haun felt that "we struck at the Nova Scotia bait too fast."[41] His logic is doubly mystifying in view of the facts that co-ops were flourishing all over the country and he himself had toured co-ops in the Midwest, including the nation's first cooperative oil well and refinery, in Phillipsburg, Kansas. The Southern States Cooperative in Richmond had 100,000 members and $28 million in annual business.[42] A co-op dairy in Murfreesboro,

Tennessee, was the largest in America, with 2,400 members, and the Farmer's Federation in Asheville had annual sales of more than $3 million.[43] Nevertheless, when the Earhart Foundation grant ran out, the Conference discontinued the project. Articles on co-ops continued in *Mountain Life and Work* into 1944 but ceased almost entirely thereafter.[44]

It is ironic that the Conference's involvement in the co-op movement came to an end during Alva W. Taylor's term as executive secretary, for he was the most progressive chief officer of the Conference during its first half century, and (with the exception of John C. Campbell) the only one capable of leading it much beyond its conservative social and political origins. In an editorial a few months after he took office in January 1942, Taylor offered a list of principles that he said were "as fundamental to our social and political system as the freedom of business enterprise has ever been":

> . . . the right of labor to a job, not merely, as Henry Ford once said, to seek a job; the right of labor to organize; . . . the right of the aged, the children, and the unemployed to a guarantee of subsistence and (in due time) of the ill to medical care; . . . the right of the children of the poor to the abolition of wage labor; . . . the right of women to equal pay for equal work; . . . the right of all consumers to cooperate under advantages in the law equal to those of . . . corporations; the right of the people to own and manage any public utilities they may wish . . . on their own behalf; . . . the right to a day for those who labor with their hands no longer than that of those who work in offices, and to a wage that lifts much of the burden of poverty from their shoulders; the right of the unemployed to work for a wage on public works.[45]

Since the tough-minded demythologizing of Commissioner Claxton a quarter of a century earlier, there had been nothing to equal Taylor's statement. Asked a decade after he had become the Conference's executive secretary how he had formed his progressive philosophy, Taylor attributed it to "my first memories on a piece of raw prairie for which my father paid . . . $10 per acre and 10% interest [to] a N. Y. loan shark [who] had bought it from the government for about one-tenth of that price."[46] In fact, there had been many other influences.

For fifteen years after his graduation from Drake University in 1896, Taylor preached and taught in the Midwest and wrote for the *Christian Century* and other periodicals. The next fifteen years found him teaching at the Bible College of the University of Missouri and increasingly involved in the peace movement, interracial affairs, the World Court, and the League of Nations. As a member of the Interchurch World Movement, he studied the steel strike of 1919 and published *The Twelve Hour Day in Steel* (1920).

Taylor had long been fascinated by the history of oppressed people and their revolutionary leaders. He wrote his 1910 University of Chicago thesis on Irish tenant farmers. About the same time, he wrote a sketch of one of his revolutionary heroes, Lev Tolstoy, and a critical piece on the Mexican leader Porfirio Díaz, who brought "development" to Mexico at great benefit to American capitalists and great cost to Mexican peasants.[47] In 1927 he wrote a sensitive article on the Mexican revolutionary priest Miguel Hidalgo y Costilla, who had helped peasants start cooperatives and cottage industries that were eventually destroyed by the "long arm of the colonial government," and who in the fall of 1810, as "a parish priest in the little town of Dolores . . . lifted the banner of revolt" that eventually led to his own death before a firing squad.[48]

In 1929, in his late fifties, Taylor became professor of social ethics at Vanderbilt University. As preacher, teacher, and editor of *Social Trends* (1928–32), he was soon active in supporting striking textile workers in Danville, Virginia; the Progressive Miners in Illinois; Harlan County, Kentucky, coal miners; and striking miners in Wilder, Tennessee, where one or two of his students were helping to organize.[49]

Taylor's efforts eventually cost him his Vanderbilt job. Aged Chancellor Kirkland, whom he described as an autocrat who had a "majority of Babbitts on his board" and favored "everything that was of yesterday and most of all . . . the scheme that gave this university millions," abolished Taylor's chair, claiming the move was necessary because of the Depression. But Taylor remained philosophical. "I am only a progressive," he said, "but even a progressive looks radical to a reactionary."[50]

For several years thereafter, Taylor taught part-time at Fisk University and worked with the League of Nations Association. For one year (1939–40), he managed the Farm Security Administration's Cumberland Homesteads resettlement project at Crossville, Tennessee, an experience that taught him some discouraging lessons about the relationship between "big business capitalism and New Deal idealism," as well as the rigidities of the Farm Security Administration bureaucracy.[51]

Taylor's association with the Southern Mountain Workers Conference apparently was slight before he became executive secretary in 1942, although he attended annual meetings as early as 1933 and wrote now and then for *Mountain Life and Work* in the late 1930s. His appointment was a brilliant stroke. His ecclesiastical and academic credentials were impeccable, his social involvements matched many of the Conference's advertised concerns (and even more of the region's actual problems), and his theology and politics were well suited to move the Conference beyond its conservative program for the mountains.

While maintaining that "the Christ way is the best way," Taylor nevertheless called himself a "good deal of a humanist." Asked the perennial fundamentalist questions about a personal God, Heaven, and the will of God, he replied that his experience had "never revealed any intervention to save me from the tragedies that have come into my own life," that "if I don't have [Heaven] within myself and . . . help to bring it to my community, I doubt if there will be any for me," and that "the best I can discover out of the experience of both myself and others is to me the will of God." As a seasoned advocate of the social gospel, he later seconded Claxton's judgment that "it is dangerous to preach too much of the gospel message."[52]

Commenting on the Anglo-Saxon myth that had been so much of the Conference's stock-in-trade, Taylor said in 1938 that it "no more tells [the] sociological story [of the mountain region] than did the romance . . . of the Old South tell that of slavery and poor whites. The romantic coloring of pure Anglo-Saxon blood, rugged mountaineer individualism, colonial customs, etc., has covered up the poverty in the coves, the mountainside farms, and the thin soil of the plateaus." The millions made out of timber-cutting by entrepreneurs, Taylor said, "were siphoned off into the cities and the centers of capital; the forest workers were left in poverty."[53]

Yet with respect to capitalism and socialism Taylor held to a closely reasoned position. He was equally capable of denouncing the "utterly unchristian principles of laissez-faire," predicting that "we have lived under a soviet of big business so long that unless some readjustments are made to give the masses a new deal, we are headed for much trouble," and yet saying that "I am for these ardent young radicals, heart and soul, but must object to the apostolic zeal that makes socialism and every other good thing synonymous."[54] His involvement in the Wilder strike crystallized his objections to doctrinaire socialism. He wanted to feed the starving families of the Wilder miners as well as to organize them, and he felt the former effort was frequently sacrificed to the latter by organizers Howard Kester and Myles Horton, whom he found excessively doctrinaire about their socialism:

> *We* got the [garden seeds] into the ground—even though we got no socialist ideas in with [them]. When we go socialist we will want a few *living* miners to dig the coal even if it is more idealistic

to let them starve for the sake of propaganda. . . . We are doing our part to "give the bosses a damned good licking" without visiting the wrath of the devils on the unfortunate unemployed . . . who happened to work in a closed mine or were too dumb or pro-hoover [*sic*] to join the union before the strike. Their kids' bellies hurt when they are empty and my book tells me to feed even the enemy.[55]

Taylor continued his social involvements as executive secretary of the Conference. His keynote address at the Highlander Folk School's tenth-anniversary celebration in the autumn of 1942 caused the *Chattanooga Times* to attack him for what it called his "leftist views" and attempts to "inflame ignorant Negroes," but inside the Conference he appeared to be causing some significant movement.[56] He formed a new Industrial Committee, and as editor he brought a new vitality to *Mountain Life and Work* with his own series of articles on socialized medical care.[57] But he chafed under the influence of the Berea group as John C. Campbell had twenty-five years earlier. "You know, as I think I have told you two or three times," he wrote to a friend in May 1944,

> I have been a little tied down under criticism from certain parties at Berea, but now I feel after two years and especially with the attitude of the Executive Board at the [recent] Asheville meeting, that I am a little less under duress from the Berea group. . . . My gratification over the action of the Board was largely that I feel they are going to be permitted to cut loose from Berea.[58]

But cutting loose from Berea did not prove possible, and Taylor withdrew at the end of 1944, to be replaced by conservative army chaplain Glyn Morris, formerly director of the Pine Mountain Settlement School.[59] The organization (by then renamed the Council of Southern Mountain Workers, to become the Council of the Southern Mountains [CSM] ten years later) had in a sense come full circle. Its conceptual and analytical confusion had been revealed by its response to the problems of labor and industrialization; its operational limits, by its halting involvement in the cooperative movement; and its inability to use its religious origins as a basis for transformation, by the brevity of Alva W. Taylor's tenure as executive director.

At length the limits manifested themselves in the lack of a vital function, which was linked to a financial crisis. Although in the spring of 1944 Taylor had said the Council was "on a mountaintop with a wide and long vista before us," the next five years witnessed a severe retrenchment.[60] Support from Berea College and the Russell Sage

Foundation was discontinued. To conserve remaining funds the Berea office was closed in 1949, and the group shared an office with the Southern Highland Handicraft Guild in Asheville. Although plans were made to continue annual meetings, there was in fact only a skeleton organization until 1951, when funds were found to reopen the Berea office. Perley F. Ayer, a New Englander then working as farm manager for the Pleasant Hill (Tennessee) Academy, became executive secretary. Ayer was to preside, during the next sixteen years, over the most turbulent period in the organization's history.[61]

Perley Ayer's "Call to Partnership"

Perley Ayer's first task was to revive the Council. Funds were only part of the problem; most of the early leaders who had set the tone of the Council and defined its programs were gone, and a new set of critical issues was arising in the region. Strip-mining was just getting under way; the coal industry was in decline, and mechanization of the mines was causing unemployment to skyrocket; migration of mountaineers to the cities was growing rapidly; in 1954 the Supreme Court was to hand down its *Brown* decision on school desegregation; and in the early 1960s there was to be a new round of major federal programs for regional reconstruction.

For the Council, however, the 1950s turned out to be a decade of muddling through: seeking operating funds, finding new staff and board members, and continuing marginal programs, most of which were adumbrated by Ayer's statement upon becoming executive secretary. The region must share, he said, "the best of its traditions, its folk tales and songs, its crafts, its natural resources . . . not only with all parts of the area, but with all America as well."[62] *Mountain Life and Work* became a collage of advertisements for weaving yarn, romantic stories by Jesse Stuart, songs and dances, and reports on conventional social-service projects. The Council's publications program, begun in the late 1950s, produced collections of folk tales, Stuart's stories, and a dulcimer instruction booklet. Attendance at annual meetings reflected much of the Council's origins but little of the postwar changes in the region. Of more than three hundred who came to the 1958 meeting, more than a third represented churches and settlement schools and a quarter more came from colleges and universities. About 10 percent came from Berea, but there were only one representative from the United Mine Workers and three each from the Highlander Center and TVA. More than half of the board represented Berea, the churches, and the settlement schools.[63] Although the Council was in an expansionist mood again, it was short of money and by 1958 had to borrow $5,000 from Berea College.

Thus the focus during Ayer's first decade was on the quaint and picturesque cultural traditions of the least industrialized and conflict-ridden sections of the region, and on continuing the missionary services of the early days. Until they were virtually forced on the Council by events of the 1960s, the fundamental structural and political questions were deferred.

The 1960s, therefore, found the Council bound both by its long-standing missionary emphases and by the more recent contradictions of Ayer's "call to partnership" in a resource colony. Several things became clear: (1) The Council's central policy of political neutrality was not tenable; (2) the largesse received from corporations, foundations, and government agencies reassured by the rhetoric of neutrality came at a high price; (3) the economic and social programs made possible by such funding (for example, the Uptown program for Appalachian migrants in Chicago) ultimately neither satisfied the donors nor proved effective in substance; and (4) timidity in policy and ineffectuality in programs eventually produced internal dissension and led to a radical transformation of the Council itself at the end of the decade.

The paradoxes of neutrality. By the early 1960s the Council was being asked frequently to take positions on controversial issues, and even Kentucky's Attorney General John Breckinridge urged the group in 1962 "not to fear politics."[64] But Perley Ayer insisted upon consensus and neutrality. The Council, he said in 1963, is "the composite of individuals and agencies willing to join forces" to do what must be done. What usually had to be done, in his view, were only those things no one strenuously objected to—hence things that threatened no one's interests.[65]

In the winter of 1963 an editorial in *Mountain Life and Work* took note of strip-mining but added, "The Council . . . never presumes to give instructions or to issue demands. Our function is that of a catalyst. [We] hope to encourage people to do whatever *they* need to do . . . for the honor and integrity of their kind." If the Council becomes identified with any political viewpoint, the editorial continued, "there goes our integrity, our purity and our support, right out the window." A Council brochure of the same general period insisted, "It is . . . essential that the CSM be seen not as a political power. . . . CSM is not interested nor willing to carry on political fights. . . . Being absolutely NON-POLITICAL provides the CSM a broad base of operations."[66]

In 1964, while the Appalachian redevelopment legislation was being debated in Congress, the Council invited a panel of government officials and businessmen to discuss it but insisted that the Council itself had "no program to push, no particular point of view to sell." The next spring, as it was becoming clear that the War on Poverty was seriously flawed, the Council retained its tone of reasonableness and neutrality. "We must try," it said, "to understand and not be content until we have all the facts we can muster." Ayer told the staff early in 1966 that the Council was "constantly being asked to support causes and . . . legislation," but he insisted that it must refrain from doing so. In an editorial in *Mountain Life and Work* a month later, he insisted that it was "unwise" to "carry out . . . programs in competition with . . . the organized school systems [or] independent of the chambers of commerce," even though vested interests such as coal companies were using the school systems to help achieve political control over many Appalachian counties and the U.S. Chamber of Commerce was actively opposing every piece of Appalachian legislation introduced in Congress.

As late as March 1968, during congressional debate on placing OEO community-action agencies under the control of local politicians, *Mountain Life and Work* set forth some of the arguments but declined to offer "any official [Council] interpretation."[67] Although real neutrality was and long had been impossible in the Council's inescapably political arena, Ayer was committed to neutrality because he conceived of the organization as a home for everyone of whatever persuasion who wanted to "help."

Ineffectual as it eventually proved to be as a base for operating programs, the policy of neutrality improved the finances of the Council rather dramatically. Although Ayer had taken over an insolvent organization, which he feared might "wither like a cucumber vine in the August sun," he lived to preside over a Council dozens of times wealthier than it had ever been. The 1952 budget of $4,600 more than tripled (to $16,500) by 1955. By 1959 it rose to $42,000, and it passed the $100,000 mark in the early 1960s. By the middle of that decade, the Council was disbursing more than a million dollars a year in public and private funds.

The costs of neutrality. The wealth came at a price. Until the Council began to be more visible as a result of the infusion of money, corporate interests in the mountains seem to have paid it little attention. But in the late 1950s corporations began contributing to and joining the Council. Ayer told the board of the Council in 1959 he had reason to feel that Ashland Oil, General Telephone of Kentucky, and Kentucky Utilities would make large contributions. Corporate memberships were soon obtained by Appalachian Power, Georgia Power, Alabama Power, Carolina Power and Light, and Kentucky Power; Kentucky Utilities, Kentucky–West Virginia Gas, and Kentucky Telephone; and the Big Sandy–Elkhorn Coal Operators' Association, the West Virginia Coal Association, Debby Coal, and Beth-Elkhorn. Funds also came from the Ford Foundation and other private philanthropies (including board member Stuart Faber's Appalachian Fund) and directly from the OEO, which awarded the Council half a million dollars in 1965 to train "community action technicians" and contributed $406,000 for new and existing programs in 1969.

When the possibility of corporate or government control over the Council was raised at a board meeting in 1966, Ayer said he was certain it could be prevented, even though government funds that year made up 69 percent of the budget. Yet the Council, when it defined itself in fund-raising statements, sometimes took a different line. In a report to the Ford Foundation only a few months after Ayer had reassured the board, the Council was described as a "counselor and program director in conjunction with the Federal government." At a January 1967 board meeting, member Albert Mock suggested that the Council "offer to place on the . . . Board a member of the management of any . . . company which would contribute money" and proposed a plan to have large industries control small "people's corporations" in the mountains.[68]

A major Council program was Mock's "Enterprise Development Project," funded by the Economic Development Administration and the Sears Foundation. A November 1967 meeting of those responsible for the project included officials of the Appalachian Power Company, Alabama Power, Kentucky Utilities, Kentucky Power, and Kentucky River Coal Sales. Five of the eight members of the Council's Regional Economic Development Commission in 1967 were executives of these companies.

Nevertheless, Ayer retained his belief that the Council could remain neutral and avoid control by those who provided its money. Announcing a $150,000 U.S. Department of Labor grant for an experimental employment project in 1965, he said that in increasing its staff to run the new programs, "the Council has been fortunate in finding men who are 'nonaligned' . . . not committed to any particular political, economic or social faction or structure. Thus their work will be as nearly as possible unencumbered by bias or prejudice of any sort."[69] It was a naive judgment at best, as the operation of the Council's heavily funded programs had already begun to show.

Programs that satisfied no one. Three efforts launched by the Council in the mid-1960s—the Chicago Southern Center; the McDowell County, West Virginia, community action program; and the Appalachian Volunteers—showed that money obtained on the basis of a dubious neutrality would produce programs that neither satisfied the donors nor served well those they were intended to help.

Since World War II the Council had taken periodic note of Appalachian migrants in Detroit, Cincinnati, Louisville, Cleveland, Dayton, Chicago, and elsewhere.[70] Until 1962 its most significant program effort had been to hold an annual Workshop on Urban Adjustment of Southern Appalachian Migrants. But in that year the ultraconservative millionaire insurance executive W. Clement Stone of Chicago (author of *The Success System That Never Fails* and a heavy Nixon contributor in the 1960s) made two grants to the Council for its migrant work. The spring 1963 issue of *Mountain Life and Work* carried a full-page statement of appreciation to Stone from Perley Ayer. "Behind every good thing . . . there are dreamers who are also doers," it said. "Without such 'never-say-die' men, the best of us may despair. . . . The Council . . . salutes Mr. W. Clement Stone and his philosophy." With the help of Stone's money, a director was hired to open a Council office in the Uptown area of Chicago—one of the largest and worst of the Appalachian migrant ghettos, a square mile between the Loop and Evanston.[71]

In *Uptown: Poor Whites in Chicago,* Todd Gitlin and Nanci Hollander describe the Uptown of the early 1960s:

> One square mile, fifty or sixty thousand residents at any one time. . . . Perhaps half were born in the South, mostly in [Appalachia]. In 1960, 21 percent of all residents were over sixty years old, and over half the housing units were one or two rooms. . . . 27 percent lacked what the census called "adequate plumbing facilities." Despite a 13 percent vacancy rate, Uptown ranked second (to black Lawndale) in population density in the city. . . . 11 percent of store spaces were vacant, 21 percent in "marginal uses" (pawn and secondhand shops, missionary churches, fly-by-night businesses), [and] 17 percent in taverns.[72]

Feeling against Uptown residents had become intense in the 1950s. Toward the end of the decade the *Chicago Sunday Tribune* ran an article on the "fightin', feudin', Southern hillbillies and their shootin' cousins." It was followed by Albert Votaw's warning in *Harper's* that a "small army of . . . migrants from the South—who are usually proud, poor, primitive, and fast with a knife" had invaded Chicago. They were, Votaw said, "the prototype of what the 'superior' American should be, white Protestants of early American Anglo-Saxon stock; but on the streets of Chicago they seem to be the American dream gone berserk."[73]

But if the American dream had gone berserk in Chicago, it was not precisely in the way (or for the reasons) Votaw supposed. Besides being "home" for fifty thousand of Votaw's hillbillies, Uptown was also headquarters for Clement Stone's insurance companies, whose home offices, Gitlin and Hollander wrote, rose "like occupying sentries over the paper-blown streets." With the help of local politicians and urban-renewal officials and policies, Stone had gained financial control over much of the area and political and ideological control over most of the rest.[74]

Operating with Stone's money, the Council's Chicago Southern Center was in a position neither to challenge his domination nor to respond to board member Philip Young's urgent request in February 1966 that Uptown migrants be consulted in designing the Center's programs.[75] While the Center was distributing food and Christmas baskets and used clothing, and organizing men's clubs and ladies' sewing groups, other organizations such as JOIN (Jobs or Income Now) were organizing rent strikes, fighting the welfare bureaucracy, challenging the class-biased policies of urban renewal, and calling attention to the use of police power against the poor.

Thus the Southern Center acquired a reputation for conservatism among many Uptown residents and organizers. Gitlin and Hollander said it offered "minimal service," and in 1969 a letter to the editor of *Mountain Life and Work* reported that organizers in Uptown "were of the opinion that the staff of the Center wants to avoid political controversy at all costs, and thus will not cooperate in community organizing efforts." The Center's Director, James R. Gresham, replied, "Criticism . . . from 'organizers in the Uptown Community' are [sic] not new to us. We are not in league with those who believe in sit-ins, marches on the police and other types of demonstrations [which are not effective with] the individualistic Southerner."[76] Five hundred miles from Appalachia, in an urban setting, the missionary approach and the Anglo-Saxon thesis were still recognizable.

The Council's work in OEO-sponsored community action proved that it was no more effective in working with those still living in the most exploited areas of the region than it was in ministering to those who had fled to the cities. In early 1964 the McDowell County (West Virginia) Development and Improvement Association, which with help from the Area Redevelopment Administration had brought a small factory to the county, asked the Council for further guidance. After a visit by Ayer's assistant Loyal Jones, the Association voted to reorganize as the "McDowell County Chapter of the West Virginia Branch" of the Council. A proposal to the newly authorized Office of Economic Opportunity brought large grants in late 1964 and early 1965 for a community-action program (CAP). By the summer of 1966 the McDowell County CAP was one of the most heavily funded in the region. In concept and operation, however, it clearly reflected the missionary origins and compromised neutrality of the Council.[77]

The CAP board was dominated by business and professional men and chaired at one time by a local businessman who declared, "The poor of McDowell County live better here than anywhere else. There is no need to stir these people up." OEO analysts found that "political action activities . . . have been few in number" and that the program concentrated on conventional social services (free vitamins, book drives, tutoring) provided by community centers run by such unrepresentative and ineffectual neighborhood councils that door prizes had to be given to entice residents to attend meetings. Most of the CAP's effort went, the investigators found, into a "socialization and retraining" program "aimed at changing the values and attitudes of the Target Group in order to give them a greater stake in the middle-class culture from which they have been isolated." OEO itself was so displeased with the CAP that it forced a partial reorganization of the agency before approving new funding early in 1967.

Related problems arose in the Council's operation of another OEO-funded venture, the Appalachian Volunteers (AVs), formed in late 1963 and early 1964 (before the advent of OEO) to use weekend and summer student volunteers to paint one-room schoolhouses in the region. As the AVs moved toward more political activities later, Ayer fired several top AV staff members. The organization itself left the Council and incorporated separately early in 1966. When OEO shifted its funds to the new independent organization, Ayer complained that the Council had been "erroneously and . . . sometimes purposely misjudged and underestimated in its dedication to the poor . . . due to our refusal to embrace a strident militancy for its own sake."[78]

The Council's problems with the Southern Center, the McDowell County CAP, and the AVs were symptomatic of the contradictions in its posture and policy. Its effort to remain "nonpolitical" left it not a broad but a narrow base of operation. Its own programs—crafts and folklore; distributing drugs, shoes, and books donated by manufacturers at tax advantages to themselves; and rationalizing social and economic dislocations such as forced out-migration—never rose above their missionary origins.[79] As a facilitator and implementer of federal programs (such as OEO), it proved more conservative than the agencies themselves. Its proindustry programs (for example, Enterprise Development) were collaborative, and it was unable to co-operate with alternative development programs proposed by others.

When Harry Caudill and Gordon Ebersole (both Council board members) organized the public power–oriented Congress for Appalachian Development in late 1966, Ayer complained that they were "aspiring to supplant and supersede" the Council. "You appear dedicated," he told them, "to the organization of pressure groups . . . and to proving your humanitarianism by the competitive and antagonistic approach." In a reply to President Philip Young, Ebersole wondered whether the Council was "interested in change or [in] supporting the status quo with a naive hope that exploitation of men and resources will end if the golden rule is repeated at each annual meeting."[80]

Dissension and reconstruction. As it became clear that significant work could not be done under Ayer's leadership and that the region's problems were more serious than ever, criticism began to arise from the board and staff. Caudill, Ebersole, and other board members pointed out repeatedly what the issues were: the welfare mess, the Vietnam War, mine health and safety, strip-mining, and absentee ownership of resources. In March 1968, staff member Isaac Vanderpool criticized the OEO programs the Council was running, charging that "short-time 'disguised' work programs for a handful of the poor . . . create false expectations for a few more people, and . . . operate most effectively as conscience soothers for the bureaus and agencies, who are lying to everyone, including themselves." The Council, Vanderpool charged, was

> . . . just as guilty of wavering back and forth as any other bureau or agency and of philosophizing while increasing numbers of Appalachian people go hungry. [Indeed] we are quite often the first organization to take up a program that is fresh from some drawing board. Our failure is that we do not stand firm as an organization; we do not use our knowledge and influence to steer clear of pointless programs. . . . The Council has a responsibility to the people of the region. We are *not* responsible to the bureaus and agencies to help them get some pet project going. Where do we really stand?[81]

Ayer saw the developing controversy not as evidence that there was legitimate disagreement over substantive issues but as a sign that "those on the left" were adopting the "techniques of power politics." It was an extension of his earlier assertion that the controversy was an "illustration of what goes wrong when an agency becomes [too] sure of what it is organized to do."[82] By late 1966 a report on Council management prepared by a special subcommittee of the board found internal staff relationships a "jumbled . . . tangle of dissonances" and discreetly recommended that Ayer step down. By the end of the year the Council was under the direction of Loyal Jones (whom Ayer had picked as his successor), but its problems were far from resolved.[83] In such an inherently unstable situation, changes were inevitable.

Though long delayed, the changes came dramatically once they arrived. Within the space of twelve months, the Council was to be substantially reconstructed at two annual meetings in 1969 and 1970.

This Land Is Our Land, and the Land of Our Children: Toward Reconstruction

I have a great deal of respect for the Council of the Southern Mountains, but time waits for . . . no organization.
A. C. Sides, Director, Clay-Jackson Community Action Group, Inc. (1968)

The Council had had a long tradition of "neutral" annual meetings. When Saul Alinsky had been mentioned as a possible speaker at the 1966 meeting, the consensus had been that the meeting was "not a place for indoctrination."[84] There had been some controversial speakers and quasi-radical activity the following year in Knoxville, but until the 1969 Fontana, North Carolina, meeting all of the annual gatherings had been relatively tame affairs, with speeches by "important" people. The Fontana meeting, however, had been planned as an opportunity for Appalachian people to "fashion [their own] strategy to deal creatively with their own present and future." Discussion was to lead to "specific, concerted and direct action."[85] Joining the usual array of social workers, academicians, professionals, and agency personnel were many of the young and the poor who had never before participated.

In two tempestuous business meetings on April 10 and 11, the Council moved far from its long-cherished neutrality. An early vote ensured full participation in all decisions for all those attending the meeting. Later votes required the Board of Directors to be composed of 51 percent poor people within three years and established new working commissions on black Appalachians, poor people's self-help, aging, and natural resources. Moving into explicitly political areas, resolutions were then passed favoring a guaranteed annual income and opposing the Vietnam War and the antiballistic-missile system. All were adopted, amid charges by conservatives that the meeting had been packed with radical "outsiders."

Reactions to the meeting varied widely. President Philip Young found the Council now in a position to "assume the role of advocacy for [all] the region's people," but West Virginia University's provost Robert F. Munn condemned the "whole sorry bit" as shrill and puerile. Conference chairman Richard Austin was excited by the "perilous but remarkable dynamics" of the meeting, but board member Oliver Terriberry found it a "total disintegration into mob rule—a shouting, cat-calling exercise liberally sprinkled with foul . . . language." Past Council President Donald Fessler concluded that it had been an "engineered operation," with innocent-looking new bylaws "designed to facilitate a takeover by non-members." Potter Charles Counts wondered aloud, "Have we been raped?" Tom Cain of United Appalachians of Cincinnati replied that "the Council was not raped, it was married—married to the poor, the blacks, the youth and the urban Appalachian; it is pregnant—not by lust, but love—and it is a pregnancy of creative and beautiful people."[86]

Those who feared that the Council had dug its own grave were at least temporarily proved wrong. Within six months Loyal Jones reported that membership was at an all-time high, and the commissions were meeting and conducting their own business. Like Ayer, however, Jones himself preferred a middle ground and feared that the Council would perish if it became a "polarized debating ground or action arena." The Council, he said, had always "depended on and supported the basic institutions of the country" and counted on "individuals of means" for its budget. But such sources, he said, "will not endlessly finance [attacks] upon themselves."[87]

Others countered that money that could be used only to support existing institutions was money better done without, but Jones's prediction of financial difficulty was nonetheless accurate. W. Clement Stone announced that his annual $25,000 would be "withheld temporarily." The Ford Foundation's action on a proposal to fund the newly active commissions was unexpectedly held up, and OEO money became unreliable.[88] If the Council was to survive, it had to serve its new constituency, find new money, and resolve its internal division. The Fontana meeting, as it turned out, was a bare beginning.

The 1970 annual meeting at Lake Junaluska, North Carolina both extended the trend of Fontana and heightened conservative fears engendered there. Before the meeting opened, handbills warned that the Council had been taken over by radicals associated with the AVs, the Southern Conference Education Fund, and Highlander Center, all of which had been targets of earlier anti-Communist propaganda.

The issues that dominated discussion were those of the student movement of the late 1960s (opposition to the war, environmental awareness, participatory democracy) accommodated to the special problems of the region. After voting down a requirement that only those who had been Council members for thirty days could take part in the business meeting, participants passed resolutions granting funds to the Black Appalachian Commission, insisting upon community control of OEO programs, calling for the abolition of strip-mining and an end to the TVA's buying of strip-mined coal, and opposing President Nixon's Family Assistance Plan. The newly formed Natural Resources Commission presented a resolution opposing a recent Corps of Engineers report on water resources in the region, which had dismissed the possibility of public power.

A resolution emanating from the Youth Commission was passed

to make the "defined operational goal" of the Council the "public control of all natural resources, all private transportation (including railroads) and all energy corporations." Another resolution called for changing the Council's main function from providing data and technical assistance to communities and industries to "active support for the struggles of working and poor people" in Appalachia.

A month after the Lake Junaluska meeting, the board met in Berea to consider what Loyal Jones called the "three crises": lack of money, disputes about who was to manage the Council (board or membership), and "confusion of purpose." The board recommended finding new sources of funds but deferred the other issues until the results of Lake Junaluska had time to "settle out." Two weeks later Jones resigned (along with several other staff members), charging that the Council had become a "narrow, reform-oriented organization."[89]

Several weeks later the board met again to consider whether the Council had in fact been killed by "reformers on the left." Board member Warren Wright said that "the specter of . . . loss of funds" was not to be feared, because money available before had been restricted to innocuous projects. Mike Smathers added that the question was "not simply whether we will get money, but for what purposes, and from whom." As for Jones's "confusion of purpose," Smathers insisted that the situation in the region did not breed consensus, hence the Council would have to learn to deal with "confrontation, conflict, and compromise." In a letter to the *Louisville Courier-Journal*, a new member named Faye Baker said simply, "If the Council falls, we will build it again."[90]

The Pain of Renewal

The steps toward reconstruction taken by the Council were infused with the idealism of the youth movement of the late 1960s and grounded in a tough-minded analysis of the politics and economics of the region. For the reconstruction to prove durable, however, both the new issue-oriented strategy and the participatory organizational structure reflected in the commissions had to work, new funds had to be found, and new coalitions had to be forged. And finally, the interpersonal conflicts engendered by the reconstruction itself had to be resolved.

To head the reorganized Council, the board chose a farmer and self-educated minister, Warren Wright, as executive director, assisted by Julian Griggs, who had helped form the Poor People's Self-Help Commission, and Isaac Vanderpool, whose earlier letter had challenged the Council's collaboration with federal agencies and who was himself the son of a Floyd County, Kentucky, coal miner. Wright had many qualities consonant with the mandate of Fontana and Lake Junaluska: awareness of the colonial status of Appalachia, eagerness to use the Council's political potential, confidence in Appalachian people, and great strength of character and integrity.

Born in a Consolidation Coal Company camp in Letcher County, Kentucky, Wright had physically prevented Bethlehem Steel's bulldozers from coming on his land in 1961. He took his case all the way to the Federal District Court, researching and writing the legal briefs himself. Wright lost his case after discovering that in "this . . . rat-infested, wolfish jungle . . . we have so long and so religiously called civilization," judges would falsify the legal record to protect the interests of corporations whose funds had ensured their election. "I have the system to thank for one thing," Wright said. "That fight made me socially alive for the first time. That's when I became a citizen of the United States."[91]

Leaving the new commissions to operate autonomously, Wright concentrated his own work on strip-mining and a "welfare system that is robbing the hell out of poor people." There is "some hell in Appalachia that . . . desperately needs to be raised, and Appalachian people plan to raise it," he said, rejecting the prevalent notion that they were too fatalistic to protect their own interests. Under Wright's editorship, articles began to appear in *Mountain Life and Work* on the region's colonial system of education, West Virginia's regressive tax structure, the Appalachian Power Company's Blue Ridge project, and the coal industry.

Wright's address to the 1971 meeting (which took as its theme "This Land Is Our Land and the Land of Our Children") was a condemnation of the core assumptions of American life the likes of which had not been heard since the brief days of Alva Taylor thirty years earlier. He began by quoting Frederick Douglass: "Those who profess to favor freedom, yet deprecate agitation, are men who . . . want the ocean without the awful roar of its many waters." Wright then lashed into the vice-president of Consolidation Coal, who, he said, had recently declared that those who opposed strip-mining were "stupid idiots, socialists, and commies." Blending the rhetorical skill of the country preacher with the political insight gained in his fight with Bethlehem Steel, he quoted the prophet Isaiah as he had never before been quoted at a Council gathering—to condemn competition and acquisitiveness as basic drives in America:

Come now, ye rich, weep and howl for your miseries that are coming upon you. Your riches are corrupted, and your garments are moth-eaten. . . . Behold the hire of the laborers who mowed your fields, which is of you kept back by fraud.

Dissent "is of divine sanction," Wright insisted. "Let those who dominate and who are . . . destroying Appalachia take note."[92]

Wright's boldness was a strong tonic for the Council, but it also began to produce opposition from some younger staff members, who felt that his relatively autocratic administrative style flew in the face of the move toward democratization and that the focus on strip-mining was at odds with the decision to have the Council serve many constituencies through its commissions. Wright himself considered the "people's movement" implied by the new tone of the Council desirable, although he doubted that it already existed. But the argument over the Council's proper role in bringing such a movement into being seemed incapable of resolution, and in mid-1971 Wright stepped down as executive director.

In actual fact, no executive director's position was implied by the evolving structure of the Council; probably no executive director, assisted by any conceivable board, could have managed the new Council. Thus, in July 1971, after Wright's departure, administrative structure finally caught up with theory when the position was abolished. A "staff coordinator" was appointed, but the administrative model was egalitarian: All members of the staff were to be equal in power and responsibility. A few months later the staff voted to limit their own salaries to those set by OEO poverty guidelines.

Some early attempts to encourage an Appalachian "people's movement" proved successful. The Council coordinated an Appalachian "March for Survival Against Unfulfilled Promises" in Washington in early November 1971, to protest the inequities and insensitivity of the welfare system and the federal bureaucracy. "We are going," participants said, "to tell the nation what it's like to feel like colonized people . . . ignorant 'hillbillys' [and] 'yesterday's people.' [We] are going to demand that [we] be treated not as a reserve cheap labor pool, but as first class citizens. [We] are going to have a say in the programs that control [our] lives." Descending with new self-confidence upon the offices the U.S. Department of Health, Education, and Welfare (HEW), OEO, the Appalachian Regional Commission, and Appalachian legislators, they demanded and ultimately got personal appearances by HEW Secretary Eliot Richardson and other officials who at first ignored or refused to talk with them.[93]

A month later the Council helped sponsor a People's Hearing on Strip Mining, at Wise, Virginia. More than two hundred people from five states heard former Council Executive Director Warren Wright declare that America's laws, courts, media, and elected representatives "will not speak for us, do not hear us, and have in simple truth, betrayed us." A people's hearing, he said, "is the only true democracy in America."[94]

The movement away from the assumptions, values, structures, and styles of action that had characterized the Council during most of its first sixty years found physical expression in the fall of 1972, when the organization moved out of Berea and into the coalfields of Dickenson County, Virginia. Insofar as the move was motivated by a desire to get physically close to the most urgent problems of Appalachia, it was a success. Highway 83 from Pound, Virginia, to the new headquarters at Clintwood crosses an area cursed with the riches of coal and looking as though it has been ripped to pieces by the fury of some cosmic malevolence. Strip-mining is rampant, and the highway (ironically called the Cumberland Scenic Trail) affords an unbroken view of blasted mountaintops, 300-foot spoil banks that can never be stabilized or reclaimed, silted streams, and thousands of acres of thick mud in the bottoms. Overloaded coal trucks rumble one after the other onto the highway, already battered full of holes and covered with mud by their predecessors.

But the move had other aims also: to help build a regional consciousness and return control of Appalachia to its own people; to generate development strategies that were not merely an extension of the tendencies of mainstream America to reproduce itself; and to "identify [local] groups, relate them to each other, get . . . information to them [and] identify coalitions which must be supported."[95] To accomplish these more substantive aims, the Council had to survive, and survival was not easy. It was complicated by difficulties inherent in the new organizational structure, the failure of widespread commitment to the Council to materialize, and eventual disharmony among the new staff.

The old staff, said new Council President Jim Somerville, was a "fat stall of cattle," well fed, well paid, accustomed to the forms of a bureaucracy, and frequently with their major allegiances outside the region. The aim was to replace them with "lean and mean" mountaineers, natives who knew the region and were willing to stay and sacrifice to get the job done. But that aim was only partly accomplished. Some of the new staff were "natives" only in the limited sense that they were born and raised inside the geographic boundaries of Appalachia. By and large, they were children of the middle class, some of whom had come to the Council by way of graduate school outside the region. At one level they were motivated by a desire to solve the problems of their own region, but at another they appear to have been trying to heal the cleavage in their own souls and to assuage the guilt that derives from knowing that one's own middle-class privileges were bought with the sweat of one's mountain brothers and sisters.[96]

One by-product of the inner conflict was a compensatory bias against all middle-class people, especially academicians and professionals. Buttressed by a prior commitment to a personalistic philosophy and an antiestablishment politics, the bias against professionals resulted in a staff with few defined areas of responsibility, no backup systems or procedures, and no lines of authority. The staff also intended, through the new structure, to avoid alienated work, sterile interpersonal relationships, and reduced potential for personal growth. Nevertheless, the new staff structure proved unable to prevent conflicts among staff members, some of whom resigned in mid-1973. A few months later the very magnitude of the task in Appalachia was urging the Council to bureaucratize itself again: to compartmentalize and delegate responsibility, establish lines of authority, formalize communication and decision-making, and codify policies and procedures. In mid-1974 a plan was considered to hire a new executive director.[97]

Problems also arose with plans for changing the Council's relationship to "the people" and whatever "people's movement" might be emerging. By mid-1972 the Council's commissions, intended as one of the primary mechanisms for establishing the new relationship, were meeting infrequently if at all and had little influence on policy. The Council's bylaws were therefore changed to replace board members drawn from the nearly defunct commissions with representatives drawn from the welfare-rights organizations, antistrip-mining groups, health-care groups, and insurgent workers' and union reform organizations that were forming in the region. Institutional membership, which had earlier been open to any group, was restricted to "Appalachian organization[s] working for a democratic and economically secure future for . . . our people."

The old Council's weakness lay in its tendency to romanticize the conservative and picturesque aspects of folk culture; to overlook the dysfunctional effects of industrialization; to identify mountain people's interests with a national self-interest that resulted in their exploitation; to remain neutral when neutrality was impossible; to cooperate and react rather than initiate and act; to ally itself with conservative and paternalistic "helping" agencies and strategies; to focus on symptoms and rely on nostrums, rather than identify causes and press for structural reform; to remain comfortably inside restrictive ideological boundaries.

The new Council's strength lay in its tough-mindedness about the sources and effects of exploitation, insistence on structural reform, willingness to engage in necessary conflict, and efforts to help local people and groups determine their own future. Yet the new Council also proved to have the defects of its qualities: a predisposition to identify exploitation solely with "outsiders," to absolve mountain people of all responsibility for their own dilemma, to reject coalitions that threatened ideological purity, and to romanticize the "struggle" aspects of regional history even as the old Council had romanticized its picturesque aspects.

The move to turn the Council into a "people's organization" reached its apex in mid-1974 at the sixty-second annual meeting, where amendments to the bylaws designed to restrict further the participation of middle-class professionals were rejected after strident debate. When one member charged that professionals were trying to take over the organization, Amy Parks of Fairmont, West Virginia, replied "I can't see nothing to take over."[98] She was not being overly pessimistic; a few months later, the Council clung tenuously to life. It had been largely an anachronism during its final decade in any case, for the focus of public attention had shifted to local issue-oriented groups at the community level, and to federal programs at the regional level.

Notes

1. See Henry D. Shapiro, *Appalachia on Our Mind: The Southern Mountains and Mountaineers in the American Consciousness, 1870–1920* (Chapel Hill: University of North Carolina Press, 1978). Both the WCTU and the Federation of Women's Clubs started mountain schools. Such schools continued to be founded into the 1920s. Olive Dame Campbell, *Southern Mountain Schools Maintained by Denominational and Independent Agencies*, rev. ed. (New York: Russell Sage Foundation, 1929), listed 120 schools. For personal accounts of some of the better-known efforts, see Lucy Furman, *Quare Women: A Story of the Kentucky Mountains* (Boston: Atlantic Monthly, 1923) (Hindman Settlement School, Knott County, Ky.); William S. Dutton, *Stay On, Stranger* (New York: Farrar, Straus & Young, 1954) (Alice Lloyd College, Pippa Passes, Ky.); Lucy Morgan, *Gift from the Hills* (Indianapolis, Ind.: Bobbs-Merrill, 1958) (Penland School in North Carolina); Harnett T. Kane, *Miracle in the Mountains* (New York: Doubleday, 1956) (Georgia's Berry Schools); and May Cravath Wharton, *Doctor Woman of the Cumberlands* (Pleasant Hill, Tenn.: Uplands, 1953) (Pleasant Hill Academy).

2. Quoted from a resolution of the Foundation's executive committee, June 20, 1908. This and subsequent quotations are from the John C. Campbell Papers in the Southern Historical Collection at the University of North

Carolina and are used by permission. Collection hereinafter cited as SHC-UNC. Born in Indiana, Campbell spent his youth in Wisconsin. Before beginning his work with the Foundation, he had taught in a mountain school at Joppa, Alabama (1895–98), and served as principal of the Pleasant Hill Academy and as dean and president of Piedmont College in Demorest, Georgia (1901–7). See Henry D. Shapiro's "Introduction" to Campbell's *The Southern Highlander and His Homeland* (Lexington: University Press of Kentucky, 1969).

3. Campbell to John M. Glenn, Russell Sage Foundation, undated (*ca.* March 20, 1912), SHC-UNC.

4. Campbell to Glenn, July 3, 1912, SHC-UNC. See also John M. Glenn, "John C. Campbell and the Conference," *Mountain Life and Work*, XIII (July 1937), 8–11. Hereinafter cited as *MLW*.

5. William A. Brown to Campbell, November 8, 1912, and Campbell to Glenn, January 17, 1913, SHC-UNC.

6. *MLW*, XXIII (Summer 1947), 1 ff.

7. Minutes of organizational meeting, and Campbell to Glenn, May 8, 1913, respectively. Both in SHC-UNC.

8. *A Condensed Report of the Southern Mountain Workers Conference, Knoxville, Tennessee, April 22-23, 1914,* SHC-UNC, and Campbell to Glenn, April 25, 1914, SHC-UNC.

9. Lydia Holman to Campbell, May 13, 1915, and Campbell to Glenn, March 20 and April 17, 1917, all SHC-UNC.

10. Correspondence of Olive Dame (Mrs. John C.) Campbell and John Glenn, 1919–24, SHC-UNC.

11. Campbell to Glenn, March 20, 1917, SHC-UNC.

12. This and subsequent quotations are from Claxton's own transcript of his address in SHC-UNC.

13. *Ibid.*, pp. 7–15. Pursuant to an order of Congress in 1907, the Department of Agriculture had completed a study of the region's water power potential in 1908. See USDA Forestry Circular 144, *The Relation of the Southern Appalachian Mountains to the Development of Water Power* (Washington, D.C.: Government Printing Office, 1908).

14. Marshall C. Allaben to Campbell, April 2, 1918, SHC-UNC.

15. Frost to Campbell, March 17, 1913, and Campbell to Glenn, March 26, 1913, both SHC-UNC. Cf. William G. Frost, "Our Contemporary Ancestors in the Southern Mountains," *Atlantic Monthly*, LXXXIII (March 1899), 311–19. Frost, a graduate of Oberlin Theological Seminary, had come to Berea in 1889. See William G. Frost, *For the Mountains: An Autobiography* (New York: Fleming H. Revell, 1937), and Shapiro, *Appalachia on Our Mind*, pp. 113–32.

16. Glenn to Campbell, April 3, 1913, and Campbell to Glenn, September 17, 1914, and May 8, 1913, respectively, all SHC-UNC.

17. Glenn to Campbell, May 13, 1913; Frost to Glenn, April 22, 1921; Glenn to Olive Dame Campbell, December 7, 1923; and Hutchins to Olive Dame Campbell, November 12, 1924. All in SHC-UNC.

18. *MLW*, I (April 1925), 20–22.

19. See, for example, Ellen Churchill Semple, "The Anglo-Saxons of the

Kentucky Mountains: A Study in Anthropogeography," *Geographical Journal,* XVIII (1901), 588–623.

20. Rev. Warren H. Wilson, in *MLW,* II (July 1926), 4. Wilson, head of the Town and Country Department of the Board of National Missions of the Presbyterian Church, U.S.A., was an early colleague of John C. Campbell.

21. *MLW,* III (July 1927), 10.

22. *Ibid.,* I (April 1925), 2–4. *Mountain Life and Work* began as technically independent of both the Conference and Berea, but from 1928 until 1950 it was (except for a few issues) edited by the executive secretary of the Conference. During the 1940s its masthead designated it as the "organ" of the Conference.

23. Report of the Thirteenth Annual Conference, March 17, 1925.

24. *MLW,* I (April 1925), 34.

25. *Ibid.,* VII (July 1930), 7.

26. Address of Spencer Miller, Jr., *MLW,* VIII (July 1932), 3–7.

27. Lois MacDonald, "Mountaineers in Mill Villages," *MLW,* IV (January 1929), 3. See also *ibid.,* IV (January 1929), 20 ff.; VII (January 1932), 30; and VII (April 1932), 1–3. On the role of churches in the famous Gastonia textile strike of 1929, see Liston Pope, *Millhands and Preachers* (New Haven: Yale University Press, 1942).

28. See, for example, *MLW,* VI (January 1931), 10; XII (April 1936), 25; XVI (Fall 1940), 15 ff.; Myles Horton, "Highlander Folk School," XVII (Spring 1941), 15–16; and XXXV (Winter 1959), 23. In later years Highlander director Horton periodically served on the Conference board.

29. *Ibid.,* XX (Spring 1944), 1.

30. *Ibid.,* XIV (October 1938), 19; and XVI (Spring 1940), 4–6. On the incorporation process, see Richard Morgan Seaman, "An Analysis of Federative Patterns in Social Organization with a Field Study of the Council of Southern Mountain Workers," unpublished Ph.D. dissertation, Northwestern University, 1947, pp. 78 ff.

31. See *MLW,* XI (October 1935), 1–3 and 20–23; XII (October 1936), 1–5; and XVI (October 1940), 24–27. Seaman, in "Analysis of Federative Patterns," pp. 127–28, notes that when incorporation was considered "There was concern as to whether 'action' could not now be added to the Council's purpose." No such addition was made, however, for fear that it would, as Executive Committee minutes expressed it, "lessen the value of the organization by making membership intolerable for some of the denominations which could not commit themselves."

32. See Marquis Childs, *Sweden: The Middle Way,* rev. ed. (New Haven, Conn.: Yale University Press, 1947).

33. John C. Campbell, *The Southern Highlander and His Homeland* (1921; reprint, Lexington: University Press of Kentucky, 1969), pp. 25 ff.

34. See *MLW,* VI (April 1931), 2 ff.; XI (July 1935), 24 ff.; XV (April 1939), 27; XV (Winter 1940), 29; XVIII (Autumn 1942), 26; XIX (Summer 1943), 17; XX (Summer 1944), 12 ff. and 35.

35. See Smith's articles in *ibid.,* XIV (October 1938), 18; XIV (January 1939), 20 ff.; and XV (July 1939), 14–19. Also Seaman, "Analysis of Federative Patterns," pp. 121 ff.

36. *MLW*, XIV (July 1938), 18 ff. When co-ops throughout the country later pooled funds for a radio series, CBS and NBC refused to sell them air time until forced to do so under pressure from Senator Norris [*ibid.*, XIX (Winter 1942), 3].

37. *Ibid.*, XV (July 1939), 31; and XVII (Summer 1941), 12 ff.

38. Ellsworth Smith, "Cooperatives—the Hope and Unknown of the Southern Highlands," *ibid.*, XV (July 1939), 14 ff. On co-ops in Nova Scotia, see M. M. Coady, *Masters of Their Own Destiny* (New York: Harper, 1938).

39. Upon his inauguration as president of Berea in 1920, Hutchins had remarked, "At a time when restlessness and the spirit of Bolshevism pervade the industrial centers of our Nation, it is reassuring to know that the Southern Mountains contain a population of . . . pure-blooded Americans . . . needing only the advantages of Christian education to become a source of strength to our national life." Quoted in Henry Shapiro, "A Strange Land and a Peculiar People: The Discovery of Appalachia, 1870–1920," unpublished Ph.D. dissertation, Rutgers University, 1967, p. 107n. Hutchins quotations not otherwise attributed are from *MLW*, XII (October 1936), 10 ff.

40. *Ibid.*, XV (Winter 1940), 26, and XV (Spring 1940), 16 ff.

41. *Ibid.*, XVII (Spring 1942), 14 ff.

42. *Ibid.*, XVIII (Autumn 1942), 14. On coops in America in the 1930s, see James B. Warbasse, *Cooperative Democracy* (New York: Harper, 1942).

43. *MLW*, XIX (Summer 1943), 18; XX (Summer 1944), 26 ff.; and XX (Winter 1944), 16. In a letter to Olive Dame Campbell of March 16, 1925 (SHC-UNC), the Federation's James G. K. McClure reported six operating warehouses and annual sales of $680,000. See McClure's "Ten Years of the Farmer's Federation," *MLW*, VI (April 1931), 23–25.

44. *Ibid.*, XIX (Autumn 1943), 48.

45. *Ibid.*, XVIII (Summer 1942), 32.

46. Letter of May 19, 1951. Information and quotations that follow are from the Alva W. Taylor papers in the Disciples of Christ Historical Society, Nashville, Tennessee, and are used by permission. See *Alva W. Taylor: a Register of His Papers in the Disciples of Christ Historical Society* (Nashville: Disciples of Christ Historical Society, 1964).

47. See *Christian Century*, December 1 and 15, 1910.

48. Alva W. Taylor, "Hidalgo: Father of Mexican Revolution," *Front Rank*, October 30, 1927.

49. Letters of December 17, 1932; May 6, 9, and 18, 1933; July 16, 1937. See Fran Ansley and Brenda Bell, "Davidson-Wilder, 1932," *Southern Exposure*, I (Winter 1974), 114 ff.

50. Letters of May 18, 1933; March 3, 12, and 31, 1934; May 3, 1934; May 16 and 19, 1936; and August 27, 1936.

51. Official Cumberlands Homesteads Correspondence, 1939–40 (in Taylor papers at the Disciples of Christ Historical Society). Quotation from letter of November 1, 1939.

52. Letter to J. M. Allen, March 28, 1942, and letter of March 3, 1948, respectively.

53. Alva W. Taylor, "Sub-marginal Standards of Living in the Southern Mountains," *MLW*, XIV (July 1938), 12–14.

54. Letters to W. J. Lhamon, December 17, 1932, and November 27, 1936; letter of March 18, 1933, respectively.

55. Letter to unidentified correspondent, May 18, 1933. Taylor had no qualms about socialist politics. See, for example, his admiring article on the socialist city government of Milwaukee in *Christian Century*, December 8, 1910. Emphasis in original.

56. *Chattanooga Times*, October 27, 1942. Taylor was by then serving as a U.S. Department of Labor arbitrator for cases in the Southeast.

57. *MLW*, XVIII (Spring 1942), 20–23; XVIII (Summer 1942), 5–14; XVIII (Autumn 1942), 21–22.

58. Letter of May 3, 1944.

59. Morris's articles appear in *MLW*, XIII (October 1937), 8–12; XIV (January 1939), 13–14; and XVII (Winter 1942), 8 ff.

60. *Ibid.*, XX (Spring 1944), 1, and XXV (Summer 1949), 4. Seaman, "Analysis of Federative Patterns," pp. 82–83, notes a decline in breadth of institutional and individual participation after 1936. Projected budgets had risen from $3,000 in 1938 to $13,000 in 1944 but were not always met (p. 110).

61. On Ayer's early work and his appointment, see *MLW*, XXIV (Winter 1948), 13; XXVII (Summer 1951), 47; and XXVII (Fall 1951), 22. Some of his speeches were published after his death in *Seeking a People Partnership* (Berea: Council of the Southern Mountains, 1969). The name of the Conference was changed in 1944 to the Council of Southern Mountain Workers, and in 1954 to the Council of the Southern Mountains. I shall refer to it henceforth as "the Council."

62. *MLW*, XXVII (Fall 1951), 22.

63. From registration list for 1958 annual meeting, and letter from Council president to board members, October 2, 1958.

64. *Middlesboro* (Ky.) *Daily News*, March 26, 1962, p. 1. See also *MLW*, XXXIX (Fall 1963), 5–9.

65. *MLW*, XXXIX (Fall 1963), 60–61.

66. "Introducing the Council of the Southern Mountains," undated mimeo.

67. See *MLW*, XL (Fall 1964), 6; XLI (Spring 1965), 5; minutes of executive staff meeting, January 9, 1966; and *MLW*, XLIV (March 1968), 11.

68. Richard B. Drake, "CSM: Current History in the Making," *MLW*, XLVI (June 1970), 9 ff.; and "Final Report from the Council of the Southern Mountains to the Ford Foundation on the Appalachian Project," July 22, 1967, p. 13 (mimeo).

69. *MLW*, XLI (Spring 1965), 27.

70. See for example *ibid.*, XXX (Summer 1954), 23; XXXIV (Fall 1958), 42 ff.; and XXXVI (Fall 1960), 52. Officially the Council had no position on migrants, but the point of view most often represented in *Mountain Life and Work* was that Appalachian people who "chose" to migrate must be helped. See Howard Beers, "The Changing Highlands," *MLW*, XXXIV (Fall 1958), 5–6, and Rupert B. Vance, "How Much Better Will the Better World Be?," *ibid.*, XLI (Fall 1965), 25 ff. Migration to urban centers increased greatly during World War II but was already significant by the mid-1930s. See

G. G. Leybourne, "Urban Adjustment of Migrants from Southern Appalachia [to Cincinnati]," *Social Forces,* XVI (1937), 238–46, and Morris G. Caldwell, "Adjustments of Mountain Families in an Urban Environment," *ibid.,* XVI (1938), 389–95.

71. See *MLW,* XXXIX (Spring 1963), 9; *ibid.,* XXXIX (Winter 1963), 35; and board minutes, February 19–22 and November 26, 1963. The Center opened in November. Representatives of the Chicago Boys Club, W. Clement Stone's insurance company, and others attended the Council's 1963 annual meeting and proposed the Center. In 1962 Stone had contributed $7,500 to the Council, one-tenth of its operating budget.

72. Todd Gitlin and Nanci Hollander, *Uptown: Poor Whites in Chicago* (New York: Harper & Row, 1970), p. xix.

73. Albert N. Votaw, "The Hillbillies Invade Chicago," *Harper's,* CCXVI (February 1958), 64–67.

74. See Gitlin and Hollander, *Uptown,* p. 331.

75. Council Executive Committee minutes, February 4, 1966.

76. Gitlin and Hollander, *Uptown,* p. 103; *MLW,* XLV (February 1969), 23. For a sympathetic view, see Bill Montgomery, "The Uptown Story," *ibid.,* XLIV (September 1968), reprinted in David S. Walls and John B. Stephenson (eds.), *Appalachia in the Sixties* (Lexington: University Press of Kentucky, 1972), pp. 144–53. In mid-1966 the Center was incorporated separately, and the Council ceased to handle funds for it at the end of 1967.

77. Funding data were drawn from *Poverty Program Information* (Washington, D.C.: Office of Economic Opportunity, 1966), II, 987–88. Subsequent discussion of the organization is based upon an OEO-funded study, *An Evaluation of the Impact of the Community Action Program upon Poverty Conditions in McDowell County* (Morgantown: West Virginia University Human Resources Institute, 1969).

78. Ayer to the OEO's Jack Ciacco, May 28, 1966, and to Sargent Shriver, May 31, 1966. For an extended discussion of the AVs, see Chapter 7.

79. See for example *MLW,* XXXV (Fall 1960), 53. Distributing used books provoked controversy. See Edward Geller, "Such Easy Charity," *Library Journal,* XC (April 15, 1965). The vitamin project was a plan, co-sponsored by the E. R. Squibb Company and the National Institutes of Health, to use vitamin-deficient Appalachian children as subjects for a research project. See the Council's Newsletter no. 2, September, 1964, and *Report for 1965,* p. 5. Also see the *Mountain Eagle,* September 17, 1964, p. 1.

80. Ayer to Ebersole, August 16, 1967, and Ebersole to Young, August 30, 1967. On the Congress for Appalachian Development, see Chapter 8.

81. *MLW,* XLIV (March 1968), 16.

82. *Ibid.,* XLIII (Spring 1967), 2, and XLII (Winter 1966), 2, respectively.

83. Quotation from report by William Ramsay to Executive Committee, September 15, 1966. See also P. F. Ayer, "Along Came Jones," *MLW,* XXXIV (1958), 33 ff. Jones joined the staff full-time in June, 1958.

84. Minutes of executive staff, January 17, 1966.

85. From the conference call in *MLW,* XLV (February 1969), 12–13.

86. All quotations from *ibid.,* XLV (May and June 1969).

87. Executive Director's Report, October–November 1969, and Loyal Jones, "1970's CSM," *MLW*, XLVI (January 1970), 7 ff.

88. The Council requested $180,000 from Ford in mid-1969 for commission staff training and projects. Difficulty in getting the money was increased by the restrictions of the Tax Reform Act of 1969. The OEO was apparently guilty of considerable duplicity in its dealings with the Council. See Ward Sinclair's article in the *Louisville Courier-Journal*, June 7, 1970.

89. *MLW*, XLVI (May 1970), 14–15, and XLVI (June 1970), 4 ff., respectively. See also articles in the *Louisville Courier-Journal*, June 3 and 8, 1970.

90. *Louisville Courier-Journal*, June 8, 1970.

91. *MLW*, XLVI (July–August 1970), 23 ff. On Wright, see *ibid.*, XLVI (October 1970), 8–12, and the *Louisville Courier-Journal and Times Magazine*, September 27, 1972.

92. *MLW*, XLVII (July–August 1971), 4 ff. Ironically, Wright's predecessor, Alva Taylor, twenty years before he himself became executive secretary, quoted the same scripture in an article on economic exploitation in America. See Alva W. Taylor, "Poverty and Wealth," *Front Rank* (undated clipping in Taylor papers, prior to April 24, 1921), pp. 8–9.

93. *MLW*, XLVII (September–October 1971), 14, and "Summary of the Welfare March on Washington," *ibid.*, XLVII (November 1971), 3–15.

94. *Ibid.*, XLVII (November 1971), 22 ff.

95. Minutes of Administrative Committee meeting, December 10, 1972.

96. The dilemma, commented upon by many Appalachian natives, has received a classic statement in Frantz Fanon's *The Wretched of the Earth* (1963; reprint, New York: Random House, 1968), pp. 148 ff. I am sensitive to the dilemma partly because I am part of the phenomenon I describe. See Preface and David E. Whisnant, "Ethnicity and the Recovery of Regional Identity in Appalachia," *Soundings*, LVI (Spring 1973), 124–38. See also Mike Smathers, "Notes of a Native Son," *MLW*, XLIX (February 1973), 19–22.

97. Minutes of Administrative Committee meeting, December 10, 1972. Kenneth Keniston noted a similar dilemma among the young staff that coordinated the Vietnam summer project in 1967. See *The Young Radicals* (New York: Harcourt Brace, 1968). His observations were corroborated by Kirkpatrick Sale's study of the Students for a Democratic Society. See his *SDS* (New York: Random House, 1973), pp. 213 ff.

98. Rex Bailey, "Mountain 'working class' plan fails," *Louisville Courier-Journal*, August 11, 1974.

PART II
THE
FEDERAL
EFFORT

CHAPTER 2

All Forms of Human Concerns:
The Tennessee Valley Authority, 1933–75

> This is the story of great change. . . . It is a story of the people and
> how they have worked to create a new valley.
> David Lilienthal, *TVA: Democracy on the March* (1944)

> TVA now controls the fate of the coal-bearing regions of Appa-
> lachia. [In] Central Appalachia, its role has been nothing short of
> disastrous.
> Harry Caudill, *My Land Is Dying* (1971)

INTRODUCING THE Tennessee Valley Authority legislation in 1933,
President Roosevelt called the Authority a project that "touches and
gives life to all forms of human concerns." A bronze plaque affixed
to TVA's first dam on the Clinch River three years later said it was
"Built for the People of the United States." The next year Roosevelt
contemplated establishing seven additional valley authorities modeled
on TVA.[1] Nebraska's "fighting liberal" Senator George W. Norris,
who introduced the TVA legislation annually for twelve years and
saw it vetoed twice (and for whom the first dam was named), died in
1944 confident that he and his colleagues had built well.

For most of its first two decades, liberals and progressives were
almost unanimous in celebrating TVA as the most idealistic and comprehensive planning effort ever attempted in the United States. The
consensus was that no other effort had ever been aimed so directly
at the basic causes of widespread social and economic problems, or
designed so imaginatively to achieve the integrated development of
the total resources of a region. Within a decade, TVA became the
national symbol of rational, humane, democratic planning and development. Foreign visitors flocked to study TVA and returned home
to emulate its approach to integrated resource development. Chairman David Lilienthal referred to TVA as "a pattern for the New
World" and envisioned "the use of TVA experience and methods in
the reconstruction of the world."[2] Such criticism as there was came
mostly from doctrinaire laissez-faire ideologues, pork-barrel politicians, and competing business interests such as private utilities and
fertilizer manufacturers.

Since about 1960, however, TVA has come under increasing criticism from liberal and progressive quarters. Much of the criticism was precipitated because of TVA's impact on Appalachia's coal mining counties, but it ultimately extended to the agency's entire operation. Although TVA's recent critics have not been wholly of one mind, the outlines of a new consensus can nevertheless be discerned: that the agency created to reconstruct the natural environment of the Tennessee Valley has itself become environmentally destructive; that an experiment in what was once proudly called "grassroots democracy" has become an unaccountable bureaucracy; that an agency that pioneered in progressive labor relations among public employees has helped to drive unionized coal operators out of business; and that the much touted TVA "yardstick" of efficiency and economy in power production has been reduced to a single-minded insistence upon producing power at the lowest dollar cost, regardless of social or environmental considerations. Shortly after TVA's fortieth anniversary, the liberal *Washington Post* columnist Nicholas Von Hoffman surveyed the criticism and succinctly called the Authority "an idea whose time has gone."

In a profoundly important sense, however, TVA's history as a public development agency has provided a persistent counterpoint to most discussions and decisions about development strategies in Appalachia since the late 1930s. Paradoxically, that has especially been the case since TVA's image began to decline in the 1960s, as a new generation of planners and developers sought models for a new round of state and federal Appalachian programs.

Whether Von Hoffman's summary judgment is fully justified is too vast a question to entertain in so brief a space. But because the history of TVA is so intimately connected to the history of development strategies in Appalachia (and public opinion concerning them), one must try to understand not only TVA's direct impact on the Appalachian portion of its service area, but also its status as a model for subsequent development efforts in the region.[3]

The Valley and the Coming of TVA, 1933–53

In the three or four decades prior to the advent of TVA, much of the great valley of the Tennessee River, stretching over six hundred miles from Knoxville through northern Alabama and then northwest to the Ohio at Paducah, Kentucky, had been reduced by waste and neglect to an economic and ecologic disaster area. Annual floods, abetted by the clear-cutting of forests and unrelieved years of row-cropping, carried irreplaceable topsoil down the river, destroyed farms and towns, and wasted valuable hydroelectric potential. Forest fires consumed thousands of acres of timber annually. Sixty-two percent of the valley's 3 million people scratched out a bare subsistence on 350,000 small (70-acre average) farms scattered over 41,000 square miles in portions of seven Appalachian states. Unaided by electricity or progressive farming techniques, their efforts earned them an average annual income only 44 percent of the national average.[4] Even the river itself was a largely wasted resource. Frequent shoals, narrows, rock reefs, and gravel bars restricted navigation to a fraction of the river's total length, and little of its hydroelectric potential had been developed.

Development efforts before 1933 had been fragmented, mostly private, single-purpose projects whose aims and operations were frequently in conflict with one another. High dams built for power production by private industries on upstream tributaries, for example, were at odds with downstream flood-control dams and the need for increased flow for navigation. The individual projects themselves seemed scattered almost randomly about the valley: a hydroelectric installation here, a navigation lock there, a flood-control dam somewhere else, and reforestation virtually nowhere.

The TVA legislation sought to replace uncoordinated, fragmentary, single-purpose development with unified, public, multipurpose development that would bring each separate project into a total harmony of design with all the others, aiming toward optimal reconstruction and development of the entire economic, social, and ecological system of the valley. Private development, which brought great benefits to a few and left little or nothing for the majority, was to yield to public development for the common good. And inherently wasteful single-purpose projects were to be supplanted by more efficient multipurpose endeavors—dams, for example, that provided an integrated system of power production, flood control, and navigation.

Unfettered by the arbitrary boundary lines of sometimes jealous and self-interested counties and states, TVA was to develop the entire valley as a natural entity. "What God has made one," said Director David E. Lilienthal in an inflated poetic figure, "man was to develop as one." Another of the three original directors, agriculturalist Harcourt A. Morgan, chose the phrase "Our Common Mooring" to denote his own early ecological understanding of the interdependence of the valley's natural systems and their relationship to its institutions. The third director (and original chairman of the board), Arthur E. Morgan, though differing from his colleagues both temperamentally and in some of his social and political views, shared with them "a picture of the world as it might be" in the Tennessee Valley.[5]

The agency created in May 1933 to implement the idealistic design had no precedent. President Roosevelt envisioned a "corporation clothed with the power of government but possessed of the flexibility and initiative of a private enterprise."[6] The description may have been more politically expedient than accurate, but the agency was unique, nevertheless. To free it from the bureaucratic rigidities of established federal departments and agencies, TVA was made an entirely separate government corporation. To allow it to build a competent staff quickly, it was exempted from both formal Civil Service regulations and informal patronage expectations. To expedite its construction timetables and increase flexibility of architectural and engineering design, it hired its own architectural and engineering staffs and construction crews. Its broad-scale managerial autonomy also included freedom from audit by the General Accounting Office and substantial freedom from congressional appropriation control by virtue of its authority to reinvest revenues from power production. To increase responsiveness to local needs and provide accountability, TVA's principal headquarters were located in the valley itself rather than in Washington; administration was to be decentralized, and there was to be constant "grassroots" input.[7]

It was an impressive creation, and its accomplishments in its primary areas of responsibility (navigation and flood control, agriculture, and power production) during its first twenty years moved some, including Chairman Lilienthal, to lyricism:

> It is a tale of a wandering and inconstant river now become a chain of broad and lovely lakes which people enjoy, and on which they can depend . . . for the movement of the barges of commerce that now nourish their business enterprises. It is a story of how waters once wasted and destructive have been controlled and now work . . . creating electric energy to lighten the burden of human drudgery. Here is a tale of fields grown old and barren with the years, which are now . . . lying green to the sun; of forests that were hacked and despoiled, now protected and refreshed with strong young trees.[8]

TVA had succeeded in a task at which many had failed before. A century of prior effort to make the Tennessee navigable—dredging, channeling, blasting, locking, and building expensive canals around the "steamboatman's hell of agony and danger" at Muscle Shoals—had resulted in only a six-foot channel below Chattanooga and a three-foot channel upriver to Knoxville by 1933. But within little more than a decade, the TVA had transformed the Tennessee into a fully navigable, nine-foot, year-round channel throughout its entire length, involving a total vertical lift through the locks of more than five hundred feet.

By TVA's twentieth anniversary, river traffic had exceeded one billion ton-miles per year, more than twenty-two times what it had been in 1928.[9] Thirteen dams on the five major tributaries (the Clinch, Holston, Little Tennessee, French Broad, and Hiwassee) and nine on the main channel of the Tennessee vastly reduced the frequency and severity of floods in the valley. In the fifteen years prior to 1951, TVA claimed, control of potential floods at Chattanooga alone resulted in aggregate savings of about $154 million.[10]

Navigation and flood control were the primary aims of the act, but an important secondary aim—to be pursued, in the words of Section 9(a), "so far as may be consistent with such purposes"—was power production. In that area also, TVA demonstrated remarkable success by the end of its first two decades. From slightly less than 750,000 kilowatts of installed hydroelectric capacity on the Tennessee and its tributaries in 1933, available capacity more than doubled to nearly 1.6 million kilowatts before 1940 and rose to 3.0 million kilowatts by 1953. By 1955 TVA had assembled what Chairman Gordon R. Clapp justly called the "largest single integrated [power generation and distribution] system" in the United States, serving 97 municipal systems and 51 rural electrical co-ops (1.3 million customers) spread over an 80,000-square-mile area in six states.[11]

Much of TVA's early hydroelectric power was consumed by the valley's farmers, only 3.5 percent of whom had electric service in 1933. By 1955, 90 percent of the farms were electrified, and residential and industrial use of electricity had increased dramatically.[12] In conjunction with reforestation, flood control, and rural electrification, the TVA's phosphate fertilizer program substantially transformed much of the agriculture of the valley. Eroded, row-cropped, inefficient, and uneconomical hardscrabble farms gave way to lush dairy farms.

The indirect spinoff benefits of TVA's primary programs in navigation, flood control, power production, agriculture and forestry were also substantial, even if they may upon occasion have been overestimated by the agency's strongest supporters.[13] As by-products of maintaining and providing social services for its own construction crews, TVA became involved in improving the general quality of life in the valley: housing, health care, libraries, recreation, adult education, and the like. And although, in the opinion of a thirty-year veteran TVA planner, the Authority was never able to develop a coherent and consistent position with regard to its role in overall planning in the valley, planning was one of its perennial concerns. The early planned town at Norris was followed by the employee village at Fontana and later programs of planning assistance to local and state agencies.[14]

Beginning in the early 1950s on Chestuee Creek, a tributary of the Hiwassee (in turn a tributary of the Tennessee) in east Tennessee and on the Beech River in the western part of the state, TVA also inaugurated what came to be called the Tributary Area Development program (TAD). Stemming from routine requests for technical assistance in two small watersheds, the program grew to encompass planning and construction projects in sixteen tributary areas. The TAD program has had its critics but nevertheless has been cited repeatedly by TVA supporters as evidence of the agency's authentic grassroots involvement and its flexible commitment to positive change in the valley.

Thus, although some of TVA's strongest recent critics have been reluctant to admit the agency's positive accomplishments, those accomplishments cannot be gainsaid. Rather than simply deny that there have been benefits, one must press on to ask, for example, whether costs have been offset by benefits, and whether the benefits themselves have been equitably distributed. Rather than merely decrying specific policy decisions, one must show how those decisions betrayed not only the abstract (and in some sense practically unattainable) ideals of TVA but also the agency's own history of social responsibility.

"An Idea Whose Time Has Gone": Recent Criticism of TVA

Criticism of the TVA idea actually reached back beyond the origins of the agency itself to the fifteen-year-long battle over what to do with the federal government's World War I dam and nitrate plants at Muscle Shoals, Alabama.[15] The heroic efforts of Senator Norris and a few colleagues (especially Alabama's Lister Hill) had turned back repeated attempts to sell or give the Muscle Shoals facilities to private interests (Henry Ford offered to buy the $190 million installation for $5 million and turn the surrounding area into a wonderland of prosperity) and eventually forced bills through Congress to create the public Tennessee Valley Authority. The first TVA bill received a pocket veto by President Coolidge in 1928, and the second was vetoed in 1931 by President Hoover, who in the early 1920s had helped lead the campaign of the National Electric Light Association (NELA) against public power.[16]

Opposition from conservatives and business interests after the passage of the act was vehement and ranged in the early years from the petty "spite lines" run hurriedly into rural communities by private power companies hoping to forestall TVA's plans to the "eighteen-company" suit carried all the way to the Supreme Court by the Tennessee Electric Power Company and other private utilities seeking to have the act itself declared unconstitutional.[17] Except for a local controversy over the building of Douglas Dam, however, TVA had about a decade of relative freedom from challenge after the constitutional cases were settled.

The Eisenhower administration brought renewed pressure on TVA from both Republicans and conservative Democrats and the friends of both in the private utilities. Begun by relatively petty means—denouncing TVA as "creeping socialism," trimming budget requests, refusing to reappoint relatively liberal Gordon Clapp as Chairman—the Eisenhower battle against TVA ("By God, if ever we could do it," he reportedly once told his Cabinet, "before we leave here, I'd like to see us sell the whole thing.") reached its apex in the celebrated Dixon-Yates scandal.

When TVA asked for funds to construct a new generating plant north of Memphis, Eisenhower refused to include funding for the project in his 1954 budget message. Instead he backed a plan by Edgar Dixon (of the Middle South Utilities holding company) and Eugene Yates (of the Southern Company) to sell power to TVA from a new privately owned plant. The Dixon-Yates proposal, which at various times also contemplated selling TVA's Shawnee plant (near Paducah) to a private utility and having the Atomic Energy Commission buy power from private utilities instead of TVA, provoked a storm of protest in Congress. Hearings stretching over many months revealed numerous conflicts of interest and eventually led to the cancellation of the Dixon-Yates contract.[18]

But the criticism TVA received during its first two decades, stemming by and large from political and ideological conservatives opposed to most forms of cooperative public enterprise, was qualitatively different from that which followed. Latter-day criticism, coming primarily from liberals and progressives, was in some sense the revolt of a child against its father, in which the child declared the father's values obsolete and his methods tyrannical, and the wounded father charged the child with forgetfulness, naïve impracticality, and ingratitude.[19]

The recent controversy over TVA paralleled (and in some cases presaged) criticism of most public agencies and policies in the 1960s and 1970s. Beginning in earnest about 1962, criticism of TVA's strip-mining practices predated the environmental movement of the mid-1960s and developed into a full-blown critique of the Authority's environmental impact. Drawing new inspiration from the anti-war and anticorporate crusades of the late 1960s, the critique further excoriated the agency's effects upon the coal industry. Later criticism, paralleling the consumer movement of the early 1970s and the scrutiny of public agencies in the wake of Watergate, charged TVA with a lack of public accountability. And in the energy conscious mid-1970s, the agency that had pioneered in setting standards for low-cost power production and rural electrification came under fire for having a power policy that was geared to an obsolete high-consumption mentality and apportioned costs inequitably among the various classes of users.

Negative environmental impact. By 1944 TVA had completed all its dams on the Tennessee River; by 1953, when the gates closed at the Fort Patrick Henry dam, most of the available hydroelectric potential of the tributaries had been developed.[20] To meet escalating power demands (especially those of the Atomic Energy Commission installations at Oak Ridge and Paducah), TVA turned to coal-fired generating plants. Although coal-fired plants had long been a part of TVA (Watts Bar was built in 1940, Johnsonville in 1949), not until the mid-1950s did they produce more power than was generated by hydroelectric installations. By the late 1960s TVA was generating about three-fourths of its electricity from coal-fired steam plants.

But the shift to steam plants involved more than a simple change in technology. To heat the gigantic boilers while maintaining low-cost power production, TVA turned to cheap strip-mined coal. By 1961, when it acquired mineral rights to more than 100,000 acres of Appalachian coal lands in east Tennessee and southeastern Kentucky, it had already stripped 25,000 acres.[21] Other acreage was steadily acquired, until by 1975 the Authority owned more than 375 million tons of reserves, including the controversial Red Bird tract in Kentucky's Daniel Boone National Forest.[22]

In addition to mining its own reserves, TVA purchased enormous quantities of strip-mined coal, including the total output of Peabody Coal's western Kentucky mines, which it used to fuel its steam plant at Paradise, Kentucky. By 1968 TVA was using 5.5 percent of the total U.S. coal output, or 1,600 carloads a day, making it the nation's largest single user of strip-mined coal.

Protests by journalists, congressmen, governors, and local community groups that TVA was causing the destruction of much of the Appalachian coal region availed little, as did court challenges by environmental groups. In 1965 board chairman Aubrey Wagner reportedly told the *New York Times*'s Ben Franklin: "Stripmining, while it is going on, looks like the devil, but . . . if you look at what these mountains were doing before this stripping, they were just growing trees that were not even being harvested!" About the same time, TVA Reclamation Director James Curry said that "stripmining is part of the American way." After private foundation officials rejected TVA's 1971 request for $415,000 to restore lands stripped under TVA contracts, the Authority inaugurated a minimal but highly publicized reclamation program. In effect, however, it continued to deny that strip-mining was a serious enough environmental or social problem to affect TVA policy substantially.[23]

In addition to destroying land by strip-mining itself, TVA's burning of generally high-sulfur strip-mined coal vastly increased the emission of sulfur dioxide (SO_2), which in its final forms as sulfates and "acid rains" is poisonous to animals, humans, and crops. By late 1974 TVA accounted for 52 percent of all utility-produced SO_2 emissions in the eight-state Environmental Protection Agency (EPA) Region IV, and 12 percent of total utility-produced emissions in the United States.

TVA nevertheless resisted EPA's demands that SO_2 "scrubbers" be installed at its steam plants, arguing instead that tall stacks should be used to disperse the undiminished emissions over a wider area. Scrubbers eventually installed at three TVA plants (Shawnee, Johnsonville, and Widow's Creek) proved remarkably effective. The Shawnee scrubber was completed in March 1972, and tests by the Bechtel Corporation for EPA found that "operation of the scrubber was entirely satisfactory throughout the [test] period." In some respects the scrubber operated successfully under conditions more severe than those anticipated in normal use. Bechtel's later (1974–75) tests of three scrubber systems at Shawnee found that all "operated with better than 99 percent particulate removal efficiency." Depending on the system used and the test conditions, SO_2 removal ranged between 70 and 87 percent.[24]

But until 1975 board chairman Aubrey Wagner nevertheless scoffed at scrubbers as a "billion dollar pig in a poke," and TVA continued to insist that it would proceed no further with scrubber installation, despite repeated EPA directives, suits by the states of Alabama and Kentucky, and growing evidence that scrubbers were being used successfully by several private utilities.

Paradoxically, while environmentalists challenged TVA's operating policies for its coal-fired steam plants, the Authority itself increasingly viewed the plants as outmoded. In the mid-1960s TVA began a move toward nuclear generating stations. Plans were soon laid to double TVA generating capacity in a single decade (1974–83), and 90 percent of the new capacity was to be supplied by new nuclear plants (Brown's Ferry in northern Alabama, Sequoyah near Chattanooga, Hartsville near Nashville, Watts Bar near Knoxville, and others). Public protests and court suits over the safety and environmental impact (storage of wastes, radiation leakage) of the plants ensued, but

TVA proceeded with the design and construction of new plants and the execution of contracts with energy conglomerates to ensure continuing supplies of uranium.

Though within its legal rights in building nuclear stations, TVA was insensitive to a growing body of public opinion. TVA officials insisted that safety problems and environmental effects of the nuclear plants were being exaggerated, but the private East Tennessee Energy Group pointed out that there had been sixty-five "abnormal incidents" at Brown's Ferry in 1973 and ninety-seven the following year (higher than for any other such plant in the country). In March 1975 a fire in some control cables at Brown's Ferry caused $6.7 million in direct damage and $120 million in lost generation, and would have resulted in a disastrous "core melt-down" if last-minute manual controls had not been applied. Several investigative reports on the fire (including one by the Nuclear Regulatory Commission) concluded that TVA had been lax in designing, operating, and maintaining the facility.[25]

Held to be even more dangerous and environmentally suspect than TVA's conventional nuclear installations was the liquid metal fast breeder reactor (LMFBR), an experimental second-generation nuclear plant scheduled to be built on the Clinch River near Knoxville. Although there was little available background of experience on which TVA and its project partners (Commonwealth Edison and the nuclear industry) could draw in designing and operating the plant, the Authority pressed ahead.[26] Suits entered against the LMFBR charged that the project should be halted because (1) reactor safety could not be guaranteed; (2) problems of radioactive waste management, transportation, and storage were insoluble; (3) the increased generating capacity was neither necessary nor cost-efficient; and (4) the potential health risks of the plutonium fuel were socially and ethically unacceptable. Local, state, and national groups (including the Natural Resources Defense Council) protested, but TVA remained committed to the project despite tripled cost estimates and suggestions that federal support might be reduced.[27]

Environmental protests against new TVA reservoir projects also arose. Construction on the $70 million Tellico dam on the Little Tennessee River was halted temporarily by environmentalists who objected to damming the "Little T," by residents of the project area who did not want to lose their homes and farms, and by a segment of the Cherokee nation opposed to flooding the ancient Cherokee capital and burying ground.

A widespread controversy developed in 1970 over TVA's plan for a $100 million series of fourteen dams and fifty-four miles of stream channelization projects on tributaries of the upper French Broad River in western North Carolina. The project, which would have flooded 11,225 acres and displaced 600 families, was the latest version of a plan that TVA had advanced as early as 1941 but abandoned for lack of local support. Fifteen years later a more desirable Soil Conservation Service proposal, which would have located dams and reservoirs primarily on national forest land, was lost in a squabble between the Forest Service and TVA. But in late 1966, TVA's new upper French Broad plan was approved by the commissioners of the five affected counties and endorsed widely by businessmen, local officials, and the media. TVA justified the plan in terms of flood control, water supply, and secondary benefits to agricultural, recreational, and industrial-commercial development.

A few months later, however, local opposition surfaced. Local state Representative Charles Taylor, in a speech to the Citizen's and Taxpayer's League, questioned the benefits claimed for the project and showed that in four western North Carolina counties where TVA tributary reservoirs had been built several decades earlier, there had actually been a subsequent decline in population, per capita income, and tax revenue. By September 1970 scattered local opposition had coalesced into the Upper French Broad Defense Association (UFBDA). Made up of farmers, professors, retired professional people, clerks, housewives, and students, UFBDA conducted careful research on the environmental, social, and economic impact of other TVA tributary projects as well as the probable effects of the upper French Broad plan.

An intensive series of public presentations quickly built UFBDA membership to more than a thousand and brought endorsements from the Sierra Club and the influential Conservation Council of North Carolina. For an August 1971 public hearing on the Mills River portion of the project, UFBDA turned out 250 of its members to testify in opposition to the plan. Sixth- and seventh-generation local residents dispensed home-cooked food from a "hospitality room," while others, many wearing UFBDA's symbolic yellow scarves, argued before hearing officers that TVA had exaggerated both the need for and the benefits of the project and underestimated its cost and negative impact. Charts and graphs showed miles of free-flowing mountain streams turned into defoliated drainage ditches; slides showed communities and productive dairy farms that would be inundated; map overlays showed the nearly three thousand acres of mud flats expected to result from reservoir drawdown.

The hearing and UFBDA's other efforts were so dramatically effective that TVA's board chairman Aubrey Wagner announced in November 1972 that the upper French Broad project had been canceled "because adequate local support and commitment no longer exist."[28]

Effects upon the coal industry. TVA's use of very large quantities of coal had a strong impact not only on the environment but also on the structure of the coal industry itself. As James Ridgeway explained the process, TVA began to offer long-term (5- to 30-year) coal-purchase contracts to a depressed coal industry in the early 1950s in order to assure itself of a steady supply of coal.[29] Until then most coal had been deep-mined and sold in the highly competitive "spot" market. But TVA's new purchasing policy helped drive coal prices down to such a level (from $4.80 in 1955 to $2.50 in 1965) that unionized deep mines were forced to yield most of the market to nonunion strip mines.

John L. Lewis had charged as early as 1956 that TVA purchasing practices were detrimental to nonunion coal operators.[30] By 1961 Pulitzer Prize journalists Nat Caldwell and Gene S. Graham had substantiated the charge in the process of exposing both Lewis's and TVA's connivance with the coal industry. Caldwell and Graham described one incident in which bargemen dodged rifle fire to run coal from western Kentucky mines past United Mine Workers of America (UMWA) pickets and unload it at TVA's Widow's Creek steam plant in the coal-rich Sequatchie Valley near Chattanooga, where small union operators had been bankrupted after being squeezed between depressed coal prices on the one hand and the necessity of paying a per-ton levy into the UMWA's welfare and retirement fund on the other. The coal for Widow's Creek came from mines purchased by Cyrus Eaton with money Lewis helped him borrow from the UMWA.[31]

TVA's coal-buying policies led to further anticompetitive integration of the coal industry, as large companies that opened strip mines to fill TVA contracts were later bought up by multinational energy conglomerates. By 1973 more than 83 percent (32 million tons) of TVA's coal was being supplied by Peabody Coal (Kennecott Copper), Island Creek (Occidental Petroleum), Falcon (Seaboard Oil), Amax (American Metal Climax), and a half-dozen somewhat smaller companies from mines that in some cases had been opened with TVA loans. The Authority's increasingly close relationship with private industry became especially clear with its $23 million loan to the Peabody Coal Company to open a deep mine on TVA reserves in western Kentucky (from which Peabody would then sell coal to TVA for $12 per ton) and its subsequent bid to purchase Peabody outright.[32]

Lack of accountability. Although there had long been problems with two of the principal mechanisms designed to ensure TVA's accountability (rural electrical cooperatives and municipal power boards), the Authority for several decades had a not entirely undeserved reputation as an accountable agency in touch with the grassroots. That reputation eroded steadily as criticism mounted in the 1960s.

The TVA board itself was, appropriately enough, the focus for much of the controversy over accountability. Although TVA's enabling legislation required that board members "profess a belief in the wisdom and feasibility of the TVA Act," there had been indications for thirty years that the board, which is appointive rather than elective, would not long remain an instrument for implementing the act in good faith and for responding to the wishes and needs of the valley's people. David Lilienthal warned in his journal as early as 1941 that it might become "a pasture for worn-out faithfuls" and an implementer of whatever policies were in favor with the current federal administration.[33]

Indeed, political considerations had influenced board appointments at least since President Roosevelt had appointed an out of office senator (James P. Pope of Tennessee) to fill Arthur Morgan's seat. In 1954 President Eisenhower replaced the relatively progressive Gordon Clapp with General Vogel in order to help ensure the TVA's acquiescence to the Dixon-Yates scheme, and in 1957 he apppointed Tennessee Republican William L. Jenkins, a defender of strip-mining who declared that "what [TVA gets]—strip or deep—is up to the coal industry." Two years later President Ford nominated James Hooper, a Mississippi businessman who was patently unqualified but whose wife was a Republican National Committeewoman. Hooper's nomination was eventually rejected by the Senate.[34]

As the board, which had become substantially the patronage pasture Lilienthal had feared, allowed the agency to drift farther away from the progressive posture of its early years, it repeatedly flouted the spirit and letter of state and federal legislation designed to ensure responsibility and accountability. Board meetings, traditionally held behind closed doors, were opened after widespread agitation by the press and the forcible ejection of some reporters who had tried to attend. Other reporters had to invoke the Freedom of Information Act to obtain data from TVA files.[35]

At length it appeared that little more than a single strand remained of the seamless web: TVA was a power producer and little more. And even that limited task, its new critics said, it accomplished less and less well.

Obsolete and regressive power policy. Insisting that there was no profitable market among poor valley farmers, private power companies in the 1920s had refused to run their lines into rural areas. In that conservative context, TVA boldly extended service to the remotest hamlets and hollows, built up demand through intensive promotion, and steadily added generating capacity to serve the new loads. By 1959, 97 percent of the valley's farms were electrified, and the American Public Power Association was studying TVA to learn how to increase demand.[36]

A by-product of the low-cost, high-use policy, however, was a regressive rate structure. To build up its load, TVA extended the lowest rates to the largest users. Thus individual owners of small businesses and homes came to subsidize large industrial users and federal installations such as Oak Ridge. In 1974, TVA was charging municipalities 8.7 mills per kilowatt, whereas industries were paying only 6 mills, and federal agencies (including atomic installations) 5 mills.[37]

But unequal sharing of costs was only part of the problem. In a period of increasing environmental and energy concern, TVA seemed to be caught in its own growth spiral. To serve high demands during peak periods, the Authority chose to build "peaking" facilities, such as the $200 million Racoon Mountain pumped-storage project, instead of taking the environmentally more desirable step of instituting pricing policies (such as peak-load pricing) that might have evened out the load.[38]

It was also questionable whether TVA actually needed all of the new generating facilities it was building. Testimony prepared by the East Tennessee Energy Group for presentation at TVA congressional oversight hearings in 1975 suggested that the Authority's demand projections overestimated the growth of population and of both residential and industrial consumption, and underestimated the effect of recession, a trend to energy conservation, and price elasticity of demand. Exaggerated demand projections, said ETEG, were used to justify building new facilities (especially the base-load nuclear plants), the cost of which was then covered by successive rate increases, which between 1967 and 1975 amounted to more than 140 percent.[39]

A final paradox is that as TVA's load has grown, its efficiency of production (based on both construction and operating costs) appears to have fallen. In 1960, James Branscome reported, TVA generated 1 kilowatt of electricity per 9,590 BTUs of heat required (from coal that averaged 11,829 BTUs per ton), but by 1975, 9,770 BTUs were required (from 10,760 BTU-per-ton-coal) to generate the same amount of power. Construction costs for TVA's Paradise steam plant were $134 per kilowatt of installed capacity, but the Duke Power Company had built a similar facility about the same time for $100 per kilowatt. Charges of TVA's inefficient production were also raised in its May 1973 Congressional appropriation hearings. Numerous private utilities had lower construction costs per kilowatt, and among the fifteen largest steam generating plants in the country, TVA's plants ranked highest in the number of employees per hundred megawatts of capacity.[40]

The Historical Roots of Current Criticism

The shift in TVA's role both in the valley and in neighboring Appalachian counties cannot be accounted for in any simple terms. The agency's history is complex, and its operation has always involved costs as well as benefits. Some crucial policy decisions (such as load building) were made decades before their potentially negative implications could be foreseen. Some were made in the knowledge that there were feasible alternatives; others were forced by combinations of historical circumstances beyond TVA's control. TVA's present posture is in any event the collective result of myriad incremental policy decisions stretching back through four decades.

As one surveys those four decades, a half-dozen factors appear to have been especially important in producing TVA's present posture: (1) internal dissension among the original board members, which fragmented critical policies and confused lines of development in the early years; (2) the early co-optation of the agency by vested interests, especially through the agriculture program; (3) a gradual narrowing of function, which derived from the successful completion of portions of the original mandate; (4) a historical change of context, which left TVA responsive more to national power demands than to the needs of the valley and the well-being of the larger Appalachian region; (5) simple naiveté; and (6) the unforeseen constraints of "self-financing."

The original board and the social vision of TVA. In one sense it is ironic that TVA ever became known as an agency with an actual mandate to bring about broad social reconstruction of the Tennessee Valley. For although both Senator George Norris and President Roosevelt envisioned a fairly comprehensive social role for TVA, its legislative mandate was in fact rather narrow. The only explicit legal basis for the social programs of TVA's early years lay in Section 22 of the law, which authorized TVA

> . . . to provide for the general welfare of the citizens . . . to make such . . . general plans for said Tennessee basin and adjoining territory as may be useful . . . in guiding and controlling . . . development [and] fostering an orderly . . . and proper physical, economic, and social development of said areas; and . . . to cooperate with the States affected thereby, or subdivisions or agencies of such states, or with cooperative or other organizations.

The disparity between Norris's and Roosevelt's expectations and TVA's narrow mandate could be resolved, therefore, only through the exercise of discretionary latitude in the administration of actual programs. Thus the composition of the original board of directors was very important; TVA's actual social role would in effect arise out of the harmony (or conflict) among the social and political views of three men: Arthur E. Morgan (the first chairman), David E. Lilienthal, and H. A. Morgan. As it turned out, the three had very different views concerning the policies TVA might best pursue to bring about social change.[41]

Arthur Morgan came to TVA from the presidency of Antioch College. Earlier he had achieved international recognition for his Miami River Valley flood-control project, which blended innovative engineering principles with sensitivity to the social dimensions of engineering design. Morgan saw TVA as a chance to use his broad experience in an actual social context to create "a picture of the world as it might be."[42] During his five years on the board (1933–38), he pushed TVA into much of what was later called its "quiet work"—education, progressive labor relations, town planning, health care, and the like.

Arthur Morgan was daring, imaginative, and creative, but he was also given to utopianism, rigid moralism, self-righteousness, and political naiveté. The latter qualities drew him quickly into conflict with David Lilienthal.

The aggressive Lilienthal came to TVA at the age of thirty-three, having already transformed the Wisconsin Public Service Commission from a moribund legitimizer of the wishes of "regulated" utilities to an effective guardian of the public interest. And although he shared much of Arthur Morgan's desire to transform the valley, he had vastly different ideas about how the transformation was to be accomplished.

When President Roosevelt referred to Arthur Morgan as a "human engineer," Lilienthal replied "I don't believe that that is the way to get a better living for people, by human engineering them. . . . Welfare work and economic revision are two different things—I don't have much confidence in the first." In less charitable moments Lilienthal referred to Morgan's social programs (such as the model village at Norris dam) as "basketweaving" and "A. E.'s screwiest brain children." "I don't have much faith in uplift,'" he told a Knoxville audience in 1937. In his view, TVA's success (and the eventual improvement of the quality of individual lives in the valley) depended upon the inevitable economic effects of infrastructure development (dams, power programs, navigation) carried on in "collaboration with business and industry."[43]

The third original board member, Harcourt A. Morgan, was sixty-six years old at the time of his appointment. "Dr. H. A." had come from Canada to Louisiana in 1889 to do agricultural research and had risen from a researcher at the University of Tennessee Agricultural Experiment Station in 1905 to the presidency of the University in 1919.[44] A man of rather conservative social views, Dr. H. A. usually joined with Lilienthal in opposing A. E. Morgan on the board.

With H. A. Morgan's cooperation, Lilienthal succeeded after only about three months (in August 1933) in arranging a three-way partition of the board's responsibilities, which curtailed A. E. Morgan's power as chairman. Thereafter, A. E. Morgan was in charge of construction, H. A. Morgan took over the agriculture program, and Lilienthal became solely responsible for the power program. Because each thereby gained control also of any social aspects of their respective programs, TVA did not develop a coherent approach to social reconstruction.

Later, again with H. A. Morgan's cooperation, Lilienthal helped maneuver A. E. Morgan into a conflict with President Roosevelt that resulted in his removal from the board in 1938. Thomas McCraw, who studied the Morgan-Lilienthal feud in detail, concluded that "there can be no doubt that the social objectives of TVA lessened after the departure of Arthur Morgan."[45]

But the significance of the Lilienthal–H. A. Morgan voting bloc and A. E. Morgan's departure reached beyond *ad hoc* opposition to a particular set of views on TVA's role in social reconstruction. After the agriculture program became Harcourt Morgan's exclusive province, the structural and political consequences of his relationship with the agriculture establishment took on greater significance. As early as 1942 Philip Selznick concluded that TVA, partly through its agriculture program, had been rather thoroughly co-opted.

Co-optation. "The corruption of ideals," Selznick wrote shortly after TVA's tenth anniversary, "is easier than their fulfillment, and is . . . more natural." In Selznick's view, TVA's official "grassroots" doctrine ultimately became "a screen for covert opportunistic adaptation" as the agency "trimmed its sails in the face of hostile pressure."[46] Through the agriculture program, Selznick argued, a right wing was built inside TVA which eventually affected all of its policies and led to more general co-optation by established interests in the valley.

The historical development of such a dynamic within TVA Selznick charged partly to the nature of organizations themselves. Organizations, he argued, are "dynamic conditioning field[s]" in which one faces the inescapable dilemma of pursuing ideal ends through concrete choice among alternative means. Such choices shape and condition both the organization itself and all of its members. As they defend and rationalize their choices, organizations come in some respects to resemble social organisms, with their own internally useful sets of values and precepts. Formulated by top management and instilled into lower-echelon managers, such precepts are used to shape the viewpoints of new personnel, to bind together technical experts who may lack conscious ideology, and (above all) to protect the organization from critics and potential competitors.

As a specific example of such a precept, Selznick focused upon TVA's idealistic "grassroots" doctrine. Although it had no explicit basis in the legislation, the doctrine was codified quite early in the agency's history.[47] Almost simultaneously, however, Selznick observed, a pragmatic *organizational* doctrine was being formulated as TVA personnel came to terms with "established local and national interests." The ideal proved to be in relatively permanent conflict with the pragmatic choices, which almost invariably had the decisive influence on policy. As Selznick understood it, the triumph of organizational over official doctrine—while never fully avoidable by any organization—was abetted in the case of TVA by both inherent weaknesses in the official doctrine itself and the capacity of established interests to influence the operationally more important organizational doctrine.

Selznick found the official grassroots doctrine to be burdened by a number of "unanalyzed abstractions"—vagueness, for example, about how local grassroots influence could practically be brought to bear on TVA, and a facile assumption that locating the agency physically in the valley would assure "participation by the people." Even more important was the contention that working through established local institutions guaranteed democratic control and grassroots participation.

The agriculture program was a pertinent case in point. Having decided to develop the forestry program independently of the land-grant colleges and extension services, Arthur Morgan initially also pressed for an independent agriculture program oriented toward self-help cooperatives, subsistence homesteads, rural zoning, and regional planning. But his urgings were squelched by the Harcourt Morgan–Lilienthal bloc. A "memorandum of understanding" executed by the end of 1934 placed TVA's agriculture program effectively in the hands of Harcourt Morgan's constituency: the agricultural extension departments of the valley's land-grant colleges. Those departments were in turn heavily influenced by both the politically attuned county agents and the local branches of the conservative American Farm Bureau. The informal "understanding" was later implemented through a system of formal contracts between TVA and the colleges. Through the TVA's Agricultural Relations Department, directed by J. C. McAmis (who reported to Harcourt Morgan), the agricultural establishment in the valley was able to exert continuous pressure upon TVA agricultural policy.

The immediate result, Selznick found, was a conservative, class-biased TVA agricultural program. "Test-demonstration" farms were usually chosen only with the approval of the extension agents, who customarily worked with the more prosperous farmers.[18] Black agricultural schools were omitted from the program entirely. Tenant farmers received virtually no attention. And neither the Farm Security Administration (FSA) nor the Soil Conservation Service (SCS)—both New Deal agencies with a more direct approach to farm problems than the Department of Agriculture and the land-grant colleges—was able to work with TVA to a significant degree.

Thus at a time when both FSA and SCS—as well as the more militant Southern Tenant Farmers Union—were grappling with the problems of poorer farmers in the valley and elsewhere in the Southeast, TVA allied itself with (and directed its programs toward) wealthier farmers and the agricultural establishment.

In effect, established agricultural interests in the valley had been given control of the agricultural program in exchange for at least tacit approval of the power program. Thus developed the H. A. Morgan–Lilienthal bloc, and thus ended Arthur Morgan's hopes for an agency more directly involved in social reconstruction above the infrastructure level. "The role and character of the TVA," Selznick concluded in 1943, "have been shaped, at least in part, by the co-optative relationship in agriculture."

Selznick's conclusion concerning TVA's early history can be extrapolated to explain much of its recent history as well. When agriculture was the most effectively organized constituency in the valley, TVA deferred to it to help save the power program; when a few years later the agriculture program was essentially complete, the valley had shifted substantially away from farming, and the power program was successful, large energy users replaced the agriculture establishment as *de facto* arbiters of policy. To save itself as an agency, TVA deferred to them, and thus began a second round of co-optation.

TVA's argument that grassroots control of the power program was guaranteed by voluntary associations such as the rural electric co-ops was ultimately not persuasive. Those associations, as Selznick pointed out, shared the burdens and responsibilities of power, but not the power itself. Selznick's conclusion was corroborated independently twenty-five years later by Victor Hobday, who studied TVA's municipal power boards. Although he took a generally positive view of TVA, Hobday concluded that municipalities using TVA power had relatively little influence upon power policy. Those policies, he found, were made almost solely by engineers, were not subject to disinterested review, and were rarely overruled by the TVA board.[49]

Narrowing of functions. The co-optation of the power program, although abetted by the nature of bureaucracy itself, nevertheless resulted substantially from conscious policy decisions. But to a degree TVA also became the unwitting victim of both its own success and historical circumstances that reached a climax in the 1950s. By 1944 the dams on the main channel of the river were complete, and all of the larger tributary projects (except Tellico) were finished by 1951. The agriculture program was established and successful within its limits, and there was a navigable channel from Knoxville to Paducah. Thus the great original symbolic work of TVA was done.

The inevitable narrowing of TVA's function implicit in the fulfilling of substantial portions of its original mandate coincided, unhappily, with both the political pressure brought to bear upon the agency during the Eisenhower years and a steadily increasing demand for electric power. Residential and industrial loads were growing, but the major source of new demand since World War II had been the atomic energy installations at Oak Ridge and (later) Paducah, the Huntsville, Alabama, rocket complex, and the Tullahoma, Tennessee, wind tunnel. Gordon Clapp, chairman of the board between 1946 and 1954, insisted that both the "expansion of economic opportunity in a competitive enterprise society" and "maintenance of our national strength to avert war and the strength to wage war if we must" required constant expansion of TVA generating capacity.[50] Thus, through conscious policy decision, political pressure, and the conjunction of historical circumstances TVA found its originally broad functions narrowed to a single one: low-cost, high-volume production of electricity. To that all other considerations became secondary.

As TVA's functions narrowed, its power policies increasingly resembled those of private utilities, reflecting a shift in priorities and perspective of which Lilienthal had warned as early as 1941. "We are in considerable danger," he noted in his journal, "of running the electricity program as if it were a private utility, a good well-organized private utility, but a utility nonetheless; ... [Some] of our top men might be surprised that I [don't] consider that this is just what is expected of them!"[51]

Change of context. The implications of the narrowing of function would have been serious enough if TVA had continued to predicate its policies (at whatever level of grassroots sensitivity) upon the original principle of unified development of the valley's resources for use by its own people.

After the mid-1940s, however, TVA was increasingly integrated into a national energy demand system. What had been intended as a broadly conceived developmental effort at length turned much of both the Tennessee Valley and the adjacent coal-bearing areas of Appalachia into a national energy reservation in which every other consideration was subordinate to large-scale power production at the lowest possible dollar cost. The so-called energy shortage and the national push toward "self-sufficiency" in energy overrode protests in the valley against more dams, strip-mining, and nuclear plants.

Naiveté. In dealing with its critics and opponents, TVA has been in most respects the canniest and least naive of agencies. Its early history offers ample evidence of the political sagacity of both David Lilienthal and Harcourt Morgan. But a persistent level of naiveté appears to have made TVA less willing to question its own policies than it might otherwise have been.

For all their differences, to take an important example, both Lilienthal and Arthur Morgan shared a conviction that essentially technical and technological solutions could be found for all social problems. Harcourt Morgan apparently assumed that superphosphates administered by agricultural extension agents from the land-grant colleges would lead to an equitable reconstruction of agriculture in the valley. Arthur Morgan too naively trusted TVA's adversaries in the private utility industry and seems to have believed that rational human engineering could overcome the fallibilities of human nature and the rigidities of entrenched institutions. David Lilienthal proclaimed that "experts as well as rivers have no politics," even though it was clear quite early that the politics of the three experts on the board conditioned their exercise of expertise.[52]

Troubled on one occasion by the problem of the equitable distribution of the benefits of TVA programs, Lilienthal said that "if we solve the problem of production, the distribution problem will almost inevitably be solved as a part of it."[53] But the agriculture program was already a powerful counterexample. And in recent years TVA has somewhat naively clung to a commitment to open-ended growth in energy use long after it had been abandoned even by many private utilities.

The unforeseen constraints of "self-financing." Until it sold its first $50 million worth of bonds in September 1960, TVA had been financed wholly through Congressional appropriations and its own revenues. But Lilienthal had suggested the possibility of self-financing through bonds as early as 1941.[54] By 1953 there were formal proposals to allow TVA to issue bonds in order to expand production capacity fast enough to meet rising demands. Although the proposals brought a warning from Chairman Clapp that "mismanagement and higher rates" would be a likely result, a seven-year debate in Congress culminated in the signing of a TVA "self-financing" act late in 1959.[55]

Although liberals and conservatives rarely agreed about TVA, they joined in supporting self-financing. Liberals theorized that it would give TVA more administrative freedom and allow it to expand generating capacity faster to meet both load demand and the competition of private utilities. But the conservative argument, though never articulated in public, was more sound: A TVA in the private bond market would be a TVA stripped of some of its primary competitive economic advantages over "investor-owned" utilities.[56] Indeed, the self-financing act in its final form forbade TVA to expand its service area and required it to repay all past federal appropriations, including interest on the "debt." As TVA's bonded indebtedness grew—especially to cover the escalating costs of its nuclear program in the 1970s—its rates rose so dramatically that they approached those of some private utilities.[57]

A final irony is that the intractability TVA displayed in responding to its recent critics was unnecessary. Its own best history provided an ideal warrant for reorienting the Authority to meet the challenges of a new set of social, economic, and environmental conditions. Its history of progressive labor relations with its own construction and operating employees could have been considered a precedent for reassessing its impact on union miners and mine operators. Its early commitment to a sophisticated understanding of the total environment (the "seamless web," the "common mooring") pointed the way toward alternative policies on strip-mining and steam-plant emissions. Its early concern (expressed at least until Arthur Morgan's departure in 1938) for the detailed social implications of its initial projects argued for paying closer attention to the social costs of its recent policy choices. Its resolute resistance to the constitutional challenges to TVA mounted by private utilities in the 1930s called into question its recent close relationships with coal producers. The symbolic low-cost power "yardstick" of its early years could have been transformed into an energy-efficiency yardstick to meet the challenge of the 1970s. And its "grassroots" doctrine (whatever its operational limitations) was a clear precedent for closer attention to accountability.

But there was little evidence that contemporary TVA policy was sensitive to the progressive tendencies of the agency's own best history. For Appalachia, that fact had two important implications: a negative direct impact upon the coal-producing counties (and to a lesser extent the tributary areas), and reduced credibility as a model for future regional development efforts. It is a sad historical irony that the federal Appalachian programs of the 1960s were initiated just as criticism of TVA began to mount.

Notes

1. See Walter M. Daniel, *Should We Have More TVAs?* (New York: Wilson, 1950); Marguerite Owen, *The Tennessee Valley Authority* (New York: Praeger, 1973), p. 234; and David E. Lilienthal, *The Journals of David E. Lilienthal* (New York: Harper & Row, 1964), I, 243.

2. Lilienthal, *Journals*, I, 554 and 563. See also Odette Keun, *A Foreigner Looks at TVA* (New York: Longmans Green, 1937); David E. Lilienthal, *TVA: Democracy on the March* (1944; reprint, Chicago: Quadrangle, 1966), pp. 196–209; and Herman Finer, *The TVA: Lessons for International Application* (New York: Da Capo, 1972). In "Political Regionalism and Administrative Regionalism," *Annals of the American Academy of Political and Social Science,* CCVII (January 1940), 138–43, Donald Davidson expressed reservations about TVA, which he said was "superimposed (however benevolently)" upon the valley.

3. This chapter treats the history of TVA only insofar as necessary to explore these two issues. Vastly greater detail is available in the extensive literature on the agency. Especially recommended are C. Herman Pritchett, *The Tennessee Valley Authority: A Study in Public Administration* (Chapel Hill: University of North Carolina Press, 1943); Philip Selznick, *TVA and the Grass Roots: A Study in the Sociology of Formal Organization* (Berkeley: University of California Press, 1949); Gordon R. Clapp, *The TVA: An Approach to the Development of a Region* (Chicago: University of Chicago Press, 1955); Preston J. Hubbard, *Origins of the TVA: The Muscle Shoals Controversy, 1920–1932* (Nashville: Vanderbilt University Press, 1961); Wilmon Henry Droze, *High Dams and Slack Waters: TVA Rebuilds a River* (Baton Rouge: Louisiana State University Press, 1965); Thomas K. McCraw, *Morgan vs. Lilienthal: The Feud Within the TVA* (Chicago: Loyola University Press, 1970) and *TVA and the Power Fight, 1933–1939* (New York: J. B. Lippincott, 1971); and Owen, *Tennessee Valley Authority.*

The account that follows is based primarily upon these sources, in addition to official TVA publications and numerous journal and newspaper articles cited hereafter. I also benefited from interviews with James Branscome, Denis Brubaker, Gene S. Graham, Aelred J. Gray, Myles Horton, and Harry Wiersema, Sr. I of course accept full responsibility for the views expressed here.

4. Clapp, *TVA: Approach,* pp. 14–15, and Owen, *Tennessee Valley Authority,* p. 19.

5. Arthur E. Morgan, *The Making of the TVA* (Buffalo: Prometheus Books, 1974), p. 197; Lilienthal, *TVA: Democracy on the March,* p. 53; McCraw, *TVA and Power Fight,* p. 17; and Selznick, *TVA and Grass Roots,* p. 43.

6. Quoted in Owen, *Tennessee Valley Authority,* p. 14.

7. Specific provisions of the act are discussed at length by Owen, *Tennessee Valley Authority, passim.* The conceptual and administrative design of the agency is examined in Selznick, *TVA and Grass Roots.*

8. Lilienthal, *TVA: Democracy on the March,* p. 1.

9. For a full discussion of the development of navigation on the river, see Droze, *High Dams and Slack Waters, passim.*; and E. P. Ericson, "River Transportation," in Roscoe C. Martin (ed.), *TVA: The First Twenty Years* (University, Ala., and Knoxville: University of Alabama Press and University of Tennessee Press, 1956), 95–107.

10. Harry E. Wiersema, Sr., "The River Control System," in Martin (ed.), *TVA: The First Twenty Years,* pp. 77–94.

11. Clapp, *TVA: Approach,* pp. 82–113.

12. *Ibid.,* p. 69. The number of farms declined precipitously during the same period, however.

13. See O. M. Derryberry, "Health"; Robert M. Howse, "Recreation"; and John V. Krutilla, "Economic Development"; in Martin (ed.), *TVA: First Twenty Years,* pp. 193–231; Lilienthal, *TVA: Democracy,* pp. 63–67; and Owen, *Tennessee Valley Authority,* pp. 119–39 and 234 ff.

14. Interview with Aelred J. Gray, October 5, 1975. See also Aelred J. Gray, "The Maturing of a Planned New Town: Norris, Tennessee," *The Tennessee Planner,* XXXII (1974), 1–25. Gray was former director of the TVA's regional planning staff.

15. See Hubbard, *Origins of TVA.* The disposition of Muscle Shoals was a national issue as early as the presidential election of 1920.

16. On the vetoes, see Judson R. King, *The Conservation Fight: From Theodore Roosevelt to the Tennessee Valley Authority* (Washington, D.C.: Public Affairs Press, 1959), pp. 174–88, 234–42.

17. On the constitutional challenges, see McCraw, *TVA and Power Fight,* pp. 108–21.

18. See Jason L. Finkle, *The President Makes a Decision: A Study of Dixon-Yates* (Ann Arbor: University of Michigan Institute of Public Administration, 1960). For typical reports of Eisenhower's opposition to the TVA, see *New York Times,* October 16, 1952, p. 1; May 14, 1953, p. 24; June 18, 1953, p. 18; March 15, 1954, p. 12; January 17, 1956, p. 1; and a summary article by Allen Drury, July 27, 1956, p. 1.

19. For summary articles on recent criticism, see *New York Times,* August 5, 1973, p. 43; and January 12, 1975, p. III-1. Also Tom Redburn, "A Good Idea Gone Sour in the Tennessee Valley," *Baltimore Sun,* December 14, 1975, p. K-3.

20. Three additional tributary projects were begun after 1967.

21. Harry E. Caudill, *My Land Is Dying* (New York: E. P. Dutton, 1971), p. 73.

22. See *New York Times,* July 2, 1961, p. III-10; March 27, 1962, p. 49; and July 3, 1968, p. 57; *Mountain Eagle,* July 25, 1974, p. 3, and August 22, 1974, p. 1; and *Louisville Courier-Journal,* November 6, 1975, p. D-1.

23. See *New York Times,* June 6, 1971; p. 107; and December 5, 1971, p. 23. For an extended discussion of TVA strip-mining practices, see Caudill, *My Land Is Dying,* pp. 67–79, and *Mountain Eagle,* June 27, July 25, August 22 and 29, and September 19, 1974. Wagner and Curry statements quoted from Caudill, *My Land Is Dying,* p. 79. The five-year, four-state reclamation project, scheduled to cost $22.8 million for 80,000 acres (an average of only $275 per acre) was revealed in TVA's 1975 *Annual Report.* See *Louisville Courier-Journal,* January 1, 1976, p. 1.

24. Research Triangle Institute, *Industrial Environmental Research Laboratory (Research Triangle Park): Annual Report, 1975* (Research Triangle Park, N.C.: Environmental Protection Agency, 1975), pp. 112–14, and Environmental Protection Agency, *EPA Alkali Scrubbing Test Facility: Advanced Program, First Progress Report* (Washington, D.C.: Environmental Protection Agency, 1975), pp. iii and 1-1 to 1-5.

25. Damage and lost-generation figures quoted from Nuclear Regulatory Commission conclusions as reported in the *Louisville Courier-Journal,* February 29, 1976, p. 1.

26. In *We Almost Lost Detroit* (New York: T. Y. Crowell, 1975), John G. Fuller investigated a near-catastrophic accident at a much smaller facility near Detroit in 1966.

27. See Amory B. Lovins, "The Case Against the Breeder Reactor," *Bulletin of the Atomic Scientists,* March 1973, pp. 29–35, and *Wall Street Journal,* June 2, 1975. I am grateful to the East Tennessee Energy Group for assistance in assembling materials on the breeder reactor.

28. "We have found," David Lilienthal noted in his journal in May 1941, "that slapping Indian or historical names on dams . . . is a good way to keep down agitation for naming them after some politician . . . and, besides, it is a nice gesture to the ghosts of the Indians" (Lilienthal, *Journals,* I, 329). On the Tellico controversy, see *New York Times,* April 15, 1969, p. 35; August 12, 1971, p. 17; and October 26, 1973, p. 5. Something close to the official TVA defense of the Tellico project may be found in Owen, pp. 204–6.

For the upper French Broad plan, see *Development of the Water Resources on the French Broad River Basin in North Carolina* (Knoxville: Tennessee Valley Authority, 1966). For UFBDA, TVA, and EPA documents and references on the controversy, I am grateful to Naomi Pullman. Substantial portions of my discussion are based upon her unpublished paper, "UFBDA and the Upper French Broad Controversy." For newspaper accounts, see *New York Times,* December 31, 1967, p. 34, and July 13, 1971, p. 30, and the following articles in *Asheville* (N.C.) *Citizen*: April 27, 1971; September 1, 1971, p. 1; September 6, 1971, p. 14; September 20, 1971. Also *Asheville Times,* November 14, 1972, p. 1.

29. James Ridgeway, *The Last Play: The Struggle to Monopolize the World's Energy Resources* (New York: E. P. Dutton, 1973), pp. 21–80. See also *New York Times,* September 29, 1951, p. 20, and Caudill, *My Land Is Dying,* pp. 70–71.

30. *New York Times,* October 3, 1956, p. 20.

31. Nat Caldwell and Gene S. Graham, "The Strange Romance Between John L. Lewis and Cyrus Eaton," *Harper's Magazine,* CCIII (December 1961), 25–32.

32. See a series of articles in the *Mountain Eagle,* October 1974—July 1975. TVA eventually withdrew its bid to purchase Peabody, which was being sold by Kennecott under court order. Actually TVA had long been involved in partnerships with private industry. The conclusion of an agreement between TVA and Alcoa concerning the Fontana dam site, Lilienthal noted in July 1941, "puts TVA virtually into partnership with a huge private concern" (Lilienthal, *Journals,* I, 353).

33. Lilienthal, *Journals,* I, 280.

34. On controversial board nominations and appointments, see *New York Times*, May 18, 1957, p. 16; September 15, 1974, p. 1; April 3, 1975, p. 1; June 12, 1975, p. 24; and July 17, 1975, p. 12.

35. See for example the *Mountain Eagle*, July 18 and 25, August 29, October 24, and December 19, 1974; and *Louisville Times*, August 22, 1974. Board meetings were opened to the public in 1975.

36. *New York Times*, April 19, 1959, p. 121, and September 28, 1958, p. 125, respectively.

37. *TVA Annual Report, 1974*, p. 42.

38. These problems and others (e.g., "fair share" and "life line" rates) were featured in *Consumer's Bill of Rights* (for TVA customers) (Knoxville: East Tennessee Energy Group, 1975). In late 1975 the Natural Resources Defense Council specifically charged that TVA's rate structure heightened negative environmental effects of power production, *Louisville Courier-Journal*, November 5, 1975, p. B-5.

39. *Mountain Eagle*, July 24, 1975, p. 1.

40. *Ibid.*, October 24, 1974, p. 3, and July 24, 1975, p. 1; and memo from Neil McBride, staff attorney for East Tennessee Research Corporation, January 2, 1975.

41. On the early board, and especially the controversy between Lilienthal and Arthur Morgan, see Owen, *Tennessee Valley Authority*, pp. 40–55; McCraw, *TVA and Power Fight*, pp. 26–46; and especially McCraw, *Morgan vs. Lilienthal*.

42. See McCraw, *Morgan vs. Lilienthal*, pp. 7 ff.; and Morgan, *Making of TVA*, p. 197.

43. Lilienthal, *Journals*, I, 66; *Knoxville News-Sentinel*, March 5, 1937 (quoted in Morgan, *Making of TVA*, p. 156); Lilienthal, *Journals*, I, 141; and *idem, TVA: Democracy*, p. 119, respectively.

44. Morgan's background is described in McCraw, *Morgan vs. Lilienthal*, pp. 12–17. Details of his relationship to the agricultural establishment are discussed in Selznick, *TVA and Grass Roots*, pp. 91 ff.

45. McCraw, *Morgan vs. Lilienthal*, pp. 108 ff.

46. Selznick, *TVA and Grass Roots*, p. x. This section is based almost solely upon Selznick's analysis, from which all quotations are taken.

47. *Ibid.*, pp. 21–45. The fullest expression is of course Lilienthal's in *TVA: Democracy*. The doctrine was loosely based upon Section 22 of the TVA Act.

48. Selznick, *TVA and Grass Roots*, cites numerous statistics and specific examples, pp. 127 ff.

49. *Ibid.*, p. 264, and Victor C. Hobday, *Sparks at the Grass Roots: Municipal Distribution of TVA Electricity in Tennessee* (Knoxville: University of Tennessee Press, 1969).

50. Clapp, *TVA: Approach*, p. 93. By 1974, 17 percent of the TVA's total production went to federal installations.

51. Lilienthal, *Journals*, I, 394.

52. Lilienthal, *TVA: Democracy*, p. 175.

53. Lilienthal, *Journals*, I, 295.

54. *Ibid.*, I, 290.

55. Owen, *Tennessee Valley Authority*, pp. 116–17. Clapp is quoted in *New York Times*, August 20, 1953, p. 36.

56. On liberal Democratic support for self-financing, see *New York Times*, May 1, 1957, p. 26, and an editorial on August 16, 1958, p. 16.

57. Estimated costs on both Brown's Ferry and Sequoyah rose more than 100 percent within several years; on Bellefonte, 34 percent in one year; on Hartsville, 59 percent in one year (East Tennessee Energy Group draft testimony for 1975 TVA Congressional oversight hearings).

CHAPTER 3

Appalachia as a Depressed Area: The Area Redevelopment Administration

In 1954 Illinois Democratic senatorial candidate Paul Douglas ended his campaign tour determined to alleviate the economic problems he had witnessed in the state's southern coal-mining counties. The "depressed areas" bill he introduced as the junior senator from Illinois did not pass Congress until four years later, and it was then vetoed by President Eisenhower. The bill passed in Congress again several years later and was again vetoed. Such problems, Eisenhower said, were best left to local initiative and the workings of the free enterprise system.

But southern Illinois was only one of many depressed areas. During the 1959 hearings Tom Gish, an eastern Kentucky editor, told the committee of a coal miner from his county, unemployed for three years, who shot himself just before Christmas so his wife and eight children could collect his Social Security benefits.[1] Eastern Kentucky and the rest of the Appalachian region in fact made up the nation's largest depressed area, and John F. Kennedy saw part of the worst of it during his West Virginia primary campaign shortly after President Eisenhower vetoed the 1960 Douglas bill.

Kennedy, who had led the Senate floor debate on Douglas's first bill, made depressed areas a major issue in the primary, and immediately after his election he appointed Douglas to head a task force to make legislative recommendations. The task force report of January 1, 1961, recommended a program of federal aid modeled on the prior Douglas bills.[2] The new bill was designated S. 1 and scheduled for action as soon as Congress convened.

On January 18, when the Senate opened hearings on S. 1, Appalachian congressmen were some of its strongest supporters. Unemployment in eastern Kentucky's Harlan and Perry Counties ran from 13 to 20 percent and was over 26 percent in the county seat of Pike County. It had climbed to around 12 percent in West Virginia's industrial towns of Huntington and Wheeling, and to between 20 and 28 percent in the smaller downstate towns of Beckley, Bluefield, and Welch. Southwest Virginia's Big Stone Gap had reported over 11 percent a year earlier, and almost 14 percent of La Follette, Tennessee, workers were jobless. Senator Estes Kefauver (D.–Tenn.) described the state's southeastern counties of Grundy, Sequatchie, and Marion as in a "critical economic depression": Mines were closed; 90 percent of the miners had been out of work for six months to a year and had therefore exhausted their unemployment benefits. UMW miners had $25 a week in union benefits; the rest had nothing.[3] Witness after witness from Appalachia, including Jennings Randolph (D.–W. Va.), John Sherman Cooper (R.–Ky.), Hugh Scott (R.–Pa.), Tennessee's Governor Buford Ellington, and Maryland's Governor Millard Tawes, urged passage of S. 1. The Pennsylvania legislature passed a special resolution of endorsement, and West Virginia's conservative Senator Robert Byrd told the committee that "a good piece of legislation is always a pleasure to talk about."

Testimony from Appalachia in the House hearings of late February and early March seconded statements already given before the Senate subcommittee. Veteran congressman Carl Perkins (D.–Ky.) pointed out that one out of every three workers in his eastern Kentucky district was unemployed.[4] The bills upon which hearings were held focused upon job training, the creation of jobs through loans to new or expanding industries, and grants and loans for related public facilities such as roads, sewers, and water systems. Although Appalachian congressmen were generally enthusiastic about the program, some who supported it also predicted that it would be of little help to the region.

Representative Cleveland Bailey, whose West Virginia district included Fayette County, where unemployment had recently been driven above 34 percent through automation of the coal mines and the closing of factories, complained of foreign trade policies that were hurting West Virginia. Forty years earlier, he said, the Anaconda Copper plant at Butte, Montana, was fueled by West Virginia coal. Now it was fueled by duty-free natural gas from Canada, while Canada levied a 50¢-per-ton duty on imported coal. The Area Redevelopment Act, he said, "will not solve our basic problems." Kentucky's Governor Bert Combs supported the bill but said that other measures, such as a highway program; water, forestry, and coal development; and increased aid to education, were needed.

Outright opponents of the bill objected that the federal government had no business intervening in the economic affairs of depressed areas. Senator Goldwater, asserting that "stout hearts and strong backs" had carried earlier generations through adversity, castigated the "phobia afflicting certain politicians and pseudo-liberal theorizers, who would substitute for our free-enterprise system the awful spectre of the planned superstate."[5] Others argued that private capital was both available and mobile enough to do the job, that federal money would go to support marginal enterprises, that the anticipated funding would be but "a drop in the bucket" compared to private capital already available, and that plants would be "pirated" from prosperous to depressed areas.

Congressmen from well-off areas, who were not enthusiastic about the bill in any case and who especially feared the pirating of industries, eventually compromised with depressed-area congressmen and agreed on an "antipirating" clause.

The Area Redevelopment Act passed the Senate on March 15, 1961, and the House endorsed it two weeks later. On May 1 the act became law (P.L. 87-27). It authorized $200 million per year in industrial loans, $175 million in loans and grants for public facilities, $4.5 million for technical assistance, and $10 million for subsistence to trainees. Federal support was limited to 65 percent of project cost, and states and local governments were required to provide a 10 percent share.

The act created the Area Redevelopment Administration (ARA) to run the programs, some of which were parceled out to the Department of Labor (job training), the Small Business Administration (commercial loans), the Department of the Interior (resource development), and elsewhere. ARA itself was housed in the Commerce Department, over the objections of both Senator Douglas and Representative Perkins, who wanted an independent agency.[6]

As ARA administrator William L. Batt explained it, the ARA approach to depressed areas development had an appealing elegance:

> The pattern functions like this: the communities are encouraged to organize for economic development, to analyze their opportunities . . . and to develop a program for action. ARA will help them to make promising resource and industry feasibility studies. When a businessman indicates interest in a specific opportunity . . . he is extended a long maturity, low interest loan. . . . This loan is often coupled with financial help to the local government to provide the public facilities necessary to service the new enterprise. It may be that the enterprise requires workers specifically trained for its operation. ARA, through the Department of Labor, provides this training; and the cycle from community planning to actual jobs is complete.[7]

Actually, however, it was not that simple. For ARA to work, a number of assumptions had to prove tenable: that the necessary jobs should be generated in the private rather than the public sector; that communities could prepare overall economic development plans (OEDPs) that would adequately locate, define, and prescribe for their needs; that community needs were synonymous with those of individual unemployed workers; that the "private sector" would and could create jobs at a justifiable cost; and that the direct benefits to the entrepreneurs who would receive most of the federal money would in fact "trickle down" to the unemployed.[8]

Appalachia and the ARA Programs

> Yancey County has in the past made some very creditable efforts—at considerable sacrifice to our citizens—to lift us out of our economic rut. The failure of these efforts has contributed to skepticism and apathy regarding the present [ARA] efforts. The slowness of ARA benefits to materialize in the western North Carolina counties is now serving to enforce this defeatist feeling. [The] optimism with which we started off has faded perceptively [*sic*]; at the last planning board meeting only three members attended.
> Yancey County planning group[9]

In the original Douglas bill, the single condition under which an area could be classified as depressed was long-term high rates of unemployment. The conditions were later broadened to include rural counties where underemployment was a significant problem (the 1960 bill included 662 such counties). But the 1961 law was so generous in its definition that within eight months about 900 counties containing one-sixth of the U.S. population had been designated, and 170 others were added soon thereafter—a total of about one-third of all counties in the country.

Although Section 5(b) directed ARA to "distribute the projects widely among the several states," the lack of both staff and adequate statistical data (in addition to political considerations) deprived the designation process of rationality. An immediate result of designating so many areas was that comparatively little money was finally available to aid seriously depressed areas such as Appalachia.

By any of the criteria used to designate depressed areas, large portions of Appalachia were qualified. One Interior Department economist located seventy-nine contiguous counties there that qualified; a high percentage of the 1,070 depressed-area counties lay within the region.[10]

For those counties, an Overall Economic Development Plan

(OEDP) was the first requirement for access to ARA funds. Required by Section 6(b), the OEDPs were to be prepared locally as communal exercises in self-awareness, descriptions of economic problems, inventories of resources, and projections of specific development strategies and projects. Although stringently objected to by some economists, OEDPs became a keystone of the ARA program.[11]

Sar Levitan, who studied a large random sample of approved OEDPs, found that although some were excellent (for example, Avery County, N.C.), many showed that communities "did not take the OEDP preparation seriously" and therefore produced superficial and poorly conceived plans that "normally involved only limited thoughtful analysis" and rarely included cost-benefit considerations. Surveying OEDPs for Kentucky, Levitan found that

> . . . most if not all . . . were prepared by the State Area Program Office [and] were stated in such general terms that . . . they could have described any area. An OEDP prepared for an agricultural county in the extreme western part of the state was almost identical with one filed for a coal mining county in the eastern part.[12]

ARA adopted a strategy of accepting inadequate OEDPs "provisionally" and in some cases hired consultants to help improve them. But because funds for that purpose were limited and the agency was under pressure to produce results, the majority of the OEDPs had to be accepted more or less as they stood.

Most project proposals asked for industrial and commercial loans under Section 6(a). The consensus seemed to be that, regardless of the nature of the county's problems, "new industry" would cure them. As Appalachia had been a prime focus during the development of the legislation on depressed areas, ARA was eager to begin producing visible results, and industrial loans were attractive in that regard.[13]

By the end of 1964 the ARA reported that about 29 percent ($79 million) of its $273 million in grants and loans had gone to Appalachia, scattered among 391 projects in all 258 counties. But ARA largesse was distributed neither equally among the states and counties nor in proportion to apparent need. More than half of all ARA Appalachian funds through 1964 went to West Virginia, and 68 percent of that was authorized for tourism projects in a small number of counties. The Appalachian portions of four states (Maryland, North Carolina, Ohio, Virginia) received 4.4 percent of the funds, although they had one-sixth of the ARA Appalachian counties. Alabama and Tennessee received 3–4 percent each, while Kentucky drew about 13 percent and relatively prosperous Pennsylvania 17 percent.

The imbalances were as pronounced in the various loan and grant categories. West Virginia and Pennsylvania together received about 61 percent of the Section 6(a) industrial loan money, while Kentucky emerged with 10–12 percent year after year. Except for Georgia, which got 8 percent, other states had to settle for 0–6 percent after the first year. Even West Virginia, which generally fared well with the ARA and which needed industries in its more rural counties, saw its share of industrial loan money fall from 54 percent the first year to 23 percent in 1964, while heavily industrialized Pennsylvania's rose from 12 percent to 38 percent. The severely depressed counties of southwestern Virginia received none at all until 1964, when one $64,650 loan was approved to open a garment factory in Norton.

ARA administrator William L. Batt predicted that 115,000 jobs would be created by the agency's projects, at a cost of about $800 each, and several of the industrial loans in Appalachia indeed met expectations. A $604,000 loan to Berwick, Pennsylvania, to purchase American Car and Foundry's abandoned factory building was expected to produce 500 jobs. It produced 553 by 1968.[14]

But other industrial loans in Appalachia frequently produced fewer jobs than anticipated, and in some cases no jobs at all. A $250,000 loan to the Tompkinsville, Kentucky, Industrial Foundation to construct a building to lease to the Hayes Garment Company was expected to create 220 jobs. Five years later Hayes employed 108 more people than it had prior to the loan. A $485,000 loan to Scranton-Lackawanna Industrial Building Company to build a structure for a new printing plant was expected to generate 100 jobs. The total number employed in Scranton's large printing industry increased by nearly two hundred during the next three years, but the increase appeared to be confined mainly to the industry's largest employer, the International Textbook Company. Eureka Printing Company actually terminated more than a hundred of its 693 employees during the same period. No new plant seems to have opened. A $20,000 loan to Hewlett Coating Company in Morgantown, West Virginia, scheduled to add twenty jobs, added fewer than ten. A $500,000 loan to Glasrock Products, Inc. in Calhoun, Georgia, was expected to add 200 jobs. Glasrock reported a total employment of 85 in 1969. One Appalachian project investigated by the General Accounting Office was ARA's $355,000 loan to the Roustabout Company of Frackville, Pennsylvania, which apparently generated none of the anticipated 180 jobs. GAO termed the loan "imprudent" in a November 1964 report.

The results were not markedly better with ARA's public facilities money. Since most public facilities loans and grants went to municipalities, industrial parks, and industrial development boards rather than to specific companies, it is generally not possible to determine how many jobs were actually created. ARA claimed in its final (1965) report that jobs generated through public facilities loans and grants cost about $3,300 each, compared to $4,100 for those arising from industrial loans.

The main issues, however, were the distribution of the money and the uses to which it was put. The Appalachian portions of three states (Maryland, North Carolina, and Ohio) received no public facilities money at all; Virginia received about $500,000 (1.2 percent); and Tennessee, Pennsylvania, and Georgia got 4–7 percent. Kentucky hovered around a reasonable 13 percent, but West Virginia rose from about 8 percent the first year to about 66 percent during the last two. The sharp rise was again due to tourism projects, which eventually claimed 81 percent of the state's public facilities money.

After the passage of the $900 million Public Works Acceleration Act in September 1962, ARA's $175 million public facilities program faded into insignificance. Few applicants, in fact, could thereafter be found for its funds—which could account for ARA's willingness to put so much of its public facilities money into a few tourism projects in West Virginia.[15]

ARA's job-training program, greeted with great warmth in parts of the region, also proved to be of little use. Mayor David Francis of Huntington had strongly supported the program before Congressional committees, urging that 10,000–15,000 unemployed persons should be trained annually in Kentucky and West Virginia. When a job-training program was later set up by ARA in Huntington, however, of the more than a thousand who were invited to participate, 640 appeared for tests and only 240 qualified for training. The Huntington experience not only suggested how small the program would be likely to be in comparison to need but also confirmed a charge made by many that it served only the cream of the crop.[16]

Practical problems with the job-training program were numerous. Many Appalachian counties began job-training projects long before they managed to get ARA approval for industrial and public facilities grants and loans that were supposed to produce jobs for the trainees. By the end of ARA's first year only about nine thousand training positions existed nationwide. West Virginia and Pennsylvania had about a thousand trainees each by June 1962, but elsewhere in the region the numbers were quite small: 101 in two eastern Kentucky counties, 65 at La Follette (Tennessee), and about 60 in Belmont County, Ohio, the recipient of large numbers of Appalachian outmigrants.[17]

Had the numbers been larger, however, it is doubtful that ARA job training would have had much impact on unemployment in the region. Training periods were short (sixteen weeks at most), and a large percentage of those enrolled were being trained for poorly paying jobs (sewing machine operators, clerk-stenographers). Planned coordination between ARA job training and new or expanded ARA plants never materialized, and many Appalachian trainees had to be shipped elsewhere to jobs: clerk-stenographers from eastern Kentucky to Washington, D.C., and machine tool operators from Bluefield, West Virginia, to the Norfolk shipyards.

There were also more fundamental problems with the job-training program, which was administered for ARA by the Departments of Labor, Agriculture, and Health, Education, and Welfare (HEW). Levitan and others have documented the validity of the commonsense observation that job training is more effective in tight labor markets than in labor-surplus (that is, depressed) areas. A comparative study of trainees and nonapplicants in east Tennessee's Campbell and Claiborne counties after several years of ARA activity concluded that improvements attributable to the program were "normally overstated," that it was not clear that retraining reduced the overall level of unemployment, that benefits even for those who completed training tended to be short-lived, and that some of the claimed benefits could not be attributed directly to the training received. Another study of 1,500 ARA trainees in West Virginia concluded that "little valid proof has yet been offered . . . of high rates of personal and societal return on the retraining investment."[18]

Some ARA Projects in Appalachia: The Cumberlands, Middle Island Creek, and the New River Gorge

> It is certain that the rescue operation [in Appalachia] should go far beyond the fumbling and red-tape-ridden efforts of the present Area Redevelopment Administration. Launched with the most laudable intentions, this agency—in the Cumberlands, at least—has accomplished little beyond a few small loans for minor business enterprises. Most community leaders lost interest in it after attending a few of the interminable planning sessions. Tedious discussions of formulae, objectives and methods discouraged interest and deepened the highlanders' cynicism and disillusionment still further.
>
> Harry M. Caudill, *Night Comes to the Cumberlands* (1963)

The reconstruction of the Appalachian region must eventually be approached through the intelligent and equitable development and use of its abundant natural resources (coal, oil, gas, timber, land, and water power) for the benefit of all its people. While ARA was hardly an ideal agency for accomplishing such a monumental task, it was significantly involved in resource-development projects, and its involvement helped to set the pattern for federal approaches to Appalachian resource development during the 1960s.

Except for several small grants to evaluate mineral resources in northern Georgia and western North Carolina, and a few minor coal-related projects elsewhere, ARA's Appalachian efforts in the area of natural resources were concentrated in West Virginia and Kentucky, and were narrowly focused on recreation and tourism.

West Virginia's New River Gorge. Only six weeks after the ARA came into being, more than a thousand people gathered in Beckley, West Virginia, to hear about area redevelopment from high officials of ten federal agencies and departments. Senator Jennings Randolph and Governor Barron shared the stage with Commerce Secretary Luther Hodges. Beckley lay in one of four southern West Virginia counties (Fayette, Mercer, Summers, and Raleigh) that presented a classic test case to ARA: high, long-term unemployment (24 percent in Fayette County), lack of manufacturing industries, low incomes, poor living conditions, and abundant natural resources.

Timber resources and hydroelectric potential were very large in the gorge, through which the New River meandered on its way to join the Kanawha south of Charleston. Recoverable reserves of coal totaled nearly 4 billion tons in Raleigh and Fayette counties, and more than 100 million in Mercer. Although production was down to roughly half what it had been in 1950, during 1962 more than $20 million worth of coal would leave the 169 deep mines mostly owned by a half-dozen companies in Fayette County (New River, Ranger Fuel, Clifftop Smokeless Coal, Allied Chemical, and others). Raleigh County had more than one hundred active mines, two-thirds of which were owned by four corporations (Winding Gulf Coals, Slab Fork Coal, Armco Steel, and Eastern Gas and Fuel Associates). Output during the coming year would exceed 6 million tons at around $5 per ton.

In Summers County there was virtually no coal, but the publicly owned Bluestone Dam, built across the New River by the Corps of Engineers in 1949, had penstocks already in place for the installation of electric-power generators. Gordon Ebersole, the Interior Department's Staff Assistant for Area Redevelopment on the Resources Program Staff, reminded the crowd in Beckley that the federal Southeastern Power Administration was authorized to distribute any power that might be generated from public facilities there or elsewhere on the New River.

Because public development of coal resources was not feasible under existing laws (not to mention the prevailing ethos), and in any event the creation of new jobs in the coal industry would depend upon an essentially unstable market, three possibilities for development in the four counties remained: public power, small industries (especially timber-related ones), and tourism. But private interests in the New River Gorge would tolerate, and thus ARA was willing to support, only the last.

Fayette County's Overall Economic Development Plan, drawn up by a committee dominated by local business and political figures, recommended increased development of coal and timber resources but also emphasized tourism. Hydroelectric power was not mentioned. OEDPs from the three other counties resembled Fayette's.

Late in September, ARA's Harold Williams asked Ebersole to arrange a tour of the New River Gorge by federal officials and to encourage the National Park Service to develop a recreation plan for the area. Ebersole continued to insist that public power development would guarantee effective use of an available public resource, produce low-cost power for residential and industrial applications, and yield much-needed revenues for public services.[19] Williams himself was receptive, but ARA and the private utilities were not. The agenda was tourism, which posed little threat to established patterns of resource ownership and control.

In February 1962 the New River Gorge Development Corporation was formed to create a "national attraction that will outdraw the Grand Canyon."[20] Newspapers in the area (*Bluefield Daily Telegraph, Hinton Daily News, Beckley Post-Herald*) endorsed the tourism approach to development. Over some objections from Interior, ARA awarded two $36,000 contracts early in 1962 to the Washington, D.C., firm of Checchi & Co. to design a development program for the four counties. Before Checchi's work even commenced, however, it was agreed that "the approach would be tourism." Interior's Resources Program Staff Director Charles Stoddard charged, moreover, that the study was entrusted to Checchi rather than to the National Park Service because ARA wanted to maximize commercial rather than esthetic values.[21]

The Checchi study concluded that it would take ten years to develop the gorge "to the point where it will make a real impact as a job creator."[22] That would ultimately require, they estimated, twelve to fifteen resorts and a first-stage investment of almost $9 million. Three initial projects were recommended: 120 rooms at the 202-acre Plum Orchard Lake in Fayette County, 240 at the somewhat larger Stephens Lake in Raleigh County, and 120 at the eight-mile-long Bluestone Lake in Summers County. The three projects were expected to generate about one job per room at the resorts themselves, and perhaps half as many indirectly, for a total of 700. Current total unemployment for the counties was more than 10,000.

On the basis of the Checchi study, ARA began to pour money into tourism projects in the New River Gorge. Nearly $10 million was allocated to the Bluestone project alone, $1.8 million more for Hawk's Nest State Park in Fayette County, and lesser amounts elsewhere.

Construction on Pipestem State Park (at Bluestone) began in 1967, and the park opened in 1970 after further loans and grants from the Economic Development Administration (EDA) brought the total federal funds expended to $13.1 million.[23]

Bluestone proved to be of relatively slight economic benefit to the area. A study of the project for EDA in 1973 revealed that only 105 permanent and 180 seasonal jobs had been created, both on the site and in the surrounding area. Although average annual incomes had increased about $1,500 for those hired, only 29 percent of the work force had bettered their situations by accepting employment in the park, and the average annual income of all employees was still slightly below $3,000 per year.[24] The recreational facilities themselves were priced beyond the reach of low-income people in the four counties: $16–24 for a lodge room, and $50 a night for a small cabin in 1974.

The Cumberland Plateau. In 1963 Harry Caudill published *Night Comes to the Cumberlands.* Its subtitle was *A Biography of a Depressed Area,* and it had a foreword by Interior Secretary Stewart Udall that called the book "a tragic tale of the abuse and mismanagement of [the] resource heritage" of the Cumberland Plateau, which included "dense forests, winding rivers, abundant game, loamy soils, and thick veins of coal." Life on the plateau, Udall said, "is an anachronism, a remembrance of an ugly chapter in our history" and evidence that "the raider spirit of the last century is still abroad, wasting irreplaceable resources and demeaning human lives."[25]

Although signed by Udall, early versions of the foreword had been drafted by Gordon Ebersole, assigned by Interior to work on resource aspects of the ARA program. ARA's and Interior's subsequent involvement on the plateau revealed that Ebersole and lower-level staff in Interior were more eager to have ARA use the plateau's abundant natural resources as a base for reconstruction than were Udall, his immediate subordinates, or ARA itself. As Udall hedged in his statement, "one may differ with details of interpretation, in probing dark areas of American life."

Late in 1961 Ebersole and John Whisman of Kentucky's Area Program Office had talked informally about the plight of the plateau. As Interior was responsible for any natural resource projects undertaken by ARA, the two men agreed that a task force should be formed to explore possibilities. Early in 1962 Secretary Udall wrote to Kentucky Governor Bert Combs that the task force would include representatives from the Bureau of Mines, the Bureau of Land Reclamation, the National Park Service, and the Southeastern Power

Administration (SEPA), a composition that implied a broad, natural-resource-oriented approach to development.

By the time the task force assembled for its first two meetings at Middlesboro, Kentucky, and Wise, Virginia, in March, however, the focus had shifted. Whisman, who had helped arrange the meetings, had begun to refer to the group as a "task force on the tourism industry."[26] Nevertheless, the group concluded that "dramatic possibilities" lay in a comprehensive approach to the problem.

Ebersole's superior, Charles Stoddard, apparently still assumed that a resources approach was to be taken. In a March 30 memo he referred to "potentials for water-based recreation" but also talked of "mine-mouth generation of power, EHV [extra-high-voltage] transmission [and] new mineral development." At a preliminary meeting in early May, a report from the Southeastern Power Administration was introduced which noted thirty-seven available hydroelectric sites in the area and demonstrated the existence of a large potential market for the power.

At the May 10–11 meeting it was still the consensus that an area larger than the plateau should be dealt with, possibly the entire Appalachian region, and that an approach more comprehensive than tourism and recreation would be required. A temporary steering committee was formed from a number of federal agencies and a representative (Whisman) from the Conference of Appalachian Governors (CAG), and plans were made to constitute the group as a federal interagency committee. On May 25 Udall informed his assistant secretaries that if the Appalachian governors decided to move ahead on a regional basis, they would be eligible for ARA assistance in undertaking "a full resource analysis of the region."[27]

Events during the next few weeks are not entirely clear from the record, but it seems while Interior and other federal agencies were pushing for a comprehensive approach to regional development, John Whisman, through his position with CAG, was struggling to control whatever planning mechanism was chosen and in any case (possibly as a result of pressure from coal operators and power companies) to make sure the approach was limited to tourism. In June Whisman won his first important victory since the Middlesboro and Wise meetings in March. At a meeting with ARA in Washington, it was decided to create "a specific tourist industry task force for the Beautiful Cumberlands [Association] tourist program."[28] Whisman's role in the relatively recent formation of the Beautiful Cumberlands Association (BCA) is not clear, but circumstantial evidence suggests that he may have been involved. In any case, a July 3, 1962, letter from Interior's Steward McBryde notified Whisman that BCA would "act as spokesman for the area."

Whisman seemed determined to limit the development approach

to tourism. The question was how many federal agencies (including ARA) could be persuaded to go along. Reactions from technical staff personnel who were actually conducting the field surveys were not favorable. An Interior mineral resources engineer informed his superior in early July that while "obviously Mr. Whisman wishes a survey devoted exclusively to a study of tourism and outdoor recreation," Interior's approach should concentrate on the "total resource picture." Another engineer assigned by Interior to SEPA reported after a tour of eastern Kentucky in late June with ARA officials that Whisman "insists that the survey . . . be limited to tourism." The engineer's own conclusion, however, was that "a power survey" (coal, hydroelectric, pumped-storage) would be preferable. Even a National Park Service memo declared, "The single-minded approach for a tourist task force . . . as proposed by Whisman is not realistic."[29]

Above the technical staff and assistant secretary level in Interior, however, Whisman had more support. On July 9, Henry Caulfield, Acting Director of the Resources Program Staff, informed his assistant secretaries that a technical team was being set up to study the Cumberlands area and that "promotion of tourism through outdoor and water-based recreation would be a principal goal." He noted, however, that other approaches, including power development, were not ruled out.[30] But Whisman was apparently confident that his agenda would prevail. As early as June 12 he had already informed BCA members that plans were firm to create an "overall development approach [with] specific emphasis on . . . a tourist industry complex, regardless of whatever developments may accrue."[31]

Although ARA was already moving fairly dramatically into tourism development in the New River Gorge, it hesitated in the Cumberlands, apparently waiting for the scheduled report from the interagency task force. The report reached ARA administrator Batt in September 1962.[32] In essence, it followed the recommendations of BCA, whose list of specific tourism projects was entered verbatim in the text. In addition, "diversification of forest industries" and "wildlife management" were recommended. On power development, the report was brief:

> The potential for hydroelectric power development in the study area is somewhat limited, but significant power can be produced as part of the multiple-purpose water-development projects. Thermal-power development, based upon the local coal resources, offers the most significant future power potential. Opportunities for pumped-storage facilities probably exist in the area, *but neither this potential nor thermal power were studied to any great degree by the task force.*[33]

On September 27, shortly after he received the report, Batt informed Interior that ARA was establishing an Appalachian Recreation and Tourism Advisory Group (ARTAG), indicating that ARA would pursue the same approach in the Cumberlands that they were already committed to in the New River Gorge. On November 8, following a meeting with the CAG in Florida four weeks earlier, Interior's Stoddard wrote to Batt that John Whisman would be in town soon to advise him on what projects should be undertaken. He suggested holding up any report to the states until he had conferred with Whisman.[34]

It turned out that ARA actually undertook relatively few projects of any kind on the plateau. Only $162,000 of the $3 million it allocated for industrial loans in eastern Kentucky went to the five plateau counties (Pike, Bell, Letcher, Harlan, and Knox) that had been studied by the various task forces and study teams. For the five Virginia counties (Wise, Lee, Scott, Buchanan, and Dickenson), there was one $64,650 grant for a garment factory in Norton. Claiborne and Campbell counties in Tennessee received, in addition to $781,387 for a men's underwear factory in Tazewell, only about $1.8 million for local water supply and sewage system improvements.[35]

The net result of ARA's actual development projects on the Cumberland Plateau was therefore nearly nil. But the Cumberlands effort was an important episode in the definition of ARA policy for other parts of the region. It also reinforced John Whisman's attempt to establish his views of Appalachian development as the legitimate ones and his drive to emerge as the official liaison between federal agencies and Appalachia. His success in influencing ARA's Cumberland Plateau involvement was in fact a principal source of the momentum that carried him to important positions with the CAG and the President's Appalachian Regional Commission, and to virtual domination of the Appalachian Regional Commission during the late 1960s.

Wood pallets, feeder pigs, and strawberries: The ARA on Middle Island Creek. Nearly two hundred miles north and slightly west of the Bluestone reservoir in the New River Gorge, halfway between the West Virginia industrial centers of Charleston and Wheeling, lie the three small rural counties of Tyler, Pleasants, and Doddridge. The three share only a few of the characteristics of the rest of rural and small-town West Virginia (small population, substandard housing; significant out-migration). Unemployment in 1961 was 6–8 percent, but the counties were economically moribund and had virtually no coal-mining activity.[36] One potentially useful though hardly spectacular resource, however, was the muddy and sluggish Middle Island Creek, flowing through all three counties on its way to join the Ohio River, which forms the northwest boundary of Tyler and Pleasants.

Years of experience with resource-development projects in general—and knowledge of the public power projects of the Pacific northwest in particular—suggested to Interior's Gordon Ebersole that the three West Virginia counties might be able to develop their common water resource. To do so, however, would require the relatively recent technique of pumped storage, since neither the topography of the counties nor the characteristics of Middle Island Creek would allow a conventional hydroelectric installation.[37]

Because pumped-storage generators could be designed to use relatively shallow ("low head") pools, Ebersole speculated that it might be possible to create a pumped-storage installation on Middle Island Creek by using reversible turbines, which would return water from the Ohio River to the storage pool. He broached the idea in late 1962 to Sam White, the Republican county attorney of Pleasants County, suggesting that either the public utility districts of the northwest or the more recent conservancy districts of neighboring Ohio might allow the three counties to develop their common resource for public use. It would have been a pioneering venture; although all four neighboring states had at least a token amount of public power, and there were about one hundred municipal systems in Ohio, West Virginia had none. White promised to take up the idea with the county courts. Ebersole was to have a feasibility study made and explore possible support from ARA.

Armed with reports on pumped-storage installations and conservancy districts, Ebersole raised the possibility of a Middle Island Creek conservancy district (and perhaps others elsewhere) at the October 31, 1962, meeting of the ARA Advisory Policy Board.[38] Although his ideas were hardly greeted enthusiastically, Ebersole was able to arrange for a preliminary engineering study, which confirmed that a 200-foot-high dam stretched 700 feet across the creek near the river would allow a one-megawatt pumped-storage installation.[39] At the board meeting immediately after the report was submitted, however, it became obvious that ARA once again was determined to steer clear of public power development. ARA's Gordon Reckord questioned whether helping to establish conservancy districts was a proper use of ARA funds, but a staff member was nevertheless asked to prepare a policy paper for discussion. The paper apparently was never prepared, and during the ensuing weeks Ebersole became increasingly frustrated by Interior's own vacillation.[40]

In the late fall, Ebersole was reprimanded informally for getting Interior "on the hook" with the Middle Island Creek project. At the same time, however, the Resources Program Staff was engaged in a "conceptual study" of the development possibilities of the area, which subsequently concluded that "further consideration" of a pumped-storage project was economically justified and noted that a smaller reservoir than had been envisioned (81 square miles) would supply 760 kilowatts of power.[41]

On February 21, 1963, ARA's deputy director informed Interior that he "must discourage the use of ARA funds for the promotion of conservancy or other types of districts." No such districts were needed, he said, and it would in any case require two to three years and a public referendum to set one up. But both judgments were unsound, as it turned out. Eastern Kentucky editor Tom Gish, who had testified at the 1959 ARA hearings, reported to Ebersole that people in his area were much interested in forming conservancy or public utility districts, and plans for the formation of such a district on Middle Island Creek were moving much faster than ARA's deputy director thought possible.[42]

Before the initial reconnaissance study of the area had even been completed, attorney Sam White had persuaded the county courts of Doddridge and Pleasants to adopt a formal order requesting ARA to provide money and assistance for "the full economic development of the Middle Island Creek Valley . . . in the fields of recreation, tourism, flood control, water supply, etc." Ten days later Tyler County adopted an identical order.[43] In January White had arranged to have a bill to create a Middle Island Creek Development Authority (MICDA) introduced into the state legislature. Two weeks after ARA had said such a process would take two to three years, the bill, H.B. 398, was enacted into law.

Although Section 7(g) of the draft bill had specified that the Authority could "construct, acquire, operate, and maintain . . . holding basins . . . generating stations, pumping stations and siphons," the bill as passed provided for (in addition to recreation and tourism facilities) only flood prevention, erosion control, and flow regulation on Middle Island Creek. Governed by a local board appointed by the county courts, the Authority had broad power to enter into contracts, acquire land, receive and spend funds, and issue notes and bonds.

Thus ARA's objections were less substantive than programmatic: ARA was opposed to getting involved in the debate over public power and resource development. It was primarily committed to encouraging tourism in the Appalachian region, as it had already demonstrated elsewhere in West Virginia and on the Cumberland Plateau. On December 14, 1962, ARA's Sherwood Gates had written to Interior's Charles Stoddard that it had "come to our attention" that plans for MICDA were afoot. His letter did not mention public power but noted that ARA planned a study of the recreation and tourism potential of the area.

When ARA finally released its report a year later, it was confined to Doddridge County and proved to have borrowed heavily from a Bureau of Outdoor Recreation (BOR) study of June 1963, which recommended a series of ten small (30- to 535-acre) recreational lakes and related facilities.[44] Field study for the ARA report appears to have been confined to brief discussions in August 1963 with one director from MICDA, several state agency officials, and officials from the Hope Natural Gas Company and the Monongahela Power Company. Drawing upon the BOR study, the ARA report stressed tourism and recreation as "one of the main potentials" for economic development in the area. In manufacturing and agriculture, it advocated setting up a wood-pallet factory, raising feeder pigs, and growing strawberries.[45] Thirteen years later, no projects of any kind had been undertaken.

The Middle Island Creek episode illustrates the complex dynamics through which ARA's commitment to a certain approach to development was justified and sustained. While it is true (despite the language of the draft version of the MICDA bill) that local initiative on Middle Island Creek was directed primarily toward tourist development and that the impulse for power development came from a small contingent in the Interior Department, it also appears that the "local" choice was not entirely local.[46] What happened, apparently, is that federal (probably ARA) officials passed the word informally that money was available for tourism projects. Finding that such money could be had, local officials proposed tourism development, and ARA in turn used the proposals to justify both a specific response to "local initiative" on Middle Island Creek and its general commitment to tourism as a development priority.

Thus at one level the issue is ultimately not what was or was not done in a specific case, nor even which approach was best, but the complex role of a major federal agency in shaping (indeed to some extent producing) public opinion as a base for justifying particular development strategies. The depth of that commitment is suggested by the fact that even when the long-delayed and severely limited positive impact of tourism development had become manifest, and the future of ARA itself had begun to be in doubt, there was no change in the policy.[47]

On October 9, 1963, ARA's Advisory Policy Board discussed combining ARA efforts with those of delegate agencies such as Interior to "make a case for tourism." An *ad hoc* committee was formed to "work out a strategy [for an] educational program." A few months later, Director Batt reported enthusiastically on a visit to the ARA's Schweitzer Basin ski resort project in Idaho, an endeavor that had drawn heavy criticism in Congress. ARA field reports on development opportunities in six eastern Kentucky counties published in late 1964 and early 1965 endorsed the tourism approach and offered few attractive alternatives. For Lee County, a bakery, coin laundries, soft-drink bottling plants, homes for the aged, and growing mushrooms in caves were also recommended.[48]

In a booklet published just before its demise in 1965, designed to provide development advice to local governments and communities, ARA cited a growing demand for recreation and tourism resources and reported that nearly $70 million of its own money had gone to tourist projects.[49] The economic effects of tourist development, actually quite well known at the time, were called "hard to define and statistically slippery." A discussion of the distribution of economic benefits noted what percentages of the tourist's dollar went to restaurants and gasoline stations but contained no information on wages and working conditions in the industry. Employment implications (dismissed in sixteen lines of the text) were called "difficult to estimate." There was merely an offhand admission that "jobs may be seasonal." A list of ARA's successful tourism projects included Bluestone, which it cited as justified by an "independent survey by a private economic consulting firm" (the Checchi study, which ARA itself had told Checchi had to be limited to tourism).

Phasing Out ARA

As early as February 1962, only nine months after the ARA legislation was signed into law, President Kennedy had become impatient with the lack of substantial progress in depressed areas and had directed ARA Director Batt to move more aggressively. The necessity of doing so in Appalachia was becoming increasingly apparent, despite Interior Secretary Udall's reply to Kennedy citing ARA's New River Gorge project as a vital effort. In October 1962, in an effort to improve its record in Appalachia, ARA set up an interagency committee (headed by Dr. Harold L. Sheppard) to work with the Conference of Appalachian Governors and hired a private research institute to prepare a development plan for the region. The CAG considered the institute's work so unsatisfactory, however, that it paid the researchers their fee and dismissed them. The interagency committee also accomplished little, and severe winter floods in the region soon forced Kennedy to declare portions of Kentucky and West Virginia disaster areas.

Apparently exasperated with ARA, Appalachian governors asked the President to establish a state-federal committee. Kennedy thereupon called a meeting of the ARA Advisory Policy Board and state representatives in the Cabinet room on April 9, in the midst of hearings on the ARA amendments. At that meeting he announced the appointment of the President's Appalachian Regional Commission (PARC). Technical assistance and staff support for PARC were to be provided by ARA.

The day before the White House meeting, Representative Carl Perkins (D.–Ky.) had introduced a bill (H.R. 5525) "to provide for a resource and economic development program for the Appalachian highlands area," including natural resource and hydroelectric development. Thus in both PARC and the Congress, the stage was set for the next round. In PARC the odds for an approach to development bolder than ARA's were not good. Two prominent members of PARC and its staff were John Whisman (Washington representative for CAG and PARC's executive secretary) and William L. Batt, Administrator of the Area Redevelopment Administration. Assigned to the Water Resources Team were Ebersole and Knowland Plucknett, both of whom had opposed the ARA's tourism plan for the Cumberland Plateau. Ebersole also served on the coal and power subteams. State representatives for the latter were all drawn from state agencies, except in West Virginia, which chose as its representative Hugh Stillman, an Appalachian Power Company official from Huntington.

The process that led from the formation of the President's Appalachian Regional Commission to the final passage of the Appalachian Regional Development Act required almost two years, however, and in the meantime the Economic Opportunity Act of 1964 became law, inaugurating the War on Poverty in Appalachia.

Notes

1. James L. Sundquist, *Politics and Policy: The Eisenhower, Kennedy and Johnson Years* (Washington, D.C.: Brookings Institution, 1968), pp. 80–81. The most complete analysis of the Area Redevelopment Administration is Sar A. Levitan, *Federal Aid to Depressed Areas: An Evaluation of the Area Redevelopment Administration* (Baltimore: Johns Hopkins University Press, 1964). Portions of my background account on the legislation are based on Levitan. The writing of this chapter was greatly facilitated by access to the private papers of Gordon K. Ebersole.

2. See *New Frontiers of the Kennedy Administration: The Texts of the Task Force Reports Prepared for the President* (Washington, D.C.: Public Affairs Press, 1961).

3. U.S. Senate, *Hearings Before a Subcommittee of the Committee on Banking and Currency on Bills to Establish an Effective Program to Alleviate Conditions*

of . . . Unemployment and Underemployment in Certain Economically Depressed Areas, January 18—February 20, 1961.

4. *Hearings Before the House Committee on Banking and Currency on H.R. 4569,* February 24—March 13, 1961.

5. Quoted in Levitan, *Federal Aid,* pp. 23–24.

6. On both the details of ARA structure and the delegation of responsibilities to other agencies, see *ibid.,* pp. 35 ff.

7. William L. Batt, "The ARA Program," in Margaret Gordon (ed.), *Poverty in America* (San Francisco: Chandler, 1970), p. 370.

8. The bill authorized only 2.6 percent of the ARA's total funds to go directly to unemployed workers (as subsistence payments during training). Sar Levitan's "Area Redevelopment: A Tool to Combat Poverty," in Gordon (ed.), *Poverty in America,* p. 377, argues that trickle-down is justified by "ample data." Experience with both ARA and the later Appalachian Regional Commission (see Chapters 5 and 6) leaves substantial room for doubt, however.

9. Quoted in Levitan, *Federal Aid,* p. 200.

10. In *ibid.,* p. 69, Levitan includes among the characteristics of chronic-labor-surplus (that is, depressed) areas "a high rate of chronic unemployment, . . . stagnating population, . . . declining labor force participation rates, low wages and income, inadequate investment in capital outlays, and substandard housing." Such other criteria as number of low-income farm families, relationship of income levels to those in prosperous areas, and rates of migration were also used from time to time in certain areas.

11. See Varden Fuller, "Rural Poverty and Development," in Gordon (ed.), *Poverty in America,* pp. 390 ff. Fuller called OEDPs a "romantic . . . and impractical idea" based on indefensible assumptions about the problems and planning resources of depressed areas and about the relationship between individual and community needs.

12. Levitan, *Federal Aid,* pp. 195–201. The director of the Area Program Office was John Whisman, whose earlier and subsequent career is treated in more detail in Chapters 5 and 6.

13. Figures that follow are drawn from ARA's "Activity Summary Report," published in U.S. House of Representatives, *Hearings Before a Subcommittee of the Committee on Banking and Currency . . . on S. 1163, a Bill to Amend Certain Provisions of the Area Redevelopment Act,* April 30—May 6, 1963, pp. 95 ff., and from ARA's annual reports for 1962–65. Figures for "Appalachia" from ARA documents can be only approximate at best, because ARA used several different boundaries for the region in its reports. The 1962 report refers to an "eight-state region" but includes a map showing ten. In 1964 the region was designated as including 258 counties in ten states: Pennsylvania (52), West Virginia (51), Kentucky (42), Tennessee (29), Alabama (20), Ohio (20), Georgia (19), North Carolina (13), Virginia (9), and Maryland (3).

14. Batt, "The ARA Program," p. 548, and *Industrial Directory of the Commonwealth of Pennsylvania* (Harrisburg, Pa.: Bureau of Statistics). Subsequent conclusions about jobs are based upon similar volumes for other Appalachian states and the *Directory of Central Atlantic States Manufactures* (Baltimore: T. K. Sanderson, 1964–65). The Berwick industrial loan was given in conjunction with a $915,000 public facilities loan.

15. The Public Works Acceleration Act was administered by ARA. See Levitan, *Federal Aid*, pp. 34 ff.

16. *Ibid.*, p. 180. Levitan notes that only one-tenth of all ARA trainees were over forty-five years old and that their levels of education were relatively high.

17. "Eight Months' Training Experience Under the Area Redevelopment Act," *Monthly Labor Review*, LXXXV (December 1962), 1375–78, and *Training for Jobs in Redevelopment Areas* (Washington, D.C.: U.S. Department of Labor, 1962).

18. Richard J. Solie, "Employment Effects of Retraining the Unemployed," *Industrial and Labor Relations Review*, XXI (January 1968), 210–25, and Gerald G. Somers, "Training the Unemployed," in Joseph M. Becker (ed.), *In Aid of the Unemployed* (Baltimore: Johns Hopkins University Press, 1965), pp. 227–51, respectively. After 1962, ARA's job-training program became subordinate to that of the new Manpower Development and Training Act, which offered seventy-two weeks' training and more liberal training allowance payments to trainees.

19. Memo from William W. Wells, Department of the Interior, November 1, 1961 and Gordon Ebersole, "Appalachia: Potential . . . With a View," *Mountain Life and Work (MLW)*, XLII (Winter 1966), 10 ff.

20. Charleston *Gazette*, February 21, 1962.

21. Stoddard memo to Director, Bureau of Outdoor Recreation, May 18, 1962.

22. *Tourism as a Job Creator: A First-Stage Program for the New River Gorge Country of West Virginia* (Washington, D.C.: Checchi & Co., 1962).

23. Letter to author from Ira S. Latimer, Jr., Director of West Virginia Department of Natural Resources, March 17, 1975.

24. *Evaluation of Impact of Tourism/Recreation Projects for Economic Development Administration* (Washington, D.C.: Centaur Management Consultants, 1973), II, D-289 ff.

25. Stewart L. Udall, "Foreword" to Harry M. Caudill, *Night Comes to the Cumberlands: A Biography of a Depressed Area* (Boston: Atlantic–Little, Brown, 1963), pp. vii–viii.

26. Among those attending the meetings were representatives of the Appalachian Power Company and Old Dominion Power Company, and the president of the Harlan Coal Operators Association.

27. Udall memo, May 25, 1962.

28. Minutes of June 13, 1962, meeting.

29. Memos from Edwin M. Thomasson, staff engineer to the Assistant Secretary for Mineral Resources, to Graham Hollister of Interior, July 2, 1962; Knowland J. Plucknett to the Assistant Secretary for Water and Power Development, July 3, 1962; and William J. Briggle of the National Park Service to Hollister, July 2, 1962, respectively.

30. Henry Caulfield memo, July 9, 1962.

31. John Whisman memo, June 12, 1962.

32. *Natural Resources Potential of the Cumberland Area, Kentucky, Tennessee, Virginia: An Interagency Task Force Report for a Conservation and Recreation Demonstration Complex*, September 1962. The task force included representatives from SEPA as well as various units of the Department of the Interior. A

representative of BCA and John Whisman were listed as having provided "liaison with State and local organizations" in Kentucky.

33. *Ibid.*, pp. 12–13. Emphasis added.

34. Letter from Charles Stoddard to Batt, November 8, 1962.

35. ARA *Annual Report, 1964*, pp. 66 ff.

36. Pleasants County had no recoverable coal reserves. Tyler and Doddridge had 600 million to 800 million tons each but had had no mining activity since at least 1950 (*West Virginia Statistical Handbook*, pp. 174 ff.). All three counties had active oil and gas wells, but the 1963 *Census of Mineral Industries* indicates that production involved relatively few jobs.

37. Pumped-storage projects use reversible pump-turbines, operated as generating units during periods of high demand. At "off-peak" periods they are reversed to pump water back into the storage pool.

38. Minutes of the ARA Advisory Policy Board, October 31, 1962.

39. Letter from Lewis G. Smith to Ebersole, November 8, 1962. One problem was that the reservoir would have had a 100-square-mile surface area, and there was opposition to such extensive flooding among local residents. Using the river as the lower pool would also have required approval by the Corps of Engineers.

40. ARA Advisory Policy Board minutes, November 14, 1962. Sections 7(d) and 8(c) of the ARA law did in fact state that no public facility loans or grants could be made for facilities that would compete with public utilities "subject to regulation by a State regulatory body"—that is, private power companies. The technical assistance and information functions (Sections 10–11) were broadly defined, however, and should have afforded ample opportunity for assistance in forming conservancy districts.

41. *Conceptual Report on Middle Island Creek Development for Pumped-Storage Power and Large-Scale Recreation for Pleasants, Tyler, and Doddridge Counties, West Virginia*, Part I, January 1963.

42. Ebersole to Charles Stoddard, August 19, 1963.

43. Orders of County Court, Pleasants, Doddridge, and Tyler Counties, November 5–16, 1962.

44. Bureau of Outdoor Recreation, *Tourism and Recreation Potential, Middle Island Creek*, June 1963.

45. *Opportunities for Economic Development in Doddridge County* (Washington, D.C.: ARA, 1963).

46. Interview with Sam White, February 6, 1975.

47. Congressional debates over ARA amendments in 1963 produced serious criticism of the tourism approach. See *Hearings Before a Subcommittee of the Committee on Banking and Currency . . . on S. 1163, a Bill to Amend Certain Provisions of the Area Redevelopment Act*, April 30—May 6, 1963. See also James Duscha, "The Depressed Areas: Two Years After," *The Progressive*, XXVII (September 1963), 29–32.

48. *Opportunities for Economic Growth in . . . Breathitt, Lee, Owsley, and Wolfe Counties*, September 1964. Other reports were prepared for Elliott (December 1964) and Bell Counties (February 1965).

49. *Recreation and Tourism Development Through Federal Programs* (Washington, D.C.: Area Redevelopment Administration, 1965).

CHAPTER 4

Appalachia and the War on Poverty: The Office of Economic Opportunity

> Let us resolve here and now that we will . . . by nineteen hundred and forty-one . . . abolish all the excess of poverty . . . in these mountains and bring people up to the full average of American opportunity.
>
> William G. Frost, speech to
> the Conference of Southern
> Mountain Workers,
> 1921

> We shall soon, with the help of God, be in sight of the day when poverty will be banished in the nation.
>
> Herbert Hoover, accepting the
> Republican Presidential
> nomination, 1928

> This administration, here and now, declares war on poverty in America.
>
> Lyndon B. Johnson, State of
> the Union message, 1964

ONE CAN HARDLY AVOID an apologetic tone in writing about the War on Poverty. During the past decade the poverty program has become almost a synonym for failure. Depending on one's politics, it was either an expensive boondoggle, a modest but poorly funded program that might have worked but didn't, or a testimony to the failure of national will and imagination in dealing with the inherent inequities of our economic system. Virtually no one maintains that it permanently changed the lot of many poor people or significantly reduced the probability of future poverty on a large scale.

And yet, in Appalachia at least, the influx of federal poverty money, poverty plans and proposals, and poverty warriors was a powerful determinant of political and social dynamics for nearly an entire decade. Choices were made in Washington about which states and counties would get Office of Economic Opportunity (OEO) money; the political fortunes of county judges, mayors, and party chairmen waxed and waned in terms of their skill in manipulating OEO programs and guidelines; communities and families locked themselves in internecine battle over OEO money and jobs; a new generation of young people schooled themselves in the Machiavellian skills necessary to survive in and turn toward their own purposes the labyrinthine complexities and Byzantine politics of a large bureaucracy. Thousands of ordinary Appalachian people, employed by OEO in counties where there were few other jobs, faced a cruel choice between political dissent and economic survival. Thousands more got an "education in disillusionment" (as Highlander Center's Myles Horton has called it) by descending upon state and national capitals by the busload to petition (seldom successfully) for a redress of their poverty program grievances.

However summarily the War on Poverty may be dismissed in terms of its stated objectives, as a political and social phenomenon it must nevertheless be looked at carefully.[1]

The Origins of the War

> [A] few years ago . . . they came over here, to this hollow and a lot of other ones. They said they were out of Charleston, and out of Washington, D.C., and they were going to get all the information together about us, and file a report, and then there'd be some laws passed or something, and we wouldn't have to live like this any more. . . . I spent [a long time] answering those questions. And do you know, that was . . . years ago. I don't remember how many. . . . Now the VISTA man, the young fellow, he means well. . . . But when he told me they were thinking of studying us again, . . . that was it. . . . He told me about the new study, and I told him about the old one, and it led to an afternoon we spent, exchanging our ideas.
>
> West Virginia man to Robert Coles in
> *Still Hungry in America*

During congressional hearings on the Economic Opportunity Act of 1964 there were those who contended that no new program was needed because the nation had always been fighting poverty. Such a position suggests a sanguine reading of American history, but it is nevertheless true that the roots of the War on Poverty reach back at least into the 1930s. Lyndon Johnson said that Franklin Roosevelt "was like a daddy to me," and Roosevelt's successor, Harry Truman, began the campaign that eventually led to Medicare. Dwight Eisenhower established the Department of Health, Education, and Welfare, and many of John F. Kennedy's proposals for social legislation had roots in prior administrations. Some programs—federal aid to education, youth employment, the domestic peace corps—found their way into the War on Poverty.[2]

President Kennedy's social legislation was stalled in Congress after the passage of the Area Redevelopment Act, and by early 1962 he had concluded that ARA itself had bogged down. In December he told Council of Economic Advisers Chairman Walter Heller he wanted a broader attack on poverty. A few months later Heller was consulting with Cabinet members and others on "measures which might be woven into a basic attack on the problems of poverty . . . as part of the 1964 legislative program." By mid-November 1963, reportedly moved by Homer Bigart's article in the *New York Times* on poverty in eastern Kentucky, Kennedy had decided that such measures would be included in his new legislative program.[3] On November 23, the day after Kennedy was assassinated, President Johnson told Walter Heller, "That's my kind of program. . . . Move full speed ahead."[4]

James L. Sundquist has noted that until 1964 the word "poverty" did not appear as a heading in either the *Congressional Record* or the *Public Papers of the Presidents*. The document that did most to ensure its presence there afterward was Chapter 2 of the 1964 *Annual Report of the Council of Economic Advisers,* which found one-fifth of the nation poor and noted that there had been no significant redistribution of income since World War II. It concluded: "We cannot leave the further wearing away of poverty solely to the general progress of the economy." Johnson, his earlier assurance to Heller reinforced by the CEA report, announced the War on Poverty in his State of the Union message on January 8 and three weeks later appointed Peace Corps Director Sargent Shriver as head of a task force to draft a legislative proposal.

The Shriver Task Force was itself a poverty case. Allotted a budget of only $30,000, it begged and borrowed staff and assistance from other agencies. At first it operated out of three unused rooms in the Peace Corps building.[5] Nevertheless, it moved quickly to draft the legislation.

When the Task Force began meeting on February 2, a single concept (later called "community action") dominated discussion; it was drawn largely from work undertaken earlier by the President's Commission on Juvenile Delinquency, chaired by Attorney General Robert F. Kennedy, and the Ford Foundation's "gray areas" program, both designed to attack poverty in urban areas.[6] Yet both President Johnson's sweeping rhetoric in his January 8 address and Shriver's own political instincts called for a broader program. Adam Yarmolinsky recalls that at the first Task Force meeting on the night of February 2 in the government green Peace Corps conference room, Shriver took a look at the "one-title" (that is, community action) poverty program and said, "It'll never fly." To flesh it out, he initiated brainstorming sessions with the Task Force staff, using Chapter 2 of the CEA report as a "text," and solicited contributions from federal departments and agencies.

The next six weeks were spent adding programs and titles, until the bill indeed began to look a bit like the "hodge-podge of a poverty poultice" one of its critics later called it. The Labor Department argued for a youth employment program similar to that in the Youth Employment Act, which had passed the Senate in 1963, and work-study provisions like those in the pending omnibus education bill. To counter the heavy urban emphasis, the Agriculture Department suggested a "rural title," which included land reform and small loans to marginal farmers. The Small Business Administration pressed for an employment and business incentives title. Within a few days the bill had grown to include most of these features as well as others: migrant programs, day care, sanitation, VISTA (drawn from the National Service Corps Act passed by the Senate in August 1963), and rehabilitation of Selective Service rejectees.[7]

As introduced into Congress on March 16, the act had six titles: I. Youth Programs (Job Corps, Work Training, Work Study); II. Community Action; III. Rural Programs (grants and loans, Family Farm Development Corporation, loans to cooperatives); IV. Employment and Investment Incentives; V. Family Unity Through Jobs (employment training for unemployed fathers); and VI. VISTA.

Appalachia in the Legislative Process

During the deliberations of both the Shriver Task Force and Congress, two images were omnipresent in the media: jobless blacks in the ghettos and poverty-stricken Appalachian whites. The former dominated discussion and planning as the Task Force concentrated on young people in general and unemployed young blacks in the cities in particular. Appalachia apparently was never treated as a distinct problem requiring special attention. Indeed, Shriver's staff had neither the knowledge nor the experience required to give due attention to the latter image.[8]

Chapter 2 of the CEA report did not treat poor Appalachians separately in its statistical data, as it did blacks and Indians. It merely noted without elaboration that the "needs of the poor are not the same in East Kentucky and West Harlem." Adam Yarmolinsky recalls that as early as Shriver's first meeting with his staff, the War on Poverty was sharply distinguished from previous Appalachian-oriented programs such as ARA. It was to be a "human development" program, aimed at "rehabilitation of people and neighborhoods, rather than . . . underdeveloped areas of the country." Yarmolinsky's Task Force colleague James Sundquist reported that in late 1963 the Bureau of the Budget was also searching for ways to "distinguish the new legislation, as dramatically as possible, from all that had gone before," including Appalachian programs.[9]

Thus neither the experience nor the instincts of the Task Force disposed it to tailor the legislation to the specific needs of the Appalachian region.[10] It was therefore up to Congress to make the sizable alterations necessary to produce even a passable fit—to address, for example, the irony of establishing Job Corps and "work experience" programs in Appalachian counties where unemployment was above 25 percent and ARA's job-training programs had already proved to be of scant value.

Hearings on H.R. 10440 began before the Subcommittee on the War on Poverty of Representative Adam Clayton Powell's Committee on Education and Labor on March 17, 1964. In twenty days of hearings, seventy-nine witnesses appeared; the printed record ran to more than seventeen hundred pages.[11] Chicago, Detroit, New Haven, Oakland, Minneapolis, and Saint Louis sent their mayors to testify. American Indians had numerous spokesmen. Testimony was taken from the Chamber of Commerce, the National Association of Manufacturers, the American Optometric Association, the Amalgamated Meat Cutters, the National Association of Social Workers, the General Federation of Women's Clubs, and the Union of American Hebrew Congregations. Congressmen from Maine, Ohio, Minnesota, Texas, Florida, Montana, and New Jersey spoke for their constituencies.

But testimony about and from Appalachia was brief, infrequent, and not very effective. When Sargent Shriver first testified, he listed 137 people who had contributed to the crafting of the legislation. That only one, Governor Terry Sanford of North Carolina, had experience with Appalachian problems foreshadowed the degree of attention the region would receive during both hearings and floor debate.[12]

The only Appalachian congressman on the Subcommittee was Carl Perkins, fifteen-year veteran Democrat from eastern Kentucky's Seventh District. Perkins's presence did little to ensure that the bill would be shaped to the needs of the region. There was no mention, for example, of the fact that some of eastern Kentucky's "poorest" counties were producing millions of tons of virtually untaxed coal yearly from unsafe mines worked by miners suffering from black lung, an occupational disease that was not compensable under federal law.

During the testimony of Secretary of Labor Willard Wirtz, Perkins read a letter from an unemployed Floyd County coal miner whose seventeen-year-old son had been forced by lack of money to drop out of high school and enlist in the army three months before graduation. But instead of pursuing the implications of the letter for thousands of other Appalachian young people and for Labor Department policy, Perkins hastened to save Wirtz any embarrassment by adding, "It is true that the [Department's] programs . . . have not reached the hardcore unemployed in the minefields [*sic*] but you have . . . done everything possible within your authority and resources."[13]

Most other Appalachian congressmen absented themselves entirely from the subcommittee's deliberations, and only two of the region's governors appeared. North Carolina's Terry Sanford and Kentucky's Edward Breathitt, both of whom testified during the second round of hearings in April, essentially endorsed the bill as it stood.[14] Breathitt, in whose state lay some of the poorest counties in the nation (in Wolfe County, 81 percent of all families had annual incomes below $3,000; more than half the families were below the poverty line in 61 percent of all Kentucky counties), said that the act "embodies for the first time on the Federal level a truly strategic attack on the total complex of problems which plague our people," adding that his endorsement was "not lightly given." Thus the official seals of two Appalachian states were placed upon a program designed primarily to address problems significantly different from those of Appalachia. Except for an appearance by Robert Holcomb, President of the National Independent Coal Operators' Association, who requested that the act be expanded to include loans to small coal operators, there was no further direct testimony from representatives of the region in the House hearings.[15]

Federal department and agency witnesses did not concern themselves with Appalachia. Interior Secretary Udall's testimony dwelt mostly upon Indians and the use of Indian lands; Commerce Secretary Hodges briefly described a Mingo County, West Virginia, wood-processing plant set up under ARA, but his remarks led to no general discussion of Appalachian problems.

One of the few occasions when it was pointed out that the needs of Appalachian people derived partly from the inherent inequities of the regional economy occurred during the testimony of Attorney General Robert F. Kennedy. The subcommittee had dwelt for some minutes on the problems of Indians when Representative Martin (R.–Neb.) cautioned, "When we get into these Federal programs, we stifle individual initiative." "Without being presumptuous, Congressman," Kennedy replied, "have you ever been to West Virginia [or] in the coal mines of eastern Kentucky? . . . Have you talked to the coal miners of West Virginia and told them what they needed was individual initiative? . . . Have you told them they should go out and get jobs when there are no jobs?"[16]

The cursory Senate hearings that followed in June did not significantly extend the House subcommittee's scant consideration of Appalachia. West Virginia's Democratic Senator Jennings Randolph, the only Appalachian member of the Select Committee on Poverty, was present only one day out of four.[17] The state's junior Senator, Robert Byrd, was a cosponsor of the bill but did not speak in its favor. Nor did any of his colleagues from Appalachian states. Conservative Representative Peter Frelinghuysen (R.–N.J.) came over from the House committee to denounce the bill as an "unnecessary, hastily conceived, sloppily drafted . . . grab bag" which in the absence of pressure from the Administration would have been "laughed out of Congress"; his testimony was countered by no Appalachian congressmen. Consideration of the region would have been omitted entirely had not Attorney General Kennedy repeated testimony he had given before the House subcommittee.[18]

In neither house were Appalachian problems discussed significantly during subsequent floor debate. The Senate passed the bill on July 23, and House debate commenced on August 5. Carl Perkins was the only representative of the region to speak in favor of passage, which came on August 8. In final form, the bill differed little from H.R. 10440, prepared by the Shriver Task Force six months earlier. President Johnson signed the bill into law on August 20, 1964, as P.L. 88-452.

P.L. 88-452 and the Structural Basis of Poverty in Appalachia

> Men are chiefly persuaded, not by the logical force of arguments, but by the disposition with which they view them.
>   Robert Lampman, *Ends and Means of Reducing Income Poverty* (1971)

Before one asks whether the Office of Economic Opportunity *was* effective in the Appalachian region, one must ask whether, given the shape of the legislation, it had any *promise* of being so. A useful clue lies in a model that Daniel Moynihan has said the Council of Economic Advisers frequently used to explain poverty, and which in fact came to underlie the programs authorized by P.L. 88-452:

Poverty
leads to
Cultural and environmental obstacles to motivation
which lead to
Poor health, inadequate education, and low mobility
limiting earning potential
which leads to
limited income opportunities
which lead to
Poverty.[19]

The CEA's model, a latter-day version of the position against which the Mountain Workers' Conference had been warned by Commissioner Claxton in 1915, had its most recent antecedent in the "culture of poverty" thesis, whose best known exponent in the mid-1960s was anthropologist Oscar Lewis. In his own explanation of the thesis, however, Lewis was careful to note the relationship between the seventy factors he thought characterized the culture of poverty (for example, provincialism, fatalism, "weak ego structure") and the political and economic context. The culture of poverty, he said, "is likely to be found where imperial conquest has smashed the native social and economic structure and held the natives, perhaps for generations, in servile status, or where feudalism is yielding to capitalism in the later evolution of a colonial economy."[20]

But the CEA model admitted the relevance of no such context, and in failing to do so it overlooked a great deal of pertinent data, especially in Appalachia. Indeed, if one looks carefully at conditions in the region, a markedly different model suggests itself:

Corporate monopolization of major resources
leads to
an inequitable and undemocratic economic and
political system
which leads to
political powerlessness, economic and cultural exploitation
and environmental destruction
which lead to
poor education and social services, minimal income,
hopelessness, and out-migration
which facilitate further
Corporate monopolization of major resources.

Although no conceivable model so simple in form could account for all the complexities of the problem, the stark contrast between the two models (and the assumptions upon which they are based) suggests why the Johnson administration, the Task Force, and Congress failed to design a poverty program that had a reasonable hope of working in Appalachia: Poverty was to be eliminated by reinforcing and extrapolating the system whose irrational and inequitable operation had destroyed the region in the first place.[21] "People refuse to believe," Adam Walinsky wrote at the conclusion of the Senate hearings, "that poverty can primarily be caused by an unequal system."[22]

The record abundantly bears out Walinsky's contention; the process that produced P.L. 88-452 involved no serious attempts at structural reform. Even the House committee's majority report said that "the philosophy behind the [act] is not that existing wealth should be redistributed but that poor people can and must be provided with opportunities to earn a decent living."[23]

The only structural reform included in the original draft, a minor one (the land-reform provision of Title III), did not survive Congress. Modeled to a degree on the Rural Resettlement program of the Farm Security Administration of the 1930s and written into the draft at the insistence of the Department of Agriculture, Section 303(a) would have allowed the federal government to buy up idle land for resale as small family farms under long-term, low-interest loans. In the House minority report Kentucky Representative M. G. Snyder and others called it "an assault on basic American precepts" that looks like "something from behind the Iron Curtain." Senator Strom Thurmond of South Carolina said it was a "Trojan horse filled with socialism and collectivism." It was removed from the bill on the floor of the Senate by a vote of 49–43.

The few witnesses who were politically secure enough to suggest a structural approach either failed to do so or equivocated. Walter Reuther's written testimony before the House subcommittee called for national health care, a strengthening of Title III (land reform), and better national economic planning, but in his oral statement he bragged that the American labor movement was "the only [one] in the whole free world that supports the Free Enterprise system."[24]

Thus both critics and supporters agreed that the aim was to channel poor people into a structurally unaltered mainstream; they differed only upon whether the bill would help achieve that end. As Elinor Graham concluded, the hearings and congressional debate were essentially a ritual that "provided for public presentation of the right phrases of the officially approved social philosophy toward poverty and the proposed legislation."[25] Hence a statement by the Republican Joint Economic Committee, intended to express opposition to the Act, could have served almost as well to express the consensus of its supporters:

> Too many of our citizens . . . live outside the mainstream of American society. . . . The greatest domestic challenge before the Nation is to accentuate and extend the vast successes of our system. . . . More progress has been made within the framework of the people's capitalism of the United States than anywhere else in the world.[26]

Operational Problems

> About a year ago, many people were saying that the War on Poverty wasn't accomplishing much. . . .
> Now, only a year later, there is another sound. In all parts of the country, from all types of institutions and all kinds of people, there is a sudden recognition that the poverty program is accomplishing great things for America.
>
> *The Quiet Revolution: 2nd*
> *Annual Report, Office of*
> *Economic Opportunity,* 1967

> I was at a meeting last week, and we all got to talking, and they had some "observers" there. That's what they called them, an expert on "community action" one of them was, and an expert on "group process" the other one was. We were all saying the same thing, what a rotten shame it is, the way things have gone in the sixties—the hopes raised and the disappointment. "You all seem discouraged, depressed," the "group process" guy said. I didn't say anything. No one did. Then he asked us if we wanted to *talk* about that, our discouragement. I couldn't take it any longer. I said, no, I didn't; but I'd like for him to go over to Washington, D.C., and get the President and some Congressmen and ask them if *they* wanted to talk about anything.
>
> Young West Virginia man to Robert Coles in
> *Migrants, Sharecroppers and Mountaineers*

The appropriations bill for the Office of Economic Opportunity passed in Congress on October 3, 1964, and on November 25 (safely past the elections) Sargent Shriver announced the funding of the first OEO projects. Within a few months, Title II Community Action agencies (CAPs) had been opened in dozens of Appalachian counties; OEO's first demonstration grant had been awarded to the Berea-based Appalachian Volunteers; and OEO program acronyms were being painted on office doors all across the region. With nearly half its first fiscal year gone before any funds were released by Congress, OEO moved to spend money quickly. In a little more than a year (by

February 1, 1966), nearly $205 million flowed into eleven Appalachian (or partly Appalachian) states.[27]

But the Appalachian campaign of the War on Poverty was not to be blessed with early success. There were at least five major problems, any one of which would have been sufficient to make success uncertain.

Insufficient money to do the job. When absolute levels of funding for OEO are discussed, a comparison is frequently made between expenditures for defense and the Vietnam War, and those for the War on Poverty and other domestic programs. "Guns and butter" is the code phrase for the argument, and the statistics can indeed be impressive. Donovan and many others have pointed out that defense appropriations ran from about $50 billion in the mid-1960s to more than $70 billion at the end of the decade and that the Vietnam War alone cost more than $20 billion in 1966. OEO appropriations did not *total* $4 billion during the first three years of operation. Emile Benoit has suggested, however, that the guns-and-butter argument is misleading, for the main obstacle to increased social welfare spending has for decades been not defense expenditures but "positive congressional dislike" of social welfare spending.[28] However the argument is ultimately viewed, the fact remains that, as Donovan and a host of other analysts of the poverty war have agreed, OEO programs were "never budgeted at anything more than a pilot-project level."[29]

How much was needed to do the job? No one knows exactly, but James Sundquist pointed out that if the spending levels of the New Haven community-action project (one of the primary models) had been extrapolated for the national effort, between $10 billion and $13 billion a year would have been needed. But Mitchell Sviridoff, who was an administrator of the New Haven program, said the city needed three times the money it had available. That would have implied a national poverty budget of $30 billion to $40 billion a year. Mollie Orshansky of the Social Security Administration calculated that bringing everyone barely to the $3,000 per year poverty level would take $12 billion a year, and Levitan and others published estimates of between $20 billion and $30 billion. Even Chapter 2 of the Council of Economic Advisers report estimated the cost at $11 billion (2 percent of the gross national product). No estimate, regardless of its basis, went below $10 billion.

OEO's actual appropriation for its first fiscal year was $0.8 billion. For fiscal 1966, OEO requested $3.4 billion, the administration cut the request to $1.75 billion, and Congress trimmed that even further.[30] Less than $6 billion was allocated to OEO for the fiscal years 1965–68. With the advent of the first Nixon Administration, the situation was to become even worse.[31]

Yet the lack of large appropriations was not OEO's only money problem. Congress treated OEO, as Levitan said, "in the manner to which the poor, whom they represented, have always been accustomed. The annual handout was given grudgingly, with many strings attached, after delaying as long as possible." OEO never knew from one year to the next how much money it would have, when it would be available, or how it could be spent. One-half of fiscal 1968 had passed before Congress approved its appropriation. Only once (in 1967) did Congress pass an appropriation for more than one fiscal year. Initially OEO tried to minimize the effects of budgetary uncertainties by temporarily shifting funds from one program to another, but Congress soon forbade the practice.

Beside these essential facts, the blunders OEO made in spending (for example, giving "start-up" grants to more community-action agencies than it could support on a continuing basis) seem minor. Charging OEO with fiscal mismanagement was a bit like charging the child of a wealthy father with mismanaging a ten-cent weekly allowance, or with not using it "effectively" to end a plague.

Administrative splitting and fragmentation. Despite its defects as a metaphor for economic and social reconstruction, the phrase "war on poverty" at least implied coordinated application of substantial resources toward the achievement of specified goals. But coordination was perhaps the least characteristic feature of the poverty war in Appalachia.

The first problem was that after mid-1965 there were two Appalachian programs instead of one (indeed, the two were planned simultaneously). John Kennedy had apparently intended a single comprehensive program for the region, as evidenced by his appointment of the President's Appalachian Regional Commission in April 1963. By some point late in 1963, however, the Johnson Administration decided to separate the "human resources" aspects from the Appalachian program and merge them with a nationwide poverty bill. When or by whom the decision was made is not clear, but it had been made by the time the Task Force began its deliberations.

During the first day of the House hearings, Representative Goodell (R.–N.Y.) asked Sargent Shriver why there had been "no mention in the bill of the Appalachia program." Shriver replied that there had been a tradeoff with "the people running the Appalachian program" and that they had "allotted to us that money [$35 million] which would have been in their proposal . . . for human resource development. They felt . . . that this program was far more likely to get results in human resource development, which they had been planning to attempt, than if they attempted it themselves."[32] "Mr. Shriver," Goodell responded, "you are not in any way hinting that this would delay the programs of the Appalachian effort, are you?" Shriver's answer was categorical: "None whatsoever, no." Queried again as to whether the $35 million promised to the poverty program from the "other" Appalachian program was to be spread all over the country, Shriver promised, "We will not take anything away from Appalachia."

In all of his later testimony, Shriver continued to assure everyone that the two Appalachian programs could work together in harmony. Questioning by Representative Perkins revealed, however, that there were areas of overlapping responsibility and possible conflict. Shriver told Perkins, for example, that in his opinion Title II could be interpreted to allow OEO to construct sewer systems and electric lines, even though the original intent was to delegate such functions to the other Appalachian program.[33]

Thus by mid-1965 two separate agencies (OEO and the Appalachian Regional Commission) were conducting antipoverty programs in the region. The two bureaucracies were uncoordinated, and even their basic approaches were antagonistic in both theory and practice. ARC's "growth center" strategy concentrated on getting people out of small communities in the hollows into "urban service centers," but OEO stressed community action to make such small communities more viable. ARC's "trickle-down" approach to development was in direct opposition to the OEO's policy of helping the "worst first." And OEO's multicounty community-action agencies sometimes became involved in jurisdictional disputes with ARC's area development districts.

Even further fragmentation was written into OEO's own legislation. Title I work training (Neighborhood Youth Corps) programs were delegated to the Manpower Administration of the Labor Department. Title II adult basic education programs went later to the Office of Education in HEW, and Title IV (Employment and Business Incentives) programs to the Small Business Administration. Much of the Job Corps program was farmed out under contract to universities and private industry. In Appalachia, administration of even the programs OEO retained was soon divided between the mid-Atlantic (II) and Southeastern (III) OEO regional offices.[34] With such fragmentation and lack of coordination, the War on Poverty in Appalachia resembled an old-fashioned street brawl more than the systematized rationality of Robert McNamara's contemporary Defense Department.

OEO and regional politics. In addition to the conceptual weaknesses of the act, the hindrances of parsimonious funding, and administrative fragmentation, part of the failure of the War on Poverty must be charged to the politics of Appalachia itself. Politics in much of the region has come to resemble that "network of rackets" which C. Wright Mills has said characterizes the economies of underdeveloped countries, in which "men get ahead and stay ahead on the expectation that things cannot be done legitimately."[35]

Corruption plagued the Appalachian effort for many reasons, including nepotism, but two outweigh all others: the domination of the political and economic system by large corporations and the skewing of political power by the welfare system.[36] To compound the problem, the two factors turn out to be strongly interdependent.

Preeminent among those factors that had reduced Appalachia to widespread poverty by the 1930s was the domination of the political, economic, and social system by corporations (railroads and coal companies in some areas; land companies in others; textile manufacturers in still others). Then under the New Deal and later welfare programs, large sums of federal money flowed into the region. Much of it was disbursed by relatively unaccountable local officials in such a way as to reinforce and extend their own political power, built originally upon their willingness to do the bidding of the corporations. Year after year, corporate support at election time was traded for favorable treatment of corporations by, for example, county judges, tax assessors, and planning boards, and votes were bought with the threat of cutting disloyal voters off the welfare rolls.

Thus long before the Economic Opportunity Act became law, many Appalachian counties had developed powerful political machines in whose interest it was to avoid the structural reforms that could have helped eliminate poverty. Their opposition to the War on Poverty appeared first in the form of the gubernatorial veto power over Titles I and II (youth programs and community action). The veto seems to have been written into the act not so much because the governors themselves were wary of the program (certainly Sanford and Breathitt testified that they were not) as because the word had come up from the county machines that were the makers and breakers of Appalachian governors.

Much of the limited potential for effectiveness that OEO had in the region was therefore frustrated by county machines, some of which siphoned off funds for unauthorized purposes; rejected programs considered contrary to their interests; hired friends, relatives, and those who voted as they were told; and used their influence in the statehouses to frustrate the efforts of reform-oriented individuals and groups.

Two titles out of six. In the spring of 1965 the Council of the Southern Mountains's Larry Greathouse enumerated some of the early problems of OEO programs in Appalachia: Headstart programs "overloaded with children from high-income families," Job Corps centers that catered to low-risk enrollees, and the use of work-training programs to buy votes. As the months passed, it became apparent that

Appalachia would have fared about as well under the original "one-title" bill considered by the Task Force as it actually did under the six-title bill that emerged from Congress. Of the six titles, only Title II (community action) and Section 603 (VISTA) had a significant impact upon the region. Several programs (for example, Neighborhood Youth Corps) put small amounts of money directly into the hands of poor people, but others were marginally useful at best.

Adam Yarmolinsky reported that the Task Force "set about to look for one program that could express the central idea of preparing poor people to do the kind of work for which society would pay them a decent wage. They found it, or thought they had, . . . in the Job Corps."[37] Sargent Shriver was reportedly so proud of the idea that he insisted that the Job Corps be administered directly from his office.

But the program was hamstrung from the start. A last-minute amendment [Section 104(c)] offered by a Mississippi congressman required Job Corps participants to take a loyalty oath, and there were persistent arguments over policy (conservation camps versus urban training centers; finding jobs versus training for jobs; male-female quotas; profit versus nonprofit management of the centers). The men's centers in Appalachia tended to concentrate on conservation, an area in which very few jobs were available. The few industries in which a limited number of jobs were to be had (such as mining) either did most of their own training or offered jobs for which little or no training was needed (as in the apparel industry).

A special drive in 1967 to recruit white youths from Appalachia (to balance the large proportion of blacks from the cities) was not successful. Total enrollment in all Jobs Corps centers peaked that year at 42,000—well below the total number of unemployed in almost any random dozen Appalachian counties. Indeed, as early as 1965 there were more than 39,000 Job Corps applicants from six Appalachian states, including more than 15,000 from Kentucky and West Virginia. Jobs Corps centers in those two states had a total capacity of 616.[38]

During floor debate on the Job Corps in 1967, Representative Carl Perkins admitted that the Corps's first few months had been "less than impressive" but said it would be "unthinkable" not to continue the program. About the same time, however, Sar Levitan was arguing that "no conclusive case has yet been established to justify the Job Corps on the basis of past performance."[39]

Adult basic education, a Title II-B program, enrolled about 15,000 persons in Kentucky in 1965, only about 5 percent of the more than 300,000 adults in the state who lacked a sixth grade education. The college-based work-study program by definition was out of reach to the majority of Appalachian young people, and work-training was of little value in a glutted labor market. Title V training for unemployed fathers afforded a few thousand men temporary work at the minimum wage trimming weeds by the roadside, cleaning out creeks, fighting forest fires, repairing roads, or (not infrequently) working on the personal property of county judges and party leaders. Although by 1967 16 percent of all Title V funds had been spent in Kentucky, only 33 percent of those "trained" found jobs, compared to 50–70 percent in cities such as Cleveland and Saint Paul. Levitan discovered that one-half of the trainees remained on public assistance after completing the program. He concluded that "there is little reason to believe that [the training] has improved the employability of a significant proportion of the first 150,000 persons enrolled in the program."[40]

The rural loan program (Title III), despite the fact that North Carolina and Kentucky were among the six largest recipients, had little lasting impact in Appalachia. The program served only a small percentage of those eligible (48,000 out of 900,000 in its first four years), and loans to individuals were limited to $2,500 (and actually averaged $1,850). The primary limitation on usefulness, however, was that the region's economy depends upon agriculture to a relatively small degree.[41]

Headstart, which was added in 1965 and took 40 percent of the CAPs' funds nationwide during the first four years, reached a greater percentage of those eligible than any other OEO program. There was some opposition from local school boards, which resented the fact that Headstart money, unlike funds for the same purpose allocated under the Elementary and Secondary Education Act of 1965, went directly to the programs rather than being funneled through their hands. But except for some problems in administration, the program was hard to fault. Its effects upon the economy of the region, however, would at best be long delayed.[42]

Thus although individual and local success stories could be cited for non–Title II programs (as they were year after year in OEO annual reports), the statistics told of minimal impact. A few programs offered immediate and temporary relief; one or two others (Headstart and the Employment and Investment Incentives program of Title IV) offered deferred benefits. But none spoke to the basic structural problems. The administration, Sidney Lens wrote during the congressional battle over OEO amendments in 1966, "has no intention of changing the *relationship* between the poor and rich. [Its] sights are set on . . . improving the lot of the poor without disturbing the prerogatives of the rich." Lens pointed out that many direct means of eliminating poverty were available: raising the minimum wage, extending the National Labor Relations Act to cover collective bargaining by agricultural workers, raising Social Security benefits, or providing a guaranteed annual income. Similar suggestions were made in the A. Philip Randolph Institute's "Freedom Budget" of October 1966.[43]

Increasing congressional constraints. Whatever the original limitations in design and overall funding, poverty warriors enjoyed considerable flexibility in spending available funds during the first year of OEO activity. As the program became more visible in local communities, however, Congress began to insist upon more specific guidelines on spending and program operation. In 1966, it specified how some CAP funds were to be expended (for example, 36 percent to Headstart) and tacked on an amendment to deny salaries to subversives or participants in riots. In 1967 the so-called Green amendment (Section 210[a], sponsored by Oregon's Democratic representative Edith Green) required that community-action agencies be states or political subdivisions of states except where specific agreements were reached to the contrary.[44]

The Green amendment was widely interpreted to signify that CAPs were to be made subject to local political control. Levitan has argued that the amendment had little direct effect, pointing out that of the nearly eight hundred units of government which subsequently took action on designating CAPs, 96.7 percent voted to continue existing agencies. The operative factor in Appalachia, however, was the widespread *belief* that CAPs that "got out of line" would be taken over by the local power structure under sanction of the Green amendment. The combined effect of the original gubernatorial veto provision of Title II and the Green amendment was that the strategic and tactical options of the CAPs grew steadily narrower.

Community Action in Appalachia

> I propose a program which relies on the traditional time-tested American methods of organized local community action to help individuals, families, and communities to help themselves.
> Lyndon B. Johnson
> 1964 Budget Message

Although it has been suggested that the concept of community action derives ultimately from such antecedents as the settlement house movement of the late nineteenth century, its immediate models were drawn from a number of early and middle 1960s pilot projects (funded mostly by the Ford Foundation's community development program) in New Haven, Boston, Oakland, New York City, Cleveland, Philadelphia, and (to a lesser extent) North Carolina.[45]

Most commentators agree that the idea was injected into the early planning discussions by David Hackett of Robert F. Kennedy's juvenile delinquency and youth crime staff in the Justice Department. Walter Heller of the Council of Economic Advisers liked the idea, but Budget Director Kermit Gordon was skeptical. His reservations were overcome during a breakfast meeting with Ford Foundation executives and some of Ford's local community development leaders, however, and subsequently he and Heller persuaded President Johnson to back the approach. "In the course of a single week in mid-December [1963]," Sundquist reported, "aid to community organizations was transformed from an incidental idea in the War on Poverty into the entire war."

Although the Task Force embellished the one-title draft bill with a number of other programs, community action remained what it was intended to be from the beginning—the backbone of the Economic Opportunity Act and the central program of OEO. Community-action allocations accounted for 30 percent of the OEO budget for 1965 and 50 percent three years later.

For all its centrality as a strategy, however, community action was never very coherent as a concept. It was in fact a cluster of concepts, gathered from the Ford Foundation experience, federal departments, existing and pending legislation (for example, the Manpower Development and Training Act of 1962), and to a small extent the theory and practice of such organizers as Saul Alinsky.

In an excellent study of two North Carolina CAP agencies, Richard L. Hoffman defined five modes of action that actually characterized various CAPs (or the same CAP at different times): (1) an Alinsky conflict-oriented mode in which change is sought by using the CAP solely to generate power for poor people; (2) a "community organizing" mode, in which poor people hold the balance of power in the CAP and use it to challenge the power structure; (3) a "third force" mode in which a fairly neutral "broker" CAP mediates between poor people and the establishment; (4) a consensus mode in which a conservative CAP sides with the establishment but countenances moderate change through a bargaining process; and (5) a services-oriented CAP that is controlled solely by the power structure.[46]

Community action agencies in Appalachia employed almost the full range of modes suggested by Hoffman, with the possible exception of the conflict-oriented Alinsky mode. No Appalachian CAP managed to employ a "pure" Alinsky mode for a significant period of time. Aspects of the Alinsky strategy could be observed from time to time in various CAPs, however. One of the first to come even close to employing it broadly was the Mingo County, West Virginia, Economic Opportunity Commission (EOC) run by a native, Huey Perry.[47]

Mingo County was literally born in conflict, carved out of Logan

County at the end of the nineteenth century as part of a plan to settle the notorious Hatfield-McCoy feud. The most important conflict in the county, however, was the even more protracted struggle of coal companies to gain control of seams so rich that the county seat of Williamson justly advertised itself as "the heart of the billion dollar coal field." In 1920 Frank Keeney's 42,000-worker West Virginia United Mine Workers district (one of the few heavily unionized districts outside the northern coal fields) became the center of the UMW's drive to organize the southern fields on a platform that included a six-hour day, a five-day week, and nationalization of the mines. Subsequent eviction of miners by operators, their harassment by Baldwin-Felts agency guards, and an escalating pattern of violence led to the so-called Matewan Massacre, which left eleven men dead in a shootout at the Matewan railway station. The miners' strike was finally broken by gangs of "gun thugs," who raided the tent colony to which the miners had moved their families after eviction, and by federal troops, which prevented food and supplies from reaching them. The war escalated as it dragged on, bringing martial law, federal troops, and the bombers of General Billy Mitchell's fledgling U.S. Army Air Service in the fall of 1921.[48]

By the 1960s political and economic control of Mingo County had passed largely to U.S. Steel, which owned one-third of the land; to other coal companies, which operated about one hundred mines in the county, producing more than $25 million worth of coal a year; and to State Senator Noah Floyd, who controlled political patronage. Floyd was a nephew of "Blind Billie" Adair, who had once controlled the county through the Board of Education. Floyd's brother Troy had been Superintendent of Schools; another brother was a welfare-program supervisor until 1967; and a brother-in-law worked for the state. Floyd's machine was financed partly through an obligatory "flower fund."

Mingo County was therefore a classic testing ground for community action: out-migration was heavy, nearly 50 percent of the inhabitants were below the poverty line, 20 percent were on welfare, and 14 percent were unemployed. Huey Perry's community action program brought him to the attention of both the national news media (which portrayed the Mingo EOC as a model agency) and the Floyd machine (to which it was anathema).

Initially Perry concentrated on improving the operation of existing welfare programs—for example, by using as community organizers poverty program workers who had previously been kept busy at such tasks as building a barbecue pit in Noah Floyd's backyard. Local community groups, supported by the EOC, agitated for better roads, schools, and hot lunches for children. Later efforts became bolder, however, as the agency moved toward a conflict strategy.

When the Gilbert Creek Community Action Group opened a co-operative grocery store, local merchants protested, and Senator Robert Byrd declared himself "absolutely against this program being used to drive our business people out of business." Byrd requested an OEO investigation of the "communist" grocery store. Reportedly at the urging of Byrd, the co-op was denied authorization to accept food stamps on the pretext that its customers owned its stock (bought at $1.00 per share) and thus could be held to be using the food-stamp program for personal profit. The impasse was broken when one share of A&P stock was purchased in the name of the co-op, thus making the same restriction applicable to the A&P chain.[49] In a telling demonstration of how pressure could be applied to the CAP program through the patronage system, R. F. Copley, manager of the co-op, was fired from his position as a school bus driver by the Board of Education because he had helped organize a union of the drivers.

The stakes in Mingo County were ultimately higher than the economic threat posed by a small co-op grocery, however. The most serious conflict grew out of the EOC-backed organization of the Mingo County Fair Elections Committee (FEC) and the Political Action League (PAL). Designed to correct flagrant and long-standing election abuses (the 1960 county census showed 19,879 voting-age adults, but there were 30,331 registered voters; some names on the rolls belonged to dead people and mine ponies), the FEC's activities eventually led to a purging of the voting rolls and federal indictment of Noah Floyd and several associates.[50]

Their power base threatened by the EOC and slates of local and state candidates backed by FEC and PAL, Floyd and his machine (apparently supported by Senator Byrd and encouraged by the Green amendment) arranged to have Perry fired and attempted to have the County Court take over the EOC. Ultimately, both OEO and incoming Governor Arch Moore backed the EOC.

John Barnes's investigation of the Mingo CAP during the summer of 1967 found a vital program, broadly representative of poor people who liked and trusted its staff and had confidence that it would improve things significantly in the county. Barnes himself concluded, however, that the CAP did not in any way affect the root causes of poverty in Mingo County. What poor people needed, he said, was a base from which to "challenge the dominant political power." The CAP could offer no such base.[51]

More typical in their approaches to community action were the CAPs in Knox County and the four-county LKLP (Letcher, Knott, Leslie, Perry) area of eastern Kentucky. Although Knox was the bolder of the two CAPs, both adopted essentially what Hoffman called the "community organizing" mode. Like Mingo, Knox County was a fertile field for change: Mechanization of the coal mines had produced high unemployment, heavy out-migration had left mostly the young and the old, and 58 percent of the families were below the poverty line. The Knox County Economic Opportunity Council (EOC) received one of the earliest CAP program development grants in mid-December 1964. Within a year OEO grants to the CAP totaled more than $1.1 million, and $365,000 more went to the Board of Education for Neighborhood Youth Corps programs. By the winter of 1965 CAP director James Kendrick declared, "A revolution has been developing silently on the banks of the Cumberland River."[52] The CAP had rather quickly created about seven hundred jobs for Knox Countians, and eight out of fourteen planned community centers were operating. With the help of an OEO manpower consultant, the Cannon community center organized a corporation, sold $1.00 shares to community residents, leased the Barbourville National Guard Armory, and started a toy factory.[53]

But the revolution Kendrick was talking about was not merely economic, and it required more than woodworking factories. The problem was to gain political and economic control of the county, and Kendrick tried to use "maximum feasible participation" in the poverty program as a first step. Each of the community centers elected a fifteen-member Neighborhood Action Council, which sent three members to the county Association of Neighborhood Councils, which in turn elected one-third of the EOC board. Several other board members were elected directly from the neighborhoods. Conceptually, it was a model of both community organization and maximum feasible participation, which Kendrick said provided "considerable power, representation, and self-determination" for Knox Countians.

So pleased was OEO with the Knox County CAP's plans and progress that it awarded a large grant to an interdisciplinary team from the University of Kentucky to study the program.[54] But the conclusions from the three-year study were not encouraging. Investigator Willis Sutton, who interviewed about 170 people, found that most thought the CAP program was helping to provide needed services, but was making little difference in the county's institutional structure or customary decision-making process. Natural leaders in the local communities tended to see the CAP as not strongly oriented toward the interests of poor people. Sutton's colleague Paul Street concluded in late 1968 that "the pattern of [political] alignments existing in the county when the community action program began was not basically affected."[55]

In a later analysis, Street concluded even more somberly that "the program [has] not basically changed the leadership of the county except perhaps to clarify who were the leaders and to narrow the leadership base. . . . The real leaders [have] consolidated their positions and [are] more firmly established than before." Street found that two years after the EOC was organized, one-third of the "target group" had never heard of it. "Instead of the community action program introducing a new alignment of ideas," he said, "it was swallowed by the old ones."[56]

The trends that Street noted had in fact come to the attention of OEO quite early. Within a little more than a year after the Knox County EOC began operation, OEO forced it to combine with seven others in the Cumberland Valley in order to break the hold of county political machines.[57]

Somewhat more conservative in applying the community organizing strategy than the Knox EOC was the four-county LKLP (Leslie, Knott, Letcher, and Perry) CAP. Lacking Kendrick's confidence that the War on Poverty could make much difference in eastern Kentucky, LKLP's director, Ed Safford, was openly skeptical of the usefulness of his own relatively well-run program when it was investigated in 1967 for the poverty subcommittee of the Senate Committee on Labor and Public Welfare. One of the four counties (Leslie) was one of the poorest in the entire nation. In another, as Harry Caudill noted in late 1966, a single firm held $160 million in TVA coal contracts, but the tax structure was so regressive that taxation produced only 8 percent of the funds required to operate the county school system. Such conditions more than justified Safford's skepticism.[58]

The Kanawha County, West Virginia, CAP was more conservative still. As successor to the Juvenile Delinquency and Youth Crime Commission's Action for Appalachian Youth project in the county, it was already organized to receive funds when the Economic Opportunity Act was signed. By the end of 1965, $1.1 million had been allocated to the CAP and other county agencies for OEO programs. Run primarily by middle-class professionals drawn from the chemical industries of Charleston, the CAP focused on the delivery of welfare services. The subcommittee investigators found social action to be "of the consensus type and . . . rarely militant" even in the Cabin Creek area, where early in the century armed miners had massed by the thousands to march upon the state capital. The CAP's "worm farm" project in the Washington area of the county, the subcommittee investigator noted drily, was "rather unusual."[59]

Perhaps the most conservative CAP for which a substantial description is available was the almost completely services-oriented Asheville-Buncombe County program in North Carolina.[60] Founded at the end of the eighteenth century, Asheville became a trading and tourist center after the opening of the Buncombe Turnpike in 1824. The coming of the railroad in 1880, the arrival of entrepreneurs E. W. Grove and George Vanderbilt at the turn of the century, and the backwash effects of the Florida land rush of the 1920s produced a sustained boom that was ultimately terminated both by the national crash of 1929 and a local scandal over fraud in the sales of waterworks bonds. The scandal left city and county bonds on the ineligible list of the New York Stock Exchange for thirty years and led to a state-imposed limit on indebtedness that hampered further development.

The long-standing crisis of public confidence and political apathy produced by the scandal allowed a tight political machine to be built under the control of City Manager Weldon Weir and Buncombe County's Democratic Sheriff Lawrence Brown. The Asheville Opportunity Corporation (the city-county CAP) was a creature of the machine, which had demonstrated its power and durability by returning the mayor, city manager, and most of the city council to office in every election for more than twenty years.

The CAP board, led by the conservative Asheville-Biltmore College president William E. Highsmith and dominated by machine politicians, hired Louisville newspaperman Ora Spaid as director. Spaid, congratulating Highsmith and the city that they had "avoided militancy on the part of [your] disadvantaged," spoke disparagingly of what he called "hurry up radicals." The CAP, he said, would offer "an incremental program" concentrating on social service delivery. In an early directive to his staff, he declared that he was "basically not a conflict-oriented person." One way Spaid chose to avoid conflict was to submit a whites-only Headstart proposal, which was abandoned later only after desperate maneuvering in the face of OEO's refusal to fund a segregated program. Inevitably, Spaid became both the captive of the machine whose antagonism he feared and isolated from the poor people the program was supposed to serve. It was in fact nearly twenty months after Spaid's arrival before the CAP added specific community action programs to its agenda.

Spaid's timid approach to community action eventually spread into neighboring Madison County, the tightly controlled preserve of the formidable Ponder brothers' political machine. An independent and moderately aggressive Madison community-action organization had been formed in 1965, but at OEO insistence it was merged with the Asheville-Buncombe CAP a year later.[61] Spaid thus found himself not only placating an additional machine but also trying to keep the separate—and still somewhat aggressive—Madison board from disturbing his delicate alliance with the Asheville machine. To gain the support of the Ponder brothers, he gave control of the Madison County's Headstart program to the school board (headed by one of the Ponders) despite explicit OEO warnings not to do so.

In 1967, after an unfavorable evaluation of the CAP by the North Carolina Fund, Spaid agreed to take a more aggressive approach to community action. The CAP board was reorganized (with 50 percent low-income representatives) and the neighborhood centers began to emphasize community organizing. Within a few months CAP-related organizing efforts led to a public housing rent strike against the Housing Authority by the all-black Hillside Tenants Association. Spaid told strike leader Carl Johnson that CAP would not lead the strike but would support it. The decision naturally evoked the wrath of the local machine, which saw CAP as departing from its legitimate calling, and inspired the distrust of the strikers, who judged Spaid to be equivocal and irresolute. Thus deprived of support from any quarter, and having failed to build an independent CAP, Spaid resigned when his contract expired in 1968.

Having studied thirty-five CAPs throughout the nation (including three in Appalachia), a Senate subcommittee team concluded in 1967 that except for a small number of communities, "the community action program does not involve a predominant commitment to the strategy of giving power to the poor, of deliberate confrontation with established powers, of purposefully created conflict. [Contrary] to the hopes of a few and the fears of many, CAP is not a social revolution."[62]

But Congressional opponents of community action were not persuaded. Both Congress and local politicians had been demanding tighter controls over CAP programs almost from the beginning. By June 1965 the U.S. Conference of Mayors was insisting that big-city mayors be allowed to approve all CAP funding within their boundaries.[63] President Johnson's March 1967 message to Congress advocated tighter controls over CAP money (which had already been cut back by OEO) and greater involvement of local power structures.

Congressional proponents of community action argued that it was endorsed by most local officials, was tailored by local needs, and was in fact helping poor people to become more self-sufficient. Critics countered that community action amounted to "social reform by force," created needless conflict between CAPs and local officials, did not substantially improve the lives of poor people, and wasted public funds. West Virginia's Senator Robert Byrd charged that the objective of community action was "to build up class consciousness and to foment unrest . . . social protest, civil rights disturbances, and anti–Vietnam war demonstrations."[64]

Much of the congressional action on OEO after early 1966, as it turned out, involved placing restrictions on Title II: the Green amendment, the Byrd amendment, specific allocation of CAP funds among programs, a prohibition against shifting funds from one program to another, and restrictions on political and other "disruptive" activity by CAP employees. OEO itself, troubled by discord and resignations among its staff and perennially fearful of congressional

budget cutting, imposed additional constraints upon local CAP spending and hiring.[65]

That community action and the War on Poverty itself had turned
out to be a conservative, and in some cases even reactionary, approach
to change was not lost on the "target population." Beginning in early
1966, dozens of CAPs in Appalachia were directly challenged by local
people: the Big Sandy, Cumberland Valley, and Harlan County CAPs
in eastern Kentucky; Raleigh, Boone, Wyoming, Nicholas, Mercer,
and Webster counties in West Virginia; Dickenson and Buchanan in
southwest Virginia; and others in scattered parts of the region. Angry
citizens began routinely to confront CAP boards, governors, and state
and federal OEO officials. Several hundred Appalachian people gathered for an "Appalachian community meeting" in Washington in
August 1966, and many of their complaints centered on the War on
Poverty. Many hundreds of those who later camped on the muddy
flats of SCLC's Resurrection City were welfare mothers and unemployed fathers who had concluded that the War on Poverty had been
lost in Appalachia.

Winding Down the War

Signs of the lost war grew year by year: Scrooge-like appropriations, budgetary and administrative constraints, political interference
at the state and federal levels, cutbacks in programs, internal dissension within OEO itself, and dwindling evidence of success. OEO's
first annual report was entitled *A Nation Aroused,* its second *The Quiet
Revolution,* and its third *The Tide of Progress.* But the fourth (1969) was
more modestly entitled *As the Seed Is Sown,* and its statistics were clearly
those of a dying agency.

The coup de grâce was dealt by the Nixon Administration, which
had steadily cut back on OEO and other social programs since early
1969. In January 1973 the President appointed ultra-conservative
Howard Phillips as OEO director and instructed him to phase out the
agency. Phillips, who was widely quoted as saying that treating the
poor as a class was "a Marxist idea," froze all pending grants and
contracts. Amid stormy congressional hearings that brought threats
of violence if programs were ended, Phillips continued a dramatic
series of moves to close down OEO—replacing all names in the OEO
building directory with one (his own) for example, and calling in
newsmen to photograph office furniture being piled in hallways.

By June 1973 U.S. District Court Judge William B. Jones had

declared Phillips to be holding his job illegally (the President had declined to submit his name for Senate confirmation), and former Appalachian Regional Commission director Alvin Arnett took his place. Phillips said that Arnett would complete "the actions we set in motion to dismember the agency as directed by the President." Arnett himself, when he came from ARC to OEO a few months earlier as Phillips's deputy, had called the assignment "the greatest opportunity I could ever have dreamed of." But in July 1973 Arnett himself told a Senate committee that he would spend all the OEO money legally appropriated, even though twenty-four hours earlier he had asked a Senate appropriations committee for zero funding for all OEO programs. In mid-1974 Arnett himself was forced to resign by the White House.[66]

Assurances from the Nixon Administration that essential OEO programs would be taken over and improved by other federal agencies were hardly convincing. The War on Poverty was clearly over, and the paradox for Appalachia was that even though the program had not been designed for the region and had never operated very effectively there, its demise imposed a significant hardship upon its people. The *Mountain Eagle* reported in February 1973 that the phase-out would withdraw $6.5 million per year in income from Kentucky and cause 3,085 jobs in antipoverty programs to disappear. Nearly a thousand of them were in four of the poorest counties (Breathitt, Lee, Owsley, and Wolfe), and 1,500 more were in the LKLP counties.

Illustrative of the immediate local impact of the OEO shutdown was the closing of the LKLP area's Millstone Sewing Center, which had opened in December 1965, after the CBS television special "Christmas in Appalachia" brought truckloads of used clothing to Letcher County. Given a small OEO grant the following spring, the Center hired thirteen women to clean, repair, and distribute the clothing from quarters on the second floor of the old community school building, leased for a dollar a year. At its peak the Center employed sixteen, had its own truck for distributing clothing, and used its proceeds to operate a community kitchen to serve meals to those who needed them. In June 1966 Governor Breathitt singled out the Center for special praise, and the 1967 Senate investigation of CAP programs cited it as an example of a good and imaginative program. But funds were steadily cut back. The staff dwindled to three, gas for the truck was later denied by the LKLP, and Center director Mabel Kiser, in her weekly column in the *Mountain Eagle* for July 19, 1973, reported that "the Millstone Sewing Center is no more."[67] Although the actual economic impact of the Center had been small, its closing dramatized the frustration and disillusionment experienced by tens of thousands in whose lives the War on Poverty intervened.

"One Day It All Hangs Together": A Retrospective Note

Writing in the early days of the War on Poverty, Daniel P. Moynihan contended that social problems such as poverty must and could be solved only by professionals "whose responsibilities [are] to think about . . . such matters." Moynihan added later that the War on Poverty was declared "not at the behest of the poor; it was declared in their interest by persons confident of their own judgment in such matters."[68]

Because they were trained to interpret the "essentially esoteric information" upon which solutions must be based, Moynihan wrote, such professionals would "rather quickly" solve the "primitive" problem of poverty and "turn to issues more demanding of human ingenuity." "Men are learning to make an industrial economy work," he said. Theories are refined by analyzing hard data, and "then one day it all more or less hangs together."

Moynihan admitted the risk of establishing a "monocracy of power" through such a process (assuming the process itself worked), but did not shrink from it. Indeed, discussing the polls and mass demonstrations through which poor people were seeking to make known their judgment that the War on Poverty was hanging together rather less than more, Moynihan observed: "The day when mile-long petitions and mass rallies were required to persuade the government that a popular demand exists that things be done differently is clearly drawing to a close. Indeed the very existence of such petitions may in time become a sign that what is being demanded is *not yet* a popular demand."[69]

Moynihan's corollary argument about the implicitly value-free and nonpolitical "professionalization" of reform was also unconvincing. The record suggests repeatedly, in fact, that the choices professionals made in designing and conducting the War on Poverty were often primarily personal and value choices, made because they finally in some inchoate way either were or were not *bothered* by poverty; did or did not *feel* that it was the fault of poor people themselves; did or did not *prefer* morally, politically, or esthetically that it should be eliminated; were or were not *willing* to relinquish some of their own prerogatives to establish an equitable social order. In the final analysis, those who designed the act—from the Task Force through the final congressional debate, and thence to the writing of OEO guidelines and subsequent amendments—opted for a normalization and extension of their own middle-class values, life-styles and assumptions about the social order. Having done so, they foreclosed the possibility of dealing constructively with the structural and systemic basis of poverty in Appalachia.

Notes

1. Readers interested in the history of the War on Poverty and critiques of its many programs will encounter no dearth of research materials. Dorothy Louise Tompkins, *Poverty in the United States During the 1960s: A Bibliography* (Berkeley, Calif.: Institute of Governmental Studies, 1970), runs to 542 pages. The printed record of the main congressional hearings on the Economic Opportunity Act alone fills about twenty thousand pages. A few hundred of the available articles and books have been abstracted in *Poverty and Human Resources Abstracts* (Ann Arbor: University of Michigan Institute of Labor and Industrial Relations, 1965–). An initial approach to the subject may be made through Sar Levitan, *The Great Society's Poor Law* (Baltimore: Johns Hopkins Press, 1969); John C. Donovan, *The Politics of Poverty* (New York: Pegasus, 1967); and James L. Sundquist (ed.), *On Fighting Poverty: Perspectives from Experience* (New York: Basic Books, 1969). Alternative views may be found in Ben B. Seligman (ed.), *Poverty as a Public Issue* (New York: Free Press, 1965); Chaim I. Waxman (ed.), *Poverty: Power and Politics* (New York: Grosset & Dunlap, 1968); and Jeremy Larner and Irving Howe (eds.), *Poverty: Views from the Left* (New York: William Morrow, 1968).

2. Donovan, *Politics of Poverty*, p. 19.

3. Heller quotation from Daniel P. Moynihan, "What Is Community Action?" *Public Interest*, no. 5 (Fall 1966), p. 4. See Homer Bigart, "Kentucky Miners: A Grim Winter," *New York Times*, October 20, 1963, pp. 1 and 79. Cf. Sundquist, *On Fighting Poverty*, p. 20.

4. Sundquist, *On Fighting Poverty*, pp. 19–23.

5. Adam Yarmolinsky, "The Beginnings of OEO," in *ibid.*, pp. 34–51.

6. For a discussion of both, see Peter Marris and Martin Rein, *Dilemmas of Social Reform: Poverty and Community Action in the United States* (Chicago: Aldine, 1973).

7. I have confined myself to the barest essentials of the complicated history of the Shriver Task Force. The legislative background of some of the bills that supplied titles for the Economic Opportunity Act may be found in U.S., Senate Committee on Labor and Public Welfare, *Economic Opportunity Act of 1964: Report No. 1218*, 88th Congress, 2d Session, 1964, pp. 4 ff.

8. Key consultants were Robert Lampman, an economist, University of Wisconsin; Paul Ylvisaker of the Ford Foundation; Mitchell Sviridoff, a New Haven community leader; David Hackett, special assistant to the Attorney General in the juvenile delinquency program; and two professors from Columbia University's School of Social Work, Richard Cloward and Lloyd Ohlin. The staff also included members from the Departments of Defense (Adam

Yarmolinsky), Labor (Daniel P. Moynihan), and Agriculture (James Sund-quist).

9. Sundquist, *On Fighting Poverty*, pp. 35–45 and 21, respectively.

10. An additional factor in Task Force deliberations, the splitting of Ap-palachian aid into two separate programs, will be discussed later. For a sum-mary of economic and social conditions in Appalachia related to the poverty legislation (unemployment, personal income, health, housing, etc.), see W. J. Page, Jr., and Earl E. Huyck, "Appalachia: Realities of Deprivation," in Seligman (ed.), *Poverty as Public Issue*, pp. 152–76.

11. U.S. House of Representatives, *Hearings Before the Subcommittee on the War on Poverty of the Committee on Education and Labor . . . on H.R. 10440: A Bill to Mobilize the Human and Financial Resources of the Nation to Combat Poverty in the United States*, 88th Congress, 2d Session, 1964. A brief legislative history of the bill may be found in Donovan, *Politics of Poverty*, pp. 33–53.

12. Sanford inaugurated the North Carolina Fund (financed by the Ford and other foundations), which set up early community-action programs in western North Carolina counties. During the House hearings, Representative Carl Perkins (D.–Ky.) said that the North Carolina experience influenced the subcommittee greatly, but it is not clear from the record that that was true.

13. House *Hearings on H.R. 10440*, Pt. 1, p. 196.

14. *Ibid.*, Pt. 2, pp. 923 ff. and 978 ff., respectively.

15. Perkins held brief hearings at Kentucky's Morehead State College, but I have discovered no written record of them.

16. House *Hearings on H.R. 10440*, Pt. 1, pp. 330–31. Testifying later before the Senate committee, Kennedy referred to the juvenile delinquency commission's experience with young people in Charleston, West Virginia, but there is no evidence that that experience had much impact upon either Task Force planning or congressional action. See Phil Hirsch, "Kanawha County Experiment Aims at Youth," *County Officer*, XXIX (June 1964), 288–89.

17. U.S. Senate, *Hearings Before the Select Committee on Poverty of the Committee on Labor and Public Welfare . . . on S. 2642*, 88th Congress, 2d Session, June 17–25, 1964. Oral testimony took about eight hours; the transcript fills less than two hundred pages.

18. It was in fact years before hearings on OEO produced much direct testimony from the region. During the 1969 hearings, for example, a com-munity-action director from southwest Virginia's Lee County (with a 69 per-cent unemployment rate) testified. Representative Perkins entered a sheaf of letters from eastern Kentuckians into the record, but most appeared to have been written by either program administrators or welfare recipients fearful that their benefits would be cut off. A Burning Fork resident wrote, "I being on the C.I.P. [CEP] program, am required to write you a letter concerning the program."

19. Moynihan, "What Is Community Action?" p. 4.

20. Lewis's essay originally appeared in *Scientific American*, CCXV (October 1966), 19–25. Quotation from the essay as reprinted in Louis A. Ferman (ed.), *Poverty in America* (Ann Arbor: University of Michigan Press, 1968), p. 413. A critique of OEO's application of the culture of poverty model in an Appalachian community may be found in George L. Hicks, "The War on

Poverty: A Southern Appalachian Case," *Journal of the Steward Anthropological Society*, III (Spring 1972), 155–69.

21. Some alternative suggestions presumably were offered by Michael Harrington, who served as a consultant to the Task Force, but Adam Yarmolinsky says Harrington's ideas had "little operational impact" on the development of the program. Harrington's suggestions may have been similar to those in his article "The Politics of Poverty," in *Dissent*, XII (Autumn 1965), 412–30, in which he proposed a "Third New Deal" whose essence would be "planned expansion of the public sector."

22. Adam Walinsky, "Keeping the Poor in Their Place: Notes on the Importance of Being One-Up," *The New Republic*, CLI (July 4, 1964), 15–18. A more extensive statement of this position is S. M. Miller and Pamela Roby, *The Future of Inequality* (New York: Basic Books, 1970).

23. House of Representatives, Committee on Education and Labor, *Report on the Economic Opportunity Act of 1964*, p. 2.

24. House *Hearings on H. R. 10440*, Pt. 1, p. 429.

25. Elinor Graham, "Poverty and the Legislative Process," in Seligman (ed.), *Poverty as Public Issue*, p. 258.

26. House *Hearings on H.R. 10440*, Pt. 3, pp. 1324 ff. "People's capitalism" is a phrase derived, presumably, from Adolph Berle, Jr., and Gardiner C. Means, *The Modern Corporation and Private Property*, rev. ed. (1932; reprint, New York: Harcourt Brace Jovanovich, 1968).

27. Alabama, Georgia, Maryland, Ohio, South Carolina, Virginia, Kentucky, North Carolina, Pennsylvania, Tennessee, and West Virginia. Nearly half the sum ($97 million) went to two central Appalachian states (Kentucky and West Virginia). Expenditure of OEO funds was very uneven. Money to big cities ran to three times the national average per poor person, and rural areas in general received less than their due proportion. Expenditures per poor person were $54.20 in West Virginia and $63.10 in Kentucky, compared to a top of $96.80 in Oregon. Other partly Appalachian states ran between $10.19 (South Carolina) and $32.87 (Pennsylvania). See Levitan, *Great Society's Poor Law*, pp. 120–21, and Andrew J. Cowart, "Antipoverty Expenditures in the American States," *Midwest Journal of Political Science*, XIII (May 1969), 219–36.

28. Emile Benoit, "The Economics and Politics of Defense Cutbacks," in Arthur I. Blaustein (ed.), *Man Against Poverty: World War III* (New York: Random House, 1968), p. 2. Benoit notes that per capita expenditures on nondefense goods and services, expressed in 1963 prices, were $83 in 1939, $75 in 1953, and $56 in 1963.

29. Donovan, *Politics of Poverty*, p. 122.

30. Levitan, *Great Society's Poor Law*, pp. 90 ff. In 1966, OEO's $1.5 billion appropriation amounted to about 0.25 percent of the GNP.

31. Cf. Sidney Lens, "Shriver's Limited War," *Commonweal*, LXXXIV (July 1, 1966), 413.

32. House *Hearings on H.R. 10440*, Pt. 1, p. 103.

33. *Ibid.*, Pt. 1, p. 62. Later OEO regulations explicitly forbade such expenditures.

34. Region II included six Appalachian states (Kentucky, Maryland, North

Carolina, Pennsylvania, Virginia, and West Virginia); Region III encompassed five (Tennessee, Georgia, Mississippi, South Carolina and Alabama). By mid-1968 half the OEO staff was in the regional offices.

35. C. Wright Mills, "The Problem of Industrial Development," in Irving L. Horowitz (ed.), *Power, Politics and People: The Collected Essays of C. Wright Mills* (New York: Oxford University Press, 1963), p. 154.

36. On eastern Kentucky, for example, see Chapter 9 and two articles by Harry Caudill: "Corporate Fiefdom, Poverty and the Dole in Appalachia," *Commonweal*, LXXXIX (January 24, 1969), 523–25, and "The Permanent Poor: The Lesson of Eastern Kentucky," *Atlantic Monthly*, CCXIII (June 1964), 49–53.

37. Yarmolinsky, "Beginnings of OEO," p. 39. See also "Controversy over the Federal Job Corps," *Congressional Digest*, vol. XLVII (January 1968).

38. *A Nation Aroused: 1st Annual Report of the Office of Economic Opportunity*, p. 73. Because statistics in OEO annual reports were not aggregated for Appalachia, I used Kentucky and West Virginia as rough approximations of demand for, and availability of, Job Corps training and other programs.

39. *Congressional Digest*, XLVII (January 1968), and *Examining the War on Poverty: Staff and Consultant Reports Prepared for the Subcommittee on Employment . . . of the Committee on Labor and Public Welfare, United States Senate*, 90th Congress, 1st Session, August 1967, I, 22. One of the few reasonably successful centers, the women's center in Huntington, West Virginia, which had placed about six hundred of its nearly eight hundred graduates, 80 percent of whom were black, was closed in May 1969. See *Appalachian Lookout*, I (May 1969), 11–12.

40. *Examination of the War on Poverty*, I, 80. See also "Happy Pappies of Handshoe Holler," *Time*, LXXXVI (November 5, 1965), 38–39. OEO job-training programs were running concurrently in the region with those of ARA and the Manpower Development and Training Act (MDTA) until the phasing out of ARA in 1965.

41. See Levitan, *Great Society's Poor Law*, pp. 227–45. The original land reform provisions of Title III could have been useful to a significant number of people in the region, but they could not have significantly changed the overall economic situation.

42. See *ibid.*, pp. 133–63, and Donovan, *Politics of Poverty*, pp. 81 ff. One of the relatively few basic criticisms of Headstart is in Madelyn L. Kafoglis, "The Economics of the Community Action Program," *Tennessee Survey of Business*, III (December 1967), 1–11.

43. Lens, "Shriver's Limited War," p. 413.

44. See Edith Green, "Who Should Administer the War on Poverty?" *American County Government*, XXXIII (January 1968), 8–10. Section 202(a) (4) of the original act specified only that community-action programs had to be conducted by "a public or private non-profit agency (other than a political party)."

45. See Sanford Kravitz, "The Community Action Program: Past, Present, and Its Future?" in Sundquist, *On Fighting Poverty*, pp. 52–69; Daniel Fox, "The Unalienated Intellectuals: The Background of Community Action,"

Mountain Life and Work (MLW), XLII (Spring 1966), 12–15; and Marris and Rein, *Dilemmas of Social Reform*, pp. 14–24.

46. Richard L. Hoffman, "Community Action: Innovative and Coordinative Strategies in the War on Poverty," unpublished Ph.D. dissertation, University of North Carolina, 1969, pp. 15 ff. For further discussion of the origin and application of the community-action concept, see Donovan, *Politics of Poverty*, pp. 35–52; Sundquist, *On Fighting Poverty*, pp. 11–16; Levitan, *Great Society's Poor Law*, pp. 109–28; and Moynihan, "What Is Community Action?" pp. 3–8. The history of community-action programs in Appalachia has not been at all well documented. The many available studies of big-city CAP programs have few counterparts in the literature on Appalachia.

47. Huey Perry, *They'll Cut Off Your Project: A Mingo County Chronicle* (New York: Praeger, 1972), is undocumented and somewhat egocentric, but the main features of its account of the EOC can be corroborated from other sources, including John Barnes's "A Case Study of the Mingo County Economic Opportunity Commission: The Use of Title II of the Economic Opportunity Act of 1964 in a Rural County in West Virginia," unpublished Ph.D. dissertation, University of Pennsylvania, 1970. Portions of the following account are based on Barnes, who used such terms as "charismatic" and "a master of strategy" to characterize Perry.

48. See Malcolm Ross, *Machine Age in the Hills* (New York: Macmillan, 1933), pp. 139–50; Nancy Sue Williams, *An Early History of Mingo County* (Williamson, W.Va.: Williamson Printing, 1960); and Maurer Maurer and Calvin F. Senning, "Billy Mitchell, the Air Service and the Mingo War," *Airpower Historian*, XII (April 1965), 37–43.

49. Byrd's statement quoted in Perry, *They'll Cut Off Your Project*, p. 105, and in Barnes, "Case Study," p. 538. None of the charges was substantiated by OEO investigations. Barnes recounts the episodes in detail on pp. 395 ff.

50. See K. W. Lee, "Fair Elections in West Virginia," in David Walls and John B. Stephenson (eds.), *Appalachia in the Sixties: Decade of Reawakening* (Lexington: University Press of Kentucky, 1972), pp. 176–83; and Barnes, "Case Study," pp. 486 ff. Further discussion of FEC and PAL follow in Chapter 7.

51. Barnes, "Case Study," pp. 389, 498.

52. *Poverty Program Information as of January 1, 1966* (Washington, D.C.: Office of Economic Opportunity, 1966), II, 326 ff., and James Kendrick, "Communities Gain Stature by Progressive Programs," *MLW*, XLI (Winter 1965), 22–23. Kendrick was a former mass-communications student from Indianapolis. His approach in Knox County demonstrates a paradox common to a number of CAPs: an attempt to use essentially conservative means to achieve progressive or radical ends.

53. Pick Conner, "Cannon Builds an Industry," *MLW*, XLIII (September 1967), 17–19.

54. *Community Action in Appalachia: An Appraisal of the War on Poverty in a Rural Setting in Southeastern Kentucky*, 3 vols. (Lexington: University of Kentucky Research Foundation, 1968).

55. Willis A. Sutton, Jr., "Differential Perceptions of Impact of a Rural

Anti-Poverty Campaign," *Social Science Quarterly*, L (December 1969), 657–67, and Paul Street, "Case Study: OEO vs. Rural Poverty," *MLW*, XLV (January 1969), 7–8, 20–22. John Fetterman, *Stinking Creek: The Portrait of a Small Mountain Community in Appalachia* (New York: E. P. Dutton, 1970), is based on a Knox County community. A colorful account of the EOC may be found on pp. 178–82.

56. Paul Street, "Community Action in an Appalachian County: Slower but Surer?" *Welfare in Review*, VIII (November–December 1970), 1–8.

57. An account of the formation and subsequent dissolution of the eight-county Cumberland Valley CAP may be found in Chapter 7.

58. *Mountain Eagle*, November 6, 1966.

59. *Examining the War on Poverty*, V, 1255–90 and 1325–55. The team also investigated the Washington-Greene County CAP in the mining district of southwestern Pennsylvania and found another relatively stable but conservative organization, which concentrated on the delivery of services to "an old Anglo-Saxon pioneer community living now on the brink of total poverty but with great pride in its heritage" *(ibid.,* pp. 1385 ff.).

60. This brief sketch and the analysis of the CAP that follows are based on Hoffman's study, "Community Action," from which all quotations are taken. Another large and conservative CAP in McDowell County, West Virginia, is treated briefly in Chapter 1.

61. The rationale, presumably, was to break the potential hold of the Ponder machine over the CAP. The tactic was similar to that used (just as unsuccessfully) in the formation of the Cumberland Valley CAP. (See Chapter 7.)

62. *Examining the War on Poverty*, IV, 889–90.

63. Elinor Graham pointed out in "Poverty and Legislative Process," pp. 266 ff., that before the act had reached President Johnson's desk, Title II had been progressively weakened by (1) providing for the gubernatorial veto; (2) removing a requirement that agencies receiving community action funds be broadly representative of the community; and (3) dropping references to comprehensive planning in favor of a "components" or piecemeal approach presumably less subject to federal monitoring or control. See also Donovan, *Politics of Poverty*, pp. 54 ff., and Levitan, *Great Society's Poor Law*, p. 115.

64. "Controversy over the Federal Anti-Poverty Community Action Program: Pro and Con," *Congressional Digest*, vol. XLVII (February 1968). See also an interview with Byrd, "What's Wrong with a Poor People's March," *U.S. News and World Report*, LXIV (May 6, 1968), 72–73.

65. Levitan reported in *Great Society's Poor Law*, pp. 122 ff., that although the original idea of community action was to have all projects initiated locally, the OEO began prepackaging some "national emphasis programs" (NEPs) to help small, poorly funded CAPs get under way. By 1968, 60 percent of all CAP funds were going to NEPs, which proved to be generally safe, respectable, and not threatening to local power structures (such as Headstart, Upward Bound, and comprehensive health services).

66. See *Mountain Eagle*, February 15, 1973, p. 1; *Louisville Courier-Journal*, February 9, 1973, p. B-1; and *Mountain Eagle*, June 28 and July 26, 1973.

67. On the earlier impact of phasing out New Deal programs in Appa-

lachia, see Joan Grafton, "Relief Liquidated: March, 1936," *MLW*, XIII (April 1937), 1–8.

68. Daniel P. Moynihan, "The Professionalization of Reform," *Public Interest*, no. 1 (Fall 1965), pp. 6–16, and *idem, Maximum Feasible Misunderstanding* (New York: Free Press, 1969), p. 25. During initial House and Senate hearings, only one poor person testified: A poor farmer was heard from briefly on Title III.

69. Moynihan, "Professionalization of Reform," pp. 15–16. Emphasis in original.

CHAPTER 5

Development by Dipsydoodling: The Design of the Appalachian Regional Commission

> [The Appalachian Regional Development Act] is very important to you. It will build highways in this region, it will build a national forest in this very area, it will work on recreation programs, it will go across the board; there isn't anything that it will not be involved in.
>
> John D. Whisman
> Hazard, Kentucky,
> September 1964

> As a watchdog of the region [the Appalachian Regional Commission is] blind and toothless. It is sorry in conception, sorry in execution.
>
> Harry M. Caudill
> April 1973

AS EARLY AS 1951, the Southern Regional Council's George Mitchell suggested that the Appalachian states should form a regional organization to deal with their common problems.[1] Although social and economic conditions worsened steadily during the decade, no such move was made. In February 1959 the Council of the Southern Mountains again called upon Appalachian governors to establish "an officially responsible interstate commission" to plan and coordinate reconstruction on a regional basis. In January of the following year the suggestion was repeated in Kentucky's *Program 60: A Decade of Action for Progress in Eastern Kentucky*.[2]

An initial step was taken on May 20, 1960, when at the invitation of Maryland's Governor Tawes Appalachian governors met in Annapolis and organized the Conference of Appalachian Governors (CAG). A second meeting in Louisville in October drew governors from nine states (Alabama, Georgia, Kentucky, Maryland, North Carolina, Pennsylvania, Tennessee, Virginia, and West Virginia), and a report prepared for the CAG by the Maryland Department of Economic Development spelled out the facts of life in the region: poverty, lack of social services, out-migration, environmental damage, and

126

regressive policies (for example, on taxation and low-wage industrial development). A resolution emanating from the October CAG meeting called for a "special regional program of development." The governors' discussions seem to have assumed that such a program would be carried out by a permanent organization created for the purpose.[3]

Thus by the fall of 1960 the impetus was strong in some quarters for both a regional organization and a regional approach to development. But it was to be five years before either was created and nearly an entire decade before a single agency was in a position to implement a comprehensive development program. In the interim, CAG tried unsuccessfully to work through ARA as the contemplated regional program was twice subsumed in ARA's and OEO's national programs. A specific program for the region (the Appalachian Regional Development Act) finally emerged from Congress in 1965.

Although the Appalachian Regional Commission created by the act was burdened with the infirmities of its several models and predecessors, it nevertheless gained during its first decade *de facto* control over a substantial majority of the state and federal development efforts in the region. It continued the "infrastructure" development of ARA after ARA's demise, outlasted OEO, and branched out into the "human resources" areas that once were OEO's exclusive domain. By 1974, having spent about $4 billion in the region, the Commission was being touted in some quarters as a model of "creative federalism" worthy of extension to other areas of the country, and in December 1975 Congress extended the life of the Commission for four additional years.

In the region itself, however, there were grave doubts about the legitimacy of ARC's aims and the effectiveness of its programs. Even ARC's own top executives on occasion privately expressed their doubts. Deputy Director Howard Bray said in 1970 that the ARC's impact upon the region had been "damn small, damn modest." Asked two years later what the Commission had accomplished, Executive Director Alvin Arnett said it had "sort of dipsy-doodled along" and that little of its expensive research had helped people at the head of the hollows.[4]

Prelude:
The President's Appalachian Regional Commission

When John F. Kennedy appointed Under Secretary of Commerce Franklin D. Roosevelt, Jr., to head the President's Appalachian Regional Commission in April 1963 and charged the Commission with preparing a "comprehensive action program" for regional economic development, the announcement was greeted with some apprehension by those who had observed previous efforts. The *Mountain Eagle*, noting Roosevelt's alleged prior service as a lobbyist for the Dominican Republic's dictator Rafael Trujillo, commented ironically that he "so successfully represented the poor and downtrodden of that woe-begone country that he was hired to do something for the poor of the Appalachian area."[5] At his confirmation hearing, Roosevelt denied the allegation, but the incident foreshadowed what proved to be a persistent suspicion in the region that beneath the liberal rhetoric of regional development was a design whose effect upon the region would not be wholly salutary.[6]

With a few veterans of the ARA policy struggles over Appalachian resource development on the PARC staff, however, early drafts of some sections of the projected report proved to be relatively bold. One noted, for example, that the "Appalachian pattern of resource exploitation resemble[s] . . . the vacuum effect of extractive exploitation found in African nations recently emerged from colonialism." But such views were in the minority on the staff, and such language therefore did not long remain in the report. Months before the final report was issued, Harry Caudill concluded from the staff studies that PARC had rejected the potential for exercising public claim on revenues from coal mining and power generation.[7]

The final product of PARC's year of deliberations, issued on April 9, 1964, after a number of delays by President Johnson, was (as Donald Rothblatt later called it) little more than a "collage of committee reports based upon political bargaining" among the various states and federal agencies.[8] Harry Caudill's judgment at the time was less charitable. PARC seemed to have decided, he said, that

> . . . gaining acceptance of the programs by the governors was more important than finding effective solutions. [They] discovered that whatever aimed at effective reorganization of the decrepit economy ran afoul of entrenched absentee-owned interests and the political power structure they dominate. So the search turned toward palliatives rather than remedies.[9]

Citing the "natural advantages" of the region's resource base, the report catalogued what it called the "realities of deprivation": low income (one out of three families below the poverty line; per capita income in various states from $200 to $1,000 below the national level of $1,900), lack of urbanization, polluted water, unemployment, eroded land, lack of education, bad housing, and a shortage of personal savings and buying power.

The report's attempt to explain this apparent paradox (rich land and poor people) without admitting the aptness of the colonial analogy led to evasive and contorted logic. It referred to absentee ownership and exploitation of coal, timber, and land, for example, as a "legacy of neglect" and hinted only briefly that the "realities of deprivation" resulted from the region's disproportionate and unrecompensed contributions toward the affluence of a nation hungry for its cheap power, raw materials, and labor.

The root confusion of the report therefore lay in its mistaken assumption that Appalachia had problems because it was not integrated into the larger economy, when in fact its problems derived primarily (as early drafts acknowledged) from its integration into the national economy for a narrow set of purposes: the extraction of low-cost raw materials, power, and labor, and the provision of a profitable market for consumer goods and services.

Thus the report projected Appalachia not as the internal colony implied by the language of its early drafts (indeed not even as having suffered unequally the dysfunctional effects of development elsewhere), but as a "region apart," which because of its isolation had failed to share in the nation's general progress and prosperity. Physical isolation and simple oversight had led to economic and cultural lag. The region's history was therefore described as "a record of traditional acts *not* performed, of American patterns *not* fulfilled." Thus a solution could come, the report asserted, only when Appalachia entered the "free enterprise orbit."

To pull the region into that orbit, PARC recommended open-ended growth and an extrapolation of most existing patterns of development. Programs were to be limited to four "priority areas": highways, resource use, flood control and water power, and "improvements in human resources." Investments ($71 million was suggested for fiscal 1965) were to be directed toward ensuring the success of conventional entrepreneurial ventures (manufacturing, retail sales, tourism, and coal and timber production).

Since minutes of PARC's deliberations have never been made public, it is not possible to reconstruct the discussions that led to such a tepid report. From some available documents relating to the issue of public power development, however, it appears that a central role may have been played by PARC's executive secretary, John D. Whisman, and by utilities lobbyists working at both state and federal levels.[10]

Whisman got his start in economic development planning in a rather unorthodox manner. While working as a sales manager for the Irvin Airchute Company (maker of free-fall parachutes) he became state president of the Kentucky Jaycees in 1956.[11] A few months later he assumed the chairmanship of a Jaycee volunteer community development program in eastern Kentucky, the Eastern Kentucky Regional Development Commission. When the national Jaycees adopted the Kentucky program the next year, Whisman moved up as chairman. After the 1957 floods in eastern Kentucky, the Jaycees' state program was adopted officially by the governor and renamed the Eastern Kentucky Regional Planning Commission. Whisman became its first executive director.

When CAG was organized, Whisman became staff chairman. A few months later he was appointed to President Kennedy's Task Force on Area Redevelopment, and subsequently to ARA's National Public Advisory Committee, on which he served while also functioning as assistant for area development to Kentucky's Governor Combs and administrator of the state's Area Program Office. When PARC was formed, Whisman served first as Kentucky's representative and later as the Commission's executive secretary.

Whisman's experience with the Eastern Kentucky Regional Planning Commission seems to have done little to move his approach to planning and development beyond its Jaycee origins. Of the Commission's nine members, two were coal company executives, two were in the oil business, one was a realtor and resort developer, one a minister, and one a doctor. The Commission's *Program 60* emphasized highways, flood control, and tourism. Its failure to address the issue of equitable resource development proved to be a predictable feature of Whisman's subsequent approach to development during his involvement with ARA and PARC.

Quite early in the PARC planning process, the water resources subteam recommended that the region's hydroelectric resources be developed, and its subteam on coal urged that mine-mouth power plants be built. Harry Caudill's plea for public power at a closed PARC meeting in Kentucky early in 1963 brought a positive response from chairman Roosevelt.[12] But inside the Commission there was opposition to the idea, and Whisman (who was reported to be frequently in the company of Kentucky Power Company representatives) began to urge that public power not be considered because it would handicap the chances of passing the projected legislation.[13]

On September 20, 1963, Harry Caudill wrote to Gordon Ebersole of PARC's technical staff that "John Whisman is doing everything in his power to discourage interest in power production." Ebersole replied that Whisman had ample support for his position inside the Commission. Although power subteam chairman Milton Chase had stated unequivocally that a public power program for the region would be economically feasible and competitive with existing power systems, Ebersole reported, both the Pennsylvania and the Georgia representatives were opposed to the idea. Whisman, Ebersole said after one PARC meeting, "reiterated his often repeated position that the whole program will go down the drain if power is made an issue."[14]

Outside the Commission, however, Whisman's views were being challenged. Early in January 1964 the Perry County (Kentucky) Industrial Development Committee wired both Roosevelt and Whisman: "It is of the utmost importance that the master plan for Eastern Kentucky be based on extensive development of electric power production. . . . Our committee offers to meet anywhere at any time with anyone to pursue further this urgently needed program."[15] A memo ten days later from Interior's Assistant Secretary for Water and Power Development charged that PARC's first draft report "commits a major oversight by not recognizing that the development of electrical power potentials . . . probably exceeds all other development objectives for re-establishing . . . the economic stability" of Appalachia. His opinion was seconded by Mark Abelson, Interior's Northeast Regional Coordinator, who urged further consideration of mine-mouth power and pumped-storage facilities.

Ebersole subsequently reported to Caudill that the power section of the report was being strengthened, but the results were meager. Indeed, the PARC's executive director, John Sweeney, said about the same time that the governors would not sign any report that included recommendations concerning public power.[16]

The PARC report was scheduled to be delivered to President Johnson late in February, but the appointment was abruptly canceled. A day later a high official of American Electric Power (a holding company that owns several operating power companies in the region, including the Appalachian Power Company) announced his company's expansion plans from the steps of the White House.[17]

PARC's own staff position on public power continued to be vacillatory. Chairman Roosevelt was widely reported to have said in a speech at Logan, West Virginia, in March that a giant electric generating plant (presumably publicly owned) would be built in the heart of the coal fields. But almost immediately afterward he issued a denial. The news director of Huntington's station WSAZ-TV reported later that the morning after the telecast which covered the speech, "the president of Appalachian Power Company called . . . to request all the film clips and tapes of Roosevelt's appearance."[18]

The final PARC report contained only a mild recommendation that the potential of public power be studied. The process that led to that recommendation proved to have high predictive value for both the subsequent debate over the legislation and the operation of the Appalachian Regional Commission.

The Appalachian Regional Development Act

While the PARC staff was still at work on its report, President Johnson announced in his January 1964 State of the Union message that in addition to the War on Poverty, "we will launch a special effort in the chronically depressed areas of Appalachia." After Johnson made a well-publicized tour of the region (spending twenty minutes talking with Tom Fletcher of Inez, Kentucky, who cared for a wife and eight children on $400 a year), the administration's legislative recommendations for an Appalachian program were introduced as H.R. 11065 and S. 2782, the Appalachian Regional Development Act of 1964.[19] The act differed little from PARC's proposals.

Hearings were held in both houses of Congress in May and June. Some members argued that poverty in the cities was the first priority, others proposed self-help, and still others argued that Appalachia should not be treated better than such depressed areas as the mining districts of Minnesota.

Iowa's Representative Fred Schwengel asked HEW Secretary Anthony Celebrezze why the administration was "pushing a bill that is discriminatory against those other areas." Celebrezze replied that the problem was "much more severe" in Appalachia and that the proposed program was preferable to "relief and dependence." To Schwengel's charge that there was "too much Federal help in [this] program to encourage these people to help themselves," Celebrezze responded that "you can't help yourself very much if you don't have a job."[20]

The only important change in the bill during hearings occurred when the Senate committee deleted a provision for a permanent corporation to furnish development funds to local areas. Opposition to the provision was led by Pennsylvania's Governor Scranton and by the Chamber of Commerce, which found it "unnecessary and competitive with free enterprise."[21] The amended bill passed the full Senate on September 25 after a projected pasture-improvement program was removed. In the House, the bill passed committee but was never brought to a vote on the floor. The attitude in the House seemed to be, as the *Courier-Journal* had noted a few months earlier, "poverty first, Appalachia later."

Besides the preoccupation with the poverty program and the feeling of some non-Appalachian urban and "depressed area" Congressmen that their constituencies were being left out of aid programs, the objections of conservatives to some of the bill's provisions also contributed to the failure of the legislation in 1964. The House subcommittee minority report objected to the provision for what it called "100 percent Federally financed socialized medical care," the highway program (which it found discriminatory), the pasture program (a threat to beef producers), and the water program (which it feared would lead to public power development).[22]

To provide continuity until the bill could be reintroduced in the next session of Congress, President Johnson established the interagency Federal Development Planning Committee for Appalachia, whose composition paralleled that of the PARC but whose function was to prepare new legislation.[23]

The 1965 bill (S. 3) was introduced early in January. It was similar to the Senate-passed 1964 bill except that authorized highway mileage was changed; the pasture development provision was refocused on erosion control; timber development funds were limited to nonprofit enterprises; and an "economic efficiency" statement was inserted to provide for concentrating investments in growth-prone areas.[24] With one additional amendment (strip-mining reclamation), the Senate committee reported the bill favorably. After adding a provision to allow New York to consider becoming an "Appalachian" state, the Senate passed the bill on February 1. The House approved the Senate bill, which was signed into law on March 7.

The Appalachian Regional Development Act of 1965 (P.L. 89-4) had three principal titles. Title I established the Appalachian Regional Commission; Title II specified major programs (highways, health, land and timber development, mining-area restoration, vocational education, housing, sewage treatment, and supplemental grants-in-aid); and Title III defined local development districts through which most programs were to be implemented. Appropriations totaled $1.1 billion for a two-year period, and the act was to remain in effect for six years.[25]

In signing the act, President Johnson called it "the truest example of creative federalism in our times." During the next several years various commentators from outside the region hailed the ARC as not only a boon to Appalachia but also a model for the nation. John Fischer admiringly called ARC Executive Director Ralph Widner a "revolutionist" who was bringing about a near-miraculous transformation of the region.[26]

But many from inside the region who knew its problems intimately and who had watched the five-year process that led from CAG through ARA and OEO to PARC and ARC with increasing skepticism were not optimistic. In a stinging criticism published only three months after the act became law, Harry Caudill called it "a grim hoax" and "a shoddy bill of goods." None of its programs, he charged, struck at the roots of the region's problems, including especially the domination of its economy by corporations. "While the politicians speak piously of Appalachian rejuvenation," he said, "they lack the guts to break the iron vise that grips the territory and its inhabitants. Any basic change would send wrathful reverberations through the boardrooms of dozens of large firms. . . . The hopes of the people have been raised. Disillusionment is sure to follow." A year later Caudill called the act "comparable to a one-teaspoonful blood transfusion for a man who has bled . . . until he has collapsed."[27]

Design Failure

The transfusion had hardly begun when the limitations in the design of the act—and thus in the operation of the Commission charged with implementing the act—became quite apparent.

The region irrationally defined. Appalachia's boundaries have been drawn so many times by so many different hands that it is futile to look for a "correct" definition of the region. Depending upon which boundary is accepted, the region includes from 190 to nearly 400 counties in from six to thirteen states.[28] ARC's boundaries, far more inclusive than any ever offered before (all of one state and parts of twelve others; 397 counties) expanded in response to increasing political pressure as federal money for Appalachia became available. The PARC report addressed itself to the problems of 340 counties in eight states; the 1965 act included eleven states and about 350 counties; fourteen counties in New York joined shortly thereafter; the 1967 amendments added twenty counties in Mississippi.[29]

Thus "ARC-Appalachia" is too large and too heterogeneous physically, economically, and politically to be dealt with effectively, even if sufficient money were available. In an attempt to reimpose order on such an unmanageably diverse collection of counties, the ARC divided the region into "four Appalachias" (Northern, Central, Southern, and "Highlands"), but even that division, reflecting a variety of extraneous considerations, did not notably increase the Commission's effectiveness. For the severely depressed Central Appalachian subregion (sixty counties in four states), a strategy of "induced urbanization" was chosen in 1967 as a result of a $350,000 study. John Whisman promised a "set of action plans" for the subregion within six months. Yet six years later only 19 percent of ARC's funds had gone to Central Appalachia.[30] The superior bargaining power of less depressed subregions had nudged the Commission toward other priorities.

The logrolling among the states that produced an "ARC-Appalachia" too large to be dealt with comprehensively or efficiently was therefore followed by further logrolling among the states finally included in the region, which prevented ARC from using its funds where the needs were greatest.

Human resources functions initially allocated to separate agency. A critical determiner of the shape of the law was its having been considered concurrently with the Economic Opportunity Act. As early as 1963, PARC recommended that, except for health facilities and vocational education, Appalachian "human resources" funds should be administered by the projected antipoverty agency. Thus the possibility of a unified approach to the region's problems was foreclosed. During congressional hearings on the Economic Opportunity Act, Sargent Shriver maintained that the split would not delay the Appalachian effort and that the two programs could work together without conflict.

Shriver's confidence was not justified, however. OEO and ARC almost immediately found themselves competing for the allegiance and services of community leaders (OEO for its Community Action Agencies and ARC for its Local Development Districts). Divergent philosophies about development also led to conflict. ARC relied on working through existing political and economic structures, but in some instances OEO community action agencies urged people at the grassroots level to challenge "local leadership." OEO's attempt to provide services "up the hollows" where people lived was also in conflict with ARC's growth center strategy, whose success depended largely upon getting people to move into town. And finally, the separation of human resources money left ARC essentially a "bricks and mortar" agency, not only lacking programs but also with a skewed staff that lacked sensitivity in critical areas.[31]

ARC's belated turning to human resources problems toward the end of its first six years of operation, after the much-publicized shutdown of OEO, was greeted with skepticism inside the region. The *Mountain Eagle* charged that the ARC had acted "as though there really were no people here."[32]

Programs not addressed to the most critical needs. The main problems of the region were unemployment (especially in the coal areas where deep mines had mechanized and many operators had turned to strip-mining); a superfluity of low-wage industrial and commercial enterprises (textile and apparel factories; resort developments) and a lack of high-grade industries; widespread corporate absentee ownership and exploitation of land, people, and resources; untaxed, unprocessed exportation of natural resources; strip-mining and environmental damage from other types of development, such as second-home resort development; lack of essential human services (health, housing, education); and heavy out-migration.

The primary needs were therefore jobs with security and good wages, producing products that would benefit both worker and community; a rise in wage levels through a better grade of industrial employment and an extension of federal minimum wage and collective bargaining regulations (for example, to cover agricultural and service workers); a curbing of environmental destruction; human services related to needs and available in rural as well as urban areas; and an end to forced out-migration.

The Commission's developmental strategy focused on stimulating an "infrastructure" of conventional economic development. It assumed that human needs would be met as the effects of such development "trickled down" to the most needy. Thus instead of working to extend minimum wage and collective bargaining laws, the Commission bent its efforts to importing more low-wage industries. As pressure for the Commission to adopt a clear policy on strip-mining mounted, States' Regional Representative John Whisman admitted belatedly that "it's going to be tough not to do something. . . . It will be hard to work out."[33] Instead of attempting to provide services in both rural and urban areas, ARC opted for a "polarizing" strategy, which required people to move into town or commute long distances to get them. And finally, numerous critics have charged that ARC policies on migration (especially some features of its highway program) amounted to a strategy of deliberate depopulation. After Executive Director Alvin Arnett toured the region for three days in 1972, he admitted that although any talk of depopulation made him "sound like Hitler," there had to be "nice places reserved for people." After suggesting that parts of the region should be given over entirely to the mining of coal, he said, "We have animal preserves. . . . My God, why don't we have human ones?"[34]

As early as 1965 I. F. Stone charged that evading critical issues was the Appalachian Regional Development Act's "one distinctive trait." Five years later Robb Burlage was still calling for "an end to the great evasions."[35] Perhaps the most critical evasion was the prohibition against public power development. The PARC report itself, while equivocating about who should develop the region's coal and water resources, nevertheless said, "Developments in the field of power could have a marked impact upon the future economic situation," and observed that "substantial development of mine-mouth power" and "water installations designed to produce peaking power" (pumped-storage projects) could prove beneficial. The report therefore urged that power development studies be undertaken by ARC.

Shortly after the PARC report was released, Kentucky's Senator John Sherman Cooper urged an extension of TVA, and Representative Carl Perkins asked Interior to conduct a study of the feasibility of using Appalachian coal in large thermal generating plants. Interior Secretary Udall subsequently wrote to PARC and offered to do so, promising personnel and technical assistance.[36]

As the 1964 legislation moved into hearings, however, pressure against any commitment to public power intensified. The Virginia delegation, bolstered by private power and coal executives, asked for specific guarantees against public power. Joseph G. Hamrick, executive assistant to the governor, told the House subcommittee that he "had a conference with two of the senior executives of Virginia Electric Power Company yesterday . . . and [we] believe that the free enterprise system has done a magnificent job of supplying the power needs of this country and . . . should continue to do so."[37] Harry Caudill was invited to testify before the Senate committee on the need for public power, but the invitation was subsequently withdrawn. Former American Electric Power Company president Philip Sporn and others kept pressure on the committees as the legislation was considered in both 1964 and 1965, and their efforts were ultimately successful.

In language supplied by the companies themselves, Section 224(b) of the 1965 act specifically prohibits public power development. A position statement from the Monongahela Power Company (of the Alleghany Power System) submitted during legislative hearings said, "We . . . recommend that the . . . bill be amended to make it clear that no appropriation or financial assistance may be used . . . to finance the cost of facilities for the generation, transmission, or distribution of electric energy."[38] Section 224(b) specifies: "Nothing in this Act shall authorize any assistance . . . to be used . . . to finance the cost of facilities for the generation, transmission, or distribution of electric energy."

In his 1965 annual report to stockholders, the Virginia Electric Power Company's board chairman said:

> You are all aware of our concern with federal encroachment in the areas of free enterprise. A real threat of this nature to the electric utilities in the East developed last year. I refer to the Appalachian legislation which, as originally proposed, contemplated federally financed generating plants in the coalfields. VEPCO and other investor-owned utilities cooperated to oppose this with all the energy at our command. I am glad to report that the Appalachian legislation as enacted forbids the use of any of the presently appropriated funds for construction of electric utilities facilities.[39]

The Commission itself subsequently refused to become involved in the issue even to the limited extent suggested by PARC. In response to an inquiry from Senator Muskie as to why the power studies recommended by PARC had not been made, ARC's Federal Co-chairman John Sweeney replied in early 1967 that the Commission had "little or no enthusiasm for the commitment of our rather scarce research funds" to studying the problems of coal resource development and electric power production. In connection with the latter, Sweeney cited "unique political problems" as a deterrent.[40]

Act embodies, and Commission has followed, regressive investment strategy. Hardly anyone denied in the 1960s that problems in Appalachia were severe, and there was wide (though not unanimous) agreement that a considerable public effort to solve them was justified. With the usual exception of conservative Democrats and Republicans, Chambers of Commerce, and the National Association of Manufacturers, there was substantial consensus that large sums of money would have to be spent. The question was how and where.

Economists, who seem to have been the only ones whose advice was taken seriously, differed.[41] Some saw the problems of the region as inseparable from the continuing national recession and unemployment of the late 1950s and early 1960s, and therefore argued that the solution had to be to stimulate "total demand" for goods and services by manipulating government spending, taxes, and credit. But others contended that the demand approach was insufficient because different regions of the country experienced both recession and recovery unequally, and because some probable effects of increases in total demand (such as inflation) would be undesirable.

This "structuralist" view led to the conclusion that special attention should be focused on the "lagging" areas. Objections to the structural approach on grounds of sheer economic efficiency (on the assumption that economic activity occurs "naturally" where it is most efficient) were lessened by a consideration of other national goals such as maintaining rural-urban balance and retaining certain social values. Thus the uneasy conclusion was reached that in areas such as Appalachia, special regional policies and programs were justified.[42] But what policies and programs?

Economists of most nonradical persuasions agreed that economic growth in the region was the general answer. But what kind of economic growth? And where within the region should it occur? At the same rate everywhere, or in some places more and faster than in others? Some argued for balanced and phased growth (that is, creation of all types of symbiotically related industries, well distributed geographically, as demand increased). But the balanced-growth approach was ultimately rejected in favor of unbalanced growth, a theory that, as Monroe Newman notes, had its origin in underdeveloped countries.

The reasons why this choice was made are technically complex, as Newman suggests, but that they were also politically and culturally revealing is a fact at which he only hints. Balanced growth was rejected partly because of an assumed "scarcity . . . of managerial and entrepreneurial ability" in the region and because it required "guidance of economic processes" too unlike "accepted approaches."[43] The first assumption followed naturally from the conventional condescending views regarding people in the region held by those outside.[44] The second is a logical consequence of the free-enterprise mandate that invariably is attached to social legislation. Thus because it required the rejection of a time-honored cultural stereotype, and because it was ideologically threatening, balanced growth was not an acceptable approach.

But the theory of unbalanced growth, by contrast, was attractive. It distinguished between "autonomous acts" toward development, which required the managerial and entrepreneurial ability held to be scarce in Appalachia, and "induced acts," which did not. According to the theory of unbalanced growth, "Progress toward development can be accelerated if scarce talents are used to undertake acts that have a high induced followership."[45] Translated into programs, it meant giving money to industrialists and businessmen rather than to poor people. It was, as Harry Caudill called it, a "cruel provision," but one that offered both broadly ideological and narrowly political advantages.[46]

Thus unbalanced growth was attractive because in practice it amounted to a simple extrapolation of processes already under way and required alteration of neither free market ideology nor existing patterns of dominance and privilege. Newman points out, in fact, that in many respects growth center theory "is similar to the theory of a market economy, which depends upon signals through the price and profit mechanism to induce business to capitalize on opportunities." Thus unbalanced growth, whose "core concept" is that "spatially unbalanced growth" must be induced in the short run if both regional economic activity and the region's participation in national prosperity are to improve in the long run, is in fact simply the hair of the dog.

Spatially unbalanced growth was to be induced first in selected "growth centers." ARC has defined a growth center as "a complex consisting of one or more communities or places which, taken together, provide or are likely to provide, a range of cultural, social, employment, trade or service functions for itself and its associated rural hinterland."[47] The theory promised that the economic benefits of investment in the centers would spill over into the surrounding "hinterlands" (a term that conveys more than a hint of cultural bias), that direct and immediate payments to businessmen and industrialists would create jobs and stimulate growth whose long-term benefits would "trickle down" to those in most immediate need, and that human services concentrated in the centers would be both cheaper than and superior to any that could be provided in rural areas.[48]

Frances Piven and Richard Cloward have noted that trickle-down theories of development go back at least to Herbert Hoover, who, as the Depression deepened, aimed his policies at "the entrepreneurial groups [bankers, railroads] that, according to official American gospel, had made the economy run before and would make it run again."[49] John Sweeney, PARC executive director and later ARC federal cochairman, told the Appalachian Trade Union Conference in 1964 that

> . . . none of us . . . conceived of this initially as a program which could in the short run make any inroads on individual conditions of poverty. . . . The Appalachian program is designed to provide that kind of investment which comes about when entrepreneurs have faith in their region to make an investment, following the traditional patterns of this country.

Six years later, as ARC approached the end of its first authorized term, Executive Director Ralph Widner reflected: "Unfortunately, development makes its first impact on upper and middle-income groups. It has a trickle-down effect to the really hard-core poor."[50]

Such assurances would have been cold comfort even if trickle-down occurred, but there is evidence that it does not. Research completed by John Delaplaine and Edward Hollander in 1970 indicated that stimulation of the "private sector" neither helped the poor immediately nor affected the growth rate as the theory predicted. The best way to stimulate growth appeared to be "direct federal subventions to the local public sector." Nevertheless, an ARC task force recommended late in 1972 that the growth center investment strategy be continued "without alteration."[51] At virtually the same time, however, a comptroller-general's study of federal expenditures in Johnson County, Kentucky, concluded that $8 million in ARC funds (most of which went for roads) had not made a "significant impact" on economic conditions in four years.[52]

Whatever the abstract merits of growth center theory, evidence that it would work acceptably in Appalachia has proved hard to come by. Stephen S. Fuller's 1969 study of state-designated growth centers in 190 counties concluded that states had chosen almost all urban areas as growth centers, regardless of their capacity for growth. But Gordon Cameron, who studied the federal role in regional economic development, concluded in 1970 that there was little empirical support for growth center strategy, regardless of how the centers were chosen. His finding was confirmed specifically with reference to Appalachia by Kenneth Shellhammer's study two years later. Another 1974 study by the comptroller-general found that Ohio "generally disagreed with the . . . growth center concept" employed by ARC and noted that Kentucky "acknowledged that the way it initially identified growth centers . . . was faulty." Ralph D. Carnathan's 1973 study of the implementation of the ARC act in three states found that in Georgia local development district (LDD) directors and state administrators "without exception were critical of the [growth center] policy. The consensus was that it tends to 'make the rich richer and the poor poorer.' " Tennessee LDD directors reported that they circumvented or ignored the policy. One North Carolina director represented the consensus of his colleagues by saying, "We don't worry about it."[53]

Federalism of ARC less creative than claimed. Title I of the Appalachian Regional Development Act established the Appalachian Regional Commission as a joint federal-state agency. ARC has thus been called a new concept in government, but it is hardly that. From the founding of the Republic until the late 1920s, as James Sundquist has pointed out, a "dual" federalism existed, which defined separate areas of responsibility for state and federal government. But with the coming of the 1930s dual federalism was increasingly displaced by a "new federalism" in which responsibility is shared.[54] The question, then, is not whether ARC is a governmental innovation but whether the approach it embodies has the virtues claimed for it, and whether in any case it is appropriate to the needs of the region.

In theory, the "creative federalism" of ARC is supposed to provide a broader base for analysis and planning; a comprehensive rather than piecemeal approach to development; increased cooperation both among the states and between the states and the federal government; improved coordination and efficiency in programs; and heightened responsiveness to the problems of the region. But in practice ARC has actually offered few of these advantages. Studies of the Commission (for instance, by Rothblatt, Newman, and Derthick) have shown repeatedly that ARC programs are rarely coordinated across state boundaries; that states prepare impressive plans to get ARC money, but spend it more or less independently of the plan; that the pattern of expenditures cannot easily be distinguished from that of conventional grants directly from the federal government to the states; and that the most pressing problems of the region are those with which ARC has been least able to deal.

One especially paradoxical feature of ARC's federalism—and the source of many of its difficulties—is a double veto provision for all programs. Section 101(b) provides that Commission decisions require the affirmative vote of the federal cochairman (appointed by the president); Section 222 requires the consent of the individual states in which programs are undertaken. The Commission contends that neither veto has ever been used, but in fact the claim applies merely to the formal veto. Proposals deemed likely to meet a state or federal veto are rarely put to a vote. State votes are changed after the fact to make decisions appear unanimous. The functional elements are thus not formal vetoes but implicit threats of vetoes and gentlemen's agreements.

An example of both the importance of the state (or "little") veto and the process by which decisions are reached was the Commission's response to the Buffalo Creek, West Virginia, disaster in 1972. When an improperly and illegally constructed slag dam collapsed during a rainstorm, a fifty-foot-high wall of water destroyed fourteen mining camps, killed more than a hundred people, and left five thousand homeless as it roared down through a narrow seventeen-mile-long valley. West Virginia Governor Arch Moore announced (as Section 222 allowed) that ARC would not be allowed in the area and said that the "only real sad part about it is that . . . West Virginia took a terrible beating which far overshadowed the beating that the individuals that lost their lives took, and I consider this an even greater tragedy than the accident itself."[55] ARC's executive director, Alvin Arnett, refused to confirm that Moore had vetoed direct Commission action but said that its involvement, if any, would be "in the realm of rehabilitation, not fault-finding." ARC eventually mounted temporary relief programs, but its overall response tended to reinforce the Pittston Coal Company's claim that the dam had burst through an "act of God." ARC's 1973 *Annual Report* called the incident a "natural disaster" comparable to tropical storm Agnes.[56]

Thus the creative federalism of the ARC frequently turns out to involve conventional political logrolling and autocratic Washington-based staff decisions. When state politics become crucial, as Harry Caudill noted at the very outset of the Commission's work, the state veto amounts to a revival of "the hoary theory of nullification." In most cases, however, as Martha Derthick recently concluded from minutes of ARC's executive sessions, "It is officials at headquarters who state what the organization's interests require and who, having stated it, win a high degree of acquiescence from most of the states. . . . The state members are prepared to do what they are told must be done to preserve the Commission and keep federal funds flowing."[57]

Instead of mounting a bold, imaginative, and aggressive attack on the problems of Appalachia, the Commission has proved to be characterized by caution, vacillation, and deference to the wishes of vested interests. "The structure of the agency," the *Mountain Eagle* concluded, "is such that . . . it can undertake only the most politically popular projects [roads, vocational schools, hospital buildings] and is blocked from tackling any of the root causes of poverty in the mountains."[58]

Commission frequently not accountable for its actions. Inherent in the idea of "creative federalism" supposedly embodied in the Commission was the assumption that the new state-federal body would be responsive and accountable to the people of the region. Lately, however, its lack of accountability has led some of its critics to refer to it as a Bureau of Indian Affairs for Appalachia.[59] But whether or not the analogy is entirely appropriate is not important, for ARC's own record suggests that it has become less and less accountable to the states, that it has preferred the opinions of hired consultants to those of the people of the region, and that its workings are increasingly hidden from public view and isolated from the normal mechanisms of accountability.

Technically, the Commission consists of the federal cochairman and the governors of the thirteen Appalachian states or, as Section 101(a) specifies, their designees. In practice it is most often the designees who actually participate in Commission proceedings ("sit at the table"), and as time has passed the designees have tended to come from lower and lower in state government hierarchies. Martha Derthick found that during the early meetings of the Commission, Federal Cochairman Sweeney was opposed to having Appalachian governors themselves sit on the Commission instead of appointing representatives. Sweeney's rationale was that "lower-ranking, less visible representatives . . . would find it easier to make . . . compromises."[60] His view prevailed, and as a result the ARC staff was left increasingly free to conduct business as it chose without consulting elected representatives of the states.

The Commission's consultations directly with the people in the region have been rare and perfunctory, even though Section 102(h) of the act requires ARC to "provide a forum for consideration of problems of the region . . . and establish and utilize, as appropriate, citizens' and *special* advisory councils and public conferences."[61] Section 106(h) of the 1964 act specified that the permanent ARC office was to be in the region, but no such provision was included in the 1965 act. The headquarters therefore remained in Washington, and no field offices were established. In the beginning there were a few natives of the region on the staff, but by 1970 almost none remained. So unfamiliar was most of the staff with the region that a bus tour was arranged at one point to allow them to see it at "first hand." Staff members themselves, apparently accepting the condescending stereotype of Appalachian people, defended their isolation by saying, for example, that "you simply have to have people who know how to think in terms of program planning . . . and they just don't exist in Appalachia."[62]

The relationship between the Commission and the states and their people was to some degree paralleled by the relationship that developed between States' Regional Representative John Whisman and the Commission itself. As early as 1965, before Whisman joined the Commission staff, the *Mountain Eagle* warned of an effort on Whisman's part "to collect to himself the tight reins of control on all Federal programs within Kentucky."[63] But Whisman had already moved beyond Kentucky through his association with the Conference of Appalachian Governors and the ARA. After he came to ARC, he proposed "National Development Legislation" that would have upgraded his own position to "states' cochairman" to parallel that of the federal cochairman. He later suggested that an Office of Regional Development be established in the Executive Office of the President, with an administrative structure similar to that of ARC.[64]

Inside the Commission itself, Whisman's unique position led to a progressive consolidation of his power. Federal cochairmen, governors, and their designees came and went as elections were won and lost, but Whisman remained year in and year out. His position was further enhanced by the departures of ARC's first executive director, Ralph Widner, late in 1971 and his successor, Alvin Arnett, in 1973.

As Whisman's power increased, ARC progressively shrouded itself against public scrutiny. A series of press accounts during 1972–73 detailed the techniques (closed meetings, unannounced meetings, "dummy" meetings staged for reporters, secret meetings, "special" meetings, "States' Sessions") used in defiance of the requirement of Section 107(3) of the act that meetings must be open to the public.[65] The policy of secrecy eventually brought complaints from ARC staff members and an announcement from the federal cochairman that he would attend no more closed meetings.

Local development districts flawed in concept and operation. There were several antecedents for the Local Development District concept, but the idea seems to have been incorporated into ARC's legislation largely through the influence of John Whisman, who had helped to organize similar Area Development Councils in eastern Kentucky in the late 1950s. Section 301 of the 1965 act established the multicounty districts (LDDs) as the primary mechanism through which the Commission's development strategy was to be implemented. By the end of its first decade ARC had divided the region into seventy LDDs comprising on the average five or six counties each and was subsidizing their administrative expenses. Late in the decade Whisman and other Commission officials were urging that the LDD concept be employed throughout the nation. When Senator Joseph Montoya of Arizona held hearings on the Public Works Development Act of 1972, which would have involved such an extension, three prominent witnesses were Whisman, former ARC executive director Widner, and Kentucky's Governor Edward Breathitt. The president of the National Association of Regional Councils called the concept "an evolution of local government and the structure of our Federal system," and an official of the Kentucky Program Development Office praised it as "a linear [*sic*] descendant of the Constitution."[66]

Proponents of the concept argued that many counties were too small and too poor to hire their own planners; that problems (with, for example, highways or waterways) crossed county lines; and that multicounty planning would prevent duplication, encourage efficient, economical coordination of effort, and allow counties to compete more successfully for scarce state and federal funds.[67] Implementation of the LDD concept varied greatly from place to place in Appalachia, however, and produced more evidence that the concept itself was flawed. Some mayors and other local officials told Sen. Montoya's committee that the system was inefficient, ineffective, unrepresentative, and unresponsive to people's needs. Rothblatt concluded that because LDDs rarely had much actual impact on local planning and development, often lacked authority, and hardly ever adequately represented the poor, they were the "weakest link in the ARC planning process."[68] Ralph Widner's successor, Alvin Arnett, wondered whether LDDs were really "the proper conduit" for federal funds, and the Commission itself in late 1973 admitted that LDDs were at a "critical juncture."[69]

Despite their conspicuous lack of success, after 1967 the LDDs in many cases had, by authority of the so-called A-95 Project Notification and Review System, virtually complete control over all federal expenditures within their boundaries. The A-95 procedure developed from a September 2, 1966, memorandum that President Johnson sent to federal agencies, declaring that "we must coordinate our efforts to prevent conflict and duplication among federally assisted comprehensive planning efforts," and directing agencies and departments to ensure such coordination in their dealings with state and local governments.[70] The President's directive was implemented by a Bureau of the Budget Circular (A-80) issued early the next year, and guidelines were further defined and tightened by a series of presidential, congressional, and Bureau of the Budget actions during the next several years.[71]

As finally formulated in OMB Circular A-95, the guidelines required that all applications for federal funds be reviewed by state or areawide "clearinghouses." Although a favorable "A-95" review" (as it came to be called) was not required, federal agencies rarely approved applications that received unfavorable reviews. And since in Appalachia the LDDs were in many cases designated as A-95 clearinghouses, they acquired something approaching veto power over applications.[72]

Summary. The Appalachian regional development legislation was conceptually and politically limited to those conventional consensus approaches capable of emerging from existing federal agencies and state politics. It left human resource development to OEO and restricted the Commission to infrastructure development. That approach was further cramped by an "economic efficiency" clause that enforced a questionable growth center and "trickle-down" strategy of development at the local level. The repeated use of the veto threat in ARC bargaining sessions further reduced the planning function to the lowest common denominator of safe projects. The ideological predispositions of ARC's upper-level staff (for example, John Whisman's opposition to natural-resources development) led to a persistent acquiescence to the "great evasions" of the act and a general lack of accountability. Operationally, the Commission's local development districts in many cases exacerbated ARC's own defects, and thus turned out to be both the most crucial and the weakest link in the system. Thus it was hardly a cause for wonder that Deputy Director Howard Bray judged the impact of ARC's programs to be "damn small, damn modest."

But Bray's evaluation applied only to the effectiveness of the programs in achieving their stated aims. In political and cultural terms, the programs had a considerably larger (and regressive) impact.

Notes

1. *Mountain Life and Work (MLW)*, XVII (Spring 1951), 19.

2. *Program 60: A Decade of Action for Progress in Eastern Kentucky* (Hazard: Eastern Kentucky Regional Planning Commission, 1960).

3. U.S. House of Representatives, *Hearings Before the Ad Hoc Subcommittee on Appalachian Regional Development of the Committee on Public Works . . . on H.R. 11065*, 88th Congress, 2d Session, May 5—June 11, 1964, pp. 271–72. See also Jerald Ter Horst, "No More Pork Barrel: The Appalachia Approach," *The Reporter*, March 11, 1965.

4. Quoted in *Mountain Eagle*, January 15, 1970, p. 2, and April 13, 1972, p. 3, respectively.

5. *Ibid.*, March 12, 1964, p. 2.

6. See *New York Times*, February 4, 1963, p. 6, and March 13, 1963, p. 7,

respectively. Roosevelt was a registered agent for Trujillo, the *Times* reported, from March 1, 1956, to February 25, 1957.

7. *Louisville Courier-Journal,* November 17, 1963, and Harry Caudill, "Appalachia: The Path from Disaster," *The Nation,* CXCVIII (March 9, 1964), 239–41.

8. Donald N. Rothblatt, *Regional Planning: The Appalachian Experience* (Lexington, Mass.: D. C. Heath, 1971), p. 60. Participating states were those that had formed CAG. Federal departments included Labor, Defense, HEW, Agriculture, Interior, and Treasury. Representatives from the Small Business Administration, the Atomic Energy Commission, TVA, NASA, and the Housing and Home Finance Agency also participated. See *Appalachia: A Report by the President's Appalachian Regional Commission, 1964* (Washington, D.C.: Government Printing Office, 1964).

9. Harry Caudill, "Misdeal in Appalachia," *Atlantic Monthly,* CCXV (June 1965), 43.

10. Rothblatt reports in *Regional Planning,* p. 51, having tried twice without success to gain access to the minutes. Whether the dynamics of bargaining were the same with respect to the public power issue as to other issues is not known, but it seems reasonable to suppose that they were.

11. This brief account of Whisman's career is based on his own autobiographical statement before the House Ad Hoc Subcommittee on the Appalachian Regional Development Act in 1964, pp. 268 ff., and an interview on July 23, 1974.

12. Undated (early 1963) Interior Department memo from Gordon K. Ebersole. On Caudill's proposal, see *Louisville Courier-Journal,* September 1, 1963; PARC Water Resources Committee, "First Draft Report on the Water Resources of Appalachia," September 1963, pp. 35 ff. (mimeo); "Summary of Recommendations of PARC Staff to the President's Appalachian Regional Commission," October 30, 1963, p. 20 (mimeo). The power subteam summary did not specifically recommend public power development.

13. *Mountain Eagle,* March 12, 1964.

14. Ebersole to Caudill, September 23, 1963.

15. *Mountain Eagle,* January 9, 1964.

16. Gordon K. Ebersole memo of March 6, 1964.

17. Appalachian had recently filed a request with the Federal Power Commission for permission to build a large private power project on the New River in central Appalachia.

18. *Louisville Courier-Journal,* March 11 and 12, 1964.

19. A legislative history of the act may be found in the *Congressional Digest,* XLIII (December 1964).

20. House *Hearings on H.R. 11065,* pp. 152–56.

21. *Louisville Courier-Journal,* June 24, 1964. For a discussion of the removal, see Martha Derthick, *Between State and Nation: Regional Organizations in the United States* (Washington, D.C.: Brookings Institution, 1974), pp. 78–80.

22. *Congressional Digest,* XLIII (December 1964), 299. Harry Caudill called the bill "hopelessly inadequate"; see *Louisville Courier-Journal,* July 5, 1964.

23. Executive Order 11186, October 23, 1964.

24. On the legislative history of the 1965 bill, see Rothblatt, *Regional Planning,* pp. 63 ff., upon which this discussion is based. The economic efficiency statement provided that the "public investments made . . . shall be concentrated in areas where there is the greatest potential for future growth, and where the expected return on public dollars will be the greatest." Although the statement was later softened somewhat, it led to the pivotal "growth center" strategy, which is discussed below.

25. For specific allocations among programs, see Rothblatt, *Regional Planning,* p. 66.

26. John Fischer, "Can Ralph Widner Save New York, Chicago, and Detroit?" *Harper's,* CCXXXVII (October 1968), 12 ff.

27. Caudill, "Misdeal in Appalachia," pp. 43–47, and "An 'Operation Bootstrap' for Eastern Kentucky," *Appalachian South,* I (Spring–Summer 1966), 16. Earlier *The Nation,* CC(February 22, 1965), 182, had called the act "a feeble step." Academic evaluators have generally found ARC promising. In addition to Rothblatt, *Regional Planning,* and Monroe Newman, *Political Economy of Appalachia: A Case Study in Regional Integration* (Lexington, Mass.: D. C. Heath, 1972), see Niles M. Hansen, *A Review of the Appalachian Regional Commission Program* (Austin: University of Texas Press, 1969), p. 5. Hansen calls ARC "the most promising regional development institution in the United States."

28. See for example John C. Campbell, *The Southern Highlander and His Homeland* (1921; reprint, Lexington: University Press of Kentucky, 1969), pp. 10–18; *Economic and Social Problems and Conditions of the Southern Appalachians* (Washington, D.C.: U.S. Department of Agriculture, 1935), pp. 10–15; and Rupert B. Vance, "The Region: A New Survey," in Thomas R. Ford (ed.), *The Southern Appalachian Region: A Survey* (Lexington: University Press of Kentucky, 1962), pp. 1–8.

29. Rothblatt, *Regional Planning,* pp. 53, 62–65; Robert G. Albright, "Others Want in on Appalachian Bill," *Washington Post,* January 22, 1965, p. 8; and "13 Upstate Counties Admitted to Appalachian Aid Program," *New York Times,* August 19, 1965, p. 31. During the 1964 hearings Representative John Baldwin (R.–Calif.) asked why Mississippi, the poorest state in the Union, was excluded. HEW Secretary Celebrezze replied that the state wasn't "in Appalachia" and did not have the same problems as the Appalachian states (*Louisville Courier-Journal,* May 20, 1964).

30. Ben Franklin, "Appalachia Grant Will Fight Resistance to Change," *New York Times,* January 6, 1967, and *Louisville Courier-Journal,* November 4, 1973, p. E-4.

31. Newman, *Political Economy,* pp. 106–7, discusses the conflict at greater length. See also Chapter 9 below.

32. *Mountain Eagle,* September 24, 1970, p. 2. Some specific ARC human resources programs are discussed in the next chapter.

33. *People's Appalachia,* I (August–September 1970), 21.

34. *Louisville Courier-Journal,* July 30, 1972, p. B-1.

35. *Mountain Eagle,* January 28, 1965, p. 2, and *People's Appalachia,* I (August–September 1970), 20 ff.

36. *Mountain Eagle,* April 30, 1964, p. 2, and April 16, 1964, p. 1; letter

from Udall to John Sweeney of PARC, April 9, 1964; letter from Henry P. Caulfield, Jr., of Interior to Sweeney, June 9, 1964.

37. House *Hearings on H.R. 11065*, p. 310. See also *Mountain Eagle,* May 28, 1964, p. 1, and *Louisville Courier-Journal,* May 27 and June 10, 1964.

38. House *Hearings on H.R. 11065*, pp. 347–48.

39. Quoted in *People's Appalachia,* I (August–September 1970), 3.

40. Letter from Sweeney to Muskie, February 20, 1967.

41. The following sketch of the theoretical argument is based upon Newman, *Political Economy,* pp. 33 ff.

42. Newman notes in *ibid.,* p. 42, that the PARC report, in its emphasis on internal factors, helped give weight to the structuralist argument. PARC opted for a "stages" theory, which holds that areas move naturally from an agricultural or extractive economic base, through manufacturing for use (and eventually export), to a "final" stage in which service industries predominate and the area "has embarked on a process of self-generative growth." For a concrete application of this theory, see the Georgia plan in *State and Regional Development Plans 1968* (Washington, D.C.: Appalachian Regional Commission, 1969), p. 110.

43. Newman, *Political Economy,* p. 44.

44. Such condescension was, for example, a prominent feature of the report prepared for CAG by the Maryland Department of Economic Development in 1960. Although this was ostensibly an economic report, its writers' cultural judgments surfaced when they noted that the region had a "general reputation for backwardness" and that its labor force was "untrained and, judging from the behavior of a migrant fringe group [presumably in Baltimore], difficult to handle" (pp. 19–20). Baltimore has a large population of Appalachian out-migrants. This view of the region's people (and its corollary that regional problems have their origin in widespread character defects) has been assumed valid by many later commentators. See for example Rothblatt, *Regional Planning,* pp. 8–14.

45. Newman, *Political Economy,* p. 44. Though technically not an official ARC spokesman, Newman has been a consultant to the Commission and was one of the writers of its report, *The Appalachian Experiment, 1965–1970,* some of the language of which he subsequently incorporated into his own book.

46. Caudill, "Misdeal in Appalachia," p. 47.

47. *State and Regional Development Plans 1968,* p. 12. There has been confusion since the beginning over what a growth center actually is. Niles Hansen's study (see note 27) concluded that "some nominal growth areas are in fact hinterlands to more viable growth areas outside their districts" (p. 3).

48. For a discussion of the means by which growth centers were chosen see Newman, *Political Economy,* pp. 57 ff.

49. Frances Fox Piven and Richard Cloward, *Regulating the Poor: The Functions of Public Welfare* (New York: Vintage, 1971), p. 50.

50. Quoted in Stephanie Harrington, "Appalachia: Beyond Free Enterprise," *Commonweal,* LXXXII (May 7, 1965), 214, and *People's Appalachia,* I (August–September 1970), 19, respectively.

51. Kathleen K. Hamm *et al.,* "The Commission Investment Strategy" (mimeo ARC report, undated, ca. mid-1972), and John W. Delaplaine and

Edward D. Hollander, "Federal Spending for Human Resources," *Growth and Change*, I (January 1970), 28–33. Delaplaine and Hollander studied seven local development districts (LDD) in nine states, including West Virginia and Kentucky.

52. Comptroller General, *The Effects of Federal Expenditures on the Economy of Johnson County, Kentucky* (1972).

53. Stephen S. Fuller, "The Appalachian Experiment: Growth or Development," unpublished Ph.D. dissertation, Cornell University, 1969; Gordon Cameron, *Regional Economic Development: the Federal Role* (Baltimore: Resources for the Future, 1970), p. 38; Kenneth Shellhammer, "Growth Center Strategy as Applied to Depressed Areas in Advanced Countries: The Case of Appalachia," unpublished Ph.D. dissertation, University of Colorado, 1972; Comptroller General, *Review of Selected Activities of Regional Commissions* (1974); and Ralph D. Carnathan, "Experiment in Regional Federalism: Implementation of the Appalachian Regional Development Act of 1965 in Georgia, North Carolina, and Tennessee," unpublished Ph.D. dissertation, University of Tennessee, 1973, pp. 123–241.

54. James L. Sundquist, *Making Federalism Work* (Washington, D.C.: Brookings Institution, 1969), pp. 6–12.

55. *New York Times*, March 12, 1972.

56. See Jim Britnell, "The Buffalo Creek Flood: A Demonstration Health Program Responds to an Emergency," *Appalachia*, V(July–August 1972), 1–7, and *1973 Annual Report of the Appalachian Regional Commission*, p. 35. *Disaster on Buffalo Creek: A Citizen's Report on Criminal Negligence in a West Virginia Mining Community* (Charleston, W.Va.: Citizens' Commission to Investigate the Buffalo Creek Disaster, n.d.) strongly refutes any claim that the incident was a natural disaster. See Ben Franklin, "From God, No Comment," *New York Times*, March 5, 1972, and Eric Frumin, "An Act of Greed, Not God," *Guardian*, March 29, 1972, pp. 16–17. Pittston eventually negotiated a $3.5 million out-of-court settlement with survivors; the suit is chronicled in Gerald M. Stern, *The Buffalo Creek Disaster* (New York: Vintage, 1977). Kai T. Erikson's *Everything in Its Path* (New York: Simon & Schuster, 1976) recounts the disaster itself.

57. Caudill, "Misdeal in Appalachia," p. 43, and Derthick, *Between State and Nation*, p. 94. Cf. Caudill, "Appalachia: The Path from Disaster," *The Nation*, March 9, 1964, p. 241. For further discussion of the veto, see Rothblatt, *Regional Planning*, pp. 131 ff.

58. *Mountain Eagle*, January 15, 1970, p. 2.

59. See *ibid.*, April 26, 1973, p. 2.

60. Memorandum from Sweeney to Tennessee Governor Buford Ellington, March 19, 1965, quoted in Derthick, *Between State and Nation*, p. 89. On the declining rank of state representatives, see p. 103 and *The Appalachian Experiment, 1965–70*, p. 94.

61. Accountability directly to the people is also supposedly provided for through the LDDs of Title III. The effectiveness of the LDD mechanism is discussed in the following section and Chapter 9.

62. ARC staff member quoted in *Mountain Eagle*, November 29, 1973, p. 1. The statement rests upon the questionable assumptions that (1) there are

in fact no such persons in the region, (2) the ARC itself is competent in this regard, and (3) the conceptual vocabulary of the ARC's planning strategy is the most useful that might be adopted for the region.

63. *Ibid.*, November 11, 1965, p. 1. Cf. earlier criticisms on January 2, 1964, p. 6, and February 4, 1965, p. 2.

64. Whisman memo of October 8, 1968, in the files of the *Louisville Courier-Journal*'s Washington bureau, and Luther J. Carter, "Appalachian Program: A Mechanism for a National Growth Policy?" *Science*, CLXIX (July 3, 1970), 32–35. The position of States' Regional Representative is not contained in the 1965 ARC act.

65. For accounts of closed and secret meetings, see the *Mountain Eagle*, December 28, 1972, p. 1; January 4, 1973, p. 2; January 18, 1973, p. 2 (on a secret meeting to discuss secret meetings); and April 5, 1973, p. 1. Reporters for the *Mountain Eagle* and the *Louisville Courier-Journal* were repeatedly barred from meetings. See *Mountain Eagle*, January 18, 1973, p. B-3. In mid-1974 an ARC directive forbade staff members to talk with the *Eagle*'s Washington reporter except in the presence of the Commission's information officer. A contemporary (but undated) document, "A Discussion of the Meetings of the Council of Appalachian Governors," apparently generated by John Whisman's office, argued that secret meetings were both legal and vital to the working of the Commission. A "Council of Appalachian Governors" appeared to have been created in name only, to legitimize the closed "States' Sessions" of the Commission. The *Louisville Courier-Journal* reported ("Dissension over Whisman Splits ARC," June 2, 1974, p. B-6) that at a poorly attended session of state representatives Whisman circulated a resolution that declared him executive secretary of the Council. After its adoption, he began to refer to closed meetings as sessions of the Council, which he said were not covered by federal or state regulations on open meetings. Governors Wallace (Ala.) and Waller (Miss.) protested, and both ARC Executive Director Teter and Federal Co-chairman Whitehead said they had never heard of the Council before.

66. See John D. Whisman, "A New Commission Tackles an Old Problem," *Mountain Life and Work*, XXX (Fall 1959), 18–19, and U.S. Senate, *Hearings Before the Subcommittee on Economic Development of the Committee on Public Works . . . on S. 3381*, April 18–26, 1972. On earlier efforts to nationalize the ARC idea under Title V of the Economic Development Act, see Don Oberdorfer, "The Proliferating Appalachias," *The Reporter*, XXXIII (September 9, 1965), 22–27.

67. These arguments are elaborated in "The Local Development District: Foundation for Regional Development," *Appalachia*, I (December 1967), 9–13; Rothblatt, *Regional Planning*, pp. 151 ff.; and the entire December 1973 issue of *Appalachia*, the Commission's public relations magazine.

68. Rothblatt, *Regional Planning*, pp. 151 ff. See an extended critical editorial in the *Louisville Courier-Journal*, April 30, 1972. On problems in a particular LDD, see Chapter 9.

69. *Mountain Eagle*, April 13, 1973, p. 3.

70. Memorandum from the President Requesting Coordination at the Federal Level, September 2, 1966.

71. Section 204(b)(1) of the Demonstration Cities and Metropolitan Development Act of 1966; Sections 401(a) and 403 of the Intergovernmental Cooperation Act of 1968; President's Memorandum of November 8, 1968, to the Bureau of the Budget; Bureau of the Budget Circulars A-82 and A-82 (Rev.) of December 18, 1967, and January 10, 1969; and Section 102(2)(c) of the National Environmental Policy Act of 1969.

72. Office of Management and Budget, "Federal and Federally Assisted Programs and Projects: Evaluation, Review and Coordination" (38 FR 32874). Igor Sikorsky, Jr., in "A-95: Deterrent to Discriminatory Zoning," *Civil Rights Digest*, V (August 1972), 17–19, reported on a progressive use of A-95 to force compliance with the Civil Rights Act.

CHAPTER 6

The Worst Last: The Programs of the Appalachian Regional Commission

> O Almighty God, who has given us this earth and has appointed men to have dominion over it; who has commanded us to make straight the highways, to lift up the valleys and make the mountains low, we ask thy blessing upon these men who do just that. Fill them with a sense of accomplishment, not just for the roads built, but for the ways opened for the lengthening of visions. . . .
> Bless these, our Nation's road builders, and their friends. . . . Amen.
>
> Official Prayer of the
> American Road Builders'
> Association

> One of the first things I was surprised by was the lack of understanding of roads. My God, I said to myself, don't they know that roads mean economic development?
>
> John Waters, Federal Co-
> chairman, Appalachian
> Regional Commission[1]

THE APPALACHIAN REGIONAL COMMISSION must seem an answer to some road builders' prayers. But the results of its programs (including the highway program itself) suggest that as an answer to the most persistent needs of a majority of the region's people and communities, the Commission leaves a great deal still to be prayed for.

The ARC's highway, industrial development, and vocational education programs (its earliest and largest) remain the most substantial evidence that instead of initiating and controlling enlightened and innovative development, the Commission acts primarily as a rationalizer and facilitator of conventional private development. When after several years' experience in those areas the Commission attempted some "people" programs, such as health care, the results were generally unsatisfactory and in some cases regressive. And as it approached its second decade of operation, some of its projected programs (tourism and enterprise development, for example) remained seriously out of phase with the region's anticipated need for affordable, effective human services; environmental reconstruction;

responsive public institutions; and the development of natural resources for the public good.[2]

Quick Start: Rationalizing Private Development

During the 1965 Senate hearings on the act, the executive vice-
president of the American Road Builders' Association testified before
the Senate Committee on Public Works that "the highway industry
is ready to move into this new program without delay."[3] It was not
an overstatement. The political bargaining that preceded the passage
of the act left highways as virtually the only program no one objected
to, and thus highway construction emerged as the principal strategy
ARC chose in order to make a "quick start" and an immediately visible
impact upon the region.

From its original $840 million authorization for 2,350 miles of
"developmental highways" and access roads, the highway program
grew in seven years to more than a $2 billion authorization for more
than 3,200 miles. Well over half of all ARC money continues to go
for highways.[4]

Criticism of the program from outside the Commission has been
strong, and even ARC's two in-house analysts, Rothblatt and Newman, have charged that no cost-benefit studies were made; that no
one knows whether spending so much for highways is preferable to
other economic development alternatives; that construction has been
"sluggish" (the system was still less than 24 percent complete as late
as June 1973); that transportation alternatives were not considered;
and that corridor locations were frequently chosen for political rather
than sound developmental reasons. Maryland, for example, which
has only three Appalachian counties and more paved roads per square
mile (and a higher per capita income) than the national average,
gained an early advantage in the bargaining over mileage and routes
through its position in the Conference of Appalachian Governors and
PARC. As a result, it received the highest per capita allocation of
ARC highway money and a principal corridor, Corridor E, the location of which caused West Virginia's Corridor H to be moved south
to avoid an embarrassingly close parallel alignment.[5]

It was hardly surprising that even stronger criticism of the highway
program came from within the region; the Commission's own studies
show that the system was designed largely without reference to the
wishes of the majority of its people. Locations and design standards
were especially criticized. Noting that the standards for the devel-

opmental highways had been set below those for the interstate system with which they were supposed to connect, editor Tom Gish called them two-lane "cowpaths to the future."[6]

Like the contemporary designers of urban expressways, the Appalachian highway planners also paid little heed to either the dysfunctional effects of highway construction or its impact upon local communities. The studies assumed that virtually any growth and development were desirable, that highways would produce both, and therefore that social values were hardly at issue.[7] The highways were designed to move raw materials and manufactured goods; human needs were at best secondary considerations.

It is not even clear that the highways produced the narrowly economic advantages claimed for them. In theory the system was intended to "open up" isolated areas to economic development and connect (and thus stimulate) ARC's designated growth centers. In practice, however, it appears that most highway-related development inside the region occurred not in the "opened up" areas but at highway interchanges near established urban centers, and that the system therefore stimulated growth not primarily in the growth centers but in peripheral metropolitan areas outside the region (Atlanta, Charlotte, Nashville, Baltimore). An Ohio State University economist and geographer found after three years of study that the ARC highway program in Ohio was ineffective. "The rich areas got richer and the poor areas did not change," Harold L. Gauthier concluded, citing a General Accounting Office study that called the development highway system in the entire region a "patch-work of highway segments which provide no . . . basis for coordinated development."[8]

Since the main justification for building highways was that they would produce the industrial and commercial development through which it was assumed the immediate human needs of the region's people would at length be served, the highway program cannot be understood apart from the Commission's other efforts to stimulate industrial development. Initial direction came from a series of industrial location studies authorized shortly after the passage of the act and prepared by the Fantus Corporation in 1966.

The Fantus studies encouraged Appalachian communities to seek more marginal industries, even though as early as 1960 the report prepared by the Maryland Department of Economic Development for the Conference of Appalachian Governors pointed out that "too large a portion of the Region's resources have been directed toward attracting weak, low-wage oriented industries such as textiles and apparel."[9] Thus the Fantus report on the capital-intensive and highly profitable chlor-alkali industry discouraged communities from seeking new chlor-alkali plants. But another report in the series called getting a mobile-home or apparel plant "a goal to which more communities can realistically aspire."[10] For the mobile-home industry, communities were advised that labor "must demonstrate good productivity, moderate wage patterns, . . . free[dom] from undue wage pressures" and have a high enough selectivity ratio "to permit screening of undesirable influences" (pp. 4, 24). The report also noted that moving plants from the Great Lakes area (where they were then concentrated), would result in large savings to manufacturers in wages and fringe benefits, because wages in the industry averaged thirty-five to sixty cents an hour lower in Appalachia.

Neither the mobile-home nor the apparel report discussed the negative effects of bringing more marginal industries into the region. Instead, they urged communities to go with the trend. Between 1958 and 1963 New York and New Jersey lost 307 apparel plants; in the same period, 184 opened in Appalachian states. In only four years (1962–66), 78 new men's clothing plants appeared in the region. Apparel plants seek, the report said, "areas of basic female underemployment where experience shows that workers respond with positive work and productivity attitudes." Communities showing "a strong commitment to organized labor" were therefore called "less suitable" locations.[11] Thus the region was offered an industry that even the report itself showed was low-wage (averaging less than $2 an hour at the time of the study), unstable (because of seasonality, import competition, frequent style changes, and other factors), labor-intensive, and antiunion.

The apparel report not only encouraged communities to believe that getting such plants was in their best interest economically but also implied that shifting the industry to Appalachia would have a progressive, indeed a civilizing, function. Implicitly blending images of immigrants who stitched away their lives in ghetto sweatshops with those of the pioneers who settled the West, the report said the apparel industry "has often [functioned] as a pioneer blazing a trail in virgin territory. Its importance to Appalachia rests not only on its ability to add purchasing power to the inhabitants, but also to socialize people into the industrial work environment" (p. 40). That ability was presumably important to ARC Executive Director Ralph Widner, who the next winter said that the "hollow culture" of Appalachia produced people "who cannot work on the production line."[12]

Consideration of social costs, environmental or political impact, the preferences of residents, occupational health and safety in the industry (for example, brown lung), or the distribution of profits and earnings in specific industries was absent from the industrial location studies. They paid careful attention, however, to the needs of the industries themselves. Translated into the vernacular, the euphemistic statement that in seeking workers, industries are sensitive to "expectable responsiveness to incentive wage patterns" meant that Appalachian workers would be expected to accept the piecework and speed-up rejected by unionized workers in areas from which apparel factories were fleeing.[13]

The emphases of the early industrial location studies and the direction of ARC's subsequent efforts were at length reflected in the actual results of industrial relocation decisions. A 1970 ARC report claimed ninety-six new plant locations and more than fifteen thousand new jobs in Central Appalachia since the passage of the Act in 1965, but Keith Dix showed that nearly 30 percent of the new plants and more than half the jobs were in textiles and apparel. The majority of other new jobs were in coal mining or other extractive enterprises that had long constituted the other principal industrial activity in the region.[14]

In a final recommendation, which revealed the interdependence of separate ARC programs, the apparel industry report urged (p. 41) that a trained labor force for the factories be provided at public expense through vocational-technical schools. It was a recommendation well attuned to the intent of the 1965 act.

Like the highway program and the industrial development effort, ARC's vocational-technical education program came into being largely because none of the governors objected and because industries wanted it. It became one of ARC's proudest accomplishments, photographed and reported on time after time in *Appalachia,* the Commission's public relations magazine.[15] Appropriations for vocational education totaled $90 million through 1969 and $160 million through 1974, and the Commission's stated goal was to build enough facilities to accommodate half the eleventh- and twelfth-grade high school population of the entire region.[16]

But it was primarily the needs of industries, and not those of the region's people, that had shaped the program. Noting the paradox that vocational training received emphasis in the 1965 act even though the region needed two hundred thousand college graduates to bring its share up to the national average, ARC's former director of youth leadership, James Branscome, said that "Appalachians have a choice of becoming skilled machine laborers, or starving." Thus in 1969 the State of South Carolina, with ARC assistance, having noted that only about one-quarter of its high school graduates had previously gone on to college, decided that college-preparatory courses should be deemphasized in favor of vocational courses.[17]

The underlying premise of the vocational education program is that it is both a public responsibility and a benefit to the region's people to provide at public expense skilled workers trained to the specialized requirements of specific industries. What industry prefers, two of the location studies point out, is "training by requisition," which is candidly defined as "public, on-the-spot training of a work force for specific jobs that must be filled when a new [plant] is about to be established."[18]

But the premise is at variance with some of the values and assumptions upon which public education has been based in the rest of the country. The Jeffersonian principle is that democracy can thrive only when each individual citizen receives an education that liberates and strengthens her or his unique human potential and develops broad critical and analytical abilities. Because the need for such an education is especially critical in an exploited region, the vocational education program is a double disservice to the region's people: It locks them into the fickle job-demand system of marginal industries and deprives them of the analytical skills needed to press for long-term reconstruction of the region.[19]

After Quick Start: People Programs

As the phase-out of the Office of Economic Opportunity proceeded under the Nixon administration, and as the limitations of the ARC's own early programs (highways, stimulation of industrial development, vocational education) became manifest, the Commission began a well-publicized attempt to develop human resources or "people" programs. In the two main areas chosen for concentration, health care and education, the results were hardly more satisfactory than with earlier programs.

Health care. Section 202 of the 1965 act authorized $69 million "for the construction, equipment, and operation of multi-county . . . health facilities" in order "to demonstrate the value of adequate health . . . facilities to the economic development of the region." By 1970 health-care programs had come to claim more of the ARC budget (7.4 percent) than any other program except highway construction. Through 1974, $215 million had been spent.

When the Commission set up a Health Advisory Committee in 1965 to begin implementing the provisions of Section 202, health and health-care problems in the region were critical: scarce and outdated facilities, few doctors, high infant mortality, malnutrition, virtual absence of preventive care, high rates of communicable disease, and special occupational diseases such as black lung (among miners) and brown lung (among textile workers). The Committee's recommended emphases (regional service, comprehensive care, demonstration of "new health service techniques") were reasonable enough, but the Commission launched no actual programs for more than two years, and there was scant evidence that health problems would be measurably improved through the new programs.[20]

The Commission's first approach, the building of new hospitals, struck Harry Caudill as a "patent absurdity" before the ink was dry on the ARC legislation. As early as 1964 *Mountain Eagle* editor Tom Gish noted that lack of operating funds had forced three hospitals to close in Letcher County, Kentucky, during the previous seven years.[21] The Advisory Committee's own report noted, in fact, that the need was not for more buildings but more services.[22] In 1967 Congress removed the restriction against supplying ARC operating funds to hospitals not constructed with Section 202 money, but such problems of allocation were only the beginning.

The basic problem of the ARC health program can be succinctly stated: The limits it set in its own guidelines prohibit truly innovative approaches, and even within the narrow limits set by the guidelines the stated objectives were not achieved.

In almost no area of human need in the region have conventional assumptions, approaches, and systems of service delivery proved adequate. But instead of moving outside conventional boundaries, ARC reinforced and extended them. As soon as the Section 202 demonstration health areas were chosen, there arose a "concern within influential segments of medical practice in the Region that the Appalachian Health Program would be a device for overturning the private practice of medicine."[23] The Commission therefore wrote into its guidelines language designed to placate local medical societies by requiring that the "development and operation of any community health service under Section 202 shall preserve and encourage all existing programs and arrangements involving the relationship between the physician and the patient."[24] To insure that the guidelines would be observed, the governing boards of the local health councils were heavily weighted with doctors and "established local leaders." As of 1970 the Commission reported that "no area has successfully obtained effective representation of the disadvantaged" on the health councils, which it said "generally represent the existing power structure."[25]

But within the program's narrow limits, what actually happened in health care? Initial studies indicated that there was little substantial change in the level or quality of available services, that medical care remained beyond the financial means of most families, and that the Commission had not successfully demonstrated any new approaches to medical care. One analyst, generally favorable in his assessment of the Commission, called the health program "a case study in the travails of attempted innovation."[26]

David Danielson's extensive study of the health program in 1970 concluded that the choice of health demonstration districts was made "in a highly politicized atmosphere"; that three years after the program was authorized $20 million in appropriated funds were uncommitted and "nothing had happened"; and that subsequent fears of a budget cut caused the Commission to spend $19.6 million in less than three months on hastily approved projects.[27] Danielson also found that the Commission rejected the usual Public Health Service requirement that health boards have 51 percent consumer representation; that one 202 agency was apparently set up primarily to get a new hospital for a clique of physicians; that 69 percent of health facilities construction money had been spent for conventional hospitals (some of which were called "gold-plated" and "lavish" even by the doctors); that there was little coordination between the multicounty demonstration health areas and the multicounty development districts; and that much publicized screening programs had not been followed up by efforts to correct the defects discovered.

Danielson concluded that the 202 program "follow[s] the lead of imperfect State and Federal programs, and buys 'more of the same' rather than trying new paths which could lead the Nation out of the maze of high-cost medical care." A 1974 study by the comptroller-general of twenty-four ARC health projects in Kentucky was more blunt: "A comprehensive regional health network, as defined by ARC," the study concluded, "has not been achieved."[28]

The Commission's black lung program provided a striking example of its inability to cope with a widespread health problem peculiar to the region.

Coal workers' pneumoconiosis (black lung) is caused when miners breathe fine particles of coal dust suspended in the air in coal mines. The dust collects in tiny nodules in the lungs, destroys lung tissue, impairs the transfer of oxygen to the blood, destroys small blood vessels, and eventually leads to enlargement of the heart and early death. Once black lung begins it can progress even without further exposure to coal dust. Ten years' work in a mine is so certain to precipitate the disease that both the United Mine Workers and the Black Lung Association have argued that it should be accepted as definitive proof that a miner has black lung.

Although ARC was not the first public agency to delay attention to black lung, it had less justification for doing so than any other except perhaps the Bureau of Mines. As early as 1813, autopsies had shown that the lungs of coal miners were blackened, and by 1833 some doctors were asserting that the condition was caused by mining.

The British government declared black lung a compensable occupational disease in 1943, established a sophisticated screening and treatment program, and by 1965 had reduced the incidence of new cases to four-fifths their former level.[29]

But in the United States it has been a different story. Although by 1950 the Public Health Service had established that coal miners were five times more prone to respiratory diseases than other workers, it did not ascertain the actual incidence of black lung until 1963. Doctors in the United States were reluctant to recognize the disease. Until 1959 Cecil's *Textbook of Medicine* denied that breathing coal dust was dangerous and suggested that it might even benefit miners by slowing silicosis (a disease they were admitted to have). As late as 1966 Harrison's *Principles of Internal Medicine* equivocated on the causes of black lung.[30] It was 1969 before Title IV of the Federal Coal Mine Health and Safety Act recognized black lung as a compensable occupational disease.[31]

The Appalachian Regional Commission did nothing in relation to black lung until the Senate Public Works Committee, in hearings on the 1969 amendments, made clear that it must. In November 1970 John Whisman presented what he called an "action plan on coal mining problems," and in 1971 the Commission initiated a series of studies for a scheduled 1972 conference. One $38,000 study, designed to discover what makes men want to work in coal mines, concluded that they did so because it was the best job available, the pay was good, and the alternatives were scarce. Another showed that black lung cost workers, companies, and consumers $50 million a year but could be prevented for $31 million per year, or a maximum of 13¢ per ton of coal mined. In January 1973, UMWA President Arnold Miller charged in a letter to ARC's Federal Cochairman Donald Whitehead that the Commission's action on black lung had been "criminally slow." A few months later the guidelines were finally approved.[32]

When the Commission finally began a black lung screening and diagnostic program early in 1973, it was beset with problems. Although a comprehensive approach was indicated ("Concentration of miners . . . has more to do with the location of coal seams than with state boundaries," Arnold Miller said), ARC's "federalism" led to a fragmented state-by-state approach. During the first half of 1973, the Commission funded three separate programs in Ohio, West Virginia, and Tennessee.[33]

ARC's black-lung programs also sought to guarantee that the entrepreneurial medical system would not be disturbed. A proposal to establish a black lung clinic at the East Tennessee Chest Disease Hospital noted that the program would be "integrated into the current miner-physician encounter system without disrupting [it] by working with the . . . dedicated but overburdened physician . . . in a supportive way." About the same time, however, the *Louisville Courier-Journal's* Kyle Vance reported that some "dedicated but overburdened" doctors in Kentucky were boosting their incomes by four thousand to ten thousand dollars a month by handling black lung claims for both miners and coal companies.[34]

The most immediate beneficiaries of the Commission's black lung program may in fact have been physicians and consultants. Late in 1972, after working on its guidelines at meetings from which reporters were barred, the Commission let two controversial contracts for assistance with its program. A contract with Macro Systems, Inc., to develop screening and diagnostic services provided a fee of $469 per day for the project director, $322 per day for a "project manager," and $184 per day for a "senior consultant." Even a research assistant was to be paid $70 per day (the equivalent of $20,000 per year). Both Macro Systems and the ARC defended the fees as reasonable.[35]

A second contract authorized American Health Profiles to supply a design for a mobile black lung screening van, a plan for its use, and an "awareness" program for potential users. Doctors working on the design were to be paid $250 per day. Many authorities questioned the suitability of mobile vans for screening because they offered little privacy, caused patients to wait outside in bad weather, were unreliable technically when delicately calibrated equipment was jarred during travel over rough mountain roads, and were perhaps less economical than fixed-site alternatives.[36] But the van was nevertheless built and was unveiled with considerable publicity by the governor of West Virginia. After remaining parked in front of the state capitol for three days (screening no miners), it departed for the midwest. The van remained the property of AHP, leading some critics to charge that the net result of the contract was for the ARC to buy AHP a black lung van.

In early 1972, recognizing the limitations of some of its earlier approaches to health care, the Commission began to place additional emphasis on what had come to be called primary care, defined by one consultant as the care "most of the people need most of the time."[37] During the ensuing two years, the ARC spent more than $7 million on thirty-seven primary care projects in eleven states (less than $95,000 per project per year), which it advertised as evidence that it was capable at last of the boldness and innovation in health care called for by Section 202.

One of the programs of which it appeared proudest was the Hot Springs (North Carolina) Health Program. In fact, however, the Commission had nothing to do with the creation of the highly successful

Hot Springs program. Its later commitment of support, though substantial, was hedged with conditions that proved difficult to meet. And some of the most important policy implications of the program had little discernible impact on larger Commission strategies for dealing with health care.

The Hot Springs Health Program was conceived and begun by Linda Mashburn, a nurse who had spent four years in the late 1960s conducting health fairs throughout the region as an employee of church groups and the Council of the Southern Mountains.[38] As a location for an experiment in providing primary health care to low-income people, Hot Springs was appropriate both practically and symbolically. Situated in one of North Carolina's far western counties, where poverty and illness were widespread and health care virtually unattainable, the town took its name from mineral springs whose reputed curative properties had drawn the wealthy to its elegant hotel and baths since the early nineteenth century.

But in the early 1970s the health needs of most of the 5,500 people who lived in Hot Springs and three surrounding townships were little better provided for than they had been 170 years earlier. A small cinderblock clinic, built across a weed-grown field from the old hotel and baths (a faded sign on the wall still advertised baths for $1.50 and a gallon of mineral water for 50 cents) by descendants of the original hotel owner, had stood empty for eight years. The county had four doctors, but none would accept Medicare or Medicaid patients. The nearest general hospital was in Asheville, thirty-five miles away by a winding mountain road.

Within a few weeks after Linda Mashburn arrived in February 1971 (and despite opposition from the county's four-doctor medical society), the old clinic building had been rented and renovated, a community organizational meeting held, and a steering committee formed. On May 1 the clinic opened, its services and policies controlled by a board elected from among community people. From a shoestring operation using all volunteer personnel and with a budget of $5,000 provided by a foundation grant, the clinic grew to a staff of seventeen in eighteen months. By 1974 it had a staff of twenty-five, and two satellite clinics had been opened in outlying areas. More than four thousand patients were paying the clinics more than seventeen thousand visits a year.[39] Services (for which patients paid according to a sliding scale) included treatment for acute and chronic illnesses, physical examinations, dental care, family planning and well-baby care, drugs, home health care, and health education in the local school system. Intensive use of paramedical personnel, especially family nurse practicioners, allowed the program to function adequately with only one full-time physician.

In September 1972, sixteen months after it opened, the Hot Springs Health Program received its first $190,000 grant from the Commission. Two annual grants of $221,000 followed. But the Commission's requirement that its health projects become self-supporting after five years resulted in an anxious visit from the North Carolina governor's ARC stand-in, J. D. Foust, in January 1975, after data in a new Hot Springs program proposal showed that Madison County could not possibly support a quality medical program solely through patient fees. A subsequent meeting of ARC-funded primary care personnel in Johnson City, Tennessee, produced a resolution stating that it was imperative that the Commission develop a plan for providing long-term support for health care to low-income people. Although long-term funding of neighborhood health centers by HEW was cited as a precedent and analogue, the proposal met with little enthusiasm from ARC planners.

Education. The Commission's first thrust in education was its vocational education program, which complemented its emphasis on highways and industrial development and implemented the early recommendation of its Education Advisory Committee that the whole secondary education curriculum in the region be revised to "increase the relevancy of regular school courses to the world of work."[40]

A later, less heavily funded effort took the form of Regional Education Service Agencies (RESAs), designated as "the first priority for action by the states" and intended to provide "economies of scale" in delivering varied services on a cooperative basis to small school systems. The programs provided by the RESAs—media services, early childhood education, special education, staff development, adult education, research—were vitally needed by Appalachian school children and their families. But the RESAs were not instituted until 1970 and received during that year less than $1 million, as against the $104 million by then committed to vocational education.[41]

The disparity between RESA funding and vocational-education funding suggests that the Commission gravitated to approaches to education not in conflict with either the expressed wishes of industries or a narrowly technocratic approach to human problems. Such a conclusion was confirmed by a recent venture in education carried out by ARC in conjunction with the RESAs: the Appalachian Education Satellite Program (AESP). Though smaller and newer than most of the Commission's other programs, AESP raised issues that had substantial predictive value as the Commission requested renewal of its legislative authorization for what John Whisman called "the payoff decade."

The AESP's history was complicated, but its aims were relatively simple: to use a Fairchild-built Application Technology Satellite

(ATS-6) launched on May 30, 1974, to beam 100 hours of instruction in reading and "career education" prepared by the University of Kentucky to 1,200 Appalachian teachers from NASA's Rosman, North Carolina, control center to receiving stations at five of the Commission's RESAs. The satellite ("one swinging spacecraft," a Fairchild executive called it), which cost the public $206 million and was scheduled to remain aloft six years, also was to send programs to the Rocky Mountain states and Alaska before its signals were redirected to Ahmedabad, India.[42] The University of Kentucky assured participants that they would "absorb a solid core of the most reliable, up-to-date knowledge in the fields of reading and career education."

A more immediate beneficiary, however, was Fairchild Industries, which built the satellite as a pilot project for its entry into the commercial satellite business. Fairchild's earnings quadrupled during the second quarter of 1974, partly as a result of revised accounting procedures related to its new commercial satellite operations.[43]

Though sophisticated technologically, AESP was naive in conception and not suited to the region's most pressing educational needs. Several critics suggested that even if its aims were defensible, they could have been accomplished more easily and cheaply by using cable television, inexpensive cassettes, or other conventional means. Even David Larimore, project director for the University of Kentucky, conceded, "We aren't doing anything that can't be done some other way." Asked late in 1974 why cable television was not used for the program, a Clinch-Powell, Tennessee, RESA official told Catherine Foster of the *La Follette Press* that "we just wanted to experiment with the program. And if you put it on commercial television or the cable, just anybody could get it. And nothing kills a program faster than the misinformation that can be spread about it. That's why we wanted to put it on the satellite."[44]

The ARC reacted defensively to the criticism. Harold E. Morse, project director, said, "I was a little suspicious like the mountain man when I first heard about the satellite, but now that I've thought about it, it's the only way to go. . . . I am convinced that telecommunications satellites will be to Appalachia what small landing strips were to outlying villages in World War II." Later Morse called AESP "the forerunner of more ambitious satellite projects to help crack the cultural isolation of Appalachia."[45] But whether the region was in fact culturally isolated, and whether, if it was, that isolation could or should be "cracked" by satellites or any other means remained open to serious question.

Although Morse maintained that "local input" was sought in designing the project, there was little evidence that significant input was obtained. Numerous critics in fact suggested that consultation with local people in Appalachia's tax-starved school districts would almost certainly have placed higher priorities on raising teachers' salaries, buying school books and clothing for children who needed them, upgrading the region's universities, or even establishing a regionwide cable television system.[46]

If one must judge from the naiveté of the program's design and content, even the relatively low-priority needs of the 1,200 middle-class master's degree candidates who received AESP appear not to have been well served. In early 1974, responding to criticism of AESP, Federal Co-chairman Donald Whitehead made public a transcript of a University of Kentucky videotape justifying and explaining the project. It is worth quoting at some length:

> [Each teaching session has] a programmed instruction feature. Each participant, equipped with . . . a panel of four buttons, will listen to hypothetical teaching situations and be asked to choose among alternative approaches to the problem posed. After pressing a button corresponding to one of the four alternatives, he or she will hear a recorded discussion of the merits of that answer. . . . On the afternoon of every fourth television session, the participant can also expect to take part, by . . . telephone, in a live television seminar keyed to the continuing course work. . . . This kind of regular two-way contact [will guarantee that] course work will apply to his or her own teaching situation. . . .
>
> What really sets this program apart, however, is that all participants will [have] access to . . . an information system that will permit [the University of Kentucky] computer center . . . to make specialized searches . . . of all available literature and instructional materials in these fields. [There will also] be telephone terminals to provide rapid access to information stored in the [University of Kentucky] system. . . . All these high-quality services will be available through the RESAs. [The University] is spending a great deal of time, effort, and expertise to insure the reliability of these systems.[47]

Thus the Commission's position remained that "satellite television has a future in Appalachia's educational system. . . . If the project proves feasible, as there is every indication it will, then it will be appropriate to consider whether educational funds available in Appalachia can most wisely be expended by expanding the project." Ironically, the videotape transcript itself warned that "all too often big projects with . . . lots of money end up as relics or curiosities. Leaving little behind, they are soon forgotten. Nor is it unusual for projected technological solutions to human problems to ignore or do violence to the individual's life and work."[48]

Program Design for the Payoff Decade: Out of Touch and Out of Phase

In mid-1973, near the end of its first eight years of operation, the Appalachian Regional Commission launched a "program design effort" calculated both to evaluate its past programs and to project new programs in anticipation of Congressional reauthorization hearings scheduled for early 1975. To accomplish the former aim, it allocated $850,000 for hiring consultants to review existing programs; to design possible new programs, it set up eight subcommittees of its own state representatives, eventually assisted by other consulting firms.[49]

But the Commission's record of improving programs designed by one contingent of consultants and found faulty by a later set was not encouraging. It seemed likely that new programs would therefore be no more useful than their predecessors. Two projected programs that suggested how problematic the "payoff decade" was likely to be in Appalachia were "culture and tourism" and "enterprise [that is, industrial site] development."[50]

Culture and Tourism. During the winter of 1748 George Washington visited the "famed warm springs" at Berkeley Springs, Virginia (now West Virginia). By 1774 the first cabin had appeared at White Sulphur Springs, and by the early nineteenth century tourism was already a growing enterprise in various parts of the region.[51] It brought wealth to a few but demeaned many more. As early as 1860 Frederick Law Olmsted's *A Journey to the Back Country* took note of mountain women picking blackberries to sell to resort hotels northeast of Asheville in the Blue Ridge mountains. In 1905, Emma Bell Miles commented in *The Spirit of the Mountains*, "Too late the mountaineer realizes that he has sold his birthright for a mess of pottage" when the hotels arrive, and "the semblance of prosperity . . . vanishes with the departure of the summer people."[52]

But tourist development has nevertheless continued to be prescribed as a "natural" strategy for improving the lot of Appalachian people, and ARC became its chief exponent after the demise of ARA. John Whisman consistently proposed tourism as a prime development strategy, from his earliest work in eastern Kentucky through the Conference of Appalachian Governors and ARA. In early 1964, before he joined ARC, he spoke enthusiastically of "Cloud City" and "Magic

Mountain," two visionary tourist complexes planned for eastern Kentucky but never built.[53] Inside ARC itself, his enthusiasm remained undiminished despite a lengthening series of reports showing that tourism was not a good development strategy.

The first report, a study completed by Robert R. Nathan and Associates only a year after the ARC was formed, pointed out that jobs generated by the tourism industry required low-level skills, that "few . . . pay a living wage," that most (75 percent) were seasonal only, and that almost none were covered by collective bargaining. At Capon Springs, Virginia, where resort activity had been important since the eighteenth century, investigators found women who were heads of households working twelve hours a day for $7.00 plus tips and living during the half-year the resort was closed on $16 per week in unemployment benefits.[54] The report concluded that the usual economic impact of tourist development was "marginal," citing Gatlinburg, Tennessee, as an example of intensive development that benefited few and exploited many. Groping for justifications for continuing such development, the report ventured that it could "raise the aspirations of local residents whose horizons are broadened by contact with outsiders."

The 1966 Robert Nathan study was actually the first step in a four-phase ARC recreation and tourism plan for the region. In addition to providing an inventory of existing recreational development, it also designated twenty-three "terminal complexes" as "focal points of . . . development over the next two decades" and chose fourteen for further analysis in the second phase market-analysis study, which was released in 1971.[55] The third and fourth phases were to include the preparation of "site development" and "implementation" plans for each of the fourteen complexes.

The 1971 market-analysis report was an ill omen for the region. Discussing the problem of environmental control, it cited Disneyland as "a new standard of total environment" to which recreational complexes should aspire.[56] It was an odd recommendation indeed for an area already blighted with more than its share of "theme parks": Hillbilly Worlds, fake Indian villages, and Tweetsie Railroads. For private tourism developers, the report recommended public subsidy. "In those complexes that are not yet developed as recreational centers," it said, "the public sector might have to pioneer the initial construction and operation of recreational facilities, until . . . markets become large enough to justify private investments." One of the terminal complexes chosen for intensive development was Boone, North Carolina, which was already experiencing serious difficulties as a result of uncontrolled private tourism development during the late 1960s. Another was the nearby Mount Rogers, Virginia, area, where local citizens were organizing to oppose further public development.

As the years passed, evidence mounted that tourism was not a desirable basis for economic development, but the Commission's policy of promoting tourism remained unchanged. As early as 1965 a study for the Commission done by Litton Industries concluded that "local income and employment multiplier effects" from such development were "practically nonexistent in areas without a sizeable city" and cautioned that jobs in the industry were seasonal.[57] The warnings were repeated by the Robert R. Nathan study of 1966 and were spelled out in detail by a three-volume study submitted to the Economic Development Administration (EDA) just as ARC formed its Culture and Tourism committee in 1973.[58]

The EDA study, which focused on the economic impact of specific tourist development projects, included five Appalachian projects already in operation. At Carter Caves, Kentucky, 28 percent of the thirty-nine jobs created were permanent, and average annual income for all jobs was $2,206. Only twelve out of one hundred jobs at Greenbo Lake State Resort Park (Kentucky) were permanent. The eighty-eight seasonal employees earned an average of $1,935 per year. The Breaks Interstate Park (Virginia and Kentucky) provided $1,793 average annual incomes for eighty-one employees, only eight of whom worked throughout the year. At the Cass Scenic Railroad (Virginia), average incomes were much higher ($4,877), but workers had raised their incomes only $1,027 on the average, and only twenty out of 140 employees had year-round jobs. At Pipestem State Park in West Virginia, built with about $13 million of ARA and EDA funds, slightly more than a third of the jobs were permanent, and employees earned an average of $2,932 per year.[59]

The chairman of ARC's Culture and Tourism committee insisted in mid-1974 that the committee's work was oriented merely toward "taking stock" rather than actually promoting tourism, but a committee staff member had earlier admitted to a reporter, "Instead of being open to what, if any, role ARC might play, we're starting with the idea of promotion."[60] To have done otherwise would in fact have been inconsistent. The Commission had already designed its highway and vocational education programs partly to reinforce an emphasis on tourist development. And it had been promoting tourism more directly through a series of contract studies stretching over ARC's entire history and costing $500,000. As early as 1969, ARC funds had built a fifty-seven-unit motel-restaurant training complex at the Tri-County Vocational Education High School and Technical Institute at Nelsonville, Ohio, and a smaller "hospitality training center" was later started at the Asheville-Buncombe Technical Institute in western North Carolina.[61] The centers were built to train Appalachian young people as functionaries in the tourism industry—motel operators at best, and maids, janitors, waitresses, and filling station attendants at worst.

Thus the dynamics of the tourism industry itself and the history of the Commission's prior involvement in tourism development both suggest that there will be more promotion and further extrapolation of existing trends. A $50,000 study prepared for ARC in 1974 by Centaur Management Consultants, which had earlier done the tourism study for EDA, recommended, in fact, that the Commission inaugurate a $300,000-a-year market research program and a $2-million-a-year television advertising campaign to provide for "continued development and expansion" of tourism in the region. The study played down environmental problems related to tourist development, which it said were associated almost solely with second-home construction.[62]

What the results of further promotion are likely to mean at the local level can be illustrated by the case of western North Carolina (the site of one of ARC's terminal complexes), where tourism has long been a principal industry.

One of the earliest centers of tourism development in western North Carolina was Watauga County. Blowing Rock became a resort center in the 1880s, and shortly thereafter Moses H. Cone (the "Blue Denim King" from Greensboro) bought and developed a 3,600-acre estate nearby. A small surge of development came with the creation of the Blue Ridge Parkway in the late 1930s, but until the end of the 1950s the county remained mostly an area of small, locally owned farms. In 1960 its population was less than 18,000 (fewer than 55 persons per square mile, compared to nearby Buncombe County's 201).

But beginning in the early 1960s, resort and second-home development boomed in the county. Local developers, such as Grandfather Mountain's Hugh Morton from neighboring Avery County, added their efforts to those of large out-of-state corporations such as Carolina Caribbean to produce the boom. Within the next few years, such large resort developments as Hound Ears, Beech Mountain, and Seven Devils had sprung up. By 1968, in an article on ARC in *Harper's*, John Fischer cited the county as one the Commission had helped save by tourism development, and ARC's 1971 marketing study recommended more tourist promotion, more motels, and new lakes ("flat water recreational resources") to attract more tourists.[63]

But all was not well in Watauga County. By 1974, a meticulous study by the North Carolina Public Interest Research Group showed that 23,350 acres of the county (roughly 12 percent of its total area) were in the hands of corporate and nonlocal owners. About half appeared to have been committed to resort development. The number of second homes had increased by 250 percent between 1960 and 1970. Half-acre lots were selling for $20,000 at the Hound Ears resort; condominiums averaged $80,000.[64]

In nine other counties, patterns were similar. For the ten-county area studied intensively, nonlocally owned land increased 26 percent between 1968 and 1973, and a majority of it was concentrated in large parcels held by out-of-state buyers. During the five-year period there had been a dramatic increase in both the volume of land sales and prices (land that sold for $100–$250 per acre in Cherokee County in 1966 was selling for $2,000–$2,500 in 1974). More than seventy thousand acres were committed to resort development in the counties. Carolina Caribbean, the G. F. Company, and Sugar Mountain owned 16,300 acres in Avery County; Liberty Life Insurance held 20,400 in Burke and Jackson; three Florida firms (Realtec, Jones, and Collier and Gonzalez) owned 26,000 in Jackson and Transylvania; Carolina Ritco, a Miami firm, held title to 35,800 in Jackson; and DuPont had acquired 11,000 in Henderson and Transylvania. There were fifty-seven parcels of more than 1,000 acres each; more than half were wholly or partly owned by out-of-state investors.

The contrast between the living standards of local people and those in the second-home developments and resorts was striking. The ten-county area had acquired 13,000 second homes by 1960 but contained 60,000 substandard locally owned homes. In 1973, there were 400 second homes in Madison County, where 66 percent of the local housing was substandard. In 1970, the median value of all owner-occupied homes was $11,700, but the average cost of a resort lot was $13,000; prices ran up to $50,000 in such places as Avery County's Invershiel.

Economic benefits of resort development to local people, the study said, had been "significantly overstated" by planners and developers. The average large resort hired only twenty-five people; and Macon County, one of the fastest developing, had experienced 27 percent out-migration in the 15- to 30-year age group during the five-year period.

The negative environmental impact was found to be severe: flooding caused by the disruption of existing drainage patterns; increased erosion and siltation from the clearing of large areas for golf courses and ski slopes; a strain on water supplies; and inadequate sewage treatment. There were, the report concluded, "no real restrictions on what a developer may do to the land." Stanley P. Whitcomb, president of the Realtec Corporation of Fort Lauderdale, which owned the 4,700-acre Connestee Falls resort in Transylvania County, said his company pledged that in its developments "nature shall not surrender to man, but . . . man shall enhance, preserve, and protect nature, our inheritance, with all the resources at our command." But Michael Epley, chief planner for Transylvania County, called the development practices at Connestee Falls "abysmal."[65]

Ironically, about the same time the North Carolina PIRG study documented the negative impact of tourist development upon local people and communities, other evidence suggested that the tourism bubble itself might burst, and ARC might be called upon to bail out faltering developments in order to salvage its own tourist development policy. In late July the Groundhog resort near Hillsville, Virginia—2,600 acres of second-home lots, condominiums, and "tennis chalets"—filed for bankruptcy.[66] Less than a month later, Carolina Caribbean's Beech Mountain resort in Avery County, North Carolina, reported financial difficulties, and Governor Holshouser (at the suggestion of Secretary of Natural and Economic Resources James Harrington, a former executive of the county's 3,000-acre Sugar Mountain resort) asked that Beech Mountain be included in the ARC's upcoming tourism study by Centaur Management Consultants.

Although Harrington insisted that no federal or state aid to Beech or other resorts was contemplated, the *Winston-Salem Journal-Sentinel* reported that the study could "serve as the basis for offers of financial aid." A month later, a *Mountain Eagle* reporter quoted Harrington as saying the Centaur study was "significant because it will document the case for public assistance to troubled resorts." Carolina Caribbean had by then reported a loss of $6 million for 1973 and was $20 million in debt. Beech Mountain's president denied a report of bankruptcy, but in mid-November the parent company admitted losses of $9.3 million for 1974 and announced the sale of its Saint Croix, Virgin Islands, property at a $3.1 million loss.[67]

A report by the *Mountain Eagle* at the end of 1974 strengthened suspicions that despite its repeated disclaimers, ARC contemplated financial assistance to resorts. A $25,000 ARC contract to the Sea Pines Resort Company in fact produced a study that recommended property tax breaks for resorts and a system of land banking "whereby the government would purchase mountain land from hard-pressed landowners and then sell or lease it back to developers." Sea Pines owned 6,750 acres of resort land in North Carolina's mountainous Clay County and had been given the study contract after hosting a May 1974 ARC staff meeting at its Hilton Head, South Carolina, resort.[68]

Thus a significant component of ARC's "program design" effort for the "payoff decade" was tied to a development strategy whose economic value to the region was marginal and whose political, cultural, social, and environmental effects were largely negative. It was a strategy borrowed from, and shown ineffective by, the early days of the Area Redevelopment Administration. Another questionable borrowed strategy surfaced in ARC's program design effort as "enterprise development."

Enterprise development. Prohibited by Section 224(b) of the 1965 act from making direct ARA-type loans or grants for industrial or commercial development, ARC had to rely on its highway and vocational education programs, as well as other indirect means, to implement its growth center and "trickle-down" strategy of serving the interests of businessmen and industrialists first and the majority of the region's people later if at all. But with its enterprise development proposal it moved toward direct subsidies, primarily through industrial site development.

In March 1974, ARC awarded a contract to Katherine Peden and Associates to design the enterprise development program. The firm, asserting quite unaccountably that ARC had had "very little contact with the business establishment" in the region since 1965, recommended amending the act to allow direct grants for industrial development. Nearly 82 percent of the $76.4 million expenditure recommended was to go for the acquisition and development of industrial sites.[69] The study also recommended that ARC set up a Private Sector Enterprise Development Advisory Committee to "make the private sector more aware of what the Commission is doing and . . . give the Commission an understanding of how it can help the private sector do more for enterprise development."

Many of the study's recommendations were formulated in a "private sector working seminar" conducted by Peden at Knoxville's Hyatt-Regency Hotel early in May. Among those who joined John Whisman and other ARC staff members for the seminar were vice-presidents of American Electric Power Company and J. P. Stevens (textiles); Beth-Elkhorn's David Zegeer (overseer of the company's Letcher County, Kentucky, strip-mining operations); and representatives of Armco Steel, Consolidated Natural Gas, Columbia Gas System, Pennsylvania Power and Light, Union Carbide, the West Virginia Coal Association, and the Westvaco Corporation.[70] The seminar produced vehement complaints against federal environmental and occupational health and safety regulations. One participant asserted, "There's no such thing as social responsibility in a business that's not making a profit." Others suggested that ARC become an "ombudsman for Appalachian businesses and industries." Although the evils of welfare programs were emphasized, there was consensus on the need for government subsidies for industrial site development.[71]

The contorted logic of the seminar was paralleled by conflicts of interest among its participants. They reached from the local and relatively recent effect of Beth-Elkhorn's influence on ARC's Kentucky River Area Development District, to the broader attempts of an American Electric Power company subsidiary to block public development of the New River's hydroelectric potential, to the long-standing regressive influence of private utilities upon Appalachian development legislation. One participant, the multinational Westvaco Corporation, which had 1973 sales of more than $650 million and operated thirty pulp, paper, and chemical plants in nine of the thirteen Appalachian states, was currently involved in eleven suits charging the company with violating antitrust laws and atmospheric emission regulations and with using discriminatory employment practices.[72]

However useful an enterprise development program might prove to be to Westvaco and others in the "private sector," the potential usefulness of site development in the region was open to question. As early as August 1968 *Mountain Life and Work* reported that a 120-acre Paintsville, Kentucky, site provided with paved roads, parking lots, fire hydrants, and lighting at public expense had been abandoned twice and was growing up in weeds. Repeated efforts had been made by the Kentucky River Area Development District over the next few years to entice a manufacturer to use two sites at Whitesburg and Jackson, also prepared at public expense. But in late 1974, three months after the enterprise development study was released, KRADD's executive director reported that both sites were still unused.[73]

The Future of ARC

Although President Nixon had proposed terminating ARC in his 1971 and 1972 budget messages, Congress continued to provide funding ($272 million for fiscal 1974).[74] But the Commission was increasingly embattled and defensive. An ARC memo of early 1974 suggested that reallocating Commission funds on a subregional basis "could provide the sizzle that sells doubters in Congress and the Nixon administration."[75]

In late 1974 the Commission announced a series of public meetings in each of its seventy local development districts ("ARC's first serious public accounting to and dialogue with Appalachia's residents," Federal Co-chairman Whitehead called them) and hired a Philadelphia public relations firm to explain ARC to the public.

The public meetings afforded scant opportunity for authentic dialogue. Meeting schedules and informational materials were delayed until the last minute, and the number of meetings was vastly reduced. Audiences consisted mainly of LDD staff personnel and local officials, who watched an ARC-prepared slide show and responded to questions designed to project the Commission in a favorable light. At the Bedford, Pennsylvania, meeting there were no coal miners or steel workers in evidence; plainclothesmen were 'reportedly hired to keep undesirables out of the December 3 meeting in Wise, Virginia. John Whisman spoke repeatedly of the ARC's coming "payoff decade," but in moments of candor he admitted that the growth center strategy "never really worked," that "regional planning and democracy are not necessarily compatible," and that he had no idea how to control strip-mining or keep coal profits in the mountains. Audience response ranged from complaisant in Asheville, North Carolina, to skeptical and restive at Bedford, to openly hostile in Wise.[76]

Legislation to reauthorize ARC until 1979 was introduced in 1975, accompanied by allusions to the Commission's "solid advances" and its "pre-eminent concern for respecting and fostering that special spirit of the Appalachian people."[77] A flurry caused by a *Courier-Journal* report of possible misuse of states' administrative funds by John Whisman subsided rather quickly after a brief investigation by the governors, and the bill moved into committee hearings.[78] The hearings themselves seemed carefully managed to ensure reauthorization. No hostile witnesses were called, and some sessions were conducted before a lone legislative aide. The Senate subcommittee's scrutiny of ARC was confined largely to a series of written questions submitted to governors and Commission officials. The questions were superficial, and answers from the states were so nearly identical in some instances as to suggest that they may have been prepared by ARC itself and merely submitted by the states.[79]

Except for a surprising assertion by West Virginia's Governor Arch Moore that "we must go beyond the outmoded concept of growth centers [because] they do not fit . . . any part of Appalachia with which I am familiar," and a cogent suggestion by Dr. Vernon Wilson of Vanderbilt University that ARC consider taking "health care services to where people live" and allowing them to be planned by the communities themselves, the hearings produced no significant analysis or criticism of the Commission. The dominant motif was expressed by South Carolina's Representative Kenneth Holland to Governor Moore: ARC "is an economic force that you need desperately. And we intend to see that you get it."[80]

On December 31, 1975, the president signed P.L. 94-188 into law, reauthorizing the Appalachian Regional Commission for four years. Congress granted the Commission authority to spend $1.02 billion on highway construction through 1981 and $640 million for non-highway projects through 1979.

Notes

1. Quoted in Robert Goodman, *After the Planners* (New York: Simon & Schuster, 1971), p. 79, and *People's Appalachia,* I (August–September 1970), 14, respectively.

2. Each observation could be substantiated by an analysis of almost any program, and each problem is observable during every period of ARC's history. But for the sake of simplicity I have chosen to consider the problems in a roughly chronological sequence, illustrating each with a specific program or programs drawn from the period in which both the problem and the program were especially prominent in the Commission's activities.

3. U.S. Senate, *Hearings Before the Committee on Public Works, U.S. Senate . . . on S. 3,* 89th Congress, 1st Session, January 10–21, 1965, p. 205.

4. See Monroe Newman, *Political Economy of Appalachia: A Case Study in Regional Integration* (Lexington, Mass.: D. C. Heath, 1972), pp. 113–21; Donald N. Rothblatt, *Regional Planning: The Appalachian Experience* (Lexington, Mass.: D. C. Heath, 1971); and *Annual Report of the Appalachian Regional Commission* (1973), pp. 16 ff.

5. Rothblatt, *Regional Planning,* p. 87. For another critical consultant's study, see Ernest H. Manuel, *The Appalachian Development Highway Program in Perspective* (Washington, D.C.: Appalachian Regional Commission, 1971, mimeo), esp. pp. 4–14, 23, 57. The main critique prior to Manuel's was John M. Munro, "Planning the Appalachian Development Highway System: Some Critical Questions," *Land Economics,* XLV (May 1969), 149–61. Some of Munro's details, but few of his arguments, were challenged by Manuel.

6. *Mountain Eagle,* August 11, 1966.

7. A pertinent example is the ARC-financed study *Capitalizing on New Development Opportunities Along the Baltimore-Cincinnati Appalachian Development Highway* (Washington, D.C.: Appalachian Regional Commission, 1968) (on Corridors D and E).

8. See Rothblatt, *Regional Planning,* pp. 86–87; Carl W. Hale and Joe Walters, "Appalachian Regional Development and the Distribution of Highway Benefits," *Growth and Change,* V (January 1974), 3–11; and *Columbus (Ohio) Citizen-Journal,* November 2, 1973, respectively.

9. *The Appalachian Region* (Annapolis: Maryland Department of Economic Development, 1960), pp. 18–22.

10. *Research Report No. 6: Industrial Location Research Studies: The Chlor-Alkali Industry* (Washington, D.C.: Appalachian Regional Commission, 1966), pp. 12–25; *Research Report No. 4: . . . Summary and Recommendations,* p. 8. Subsequent quotations are from *Report No. 11: . . . The Mobile Home and Special Purpose Vehicle Industries* and *Report No. 3: . . . the Apparel Industry.* The reports were prepared under an ARC contract by the Area Research Division of the Fantus Corporation of New York. Technically, these and other consultants' reports cited subsequently do not necessarily represent the Commission's official position, but functionally it is difficult to discern substantial differ-

ences between them and official ARC documents, reports, programs, and development grants. In most cases parameters of such studies are set by the Commission before the studies themselves are undertaken.

11. *Report No. 3: The Apparel Industry*, pp. 22–30. In 1964, in order to encourage a certain garment manufacturer to locate in the area, Whitesburg, Kentucky, passed a "right to work" ordinance requested by the company. The ordinance and the company's request were denounced by the *Mountain Eagle*, and the ordinance was later repealed (August 13, p. 1, and August 20, p. 2).

12. *New York Times*, January 6, 1967.

13. *Report No. 4: Summary and Recommendations*, p. 15. "Speed-up" is the practice of running machines or production lines at faster rates than workers have become accustomed to, in order to achieve higher production rates without additional cost to the manufacturer.

14. *Appalachia*, vol. III (April 1970), and Keith Dix, "Appalachia: Third World Pillage?" *People's Appalachia*, I (August–September 1970), 9–13.

15. Richard Powers's evaluation study, *The Vocational Education Program in Appalachia from Fiscal 1966 Through Fiscal 1969: An Appraisal* (Washington, D.C.: Appalachian Regional Commission, 1971) (mimeo), p. 9, calls the program a success. See *Appalachia*, I (May 1968), 18 ff.; I (August 1968), 28 f.; II (November 1968), 23 ff.; II (February 1969), 13; III (August 1970), 1–8; VI (June–July 1973), 1–21; and *The Status of Secondary Vocational Education in Appalachia* (Washington, D.C.: Appalachian Regional Commission, 1968).

16. *The Appalachian Experiment, 1965–1970* (Washington, D.C.: Appalachian Regional Commission, 1971), p. 57, and 1973 *Annual Report*, pp. 17 and 33, respectively.

17. *People's Appalachia*, I (August–September 1970), 23. Cf. Harry Caudill's objections in "Misdeal in Appalachia," *Atlantic Monthly*, CCXV (June 1965), p. 45, and *State and Regional Development Plans in Appalachia, 1968* (Washington, D.C.: Appalachian Regional Commission, 1969), p. 123.

18. *Report No. 10: . . . Materials Handling Equipment*, p. 29, and *Summary and Recommendations*, pp. 14–25.

19. An alternative analysis of the traditional educational system holds that instead of reflecting the Jeffersonian ideal, its chief function has been to socialize students into the materialistic, nationalistic, and philistine values of the culture. In either case, the ARC vocational-education program extrapolates the less desirable features of our educational philosophy and experience.

20. See *Appalachia*, I (December 1967—January 1968), 1–4.

21. Caudill, "Misdeal in Appalachia," p. 46, and *Mountain Eagle*, January 2, 1964, p. 2 (cf. January 15, 1970, p. 2, for a later criticism of ARC's "bricks and mortar" approach to health care).

22. See *The Appalachian Experiment, 1965–1970*, pp. 62–63. Nevertheless, the report noted, 58 percent of the Section 202 funds through fiscal 1970 went for new construction. James Branscome reported in late 1972 that a new hospital built with ARC funds in Jellico, Tennessee, did not open for three years because staff could not be found. *Mountain Eagle* (November 1972), p. 3.

23. *The Appalachian Experiment, 1965–1970,* p. 63. As of 1970 there were twelve 202 areas in all Appalachian states except New York.

24. *Ibid.,* p. 63. Cf. *State and Regional Development Plans in Appalachia in 1968* (Washington, D.C.: Appalachian Regional Commission, 1969), pp. 67–68, and Newman, *Political Economy,* p. 140. Jack E. McVey, "Eastern Kentucky Cardiopulmonary Diagnostic Program" (mimeo report to ARC, 1973), p. 25, notes that the recommended program "seeks to augment and support the present health care system in Appalachia, not replace it."

25. *The Appalachian Experiment, 1965–1970,* p. 63. A new policy adopted late in 1972 was aimed at making hospital boards (but not health councils) more representative. See *Louisville Courier-Journal,* October 10, 1972, p. B-1. On the political and cultural assumptions and problems associated with changing the health-care system in the region, see an article by James Branscome in *Mountain Eagle,* November 9, 1972, p. 3.

26. Newman, *Political Economy of Appalachia,* p. 140.

27. David A. Danielson, *The First Years of the Appalachian Health Program* (Washington, D.C.: Appalachian Regional Commission, 1970, mimeo), pp. 22 and 44.

28. *Ibid.,* p. 64, and *Review of Selected Activities of Regional Commissions* (Washington, D.C.: Comptroller-General, 1974), pp. 22–24.

29. See Brit Hume, *Death and the Mines: Rebellion and Murder in the UMW* (New York: Grossman, 1971), p. 67, and Estie Stoll, "Coal Mining: The Way to a Dusty Death," *The Sciences,* August–September, 1971, p. 29.

30. Stoll, "Coal Mining," pp. 6, 29–30, and T. R. Harrison (ed.), *Principles of Internal Medicine* (New York: McGraw-Hill, 1966), pp. 935–36. Estie Stoll pointed out that in 1963 the Public Health Service spent $100,000 for a black lung study, and the European Coal and Steel Community spent $9 million in research on the disease. When expenditures in the United States finally totaled $1 million in 1966, the ECSC annual budget was $20 million. For further comparisons between U.S. and European practices, see *Coal Patrol,* no. 13 (May 16, 1971), pp. 1–2, and no. 19 (January 24, 1972), pp. 6 ff.

31. On delays in providing benefits under the act, see Arthur E. Hess, "Disability Procedures: Statement of Steps and Rationale for Action Taken . . ." *Papers and Proceedings of the National Conference on Medicine and the Federal Coal Mine Health and Safety Act of 1969* (Washington, D.C.: 1970), pp. 41–50, and *Louisville Courier-Journal,* June 18, 1974, p. 11.

32. Danielson, *The First Years of the Appalachian Health Program,* p. 24; Bill Peterson, "Action Plan on Coalmine Problems Shows Scant Results," *Louisville Courier-Journal,* April 10, 1973, p. 13; Lucille Langlois, *The Cost and Prevention of Coal Workers' Pneumoconiosis* (Washington, D.C.: Appalachian Regional Commission, 1971, mimeo); and Miller to Whitehead, January 10, 1973 (cf. *Louisville Courier-Journal,* January 19, 1973, p. B-1). In the interim, miners themselves organized the Black Lung Association, struck repeatedly over black lung legislation and benefits, and elected Miller as reform president of the UMWA. See Hume, *Death and the Mines,* pp. 94 ff.

33. McVey's report, "Eastern Kentucky Cardiopulmonary Diagnostic Program," recommended that ARC set up a central Department of Coal Health and Safety in the Region.

34. *Louisville Courier-Journal,* July 21, 1973.

35. See *Mountain Eagle,* October 26, 1972, p. 1. The contract (No. 73-52) was for $39,100. The controversy was reported on in *Mountain Eagle,* January 11, 1973, pp. 1, 19; *Charleston* (W.Va.) *Gazette,* January 16, 1973; and *Louisville Courier-Journal,* January 13, 1973, p. B-16, and March 28, 1973, p. B-1.

36. The American Health Profiles contract was No. 73-64 (for $23,000). Among those objecting to black lung vans was UMW President Arnold Miller.

37. *The Scope of Primary Care and Emergency Medical Services,* undated ARC mimeo report, ca. April 1974.

38. Information on the Hot Springs program is taken primarily from a series of interviews in August 1974 and February 1975.

39. Priscilla Guild, "Summary Descriptive Report: Hot Springs Health Program," mimeo report, University of North Carolina School of Public Health, April 1974.

40. *The Appalachian Experiment, 1965–1970,* p. 56. The Committee was established in August 1966; its report appeared in December 1967.

41. *Ibid.,* pp. 57 ff., and *Annual Report of the Appalachian Regional Commission, 1970,* pp. 60 ff.

42. Fairchild quotation from *Louisville Courier-Journal,* January 27, 1974, p. 1. Other information on the AESP is from a series of articles by Phil Primack and Anita Parlow in the *Mountain Eagle,* January 17—March 21, 1974; an unpublished investigative report by Anita Parlow; official Commission documents; interviews with Commission officials; *Appalachia,* VII (June 1974), 1–9; and *Communications Technology for Education and Health Care in Appalachia,* prepared for ARC by Washington University's Center for Development Technology in July 1972. The ATS-6 project originated in, and was funded by, the National Institutes of Education (formerly the National Center for Educational Technology in the Office of Education). A $2.2 million grant from the Institutes enabled ARC to participate.

43. *Washington Star-News,* July 24, 1974, p. 16.

44. *Louisville Courier-Journal,* January 27, 1974, p. 1. *La Follette Press* report reprinted in *Mountain Eagle,* October 17, 1974, p. 5. The Center for Development Technology report showed that, as in the rest of the country, about 80 percent of the homes in the region were served by educational television.

45. *Richmond* (Va.) *Times-Dispatch,* January 31, 1974.

46. Cf. *La Follette Press* article cited above, which raises these priorities.

47. *Mountain Eagle,* February 21, 1974, p. 4, partially reprinted in *Appalachia,* VII (June–July 1974), p. 6.

48. *Ibid.,* pp. 7–9, and transcript.

49. For a criticism of ARC's reliance upon consultants, see *Charleston* (W.Va.) *Gazette,* November 23, 1973.

50. Others were health and job development; environment and natural resources; transportation, housing, and community development; education; and institutional and development strategy.

51. See John W. Morris, "The Potential of Tourism," in Thomas W. Ford (ed.), *The Southern Appalachian Region: A Survey* (Lexington: University Press of Kentucky, 1962), p. 138.

52. Emma Bell Miles, *The Spirit of the Mountains* (1905; reprint, Knoxville: University of Tennessee Press, 1975), pp. 195–96.

53. *Mountain Eagle,* February 20, 1964, p. 1.

54. Robert R. Nathan and Associates, *Research Report No. 2: Recreation as an Industry* (Washington, D.C.: Appalachian Regional Commission, 1966), p. 73 and *passim.* See a response by Powell Lindsay, "Tourism Not Answer to Ills of Appalachia," *Knoxville News-Sentinel,* January 22, 1967.

55. *Research Report No. 14: Recreational Potential in the Appalachian Highlands: A Market Analysis* (Washington, D.C.: Appalachian Regional Commission, 1971). See also "Recreation Areas Designated in Appalachian Highlands," *Appalachia,* II (October 1968), 11–16, and II (August 1969), 18. There is a close relationship between the ARC's tourism and highway programs. *Research Report No. 13: Highway Transportation and Economic Development* (Washington, D.C.: Appalachian Regional Commission, 1970) notes: "Several [highway] corridors were selected to open up large areas of Appalachia with significant potential for recreation development. Corridors A [Atlanta to Asheville] and K [Chattanooga to Asheville] were chosen in part to achieve this objective" (p. 6).

56. *Research Report No. 14,* p. 80. Early in 1974 Tennessee had a request before the Commission to assist with recreation and tourism projects. Plans were to be prepared by Leisure Systems, Inc. (LSI), of Fort Lauderdale, Florida, under the direction of Elliot L. Lewis, who had previously done large-scale work for Disney and whose other recent projects had included ghost towns. LSI's proposal (which led to contract No. 74-117 for $87,120) said the firm could offer a "totally unique . . . synergistic interaction of creative conceptual skills and sound market and financial analysis." They proposed to interview tourist development operators and investors but not citizens of the affected areas.

57. *A Preliminary Analysis for an Economic Development Plan* (Washington, D.C.: Litton Industries, 1965), p. 115.

58. *Evaluation of Tourism/Recreation Projects for the Economic Development Administration* (Washington, D.C.: Centaur Management Consultants, 1973).

59. Figures are from *ibid.,* II, D-23 ff., 34 ff., 267 ff., 278 ff., and 289 ff.

60. Interview with J. D. Foust, July 3, 1974, and *Mountain Eagle,* March 7, 1974, p. 1, respectively.

61. Richard Powers, "The Vocational Education Program in Appalachia from Fiscal 1966 Through Fiscal 1969: An Appraisal" (Washington, D.C.: Appalachian Regional Commission, 1971, mimeo), appendix, p. 2, and interview with J. D. Foust, July 3, 1974, respectively.

62. *Tourism Policy Study for Appalachia* (Washington, D.C.: Centaur Management Consultants, 1975), pp. ii–xi. Centaur noted that its data on promotion were taken partly from Florida "to allow comparison . . . with a well-developed, or mature, tourism area."

63. John Fischer, "Can Ralph Widner Save New York, Chicago, and Detroit?" *Harper's,* CCXXXVII (October 1968), 2 ff., and *Recreational Potential for the Appalachian Highlands,* p. 129, respectively.

64. *The Impact of Recreational Development in the North Carolina Mountains*

(Durham, N.C.: North Carolina Public Interest Research Group, 1975). The PIRG study was based upon local land ownership records in county court houses, corporate records, and other data.

65. *Ibid.,* p. 26. See also *Southern Exposure,* II (Fall 1974), *passim,* for related articles on tourism in western North Carolina.

66. *Winston-Salem* (N.C.) *Journal-Sentinel,* July 26, 1974.

67. *Ibid.,* August 13, 1974; *Mountain Eagle,* September 12, 1974, p. 3; and *Durham* (N.C.) *Morning Herald,* November 13, 1974. The Centaur study confirmed the probability of bankruptcy for Beech Mountain.

68. James Branscome, "ARC Considering Recreation Study Proposal for Area," *Mountain Eagle,* December 26, 1974, p. 1. Branscome also noted that former South Carolina governor (and ARC states' co-chairman) Robert McNair and Jimmy Konduras (a former ARC governor's representative) were attorneys for Sea Pines.

69. *An Enterprise Development Program for Appalachia* (Louisville: Katherine G. Peden and Associates, 1974).

70. My letter of September 23, 1974, to Katherine Peden and Associates, asking how participants for the seminar were chosen, elicited no reply.

71. *An Enterprise Development Program,* pp. 179–80.

72. *1973 Annual Report: Westvaco on the Move* (New York: Westvaco Corp., 1974), p. 27, and telephone interview with A. T. Brust, Westvaco Public Relations Manager, September 23, 1974. Westvaco's earnings were up 269 percent over the previous year.

73. *Mountain Life and Work (MLW),* XLIV (August 1968), 21, and "Report of Executive Director, Kentucky River Area Development District," October 24, 1974, p. 2.

74. *Louisville Courier-Journal,* January 30, 1973, p. 4, and *Mountain Eagle,* January 18 and February 8, 1973.

75. *Louisville Courier-Journal,* January 27, 1974, p. B-1.

76. See a series of reports in the *Mountain Eagle,* August 8, September 19 and 26, October 3 and 31, November 7, and December 12, 1974.

77. *Congressional Record,* CXXI (April 23, 1975), 6537 ff.

78. On the allegations against Whisman, see *Louisville Courier-Journal,* March 17 and 25, 1975; *Congressional Record,* CXXI (April 23, 1975), 6539; U.S. House of Representatives, *Hearings Before the Subcommittee on Economic Development of the Committee on Public Works and Transportation . . . to Extend the Appalachian Regional Development Act of 1965,* 94th Cong., 1st Session, March 18–20, 1975, *passim;* and U.S. Senate, *Hearings Before the Subcommittee on Economic Development of the Committee on Public Works [on] Extension of the Appalachian Regional Development Act,* 94th Congress, 1st Session, March 10—June 3, 1975, Parts I and II, *passim.*

   Although an audit cleared Whisman of charges that he had mismanaged funds, controversy over his role in the Commission continued. The ARC statute was subsequently revised to deny the states' regional representative veto power over ARC spending, and a three-man committee of governors was appointed to review Whisman's role. The *Louisville Courier-Journal,* May 27, 1976, p. 1, quoted Kentucky Governor Julian Carroll as saying, "My suggestion to [Whisman] is he ought to be looking for a job." See also James

Herzog, "Whisman Has Lost Power, May Lose Job in ARC Changes," *ibid.*, April 13, 1976, p. B-5.

79. Senate, *Hearings on Extension*, Part II. To a question on the ARC's development plan, identical answers were submitted by Kentucky (p. 35), Maryland (p. 120), Ohio (p. 150), Pennsylvania (p. 174), and West Virginia (p. 268). Identical responses to a question concerning early criticisms of the highway program by Professor John Munro came from Kentucky (p. 52), Maryland (p. 129), Ohio (p. 164), Pennsylvania (p. 183), South Carolina (p. 199), and West Virginia (p. 301).

80. House *Hearings to Extend*, p. 139.

PART III

REACTIONS AND ALTERNATIVES

CHAPTER 7

One-Eye in the Land of the Blind:
The Appalachian Volunteers

> First thing I knowed, there was an organization called the Appalachian Volunteers, over in Berea, Kentucky. And you'd look out and you'd see jeeps comin' up the hollers, Scouts, Volkswagens, you know, foreign things to us, you know . . . long hair, miniskirts, beards, horn-rimmed glasses. The damn mountains . . . was swarming with Appalachian Volunteers.
> Native eastern-Kentucky organizer

FOR MORE THAN a hundred years, students have found the Southern Appalachian mountains an appealing place to exercise their idealistic impulses. When Berea College opened its doors in 1855, the first teachers were Oberlin College students, hired to teach during their winter vacations. Mount Holyoke students went to teach in Kentucky's "blab schools" in the 1880s; Middlebury College was encouraging its students in 1914 to "take their education back to the mountains"; a Swarthmore girl was working for John C. Campbell in the Asheville office of the Southern Highlands Division in 1915; and Pine Mountain Settlement School's Katherine Pettit wrote to Campbell in 1916 about "Miss Cathcart, our Illinois college girl." Some of the settlement schools and colleges in the region were founded by those (frequently women) who first came as students challenged by the need for education, medical care, and (so they perennially felt) spiritual and cultural enlightenment in the mountains.[1]

Contrary to the stereotypes of mountain people as universally "clannish" and "suspicious of outsiders," students were usually welcomed into communities except where their presence and activities exacerbated already existing political conflict or threatened economic power relationships. In February 1932, for example, in the midst of the mine wars in the coalfields, eighty students from New York—many of them members of the socialist League for Industrial Democracy (LID) and the more radical National Students League—set out by bus for eastern Kentucky's "bloody Harlan" County. Headed north from Knoxville on the last leg of their journey, they were met at Cumberland Gap by the sheriff of Bell County and an armed posse of 150 men. The sheriff took them to the Middlesboro courthouse, questioned them, and summarily ejected them from the state. A month or so later another busload was stopped at Cumberland Gap (which had become a sort of Scylla and Charybdis for radical students entering the mountains) and taken before a kangaroo court in the same courthouse. Disdaining even the semblance of due process in ordering the students out of the state, Colonel Reed Patterson, a mine-owner and attorney, warned them that "the white streams of these mountains will run red with communist blood before we surrender our country."[2] In West Virginia, however, where miners themselves had a tradition of militant union activity, student members of both the LID and Pioneer Youth managed to conduct educational and recreational programs for coal-camp children even in the midst of class warfare. Elsewhere in the mountains (for example, Marion, N.C.) Pioneer Youth ran camps for the children of blacklisted textile workers.[3]

The Appalachian Volunteers (AVs) were thus born of a tradition that had both conservative and radical strains, and their efforts eventually partook of both. Early in 1964, when the fledgling organization was confining itself to painting one-room schoolhouses in eastern Kentucky and most AVs were from colleges and universities inside the region, the *Louisville Courier-Journal* said they were doing "more good per dollar spent than any group, governmental or private, in the history of depressed areas." But by 1967, when a more radical strain had surfaced and the AV staff was made up mostly of outsiders, the conservative *Lexington Herald* struck an explicit parallel between the AVs and the troubles of an earlier time:

> In the 1930s groups of radical writers, Communists and just plain publicity seekers converged on southeastern Kentucky bent on "helping" the coal miners and poor families. . . .
>
> The poor . . . actually were exploited by these uninvited visitors who by devious means sought to stir up trouble and make the people unhappy with their lot. . . .
>
> Is Appalachia again being invaded by self-appointed helpers of the poor? . . .
>
> This is no time for fly-by-night organizers and radical bearded students who know nothing of the problems of Appalachia to be going among the people and stirring them up. [These] busybodies . . . can render the best service by returning immediately to their classrooms.[4]

As the AVs extended the two traditions of student activity in the mountains for six years during the turbulent late 1960s, they both carried forward the long history of missionary efforts in the region and at length presented what proved to be one of many organized challenges to the federal programs of the decade.[5]

Fathers and Sons: The AVs and the Council of the Southern Mountains

After fifty years of more or less marginal work in the region, the Council of the Southern Mountains in 1963 was on the verge of its most heavily funded and influential period of activity. Problems in the region had been forced onto the front pages by John F. Kennedy's West Virginia primary campaign of 1960, and there were growing unemployment and unrest among coal miners, especially in eastern Kentucky. Federal money had already begun to flow through the Area Redevelopment Administration, and additional antipoverty legislation was being projected. Perennially hard pressed for funds, the Council turned to the federal programs.

Although as early as June 1963 the Council had asked the Ford Foundation for money for "a volunteer-type of [organization for] young people in education and social service," the immediate impetus for establishing the Appalachian Volunteers seems to have come from Richard Boone of the White House special projects staff. Boone asked the Council's Milton Ogle if he could get Kentucky college students to spend Saturdays as an unofficial domestic peace corps in the state's eastern counties, in conjunction with President Kennedy's program to winterize schools and homes.[6]

There were eight hundred one- and two-room schools in forty-four eastern Kentucky counties (Pike had 75, Floyd 64, Perry 51, Clay 49, and Leslie 48), most of which were in poor repair. Fixing them up appealed to the spirit of voluntarism, self-help, neighborliness, and paternalism that had long characterized the Council. Twenty years earlier, in fact, the Council had conducted an almost identical schoolhouse painting project in cooperation with settlement schools and the American Friends Service Committee. During the summers of 1943–45, students repaired schoolhouses in Wolfe, Knott, Harlan and Leslie counties, and *Mountain Life and Work* speculated:

> If, in this program of work camps in which young people from one part of the United States are willing to pay their own way to work . . . in another part of the country . . . , we can help create bonds of interest and affection, we will have done much

toward the future understanding of the mountain region and perhaps have called attention to some of the ways in which, non-violently, the economic and social problems of the region can be solved.[7]

The first call for volunteers in 1964 brought responses from nearly a thousand students (mostly from within the region) and hundreds of local community people. On the second Saturday in January, the first volunteers renovated a one-room school on Upper Jones Creek in Harlan County, installing a new floor and sheetrock on walls, fixing windows, and putting on a new coat of paint. Later in the month, Richard Boone addressed the "founding conference" of the Appalachian Volunteers at Pine Mountain Settlement School.[8] By the end of the winter, volunteers, working on Saturdays and using materials donated by manufacturers and local businesses, had renovated forty-four schoolhouses. During the next several years, they renovated several hundred.

In March 1964 the Johnson administration arranged for a six-month, $50,000 ARA grant to expand the AV effort. Chosen to head the AVs was thirty-year-old Milton Ogle, who had come to Berea from a rural Virginia county, stayed on after graduation to manage the student industries broom factory, and then become "community development counselor" with the Council.[9] Aided by the ARA money, Ogle expanded the program along the lines already established. Dr. Luther Ambrose, a retired Berea education professor, was hired as supervisor of field operations; Flem Messer, a poor Clay County boy who dropped out of school in the fourth grade at the age of fifteen and later had gone on to finish college, was hired as a field worker. Also hired was Jack Rivel, a New Jersey native who had gone to Union College in Barbourville and then to work with the "Lend a Hand" project on nearby Stinking Creek.[10]

During the ensuing months, recreational and "educational enrichment" programs and community meetings to plan development projects were added to the AV agenda, but the organization did not depart from the self-help approach Ogle and Messer had learned as youngsters and relearned at Berea College. In an October 1964 letter soliciting renovation materials from businesses, Ogle stated what amounted to the AVs' central premise: "Deprived people cannot be helped; they must help themselves."[11]

Ogle and others were presumably aware that the coal counties where schoolhouses were being renovated had become a powder keg as unemployment rose to record levels, that the UMWA had withdrawn welfare cards and closed its miners' hospitals, and that "roving pickets" had shut down dozens of nonunion mines. Nevertheless, they insisted that self-help projects were necessary to gain the good will of officials in the feudal counties.[12] Indeed, as some of those officials became uneasy about alleged connections between the AVs and more militant groups, the AV board assured them that the organization "favors no political or social point of view and takes part in no campaigns or promotions." The Council informed its own membership that it had "issue[d] a statement to eastern Kentucky newspapers . . . because [the AVs] had been confused . . . with another, footless, pointless aggregation of 'rousers' from outside the mountains who [are causing] considerable confusion in some mining towns." The AVs, the statement continued, "hope to change the bad conditions [but] they do not enter into every . . . embroglio that may arise out of people's reactions to those conditions."[13]

The few critics of the early AVs were thus reassured, and as the program expanded there was nearly unanimous approval from the press and public officials. In cooperation with the national PTA, the AVs placed a million books and 250 sets of new encyclopedias in school houses, and the American Legion donated twenty-one dozen American flags.[14] An editorial in the *Louisville Courier-Journal* contrasted the AVs with the Appalachian Committee for Full Employment, which it called out-of-state people "whose backing and purposes are rather vague" and who have mistakenly chosen "to see the plight of the jobless miner as the result of a plot by greedy employers and cynical public officials." The *Courier-Journal* gave its blessing to the AVs.[15]

All funds for the initial AV operations, except for the ARA grant, had come from private sources, mostly in the form of donated materials. After late 1964, however, the money came primarily from OEO. In December the first OEO demonstration grant approved (for $300,000) went to the AVs. In mid-1965 another $138,530 grant allowed further expansion. By then the staff had grown to ten, and there were four field offices outside Berea (Morehead, Manchester, Barbourville, and Prestonsburg). Plans were laid to initiate a "community intern" program, to establish "outpost education" centers, and to begin work in Tennessee, Virginia, and West Virginia. OEO also assigned 150 VISTA volunteers to the AVs for work during the summer of 1965. Supervised by AV "fieldmen," they worked for the most part on schoolhouses, tutoring and recreational programs, and craft groups. By both the Council and OEO, the AVs were considered a showcase program—evidence that the cynics were wrong, that the War on Poverty was working, and that good will and peaceful cooperation could produce meaningful social change.

Problems with such a conclusion had already begun to show up inside both the AVs and the Council, however. Idealistic students sent to paint schoolhouses soon discovered that fathers were unemployed, health care was all but unavailable, schoolteachers lost their jobs if they challenged the county Board of Education, road repairs were correlated closely with voting patterns, and coal operators controlled county politics. As both students and the AV staff began to cast about for alternatives to painting over the facts of life in eastern Kentucky, there was increasing talk of community organization and a decreasing emphasis upon conventional self-help.

The shift in emphasis came partly from the very nature of community involvement itself but also from some new staff members whose arrival had tipped the balance from indigenous staff and volunteers toward a preponderance of outsiders. From Harvard and a summer as a SNCC worker in Mississippi came Gibbs Kinderman; from New York's Lower East Side via the Harvard faculty came psychologist Dr. Daniel Fox.[16] Both Fox and Kinderman were bright, articulate, forceful, well connected, and (several staff members recall) rather openly manipulative. More personable than either was Alan Zuckerman, a Boston native who had worked for both the Labor Department and OEO.

Other diverse experiences, styles, and perspectives were introduced by Bill Wells, a Quaker and a physician's son from California; Tom Rhodenbaugh, from a Catholic working-class family in Akron, lately involved in community work in Chicago's Uptown and West Side; Mike Kline, a middle-class, suburban Virginia son of a government bureaucrat; Doug Yarrow, a Quaker graduate of Carleton College; Joe Mulloy, a plumber's son from Louisville; and Steve Daughterty, son of a class-conscious United Electrical Workers shop steward from Cincinnati. By mid-1965 the AV staff was, as the Council's Loyal Jones later recalled, a "strange conglomeration of people."

The strangeness of the conglomeration and the diverse theories and approaches to political and social change it spawned eventually caused problems within the AV organization itself. But for the time being the greatest tension was between the AVs and the Council. Throughout late 1965 and early 1966 relations steadily deteriorated, as the AV program in some ways began to overshadow the Council itself. Press coverage was laudatory; the staff was growing; OEO money was increasing ($421,000 in fiscal 1965); and the weekend program had been expanded to a summer program.

The AV staff, increasingly frustrated by the Council's conservatism and Director Perley Ayer's administrative style, began to discuss autonomy. For some months there was a tentative plan (talked over quite amicably with the Council) to make the AVs semi-autonomous and move the office to Bristol, Tennessee. Faced with what he considered to be mounting evidence of insubordination in late April

1966, however, Ayer summarily fired Fox and Ogle. The entire thir-teen-member AV staff thereupon resigned, and the next day the AVs were reorganized as a separate nonprofit corporation. Within a few days, OEO money granted to the Council for use in AV programs had been turned over to the new organization, and the AV office moved to Bristol.[17]

AV Magic: May 1966 to April 1967

> Deep in the mythological substratum of American life is the image of the "summer romance," an image of coming together. . . . The summer is, for Americans, a time when harmonies are possible that cannot be achieved during the workaday year.
> Kenneth Keniston, *The Young Radicals*

The bylaws adopted ten days after the AVs incorporated were cavalier in their statement of aims. "Since the Appalachian Volunteers are opposed in principle to frozen purposes," they said, "the goals and methods of the organization will change in response to the needs of the Appalachian region." The AVs' aims changed almost contin-ually during the ensuing years, but only partially in response to the needs of the region. In a metaphor that revealed a good deal about the organization's view of the region, staff member Gibbs Kinderman said, "The Appalachian Volunteers demonstrate conclusively the truth of the old adage: In the land of the blind, one-eye is king."[18] And although the AVs were in some respects highly successful during their first year of independence, the effects of their rather lofty self-image began to show up quite early.

Within a few days after the move to Bristol, nearly five hundred VISTA volunteers assigned to the AVs for the summer convened for a ten-day training session at East Tennessee State University.[19] They came from all over the country (a substantial number from inside the region itself), represented almost every social class, and had the most diverse motives and degrees of emotional stability. Sent into com-munities that were in some cases already experiencing internal con-flict, their appearance and behavior ranged from conservative and conventional to bizarre and irrational. Their activities (fix-up, tutor-ing, and recreation in most cases) were rarely supervised closely. Some AV fieldmen were responsible for 50–60 VISTAs; a few later de-scribed the experience as "ridiculous," "a circus," and "a disaster." By the end of the summer it was apparent that as a tactic for bringing about change in the region, invasion by battalions of summer vol-unteers was not very useful.

Although the AVs continued to use summer volunteers for several years, the 1966 program was in effect a holdover from the Council-sponsored phase. Already in motion were other currents that would soon predominate. In a proposal to the OEO of October 1965, the AVs requested funds to train "community action interns," local people who would work as community organizers under the direction of AV fieldmen, and to establish "Outpost Education Centers" intended to be used as work-study-living spaces for community action and education. The following February the OEO released funds for twenty interns and five outposts.[20]

With the new programs, the AVs hoped to demonstrate that "the poor can act responsibly in their own behalf" and that "community action programs can be organized to utilize their strengths and meet their felt needs." The irony of acting responsibly in one's own behalf under someone else's direction did not become clear until later. For the time being, the new programs seemed merely a positive way of saying what was by then being said more critically all across the country: OEO's community action agencies (CAPs) were not working, were not serving those they had been designed (however poorly) to serve, and were not controlled by poor people. Instead, they were in many cases dominated by courthouse cliques and county school superintendents who were using them as a patronage mechanism.

The AVs initially intended simply to force the CAPs to implement both the "maximum feasible participation" mandate of the legislation and OEO's own recent guideline mandating that poor people make up one-third of every CAP board. AV activity was concentrated primarily in the eight-county Cumberland Valley area of southwestern Kentucky and a six- or seven-county area in southern West Virginia.

The Cumberland Valley counties (Harlan, Knox, Bell, Clay, Jackson, Whitley, Laurel, and Rockcastle) were rich in coal and other natural resources, but their people were some of the poorest in the United States. County political machines had quickly taken over the early single-county CAPs set up by OEO. Proceeding on the assumption that single-county machines would not be able to control a multicounty CAP, OEO in 1965 merged the single-county units into the eight-county Cumberland Valley CAP. But OEO's assumption did not turn out to be tenable. The only base poor people had was indeed in their own counties. But school superintendents, who (like Harlan County's James Cawood) were usually high-ranking functionaries in county political machines, had long been organized across county lines through their professional associations. They therefore quickly acquired control of the eight-county CAP. Poor people, for whom it took half a day to drive from Rockcastle County to Harlan County, were no match for the machine

Working with sympathetic members of the CAP staff and with VISTAs assigned to both the CAP and the AVs, AV fieldmen began in the summer of 1966 to organize people in the Cumberland Valley to challenge the eight-county CAP.[21] Community caucuses were held, and busloads of people were taken to meetings. By late summer the OEO quota for poor people on the board was filled, after a struggle by both sides to see that the "right" poor people were elected.

But with unemployment at record levels, control of the CAP was vital to the school superintendents and county judges who remained on the board. The continuing conflict reached a climax at a public hearing in Barbourville, attended by both OEO officials and several hundred angry poor people. In late February 1967, OEO defunded the eight-county CAP and re-established one- and two-county units. For a time thereafter the AVs were able to work closely with CAPs in the valley, as they were almost nowhere else.[22]

In the southern West Virginia counties (Raleigh, Mercer, Mc-Dowell, Boone, Mingo, Clay, Wyoming), the economic and political situation was not so desperate. Local people, kept more aware politically by a strong union tradition, were forming community organizations around issues of strip-mining, better roads, and schools. Unemployment was not as high as in the worst eastern Kentucky counties, and the area was somewhat more prosperous. The CAPs were therefore not so important a cog in the system of political control and patronage, but they were the focus for early AV work in West Virginia nevertheless.

Sent to open up AV work in the state in early 1966 were Gibbs Kinderman and Doug Yarrow, whose personal styles and approaches to organizing were quite different. Yarrow, who went to Mingo County, was nondirective; Kinderman was opportunistic and, even by his own admission, somewhat authoritarian and manipulative.

Instead of painting school houses or organizing co-ops, as the Kentucky AVs had done during their early months, Kindermann began with a strategy of reinforcing poor people's organizations and forcing the CAPs to do their job. Using dozens of tightly organized and closely supervised VISTAs to assist local groups and gather information on issues, he hoped to build political power that would cut across local community lines by focusing on issues that affected everyone. The power would be directed, at least initially, against the CAPs.

Most of the CAPs were ineffectual enough to be likely targets for hostility. The most vulnerable appeared to be the Raleigh County agency, whose director was a retired school principal. Its budget was only half as large as the nearby Mingo CAP and only one-tenth that of the $1-million-per-year Kanawha and McDowell agencies. By mid-July pressure on the Raleigh CAP (bolstered by mass meetings of two hundred to three hundred community people) forced the director to resign. Elected as president of the board was "people's candidate" Chester Workman; the AVs' Kinderman became CAP director.

The next summer local people, again encouraged and supported by Steve Kramer and other AVs, took over the Wyoming County CAP and nearly succeeded in another attempt in Nicholas County. A conflict emerged between the AVs and the Mingo County CAP when Director Huey Perry decided to resign at the end of July, and the AVs made some moves toward installing their own candidate as his successor. They were unsuccessful, however, and for a time there was serious talk of using CAP political connections to have the AVs removed from the county. Local community action groups failed to support such a move, however, and by November the AVs were working harmoniously with the CAP.[23]

For many months the CAP-takeover strategy remained a major AV priority, and strategic pointers continued to be taken from the "Kinderman model"—the successful takeover in Raleigh County. Some AVs, however, particularly in Kentucky, began to consider the model heavy-handed, arrogant, and ill suited to the needs of the region. They argued:

1. Where a takeover attempt worked, it was fine, but where it failed (as it had in several places, including the only two counties where the AVs were involved in southwest Virginia) local people were left confused, bitter, disorganized, and sometimes deprived of the patronage jobs that had at least kept food on the table.

2. The large, well-funded and therefore most important CAPs (such as the Big Sandy CAP in northeastern Kentucky) were least likely to be taken over.

3. The so-called Green amendment to the Economic Opportunity Act, passed in 1966, provided a legal basis for county machines to retain control of CAPs.

4. With the escalation of the Vietnam War, control of the War on Poverty was no longer worth fighting for, if indeed it had ever been.

There were those who had believed from the start, in fact, that the AVs should never have taken the War on Poverty seriously. In his pungently written "Report from Verda" in late 1966, Harlan County field coordinator Steve Daugherty detailed the frustrations of trying to force some accountability on one CAP: a school superintendent who controlled the CAP and served at the same time as head of the county planning board, a cynical and manipulative staff, a populace demoralized by years of forced dependency, and OEO's own political decision to continue to fund the county machine through the CAP while denying funds to local poor people whose actions even verged on being "political." The game, Daugherty decided, wasn't worth the candle.

Later, a more fundamental objection to the CAP-takeover strategy was advanced by those (including Daugherty) who argued—contrary to the romantic rhetoric of "maximum feasible participation"—that the unemployed "hard core" poor on whom OEO focused its efforts were neither the easiest group to organize nor the most progressive politically when effective organization was achieved. In West Virginia in particular it also turned out to be a fundamental error to concentrate upon taking over the marginal CAPs rather than working with the stronger and more durable miners' union.

Arguments against the CAP-takeover strategy were further buttressed by the existence of alternative strategies. From very early in its post-Council history (the bylaws statement about "frozen purposes" was prophetic), the AVs had in fact been little more than an umbrella under which various individuals and factions pursued diverse approaches to community and regional problems.[24] Besides the CAP strategy, at least three others were important:

1. *Self-help (or "grassroots economic development").* With its origins in the period of schoolhouse painting and "enrichment" programs, this strategy persisted in several guises throughout the history of the AVs. Woodworking shops, sewing and quilting groups, and craft co-ops were started by the dozens. Evergreen Christmas decorations made by poor people were at one time being hauled out of Wolfe County, Kentucky, by the truckload.

By its most partisan supporters, who projected schemes for multimillion-dollar production and marketing co-ops and scores of small, locally owned industries (for example, the Grassroots Industrial Development Corporation proposed for Breathitt and other eastern Kentucky counties), grassroots economic development was viewed as the bedrock upon which hope for change in the region must rest.[25] Others felt that it not only was of little use economically in a region owned and controlled by multinational energy corporations but also diverted attention from the necessity of structural change.

2. *Community organizing.* Although sometimes used loosely to refer to the whole range of AV activities, in its more specific sense "community organizing" meant forming local, countywide, and (in a few cases) multicounty citizens' associations. At various times the strategy appealed across almost the entire ideological spectrum of the AV staff. Conservatives thought it would lead to the formation of (or reinforcement of existing) self-help economic development projects. Those who took the War on Poverty seriously thought community

organizing would help ensure maximum feasible participation. For those more radically inclined, it seemed to offer a possible base for alternative politics.[26]

The many citizens' associations formed throughout the history of the AVs addressed a wide variety of problems: school lunches, welfare rights, roads, water supplies, housing, health care. In most cases the problems were local, and specific solutions were available even if infrequently implemented. The Highway 979 association, formed by the AVs working in twelve Floyd County, Kentucky, communities, organized a water district, operated a community printing company, and published a newspaper *(The Hawkeye)* so outspoken in its criticism of the local establishment (school superintendent Charles Clark, county judge Henry Stumbo, and Big Sandy CAP director Harry Eastburn) that it was eventually burned out. In Dickenson County, Virginia, where the Pittston Coal Company owned 90 percent of the coal and 50 percent of the population were on welfare and Social Security, the citizens' association forced a referendum to change the form of the county government.[27]

Up to a point, the community organizing approach proved sensible and useful. It arose out of felt needs (for example, hungry school children), produced concrete results (hot lunch programs) fairly quickly in some cases, and gave people a new sense of power over the immediate circumstances of their lives. But it was still based on geographical boundaries that were frequently arbitrary, and it was predisposed to do battle with established local political machines and agencies, even when the very act of battle confirmed the legal legitimacy (if not the moral authority) of the establishment.

3. *Issue-organizing.* By late 1966 there were already moves among some AVs for an approach to organizing more promising than what had come to be called the "bandaid" approach (self-help economic development and community organizing)—one that would lead to broader coalitions, more durable organization, and perhaps bolder political action. Such moves were also under way in some of the citizens' associations themselves. A group of citizens, troubled about welfare rights and impatient with the relative conservatism of the Highway 979 association, formed the more militant Eastern Kentucky Welfare Rights Organization (EKWRO) and moved to cooperate with the newly formed Kentucky Mountain WRO in Harlan County.

Such activity and analogous moves in connection with other issues suggested that community organization might be replaced, or at least augmented, by what came to be called "issue organizing"—organizing around issues, such as welfare rights, black lung, and strip-mining, that affected large numbers of people in many areas. Arguments for issue organizing drew strength from both within and beyond the region. The National Welfare Rights Organization, formed in 1966, had 350 local groups and more than 100,000 members by 1969.[28] Although issue organizing never entirely replaced the earlier and more conservative approaches among the AVs, it emerged as the primary focus after late 1966.

By allowing individual fieldmen to use organizing approaches they found personally congenial and judged appropriate to local conditions, AV director Milton Ogle had built a loose and multifaceted organization whose strength lay in its diversity of approach and its ability to attract bright young people, engage their idealism, and channel their energies toward challenging the legitimacy (if not the power) of finely articulated systems of nepotism, patronage, bureaucracy, open corruption, and covert corporate control.

But some staff members argued that the AVs had in the process become unfocused, uncoordinated, and ineffective. Some AVs (Mike Clark, Steve Daugherty, Sue Kobak, Sam Howie, and others), strongly influenced by Myles Horton's Highlander Center, thought organizing should be nondirective and "from the bottom up." Others (usually, but not always, from upper-middle-class families outside the region) felt that more directive or even manipultive "top down" approaches were justified.[29] The judgment was widely shared, however, that the AVs were involved in a good deal of frenetic and useless activity, were spread too thinly, had virtually no coordination or central direction, and lacked an effective training program for either new AVs or AV-VISTAs. Much energy was being dissipated; some possibly avoidable strife was occurring in local communities; and (perhaps above all) no coherent theory or politics was being developed for the long haul.

Hired on April 1, 1967, to address at least two of those problems (strategy and training) was Alan McSurely. McSurely was known to a few AVs, but he came primarily upon the recommendation of Mike Kline, who had worked with him several years earlier as a juvenile court counselor in suburban Fairfax, Virginia. McSurely had subsequently built a reputation as an effective organizer with the poverty program in Washington, D.C., an experience that had moved him leftward politically. By the time he came to the AVs, he was convinced of the need for a fundamental transformation of the nation's political and economic system, pertinent models for which he located in aspects of both socialism and communism.

McSurely spelled out some of his ideas in a paper entitled "A New Political Union," which he brought along with him to the AVs. He presented the paper as merely a "discussion draft" in which "no word, idea, or theory . . . is sacred" but added that "now is the time to change the words, ideas, and theories—because when the struggle heats up, we must live and die with those ideas we have finally chosen."[30] In view of the "irrelevancy and ineffectiveness" of both major parties, the "inability and unwillingness of the capitalist ruling class to make good on any of [its] promises," the extension of corporate control, and the growth of alienation and despair, he said, "taking national power" was necessary.

Although McSurely's analysis was no more radical than that of some other AV staff members, it was more programmatic. He laid down a national platform, outlined the organization of a National Central Committee, and warned that organizers "must begin preparing themselves to administrate the housing, transportation, steel production, and other programs after we gain national power." Those who might have been put off by the doctrinaire rhetoric he sought to reassure by noting that "Leftists are lovers. We are sensitive, sympathetic, forgiving, and artistic. . . . We like to trust, to empathize, and to give everyone several choices." On the other hand, he said, "revolutions, by definition, cannot be loving . . . or artistic. One must set his goals, determine the theory he is going to operate on, and then *never, never veer* from this path" (italics in original). It was, as former AV staff member Tom Bethell called it later, "a mix of hard-headed political planning and the most gossamer utopianism."

McSurely gave several copies of the paper to other AVs, and one came into the hands of a recently hired economist, Gary Bickel, who considered himself a radical but whom almost everyone else considered a very conservative fellow committed mainly to self-help economic development. To Bickel the paper seemed a sinister "Marxist-Leninist" tract whose author had no place in the AVs—a judgment he incorporated into a heavily annotated copy he circulated among AVs, VISTAs, and local community people. Director Ogle, to whom Bickel gave a copy at the end of McSurely's first week, found it "a totally simple, almost naive plan for rigid domination of a people by a small group."[31] Almost immediately, Ogle restricted McSurely's duties to the writing of some training materials, and two weeks later he fired him.

The AV staff were by no means of one mind about McSurely. Some felt that his ideas deserved discussion and that he should have been given a chance to prove himself. Three circumstances nevertheless combined to force his ouster. Each in some way foreshadowed the future of the AVs: (1) Some of the more nondirective AVs thought McSurely's paper too doctrinaire and programmatic. Their reaction suggested that further polarization over politics and organizing strategy was likely. (2) Perhaps encouraged by Bickel, some local people (including a number employed by the AVs as "community interns") decided that McSurely was "a Communist." The *Lexington Herald's* red-baiting editorial published eight weeks before the firing thus could not be lightly dismissed. (3) McSurely's continued presence on the staff was felt to jeopardize the AVs' foundation funding, which was becoming increasingly important as OEO money became less certain. As long as McSurely stayed, some argued, the AVs had an "image problem." Harvard psychiatrist Robert Coles, who served officially as consultant to the AVs and unofficially as their contact person with several foundations (especially Field and New World), reportedly read McSurely's paper and protested strongly to Ogle.[32]

The magic of the AV summers and its first year of independence was over. The firing of McSurely itself did not end it, but it highlighted the fact that organizational factionalism, anticommunism, the power of the funding agencies, and coal-dominated local politics were closing in as determinants of AV strategy and activities. They had been there all along, of course, but the AVs had managed—with luck, *chutzpah,* and the disarming appeal of youth—to avoid their direst effects.

Conflict over Issue-Organizing: Eastern Kentucky, Summer 1967

> A well-organized and well-financed effort is being made to promote and spread the communistic theory of violent and forceful overthrow of the government of Pike County.
>
> Pike County, Kentucky, grand jury,
> September 11, 1967

Strip-mining was known in eastern Kentucky as early as 1905, when the Lilly-Jellico Coal Company's Vulcan steam shovel gouged its first bites out of the Laurel County landscape. But except for a brief period during World War II it accounted for a minute percentage of total coal production until the advent of a long-term contract offered by TVA to feed its new steam plants more than a half-century later.[33] By the time the AVs were formed in 1963, eastern Kentucky was already well on its way to becoming a strip-mine wasteland of gashed mountainsides, boulder-strewn and silt-covered cornfields, acid-poisoned wells, and silted streams.

Pressure generated by local residents in Kentucky was already sufficient by 1954 to force the state legislature to pass an anti–strip-mining law. By 1966 it had been strengthened with enough amendments to make it the toughest strip-mining law in the country.[34] But the provisions of the law were so cavalierly disregarded that many local people began to take more direct action. Their increasing militance drew individual AVs (and eventually the organization itself) into the fray. But it is nevertheless a measure of the legitimacy of the AVs' claim to having the "one good eye in the land of the blind" that it took them nearly three years to see how critical the issue was. Indeed, it never became a priority with a majority of the AV staff.

Steve Daugherty was beginning to organize around the issue in Harlan County in 1966, and by late summer AVs in Raleigh County, West Virginia, were helping with an anti–strip-mining suit by Clear Creek residents against the Princess Susan Coal Company. Letcher County, Kentucky, farmer John Brown told a *St. Louis Post-Dispatch* reporter that AV-VISTA Mike Shields had helped him "a right smart" in his 1967 battle with strip-mine operator Don Nicewander.[35]

For the AVs, however, the eye of the strip-mining storm eventually centered over Pike County, which was so baronial in its social and economic structure that *Louisville Courier-Journal* reporter Bill Peterson counted more than fifty coal millionaires in the tiny county seat of Pikeville, Bruce Jackson toted up forty prosperous lawyers, and Poor Bottom resident Edith Easterling (the AV field representative) said many people were so frightened of county authorities that they hadn't been out of the hollows in twenty years.[36]

The AVs came into Pike County after their schoolhouse-painting phase was history. Their work centered in Poor Bottom (near the abandoned mining town of Hellier in the south end of the county), and around Island Creek. The Marrowbone Folk School, organized at Poor Bottom on June 1967 as a community center, was not initially viewed as a threat by the established order. But on Island Creek the bulldozers were tearing the mountains apart, and AV Joe Mulloy was helping to organize a local chapter of the militant Appalachian Group to Save the Land and People.

Mulloy, from a conservative Catholic working-class family in Louisville's West End, was drawn into AV work in eastern Kentucky because his mother's people—including his uncle Cliff Carlisle, a superb traditional musician of the 1930s and 1940s, whom he greatly admired—were born and raised there. The futility of painting schoolhouses was soon borne in upon Mulloy by working with radical mine foreman John Tiller in southwest Virginia; accompanying local Appalachian people to Washington for a protest march; talking with Myles Horton of Highlander Center; and (after March 1967, when he moved to Pike County) discussing politics with Alan McSurely, who was living there as a staff member of the Southern Conference Education Fund (SCEF). Through McSurely, Mulloy also met Anne and Carl Braden of SCEF; Hamish Sinclair, who had worked with striking miners in Perry County in the early 1960s; and Bernardine Dohrn, then with the National Lawyers Guild but later with SDS.[37]

On June 29, 1967, Island Creek farmer Jink Ray and about two dozen of his neighbors (including Mulloy and his wife, Karen) stood in front of a bulldozer sent by the Puritan Coal Company to strip land Ray had farmed for forty-six years.[38] During the early days of July the scene was repeated every morning. Defying a court order, Ray stood his ground until Governor Breathitt suspended Puritan's permit on July 18 and revoked it altogether on August 1. Among strip-mining opponents throughout the region, some of whom had taken to dynamiting bulldozers in Knott County that summer, Ray became something of a folk hero.[39] One of Puritan's bulldozer operators concluded that "the days of strip-mining is numbered."

It was too sanguine a view. The powerful Independent Coal Operators' Association (ICOA), guided by Pikeville Chamber of Commerce president Robert Holcomb, had not been idle while Ray sparred with Puritan, Knott Countians blew up bulldozers, and the governor pledged his support to a large anti–strip-mining rally at Owensboro in July. The ICOA, working with county officials (the distinction between them was mostly formal), concluded that Mulloy and McSurely had to go. "We know these people are Communists," Holcomb said. "They intend to take over the county." Pressure was hardly subtle once it began to be applied: Telephone service to both homes was discontinued; Mulloy's auto insurance was canceled, and he was visited by the Pike County sheriff and Chamber of Commerce officials who entertained him with stories of violence encountered by others who had political and social views similar to his.

Shortly after 7 P.M. on August 11 (following a meeting attended by Holcomb, Big Sandy CAP director Harry Eastburn, Judge Bill Pauley, coal operators, and other interested parties), Alan and Margaret McSurely were arrested and charged with sedition under a 1920s statute (KRS 432.040). Just after midnight the scene was repeated at the Mulloys', where books seized (*Quotations of Chairman Mao, Great Russian Short Stories, The Essential Works of Lenin, Catch-22*) were called "a Communist library out of this world" by Thomas Ratliff, who was Pike County Commonwealth Attorney, Republican candidate for lieutenant governor, and a former coal operator and president of ICOA.[40] Two nights later the McSurelys' home was dynamited.

On August 18 the sedition cases were referred to the Pike County grand jury, which returned indictments against the McSurelys, Mulloy, and SCEF's Anne and Carl Braden on September 11. Three days later a federal court declared the sedition statute unconstitutional and dismissed the charges. Neither the McSurelys' nor Mulloy's troubles were over, however. Mulloy was to be fired by the AVs a year later, and for several years the McSurelys remained locked in a complicated battle with Senator John McClellan's Permanent Subcommittee on Investigations.[41]

Aftermath of Pikeville: The AVs and OEO

On July 21, 1967, scarcely a month after Jink Ray and his neighbors stopped the bulldozers for the first time, and in the midst of growing anti–Vietnam War protests on the campuses and militance in the ghettos, Sargent Shriver sent down through the War on Poverty chain of command a memo warning that "every OEO employee and every employee of an OEO grantee [must] scrupulously avoid participation . . . in any activities which threaten public order in any community." Director Ogle forwarded Shriver's memo to his staff, adding his own admonition that "we should be on our guard not to be swept up in this situation."

By the time Mulloy was arrested, the AVs had received about $2.5 million from OEO. To support a staff (including AV-VISTAs) that hovered around one hundred, they depended on OEO for 90 percent of their budget.[42] The AVs were also a showcase program for the increasingly beleaguered OEO, not only running their own OEO-funded programs but also training Peace Corps volunteers for such farflung poverty outposts as Micronesia, Senegal, and Tanzania. OEO needed the AVs for good public relations; the AVs needed OEO to survive.

As the crises of 1967 piled up, relations between the AVs and the middle levels of the OEO bureaucracy remained cordial, but those with the Washington office at the top and the CAPs at the bottom became increasingly strained. Instances in which AVs worked harmoniously with CAPs had always been rare and usually involved either a marginally progressive CAP working with relatively conservative AVs on projects (educational enrichment, water systems, co-ops) that endangered neither CAP nor county machine, or a newly reconstituted CAP in which poor people themselves temporarily held the balance of power (for example, in the Cumberland Valley). As early as 1966, conservative CAPs threatened by politically oriented AVs were complaining to the OEO. The success of the AVs in helping to transfer control of a few CAPs to insurgent poor people's groups helped solidify opposition to the AVs among conservative CAP directors, who saw the Pikeville conflict as the chance they had been waiting for.

One of the most powerful and reactionary CAPs in the AV sphere of operations was the Big Sandy (Pike, Floyd, Martin, Johnson, and Magoffin counties) agency run by Harry Eastburn. Eastburn attended the Pikeville strategy meeting at which it was decided to arrest Joe

Mulloy as a first step toward ridding Pike County of AVs. On September 8, after Mulloy and the McSurelys were indicted by the grand jury, other CAP directors joined in the opposition. Eighteen out of the twenty-four directors in the state signed a statement issued by Al Whitehouse of the state OEO office, condemning the "open rebellion" of the AVs against the CAPs and demanding that all AV activities be made subject to CAP approval.

The Pikeville incident created a minor panic in OEO's national office. Its fate, after all, was in the hands of eastern Kentucky Representative Carl Perkins's House Education and Labor Committee. Responding to a demand from Kentucky Governor Breathitt only a week after the arrests, Shriver announced that AV funds would terminate on September 1 and that the VISTA program might also be eliminated.[43] OEO investigators were dispatched not only to Kentucky but also to West Virginia, where Governor Hulett Smith had raised charges of "immoral conduct" and "promiscuity [across] racial lines" and had demanded that AVs and VISTAs be removed from the state.

At the same time, however, some lower-level OEO officials were maneuvering to continue AV funding. Lawrence E. Williams, mid-Atlantic regional CAP administrator, wrote a bitter memorandum (marked "administratively confidential") to Shriver charging that the CAPs in eastern Kentucky were "ineffectual extensions of the 'power structure,'" that the charges they had raised against the AVs were politically motivated, and that "by the action already taken, we have put OEO in bed with the courthouse crowd."[44] Other statements and letters emanating from state, national, and regional OEO offices contradicted and "clarified" each other repeatedly. In early September, James Ridgeway reported in the *New Republic:* "Quite literally, nobody at OEO knows what its policy is" on the AVs.[45]

It was clear, nevertheless, that the OEO-AV honeymoon of 1964–65, and even the curious period of 1965–66 when the AVs helped lend credibility to the overall OEO program by opposing its reactionary features at the local level, had been supplanted by openly crossed purposes, confusion, and mutual distrust. The AVs themselves, insisting that Mulloy was not guilty of sedition, refused to fire him as the governor demanded and vowed that "with or without Federal funds, the Appalachian Volunteers will remain in Kentucky."[46] But OEO funds were in fact essential, and Ogle undoubtedly knew that the AVs' two major OEO grants (due to expire in April and May of the following year) could not be renewed without considerable difficulty.

Indeed, the AVs' organizational solidarity and resolve implied by their insistence that they would "remain in Kentucky" hardly existed in fact, whatever their relationship to OEO. Nor did external pressure on the AVs cease when the sedition charges were dropped. Internal stress broke into the open late in 1967 and focused again on Joe Mulloy. External pressure reached its peak late the next year.

Pragmatism, Principle, and Survival: The Firing of Joe Mulloy

> They said it would be better if the AVs died anyway. And I said, well, but my mother's furnace isn't paid for. And they couldn't understand what I was taking about.
>
> Native AV

Joe Mulloy was the only AV fieldman registered with a Kentucky draft board. As the Pike County struggle deepened, the board, which had kept a file on his activities, revoked his 2-A deferment and refused to consider his application to be declared a conscientious objector. Under the influence of SCEF's Anne and Carl Braden and some AVs who were Quakers, Mulloy decided to refuse induction and perhaps to accompany the refusal with actions calculated to generate publicity. Informed of his plan, Ogle and assistant director for Kentucky David Walls urged Mulloy to resign from the AVs. Ogle argued that Mulloy's objection to the war was largely a personal matter, that most mountain people did not agree with his position, and that the AV organization should not be called upon (especially just then) to take a position on the war and the draft. Walls added that Mulloy had no "moral right to force others to support his views against their wishes."[47] But Mulloy refused to resign, the lines were drawn, and factions formed.

Some AVs agreed with Walls and Ogle. Others felt that Mulloy's position was sound from both a personal and an organizational perspective: The war was morally wrong and was preventing attention to domestic problems. To support Mulloy, they argued, would move the AVs beyond their myopic, confused, and parochial approach to the region's problems and toward an analysis that comprehended the connections between U.S. imperialism, multinational energy corporations, despotic county machines beholden to coal companies (fast being bought up by oil companies), and poor people up the strip-mined hollows whose sons were dying in disproportionate numbers in the rice paddies of Vietnam. A third faction consisted mainly of local people (VISTAs, community interns) who did not yet oppose the war or the draft and who needed their AV jobs ("my mother's furnace isn't paid for") as many of the well-educated and well-connected fieldmen did not.

Pragmatism, principle, survival—crudely put, those were the options when the question of whether to fire Joe Mulloy came to a vote at a staff meeting at Jenny Wiley State Park in early December. The vote (20–19 in favor of firing) was taken amid charges of procedural irregularity and rumors that some of the local staff had been reminded that their jobs would disappear if Mulloy remained on the staff and the AVs lost their funding. In an odd way, it was homestyle Appalachian politics.

In a statement issued immediately after the firing, Milton Ogle said that Mulloy's decision on the draft rendered him "ineffective to work with the people of the Appalachian mountains." Mulloy, citing the nation's domestic problems and the ironic fact that it was mostly blacks and poor whites who were fighting the war, countered that the United States had too many problems of its own "for us to play policeman to the world."[48]

The 20–19 split came roughly between a coalition of pragmatists and the local "survival" faction, and those who held to principle.[49] The choice was most agonizing for people like Sue Easterling Kobak, who abstained from voting because she thought Mulloy should not be fired but also knew how badly the local AVs (including her mother) needed their jobs. Another local staff person who reportedly had lost his job in a Pike County mine for defending Mulloy against the sedition charges voted to fire him four months later at Jenny Wiley Park. Voting against the firing, nevertheless, was a native eastern-Kentucky organizer who was a veteran and had at various times been a miner, a CAP employee, and a cynically bemused participant in President Johnson's "happy pappy" make-work program for unemployed fathers.

Responses to the firing ranged from far-fetched and fatuous defenses ("if professional athletes . . . associate with known professional gamblers," assistant AV director George Woodring wrote, "they can summarily be prevented from pursuing their livelihood") to polite protest (from the West Virginia staff) to several resignations. The firing shows, Tom Bethell said in his letter of resignation,

> . . . how miserably the [AV] organization fails to practice what it . . . preaches. We talk endlessly about educating people to make their own decisions about the issues that affect their lives. We do not stipulate that their decisions be . . . noncontroversial. To deny to a staff member the same things that we ask him to teach is to make the [AV] program . . . a sorry testimony to hypocrisy.[50]

Hunkering Down: 1968–69

> The AVs are not about to go out of business, as some of our adversaries had hoped.
>> AV Quarterly Report, November, 1968

> As I am the only AV in Whitley County, I can't do too much mass organizing.
>> AV field-staff report, November 1968

It had been a hard year. Some key staff members had resigned; OEO funding was endangered; factions had formed; the AVs had been more or less successfully red-baited in Pikeville (and had red-baited themselves over Alan McSurely). Continued survival was problematic, and the AVs became cautious. A staff memo circulated a few months after the sedition arrests said, "We cannot afford another Pikeville."[51]

Early in 1968, OEO conducted several investigations of the AVs. On April 4 the mid-Atlantic regional director sent a long memo to Acting OEO Director Bertrand Harding saying that West Virginia Governor Smith's charges against the AVs were "ill-founded" and those raised in Kentucky were politically motivated. He recommended continued funding. At the end of June a nine-member OEO team surveyed the AVs in eastern Kentucky at the request of the new governor, Louie B. Nunn. Their report was also generally favorable but advocated closer coordination with CAPs and county officials.[52]

But the freewheeling days of the AVs were clearly over; what little OEO money they could count on in the future would be tightly controlled and would depend on patching up relationships with the CAPs. Overtures to Harry Eastburn's Big Sandy CAP shortly after the OEO report were ineffectual, however. Eastburn refused to support an AV request for OEO funding.

After Pikeville, the only bright spots for the AVs were in West Virginia, where in late 1967 and early 1968 they helped establish the Fair Elections Committee (FEC) in Mingo County and the Political Action League (PAL) in Raleigh, Mingo, and Wyoming counties.[53]

The FEC undertook the monumental task of reforming the elections system in Mingo County, where mine ponies and dead people regularly "voted," the number of registered voters was nearly equal to the total population of the county, and a variety of fraudulent electoral practices had been used for decades by the county political machine. The AVs supported and worked with FEC and PAL (which endorsed and campaigned for a slate of reform candidates in the May primary) but stayed behind the scenes. Bill Schechter, AV field representative in Mingo County, even took the precaution of temporarily leaving the AV staff to work with FEC.[54]

Despite the success of FEC, however, and a general rise in the tendency to self-determination among local people, the AVs' David Biesmeyer reported, after a week of surveying AV work in West Virginia in February, a general "demoralization and disorganization" and a "lack of agreement on goals and techniques." For all practical purposes, AV work in West Virginia ended by midsummer, as various staff members took extended vacations, withdrew, or shifted their energies into the gubernatorial campaign of reform Democrat Paul Kaufman and the race of Jay Rockefeller for Secretary of State.

In late summer, the AVs had their final and most dramatic confrontation with the political power structure in eastern Kentucky. Although the AVs had technically been cleared of guilt in the Pikeville fracas, their adversaries continued to smolder. Governor-elect Nunn had promised upon taking office to rid the state of SCEF (lumped together with the AVs by the Pikeville indictments), and the following spring he created the Kentucky Committee on Un-American Activities. With a budget larger than all other legislative committees combined, KUAC moved on the AVs in Pike County in October, apparently at the request of Robert Holcomb, who had been instrumental in the sedition arrests.

By early September, KUAC investigators were questioning AVs involved in a dispute over the rate structure of a proposed water system for the Marrowbone Creek area. Opposition to features of the system considered biased against poor people was being led by the Pike County Citizens Association (PCCA) and AV field representative Edith Easterling. Other KUAC investigators interrogated AV acting director David Walls, and a public hearing was scheduled in Pikeville for October 14–16.[55]

As an organization, the AVs refused to appear before KUAC, but they were nevertheless the primary focus of the hearings. Accused by one witness of creating "strife and malice" in the county, they were defended by PCCA's Reverend James Hamilton as "the nicest bunch of young people we ever had in the community." Asked whether she was a Communist, Edith Easterling replied, "I am a Republican, and whoever seen a Communist Republican?" She went on to apologize to the people of the county for having helped to elect "that dirty courthouse bunch."

After hearing a number of hostile witnesses, however, KUAC concluded that the "poorly supervised" and "overfinanced" AVs were trying to sabotage the Marrowbone water system, were endangering the local CAPs, and should be "permanently discontinued."[56]

They needn't have bothered. The AVs were on their last legs. The staff was down to thirty-five (from eighty in May 1968), and although a request had been filed with OEO for a half-million-dollar grant for 1969, there was little hope it would be forthcoming. Walls was optimistically attempting to start some new programs (most notably a legal services program led by Yale lawyer Howard Thorkelson), replacing departing "outsider" AVs with local people, redefining the organization to focus on providing "technical and educational services to [community] groups," and scrambling for private foundation money.[57] Sam Howie, returning to the AVs after a few months on the Highlander Center staff, said he was "convinced that there is a true ground [for organizing] somewhere between open revolution and community development and that [the AVs] are the people to find it."[58]

But it was too late. On Devember 19, Walls wrote to West Virginia field director Eric Metzner that the AVs would discontinue operations there on January 1, 1969. The 1969 OEO budget included $116,000 for the AVs in Kentucky, but Governor Nunn vowed not to approve it. On December 31 Walls was in Washington, literally going from door to door in OEO and trying vainly to get the funds released.[59]

During the early months of 1969, Walls sent out reams of proposals to private foundations (especially those with whom Robert Coles was felt to have influence), but money was not to be had. On July 3 Walls wrote to Richard Boone, who had planted the original idea for the organization, "the AVs live!" But later in the same letter he admitted, "I'm currently working for subsistence—$25/week." Walls resigned in May 1970, and a few months later the program was closed down entirely.

Retrospective

Strategically, the AVs had little lasting positive effect upon the Appalachian region. The CAP-takeover strategy, whatever its merits, was rendered obsolete by cutbacks in OEO itself; most county political machines remained relatively intact; strip-mining statutes were not adequately enforced; and most co-ops and community organizations were short-lived.

At the personal level, however, there were positive and lasting—if scattered—benefits. A few local young people, bright and energetic but trapped by circumstances, "broke out" through their association with the AVs. One young woman recalled, "Life was really lonely for me in the mountains, and the school system was very frustrating" before she was drawn into the AV chapter at Morehead State University, where she was strongly influenced by an AV fieldman:

> I spent a lot of time with him, just talking. He was a Quaker . . . and I wanted to know what being a Quaker was. . . . And so I spent a lot of time . . . just being a nuisance. . . . I was one of those Appalachians he had to give some attention to. . . . I would ask him questions a lot. He thought I was strange [and] I had never met anybody like [him] in my life. . . . Finally he got so tired of fooling with me that he got the AVs to give me a Scout and a credit card, so I could do whatever I wanted to. . . . It was sort of like a real awakening . . . to open myself up and feel comfortable with people from a different class than I was from. . . . I felt really loved and appreciated for who I was.

She quickly added, however, that her experience was probably not typical. Few Appalalchian young people were in fact ever on the AV staff.

Effects upon older people who served as community interns or were active in other early AV work seem to have been both more numerous and more positive. Some later became leaders in the black-lung and UMWA reform movements; others organized alternative health care activities (such as those in the Mud Creek area of Floyd County). Still others, such as Jink Ray of Island Creek; John Tiller of Dickenson County, Virginia; Chester Workman of Raleigh County, West Virginia; and Edith Easterling of Pike County, seem to have found significant support for work they were already doing.[60]

The effect of the AVs upon existing community organizations was mixed at best. A case in point is the Breathitt County, Kentucky, Grassroots Citizens Committee for Community Action (GCCA). Although OEO claimed that the impetus for GCCA came from a young AV-VISTA, it seems to have come instead from a young unemployed native eastern-Kentucky father. "I set up all night figuring how to get an organization going," he recalls:

> I had never done anything like this before. I didn't know shit about organizing. But I knowed that to have an organization you had to have people. So I devised a little strategy. I wanted to make it a countywide thing. . . . So I set down and put it on paper what to do: just to go to communities and talk about—say, look now, we got all these damn problems, you got no damn jobs, half of you'ns ain't got no roads, half of us ain't got nothing to eat, and we gotta do something about it. We got to get together

and we got to get a damn organization started to put some pressure on somebody, somewhere.[61]

The result was GCCA, which within a short time became a large and effective organization. As such, its organizer recalled, it came to the attention of the AVs, who moved in to "help" and "support" it. Disgusted with the AVs' urging GCCA to apply for federal grants and start co-ops (which he felt diverted attention from more basic issues), the native organizer left. Although in their October 1967 report the AVs said their relationship to GCCA "has been and will be one of technical assistance and support," an AV-VISTA who worked in the county in 1966–67 recalled later that GCCA was in fact being run by the AVs.[62]

Interaction between the AVs and the militant Appalachian Group to Save the Land and People (AGSLP) was both more important and more complicated. Before the AVs arrived on the scene, AGSLP—born out of the defiance of Uncle Dan Gibson and the Widow Combs in Knott County's Clear Creek Valley in 1965—was a viable and effective organization, but it was not without its problems.[63] Factions had formed in the argument over anti–strip-mining tactics, and a late 1965 attempt to forge an alliance with the militant roving pickets failed because some AGSLP members could not move from the single issue of strip-mining to larger political strategies. After the passage of the 1966 Kentucky strip-mining law, therefore, AGSLP lost considerable momentum.

In May 1967, some Pike County AVs met with AGSLP members in Knott County and decided to form new chapters in other counties. Within a year chapters had been organized in Breathitt, Pike, Floyd, and Harlan. Although the AVs later claimed credit for revitalizing AGSLP, their actual involvement was not very substantial, especially since most of the work after late 1967 was done by former AVs who had resigned over the firing of Joe Mulloy.[64]

A young native organizer who worked with AGSLP while on the AV staff in 1968 concluded that one effect of the AV influence was to reinforce the "reasonable" (and less effective) faction within AGSLP by emphasizing legal and administrative approaches instead of the direct action out of which the organization had been born:

> [The AVs] said you don't learn nothin' from that kind of experience, you know. You learn by takin' people to Frankfort and set down with a state representative, who was a coal operator. . . . You don't learn by goin' up and throwin' people off of bulldozers. Well, you don't stop stripmining in Frankfort, either. . . . When they throwed 'em off the damn mountain,

they did learn something. The strip operators learned something, too.

The effect of the AVs on existing organizations in the region (at least the more militant ones) was therefore less than wholly salutary. Whatever their intentions, the AVs tampered more or less blindly with the groups' internal dynamics, urged them toward more "legitimate" tactics, and in some cases hired away their leaders. A final irony was that when the political heat was turned on the AVs, they tended to solicit the support of local groups to protect themselves—asking them to attend hearings, write letters, and sign petitions. Offering the requested support then made local groups guilty by association.

A more admirable aspect of the AV legacy is the work done by a number of organizations that grew out of the AVs. One of the last programs of the expiring AVs was the Appalachian Justice Project organized by Howard Thorkelson, who came to the AVs in August 1968 from Columbia University's Center on Social Welfare Policy and Law.[65] Later separated from the AVs, first as the Mountain Legal Rights Association and then as Mountain People's Rights, Thorkelson's group worked on legal problems associated with access to federal programs. Two other groups organized with the assistance of former AVs and AV-VISTAs were the Coal Miners Legal Defense Fund, which represented miners in disability claims against coal companies, and the Appalachian Research and Defense Fund (APPALRED), a public interest law firm in Charleston, West Virginia. Designs for Rural Action, formed in 1969 by former AVs Gibbs Kinderman and Tom Rhodenbaugh, offered support to the Black Lung Association after the murder of UMWA president Tony Boyle's challenger Jock Yablonski. DRA hired harassed activist (and future UMWA president) Arnold Miller from the flooded section of the mine to which he had been assigned by company officials, who resented his involvement in the black lung movement. DRA also assisted welfare rights, legal rights, and antidraft groups in West Virginia. With the exception of APPALRED, however, almost none of the organizations begun by former AVs survived for more than two or three years.

Paradoxically, the most permanent effect of the AVs may have been registered not on the region itself, on existing regional organizations, or on the few indigenous young people who were significantly involved, but on a dozen or so aggressive and well-trained young men from outside the region. For them the AVs functioned as an important switch-point in their personal development. Tom Bethell came to Appalachia from Harvard in 1963, became the AV information director several years later, left the AVs and set up Appalachia Information, Inc. (with help from DRA), which published the splendidly researched *Coal Patrol* (1970–72), and then became Research Director in Arnold Miller's reform UMWA. AV-VISTA Rick Bank made a similar move from the AVs through the Coal Miners Legal Defense Fund to Miller's legal staff. Tom Rhodenbaugh also joined the UMWA staff, as did West Virginia AV David Biesmeyer. Harvey and Naomi Cohen and Bruce Boyens became attorneys for the UMWA's District 17 in West Virginia. Bill Schechter, who worked on both the Political Action League and the Fair Elections Committee while an AV, later moved to the UMWA's political office (COMPAC) in West Virginia. Milton Ogle went to the APPALRED staff, Doug Yarrow to the editorial staff of the Beckley, West Virginia, newspaper, and Gibbs Kinderman to head the Mountaineer Family Health Plan in Raleigh County.

In a limited sense, such channeling resulted in a gain for the region. Important policy and administrative positions were filled by young people whose politics tended toward liberal reformism, who had some understanding of the political economy of the region, and who presumably intended to resist the dictates of entrenched power blocs. But there were serious losses as well, some of which differed little from those that attended prior waves of missionary activity, and many of which were produced by attitudes and assumptions like those common among early missionaries.

In addition to sharing many of the paternalistic attitudes that had characterized earlier missionaries, however, the AVs were burdened by two that were particularly unfortunate during the late 1960s. Although the region has a substantial black population (about 6 percent, depending on how the region is defined) and many black communities, the AVs related to blacks hardly at all and had none on the staff. The organization's attitude toward women was equally unfortunate, particularly in view of the fact that women had long been leaders in a variety of progressive communities, organizations, and movements in the mountains. But because the AVs were dominated entirely by white males, blacks were left out altogether and white women ordinarily either did menial office tasks or were assigned the drudgery of house-to-house local organizing, for which the "fieldmen" eventually got credit if the effort was successful.

The *macho* spirit of competition that prevailed among fieldmen not only was abusive to women but also prevented the AVs from seriously encouraging indigenous leadership, male or female. Fieldmen were characteristically placed in superior positions vis-à-vis local people; middle-aged lifelong residents of the region thus became three-to-five-thousand-dollar-a-year "interns" to twenty-two-year-old inexperienced outsiders hired as fieldmen at six thousand to eight thousand a year or more.

The inequities persisted beyond the demise of the AVs. When the organization folded, local people who had been on the staff picked up as best they could. But with a few notable exceptions, the fieldmen returned to graduate school, resumed their careers, or (newly credentialed by their AV experience) moved into well-paying jobs in the emerging reform bureaucracy.

One of the most respected missionaries ever to come into the mountains was Deaconess Binns, whose work in southwest Virginia's Dickenson County was supported by the Episcopal church, which in turn received its local funds from executives in the coal and lumber industries. Deaconess Binns first came into the mountains around 1915 as one of about three hundred student volunteers sent from the Episcopalian deaconess school in New York. She soon returned to stay and spent nearly half a century working for a dollar a year among the mountain people around the town of Nora.[66] Six months after she retired, John Kobak, a wealthy New Englander, came to Dickenson County as an AV. The continuity between his work and that of Deaconess Binns was not lost upon the young mountain woman he met there, worked with as an AV, and later married: John "was not aware at all that he was just picking up where she left off. And she had been there since the turn of the century. Where she had quit taking people to the doctor, he started."

But John Kobak and some other AVs eventually edged toward a more political analysis and strategy than had ever been achieved by their predecessors in good works and self-help. That they did was both their promise and their doom in a region where corporations and their kept politicians had accumulated a hundred years' experience in co-opting, controlling, or destroying any organization, ecclesiastical or secular, that even marginally challenged the status quo.

Notes

1. Henry D. Shapiro, "A Strange Land and a Peculiar People: The Discovery of Appalachia, 1870–1920," unpublished Ph.D. dissertation, Rutgers University, 1967, p. 234; letter from Laura Maria Miller, Grout Family Papers, Duke University manuscript collection; John C. Campbell to John Glenn, January 21 and July 22, 1915; Katherine Pettit to Campbell, March 20, 1916. Campbell and Pettit letters in Southern Historical Collection, University of North Carolina.

2. The students' activities were covered by the national press. See "Investigating Investigators in Kentucky," *Literary Digest,* April 16, 1932, pp. 38–39; Joseph P. Lash, "Students in Kentucky," *The New Republic,* LXX (April 20, 1932), 267 ff.; Herbert Solow, "Modern Education," *The Nation,* CXXXIV (April 27, 1932), 493; Joseph D. McGoldrick, "College Students and Kentucky

Miners," *American Scholar,* I (1932), 363–65; and G. Carritt, "American Students and Kentucky Gunmen," *New Statesman and Nation,* III (1932), 703–4. In the 1960s, the LID fathered the Students for a Democratic Society (SDS), which again sent students into eastern Kentucky's Perry County.

3. See three articles by Lucille Kohn: "Solidarity in Kanawha Valley," *Labor Age,* XX (September 1931), 11; "There Are Classes in the West Virginia Hills," XXI (September 1932), 11; and "Pioneer Youth and the Labor Movement," XXI (November 1932), 20. See also *Pioneer Youth of America: 1924–1939* (n.d., n.p.) and Archie Green, *Only a Miner* (Urbana: University of Illinois Press, 1972), p. 257.

4. *Louisville Courier-Journal,* March 10, 1964, and *Lexington Herald,* February 26, 1967, respectively.

5. In addition to the published and other documentary sources cited throughout, this chapter is based on interviews with former Appalachian Volunteer staff, VISTA volunteers assigned to the AVs, and others who were associated with or knowledgeable about it (all interviews conducted in 1974): Douglas Arnett, Gary Bickel, James Branscome, Robb Burlage, Michael Clark, Gene Conti, Steve Daugherty, Edith Easterling, Sam Howie, Loyal Jones, Gibbs Kinderman, Sue Kobak, Charles Maggard, Alan McSurely, Flem Messer, Eric Metzner, Joseph Mulloy, Milton Ogle, Ann Pollard, Thomas Rhodenbaugh, David Walls, and Douglas Yarrow. I am grateful for their cooperation, but I am of course solely responsible for the views expressed here.

6. Final Report of the Council of the Southern Mountains to the Ford Foundation on the Appalachian Project, July 22, 1967; *Christian Science Monitor,* January 27, 1965, p. 1-C. Using college students to aid domestic "depressed areas" had been considered in several quarters since the Peace Corps was funded by Congress in late 1961. Criticism of the colonialist implications of the Peace Corps did not surface until later. See Marshall Windmiller, *The Peace Corps and Pax Americana* (Washington, D.C.: Public Affairs Press, 1970).

7. *Mountain Life and Work (MLW),* XXI (Fall 1945), 20–24.

8. See Philip Conn, "Appalachian Volunteers (AV): An Experiment in Community Development," unpublished thesis, The Hague, 1966, p. 14, and Gibbs Kinderman, "Appalachian Volunteers Will Expand Activities in 1965," *MLW,* XLI (Spring 1965), 25.

9. See Milton Ogle, "In the Land of the Sky—the Sky's the Limit," *MLW,* XXXV (Winter 1959), 7–16. Ogle's "Report to the [Council] Economic Development Committee" of February 26, 1960, suggests that his views on development were conventional but not overly conservative by the standards of the time.

10. See John Fetterman, *Stinking Creek* (1967; reprint, New York: E. P. Dutton, 1970), pp. 163 ff.

11. Quoted in Billy D. Horton, "The Appalachian Volunteers: A Case Study in Community Organization and Conflict," unpublished M.A. thesis, University of Kentucky, 1971, p. 48. Philip Conn, who was involved in the organization of the AVs, took the position that mountain people were ignorant, unsophisticated, cut off from and unable to cope with "modern life," traditionalistic, fatalistic, and self-destructively individualistic (see his thesis, note 8 above).

12. On the roving pickets, see John Ed Pearce, "The Superfluous People of Hazard, Kentucky," *The Reporter*, XXVIII (January 3, 1963), 33–35; Stephanie Gervis, "Gray Spring in Hazard," *Commonweal*, LXXVIII (May 1963), 220–22; and Dan Wakefield, "In Hazard," *Commentary*, XXXVI (September 1963), 209–17.

13. Horton. "Appalachian Volunteers," p. 55; and Council Newsletter no. 2, September 1964, p. 2, respectively. The AV board included representatives from each college AV chapter, eight "adults," and the AV staff. Provisions were made in December 1964 to include community representatives, but apparently few ever served. Presumably the "rousers" referred to were students supporting the Hazard miners in connection with the SDS Economic Research and Action Project (ERAP) to "organize the poor and unemployed." See Kirkpatrick Sale, *SDS* (New York: Random House, 1973), pp. 101–34.

14. The Legion was duly cautious, however. A letter from Kentucky adjutant Ray Breyer to Ogle on November 24, 1964, said, "while your request for . . . flags fulfills one of the basic principles of the Preamble (to promote 100 percent Americanism), final approval must be given by the Department Executive Committee."

15. *Louisville Courier-Journal*, November 18, 1964. The "out-of-state" charge against ACFE derived from the fact that it drew support from the Committee for Miners formed in June 1963 by Stanley Aronowitz and others. On the Committee for Miners, see Hamish Sinclair, "Hazard, Ky.: Committee for Miners," *Studies on the Left*, V (Summer 1965), 87–107, and *idem*, "Hazard, Ky.: Document of the Struggle," *Radical America*, II (January–February 1968), 1–24. On the ACFE, formed in January 1964, see Everette Tharpe, "Appalachian Committee for Full Employment: Background and Purpose," *Appalachian South*, I (Summer 1965), 44–46.

16. Two long statements from Fox concerning his AV experience may be found in *Mountain Eagle*, August 4 and December 10, 1966. In the former he expressed "private doubts about the theory and practice of volunteer organizations"; in the latter he commented upon the "lousy systems and fine people" he encountered in the region.

17. Memo from Ayer to AV staff and letter from Ayer to Ogle, both May 2, 1966. See also *Louisville Courier-Journal*, May 6, 1966, p. B-3, and *Mountain Eagle*, May 5, 1966, p. 1.

18. Quoted in Conn, "Appalachian Volunteers," p. 20.

19. One account of the session may be found in Robert Coles and Joseph Brenner, "American Youth in a Social Struggle: The Appalachian Volunteers," *American Journal of Orthopsychiatry*, XXXVIII (January 1968), 44–45. Coles's later reflections on the AVs appear in "A Fashionable Kind of Slander," *Atlantic Monthly*, CCXXVI (November 1970), 53–55.

20. Horton, "Appalachian Volunteers," pp. 71 ff.

21. The CAP staff members were Douglas Arnett, Richard Guske, and James Kendrick, formerly of the Clay, Jackson, and Knox county CAPs, respectively. On Kendrick, see Fetterman, *Stinking Creek*, pp. 178 ff. The AVs' most effective work seems to have been done by Steve Daugherty, who worked out of the Evarts (Harlan County) education outpost, but there was significant activity also in Rockcastle (Zi Graves), Whitley (Larry Qualls), and Bell (Art Ankeny). Qualls and Ankeny worked out of the Whitley-Bell outpost. The

other outposts were in Letcher County (Carcassonne) and Breathitt-Wolfe.

22. "The Program of the Appalachian Volunteers: The Cumberland Valley Project" (mimeo), March 1969; *Louisville Courier-Journal*, March 27, 1967.

23. John Barnes, "A Case Study of the Mingo County Economic Opportunity Commission," unpublished Ph.D. dissertation, University of Pennsylvania, 1970.

24. The distinctions that follow are useful for the purposes of discussion only. Each approach or strategy necessarily partook to some degree of one or more of the others. There was in some sense a temporal "progression" from the first to the third type, but each was present all along, and "later" forms preceded "earlier" ones in some areas.

25. On craft groups and co-ops, see the AVs' *Quarterly Report*, October 1967, pp. 31–44, and *VISTA Volunteer*, III (July 1967), 24–27, and IV (November 1968), 4–25. For the partisan position, see two articles by Ben Poage: "Federal Help for Co-ops," *Appalachian Lookout*, I (December 1968), 10–11, and "A Look at Southern Co-ops," I (March 1969), 16–21. Alan McSurely challenged Poage from a Marxist perspective in *Appalachian Lookout*, I (March 1969), 16–17.

26. Single-community associations included Clover Fork Independent Citizens and the Verda Advisory Committee (Harlan County), Highway 979 Community Action Council (Floyd County), the Tioga citizens' association (Nicholas County, West Virginia), and others. There were single-county associations in Wyoming and Nicholas counties, West Virginia; Dickenson County, Virginia (Citizens Committee for Community Action); and Pike County, Kentucky (Pike County Citizens Association). The Grassroots Citizens Committee for Action operated in two Kentucky counties (Breathitt and Wolfe), as did the Jackson-Clay and Whitley-Bell associations. United Appalachian Communities, based in the Cumberland Valley counties, was very short-lived. Some associations were started by AVs and left to local people to operate. In other cases (for example, Grassroots), the AVs in effect took over existing citizens' groups.

27. Linda Johnson and Sue Kobak, "Government Sponsored Grassroots Organizing," unpublished typescript report (January 1973). A judge close to the county bosses prevented the referendum from coming to a vote.

28. Frances Fox Piven and Richard Cloward, *Regulating the Poor: The Functions of Public Welfare* (New York: Vintage, 1971), pp. 320–40.

29. For a discussion of the Highlander philosophy and approach to organizing, see Frank Adams, *Unearthing Seeds of Fire: The Idea of Highlander* (Winston-Salem, N.C.: John F. Blair, 1975), and "A Talk with Myles Horton," *Appalachian Lookout*, I (January–February 1969), 3–5. Horton participated in a number of AV training sessions.

30. Alan McSurely, "A New Political Union" (typescript dated January 17, 1967). Subsequent quotations are from this source.

31. Letter to Robert Coles, April 29, 1967, Berea College Library. McSurely's reflections on his experience with the AVs and later in Pike County may be found in "How to Create Instant Socialism: Ace Organizer Confesses," *Progressive Labor*, VII (August 1969), 32–35.

32. Details of the incident are not entirely clear. Coles had been an AV consultant at least since the summer of 1965. Many letters from the AVs to Coles in the AV archive at Berea College refer to his conversations with foundation officials on their behalf. Ogle's letter to Coles of April 29, 1967, refers to a letter from Coles on April 26, objecting to McSurely. Coles's letter is not in the file, however, and Coles's assistant informed me on November 12, 1974, that he was unable to find it. The Field Foundation granted the AVs $40,000 in December 1967.

33. Harry Caudill, *My Land Is Dying* (New York: E. P. Dutton, 1971), pp. 57 ff., and Robert F. Munn, "The Development of Stripmining in Southern Appalachia," *Appalachian Journal*, III (Autumn 1975), 87–93. See also Robert F. Munn, *Strip Mining: An Annotated Bibliography* (Morgantown: West Virginia University Library, 1973).

34. Caudill, *My Land Is Dying*, pp. 101 ff.

35. *Charleston Gazette-Mail*, August 7, 1966; and James C. Millstone, "Stripmining Feud in Kentucky," *Congressional Record*, CXIII (August 17, 1967), 29114. Several AVs and AV-VISTAs worked with state legislators on the 1967 West Virginia strip-mining law.

36. Bill Peterson, *Coaltown Revisited* (Chicago: Regnery, 1972), p. 137; Bruce Jackson, "In the Valley of the Shadows: Kentucky," *Transaction*, VIII (June 1971), 28–38; and Gene L. Mason, "The 'Subversive' Poor," *The Nation*, CCVII (December 30, 1968), 721–24.

37. George Vecsey's *One Sunset a Week: The Story of a Coal Miner* (New York: Saturday Review Press, 1974) is based on John Tiller's life. On the shift in Mulloy's views, see Joseph Mulloy, "The Appalachian Story," *Bill of Rights Journal*, II (December 1969), 31–32.

38. The account of the Jink Ray episode and its aftermath for Joe Mulloy and Alan McSurely is based upon (in addition to interviews already cited) Paul Good, "Kentucky's Coal Beds of Sedition," *The Nation*, CCV (September 4, 1967), 166–69; Gene L. Mason, "The 'Subversive' Poor," pp. 721–24; James C. Millstone, reprints of a series of *St. Louis Post-Dispatch* articles (September 17–20, 1967) in the *Congressional Record*, CXIII (October 17, 1967), 29111–15; *New York Times*, August and September 1967; Bruce Jackson, "In the Valley of the Shadows: Kentucky," *Transaction*, VIII (June 1971), 28–38; Horton, "The Appalachian Volunteers," pp. 84–98, 107–23; and the Appalachian Volunteers' *Quarterly Report*, October 1967, pp. 24–29. Because this period in the history of the AVs has been written about so extensively, only the briefest outline will be presented here.

39. See Jim Wayne Miller, "The Ballad of Jink Ray," in *Appalachian People's History Book* (Louisville: Southern Conference Education Fund, n.d.), pp. 99–100; Caudill, *My Land Is Dying*, p. 87; and David E. Whisnant, "The Folk Hero and Appalachian Struggle History," *New South*, XXVIII (Fall 1973), 30–47.

40. Bibles, Goldwater's *The Conscience of a Conservative*, works by Thomas Merton, and other books were left. Margaret McSurely's offense was having worked for SNCC in 1964.

41. The McSurelys' case is discussed at length in Walter Goodman, "The Senate *v.* Alan and Margaret McSurely," *New York Times Magazine*, January

10, 1971, and one instalment of Richard Harris, "Annals of the Law: The Fourth Amendment," *The New Yorker*, November 3–24, 1975.

42. Millstone, *Congressional Record*, CXIII (October 17, 1967), 29114, and Appalachian Volunteers' *Quarterly Report*, October 1967.

43. Kentucky CAP directors were divided in their response to the AVs. Late in August thirteen directors sent a telegram to Shriver protesting the termination of funds without a hearing. *Louisville Courier-Journal*, August 24, 1967, p. B-1.

44. Undated memo, author's file.

45. James Ridgeway, "Sedition in Kentucky," *The New Republic*, CLVII (September 2, 1967), 10–11.

46. *New York Times*, August 20, 1967, p. 34.

47. Memo dated November 6, 1967.

48. Ogle's and Mulloy's statements appear in *Mountain Eagle*, December 7, 1967, p. 4.

49. The terms obscure some of the actual complexities. Those who espoused the principled position, for example, also argued that it was in fact the soundest pragmatically and offered in the long run the greatest survival value for local people. Some of the pragmatists saw their own position as deeply principled: Local people, David Walls argued in a long memo, "have the right to choose the issues for which they will . . . fight."

50. Memo from George Woodring to Ogle, December 13, and Thomas Bethell's letter of resignation, December 5, 1967, respectively.

51. Quoted in Horton, "Appalachian Volunteers," p. 99.

52. "Evaluation Report of the Appalachian Volunteers in Eastern Kentucky, June 24 to July 3, 1968" (mimeo), August 1, 1968.

53. A conscious model for PAL, according to Gibbs Kinderman, was the Farmers Non-partisan League of North Dakota, which in the second decade of this century successfully broke the monopoly control enjoyed by railroads, banks, and grain speculators. The League was destroyed in the post–World War I "red scare."

54. Letter from Ogle to Schechter, May 7, 1968, and Washington *Evening Star*, April 30, 1968. For extended accounts of both FEC and PAL, see Huey Perry, *They'll Cut Off Your Project: A Mingo County Chronicle* (New York: Praeger, 1972), pp. 136 ff.; and K. W. Lee, "Fair Elections in West Virginia," in David S. Walls and John B. Stephenson (eds.), *Appalachia in the Sixties: Decade of Reawakening* (Lexington: University Press of Kentucky, 1972), pp. 164–76.

55. *Appalachian Lookout*, I (December 1968), 14–23. Milton Ogle resigned in September. Walls came to the AVs in 1966 after employment with both OEO and HEW. On the water system controversy and the hearings, see *Louisville Courier-Journal*, October 14 and 16, 1968.

56. KUAC report of November 27, 1968, reprinted in *Appalachian Lookout*, I (January–February 1969), 11–13. Additional hearings were held on December 2–3.

57. Letter of October 10, 1968, to New World Foundation. See also David Walls, "The AVs: Coming of Age in Appalachia," *Appalachian Lookout*, I (December 1968), 24.

58. AV Field Staff Report, November 13, 1968.

59. Ward Sinclair, "AV Leader Stymied in Washington Funds Hunt," *Louisville Courier-Journal*, December 31, 1968.

60. The support sometimes came at a considerable cost, however. Edith Easterling was fired by the AVs in 1969 as a result of a controversy engendered by recently hired AV organizer Tom Ramsey. Ramsey's own apparently exaggerated account of his Pike County organizing appears to have been the basis for the statement of organizer "Bill Talcott" in Studs Terkel's *Working* (New York: Pantheon, 1974), pp. 352–56. A thorough analysis of the effect of the AVs on individuals in the region would require resources for research and interviewing far beyond those available to me here. My remarks should therefore be taken as suggestive only.

61. Interview, October 23, 1974.

62. Those primarily involved were apparently Mike Kline and Mike Reuss, son of Wisconsin congressman Henry Reuss. A community newspaper published by GCCA was edited by a local AV-VISTA but written by AVs.

63. On the formation and activities of the AGSLP, see Caudill, *My Land Is Dying*, pp. 76–83.

64. On the AVs and the AGSLP, see the AVs' *Quarterly Report*, October 1967, pp. 31–37; Horton, "Appalachian Volunteers," p. 84; and Good, "Kentucky's Coal Beds of Sedition," pp. 167–68.

65. See Howard Thorkelson, "Hunger and the Federal Food Program," in Jeremy Larner and Irving Howe (eds.), *Poverty: Views from the Left* (New York: William Morrow, 1968), pp. 184 ff.

66. Helen Lewis, Sue Kobak, and Linda Johnson, "Family, Religion and Colonialism in Central Appalachia," in Jim Axelrod (ed.), *Growin' Up Country* (Clintwood, Va.: Council of the Southern Mountains, 1973), pp. 131–56.

CHAPTER 8

Power for the People: The Congress for Appalachian Development

By LATE SUMMER OF 1965, it was clear that none of the development efforts ever employed in the Appalachian region had substantially improved the lives of a majority of its people. Much of their failure to do so was caused by their having evaded three central issues: the use of the region's abundant natural resources as a base for economic and social reconstruction; the democratic control of those resources; and the equitable allocation of publicly produced, resource-derived benefits for the individual and common good of all of the region's people.

The earliest development plan for the region had been sketched forty years earlier by the cautious Conference of Southern Mountain Workers, whose tentative efforts in cooperative economic development had been delayed until the eve of World War II and had not even then addressed the issue of cooperative or democratic resource development. By the mid-1960s the organization's board and policies were so significantly influenced by deference to the region's private utilities, coal companies, and chambers of commerce that issues such as public power, strip-mining, and alternative economic development were usually sidestepped.

The Tennessee Valley Authority—after an impressive twenty-year effort in comprehensive resource development—succumbed to internal and external pressures, narrowed its functions, and committed itself to a power policy whose effect on coal-bearing central Appalachia was devastating.

With federal programs that followed TVA, the region was little better off than it had been with the early efforts of the Conference

of Southern Mountain Workers. The Area Redevelopment Administration failed entirely to face the issue of resource development.
The Economic Opportunity Act of 1964 included no authority for
dealing with natural resources or public facilities such as hydroelectric
systems. The Appalachian Regional Commission, created largely to
continue the "infrastructure" development initiated by the defunct
ARA and denied to OEO, demonstrated from its earliest days that
it intended to keep its hands off the politically delicate questions of
strip-mining, water and steam power, and public control of natural
resources.

An Alternative Approach

Beginning about 1962, a crucial role in focusing the issue of resource development (and specifically of public power) in Appalachia
was played by Harry Caudill and Gordon K. Ebersole, one a native
of the region and the other an outsider who had hardly seen it until
a short time before.[1]

Born in Nebraska, where most power facilities were publicly
owned, Ebersole first worked as a civil engineer on the Grand Coulee
Dam. After service with the Corps of Engineers in World War II, he
returned to public development projects in the Missouri Basin. Trans-
ferred to Washington, D.C., with the Bureau of Reclamation in 1950,
he spent ten years working both in the United States and abroad with
Point Four (later AID) resource development projects. His subsequent
position as Staff Assistant for Area Redevelopment on the Resources
Program Staff of the Interior Department first brought him into
contact with the problems of Appalachia.

From early in his professional career, Ebersole had been aware
of both the potential of public resource development and the efforts
of private utilities to forestall such development. As a young engineer
he had read *Giant Power*, an indictment of the monopolistic tendencies
of private power companies and an early blueprint for public power
written by Morris L. Cooke, who had directed Pennsylvania Governor
Gifford Pinchot's Giant Power Survey Board.[2] Later he watched the
fifteen-year, one-man campaign of editor Rufus Woods of the *Wen-
atchee* (Washington) *Daily World*, which led to the building of Grand
Coulee Dam.[3] But in the 1940s he also saw Congress refuse to reconfirm Leland Olds, a vigorous and effective guardian of the public
interest, as chairman of FPC.

In the 1920s Olds had drafted (as an appointee of then Governor

Franklin D. Roosevelt) exemplary laws regulating private utilities in the State of New York. Further experience as head of the State Power Authority preceded his appointment to the FPC by Roosevelt in 1939, a position from which he sought to curb the antisocial practices of private utilities. President Truman nominated Olds for a third term in 1949, but corporate interests and their congressional allies successfully red-baited him by dredging up anti–free enterprise statements he had written twenty-five years earlier.

The sacking of Olds was the beginning of a long decline for FPC. It coincided with the midpoint of Ebersole's own career and convinced him that it was "now or never" for public power as President Eisenhower cut back on the FPC staff and installed commissioners friendly to private utilities. Eisenhower's Secretary of the Interior, Douglas McKay, promulgated revised power guidelines that led to the giving away of valuable power sites to private interests.[1]

Gordon Ebersole came to Washington with the Bureau of Reclamation only a few months after Congress refused to reconfirm Leland Olds. The subsequent machinations of the Eisenhower administration ran counter not only to his ethics and politics but also to his experience in public power development. When he became associated with the Interior Department following his Point Four and AID experience overseas, he was eager to demonstrate that, in the changed political climate of the Kennedy administration, public power and resource development was a viable approach to the rehabilitation of depressed areas.

In early 1962 Ebersole joined a group of Area Redevelopment Administration, TVA, and other officials on an Appalachian tour at the request of the Conference of Appalachian Governors. On a subsequent trip as a member of the power, coal, and water resources teams of the President's Appalachian Regional Commission, he met Whitesburg lawyer Harry Caudill, who showed him the devastation of Letcher County, Kentucky. To Ebersole, such areas seemed virtually tailor-made for public power and resource development. But Caudill was not sure.

Caudill's *Night Comes to the Cumberlands*, then in press, condemned the colonial domination of the region by "industrial overlords who robbed and ravaged the land" for generations. He spoke of the "fumbling and red-tape ridden efforts of the Area Redevelopment Administration," but he held no particular brief for public power. The uses Caudill envisioned for a proposed series of lakes on the Cumberland plateau included water supply and recreation, but power generation was not mentioned.

"When *Night Comes to the Cumberlands* was written," Caudill told a Berea College audience in October 1963, "I had grave doubts about the desirability of a major Appalachian power development." Presumably his doubts stemmed partly from the recent change in TVA's role in the region, even though he felt that "the subversion of the TVA in recent years . . . detracts nothing from the illustrious accomplishments of its first two decades," which seemed to him a "Showpiece of effective planning and accomplishment."[5] Thus, except for a brief reference to the reconstruction of the mining districts of Wales in the 1920s and 1930s, the conservation aspects of the Tennessee Valley experiment served as the primary model for the Southern Mountain Authority Caudill proposed in the final chapter of his book.

Through conversations with Ebersole and others during the ensuing months, however, Caudill reconsidered the issue of public power as he became aware of models other than TVA. At length he began to refer to the possibility of power development in the region through a "self-financing public corporation," but he was not sure what such a corporation should look like. In early September 1963, he was quoted in the *Louisville Courier-Journal* as considering both TVA and the Columbia River project as possible models. In a letter to President Johnson in December, he referred to "a public corporation similar to TVA," but in March 1964 he wrote in the *Nation* of the Columbia River experience again. Three months later in the *Atlantic Monthly*, he called for "a modernized version of TVA."[6]

Ebersole urged that what was needed was a model of public development free of the heavy encumbrances carried by TVA: its dwindling accountability, its encouragement of strip-mining through long-term coal-buying contracts, and its more than local reputation among conservatives as an alien socialistic experiment. The model he judged most applicable was the public utility districts (PUDs) of the Pacific Northwest. "It isn't enough," he wrote to Caudill, "to say you want another TVA which politically speaking gets everybody's bristles up. . . . Think how much more effective you could [be] if you saw the five dams on the Columbia River built by PUDs, and related [their] experience to eastern Kentucky rather than that of TVA which everyone knows is something honest citizens shouldn't even talk about." At length the PUD model came to dominate Ebersole's and Caudill's emerging campaign for public power development.[7]

The Public Utility District Model

In the 1920s electric power in the Pacific Northwest was monopolized by Eastern holding companies such as Electric Bond and Share, Stone and Webster, and American Power and Light, which were providing inadequate and expensive service for rural dwellers, often charging customers as much as $1,000 per mile for the installation of distribution lines.[8] In 1926 the Washington State Grange appointed an "electrical power development committee" to study alternative power systems and draft a model legislative bill. The committee reported in 1927 that the hydroelectric resources of the state "will either be developed by the public for the good of all the people . . . or by private corporations for the exploitation of present and future citizens. . . . It is the last great resource which may still be conserved for the common good."

The Grange bill to establish Public Utility Districts failed to pass in the legislature but passed the next year in a referendum supported by bankrupt farmers and opposed by private utilities, which (as a Federal Power Commission investigation showed ten years later) listed their expenditures as tax-deductible advertising. Beaten in the referendum, the private utilities filed suit to test the constitutionality of the PUD law. But the law had a solid legal basis and was upheld.

Public power was born, however, not with the coming of the PUDs but in the same year, 1882, in which central station electric power became a reality in the United States. In that year, there were only four publicly owned municipal systems, but public power planks began to appear regularly in reform party platforms in the 1890s. Jacksonville, Florida, had a public system by 1893, Seattle by 1905, Tacoma by 1910, and Los Angeles by 1911. By 1910 there were more than 1,500 municipal systems, and that number doubled by 1923. In 1965, the year the Appalachian Regional Development Act passed in Congress with a prohibition against public power, the Jacksonville municipal was paying off debts on a $30 million city coliseum and supplying more than 60 percent of total city operating revenues.[9] A decade later, the western Kentucky city of Madisonville, whose government had been financed entirely by its municipal power system for more than twenty years, instituted a small property tax only in order to qualify for federal revenue-sharing funds.[10]

The legal precedents set by the municipals were further reinforced by the federal government's activities in the area of public power after the turn of the century. The federal power program began in 1902 as part of an effort to develop arid lands in the west. The General Dam acts of 1906 and 1910 authorized construction of dams for irrigation and power generation, brought some uniformity in regulation, and imposed fifty-year limits on licenses. The Federal Power Commission was established by the Federal Water Power Act of 1920, with authority to license construction of hydroelectric plants on public lands or navigable streams; fifteen years later it was allowed to regulate power rates. Construction of Hoover Dam (the first federal "peacetime multiple-purpose" power project) was authorized in 1928, and in a single year, 1933, both the TVA and the Columbia River projects were authorized. The Rural Electrification Administration (REA) was established in 1935, and within seven years more both the Southwestern and Southeastern Power Administrations had been brought into being.

Hence the PUDs in the Pacific Northwest came into existence at a critical time in the history of public power: after the legal precedents had been established, on the eve of increased federal involvement in the area, and while the municipals were both numerous and strong. The first PUD in Washington State was actually formed in 1935, and the last in 1940, after which the private utilities improved their service and lowered rates in order to head off any future PUDs.

In concept, the PUD is relatively simple Normally a PUD law authorizes a publicly controlled body to issue revenue-producing bonds, receive and disburse funds, acquire real estate (by condemnation if necessary), construct dams and other power generation and distribution facilities, and sell electric power. Many PUDs in the Northwest are distribution facilities only, buying their power from the Bonneville Power Administration. All PUDs pay a specified portion of their receipts into the general revenue funds of their counties. As nonprofit enterprises, they supply electricity to their customers at about half the rate charged by private utilities, while paying off their own indebtedness to bondholders.

The PUD mechanism achieved impressive results in poor Washington counties. In the mid-1960s, tiny Lewis County, with a population of 35,000 farmers, loggers, and cattlemen and no industry, was operating a $2-million-per-year PUD that was providing nearly a quarter of a million dollars annually in revenues for the county, including $125,000 to support its public schools. Chelan County, also quite small, started its PUD in 1936 and purchased its first transmission lines nine years later. Within a few years it had bought out some existing power systems, built a 249,000-kilowatt generating facility at Rock Island, and financed construction of its own Rocky Reach Dam by selling $263 million worth of revenue bonds. The 800,000-kilowatt Rocky Reach project became a model of activity in the public interest; its powerhouse even included a museum of artifacts excavated during construction of the dam. Power from the project, available by 1961, attracted manufacturing installations by Alcoa, Dow Chemical, the Vanadium Corporation, and others. By 1967 twenty-two Washington PUDs were supplying electric power to 280,000 customers.

PUDs in Appalachia:
The Congress for Appalachian Development

Stymied in his attempts to get ARA and Interior involved in public power development in Appalachia, but encouraged by his ongoing conversations with Harry Caudill about PUDs, Gordon Ebersole retired from government service and began to cast about for other organizational contexts in which such efforts might be more productive. As a board member of the Council of the Southern Mountains, he recalled his Columbia River experience in the winter 1966 issue of *Mountain Life and Work:*

> Last spring my wife and I revisited the Columbia Basin in Eastern Washington where I had begun my engineering career in 1935. The sage brush and sand dunes had given way to lush green fields, and prosperous homes dominated a landscape that had known only the homesteader's shack and a few dusty roads. A long, low dam recaptured drainage wastes to be used below. . . . A region had been transformed in a generation—how did it happen and what does it mean to Appalachia?

Why, Ebersole asked, "is the Nation's richest natural resource area the poorest in terms of human development? The answer lies . . . in a colonialism that since World War II has been thrown off by nations around the world [but] still exists within our own boundaries." Recounting his experience with ARA in the New River Gorge, where the power of corporations had proved such an effective deterrent to public development, he suggested that PUDs might be a way to turn public resources to public benefit.

Ebersole and Caudill had by then been working together for about three years, and a few weeks later Caudill made explicit and programmatic what Ebersole had suggested more generally. In an article entitled "A New Plan for a Southern Mountain Authority," he argued that mountaineers must now do for themselves or be done for. Filling in the details of Ebersole's broad charge of colonialism, he noted that 90 percent of the mineral wealth of some counties was owned by absentee corporations such as the Philadelphia-based Virginia Iron and Coke Company, which in 1964 retained an after-taxes profit amounting to 61 percent of its income. Perry County, Kentucky, he said, was holding $72,000 in delinquent coal company tax bills, while a single mining combine in the county had orders for $112 million worth of coal.

Contrasting Perry County with Washington's transformed Chelan and Grant counties, Caudill outlined an Appalachian PUD effort. He proposed that the Kentucky legislature create a forty-four–county Eastern Kentucky Development District, which could issue bonds and buy back coal lands from absentee owners at the prices their owners had sworn before complaisant tax assessors they were worth—usually far below fair market value. The District would then build hydroelectric and steam-powered generating plants, sell electricity to urban load centers and new industries in the mountains, and plow back part of its revenues into regional development—schools, roads, hospitals, libraries, and environmental improvements. "Washington opted for life and turned its back on death," Caudill said. "Kentucky mountaineers have a far brighter prospect than their fellow citizens in the western valleys . . . because their land is so much richer." For the region as a whole, Caudill envisioned a PUD-like authority formed by interstate compact.[11]

In writing of the Washington experience, Caudill decried the fact that mountain people had for so long cooperated in their own exploitation by electing demagogues to public office and acquiescing to their reactionary policies. But one mountaineer whom the description did not fit was Ed Fraley of Bristol, Virginia. In the 1880s Fraley's father, with a large family to support and an annual income that hovered near zero, sold mineral rights to his sixty-five acres of land near Norton, Virginia, for fifty cents an acre. The transaction became a point of departure for Ed Fraley's political understanding of the region and its people. As a young hardware store owner, he traveled to visit jailed mountaineer migrants who were participating in the violent Gastonia, North Carolina, textile strike of 1929. Three years later he accompanied a Norton newspaperman, Bruce Crawford of *Crawford's Weekly,* into Harlan County during the mine wars, where both men attended the Dreiser hearings and Crawford was shot and wounded by a company guard. Fraley's radical view of Appalachian problems was further reinforced by visits to Russia in the mid-1930s and again in the mid-1960s.[12]

After reading *Night Comes to the Cumberlands* in 1963, Fraley wrote to Harry Caudill to urge some effort at curbing absentee ownership in the region. Two years later he suggested a bond-financed public takeover of coal lands in order to "break the colonial relationship now existing between New York corporations and the Appalachian counties."[13] Caudill's PUD articles the next year impelled Fraley to call a meeting of those who found the idea attractive. Held in Bristol in September 1966, it drew about two dozen people: Ebersole, Caudill, Don West of the Appalachian South Folklife Center, Milton Ogle of the Appalachian Volunteers, Charleston newspaperman Bill Blizzard (son of the famous Bill Blizzard, who led early union struggles in

West Virginia's Kanawha River valley), West Virginia State Senator Paul Kaufman, *Mountain Eagle* editor Tom Gish, Myles Horton of Highlander Center, and others.

At the Bristol meeting, Harry Caudill spoke on PUDs and Paul Kaufman on the political restructuring required for public ownership of resources. Lewis G. Smith of the Bureau of Reclamation, who had worked with Ebersole for years—most recently on ARA's Middle Island Creek project—presented plans for new towns on the Cumberland Plateau.

Participants disagreed about what action or direction the group should take. Bill Blizzard, whose recent article on West Virginia's regressive tax structure had also formed part of the impetus for the meeting, had understood that the main topic for discussion was to be tax structure and found Smith's new town scheme grandiose and diversionary. Lloyd Davis of West Virginia University thought a "holding company" of strong leadership at the top was essential to the success of any PUD effort; Myles Horton of Highlander, Tom Gish of the *Mountain Eagle,* and Richard Austin of the Presbyterian West Virginia Mountain Project contended that grassroots support was essential.[14]

A steeering committee reflecting the various points of view met on October 15 in Charleston and decided to incorporate the group in West Virginia as the Congress for Appalachian Development (CAD) for the purpose of "restoring self-government in the Appalachian mountains in order to wisely conserve and develop the human and natural resources of the region for the common benefit of all the people." Richard Davies, an economic consultant, told the group that the PUD idea seemed wholly applicable to Appalachia. Despite his reservations, Bill Blizzard wrote an enthusiastic account of the new group's purposes and prospects.[15]

But the public statement CAD issued after the Charleston meeting bespoke a greater unanimity than existed in fact. Lewis Smith's new town plan, presented again in Charleston, had been received quite ambivalently; the "down from the top by experts" versus "up from the bottom by the people" disagreement over organizing strategy was not resolved; the relative priority of PUDs and tax reform was debated; and the effects of new industry attracted by low-cost power were judged beneficial by some and of questionable value by others.

The CAD idea nevertheless steadily gained public attention. A meeting in Abingdon, Virginia, on January 21, 1967, attracted nearly 150 people, including representatives from Interior, HUD, TVA, OEO, the Council of the Southern Mountains, state legislatures, and development experts of all shades of opinion. Kirby Billingsley, manager of the Chelan County PUD and president of the American Public

Power Association, spoke on the Washington PUD experience to the crowd gathered beneath crystal chandeliers in the 130-year-old Martha Washington Inn. Billingsley had a double interest in CAD, since his own father had migrated from Appalachia to the Northwest when the topsoil on the family farm washed away.[16]

Lewis Smith presented his new town plan yet again, using a twenty-four-foot-long map prepared at his own expense. Smith's plan, by now called the Appalachian Light Industrial Village Endeavor (ALIVE), envisioned about two hundred lakes on the Cumberland Plateau surrounded by "new, semi-rural towns" offering a "park-like living and work environment." Industrial sites were to be grouped on the main arterial ridges, "group cultural areas" on the laterals, and residential areas at ridge ends near the lakes. Smith offered his plan as a major CAD project.

The group elected Harry Caudill as chairman and Ebersole as temporary executive secretary. Ebersole agreed to serve without pay until funds became available for a salary. A unanimous resolution called for "a frank recognition of the fact that Appalachia is in . . . servile bondage to absentee industrial and financial interests" and recommended "acquisition by the Appalachian people of the region's vast resources." Myles Horton suggested that some "one-gallus people" be put on the CAD board, raising again the issue of grassroots support. The elected board included one ex-miner (Carl Johnson) and a Kentucky community leader (Mabel Kiser, who directed Letcher County's OEO-funded Millstone Sewing Center), but the rest were "two-gallus" people: a doctor, two professors, an editor, a preacher, and a lawyer.

Press reaction to the organization of the CAD and to its program for the region was generally positive. The *Knoxville News-Sentinel* ventured that "Imagination of this kind . . . could be the salvation of the mountain region." Statements subsequently made by Robert F. Kennedy about the desirability of generating mine-mouth power in Appalachia for distribution to urban load centers helped lend national significance to CAD's efforts. Ben Franklin's enthusiastic article in the *New York Times* late in March was widely reprinted in regional newspapers, and there were signs that *Fortune* and the *Wall Street Journal* intended to run feature articles on CAD.[17]

Negative press reaction was sparse and—except for a March 29 editorial in the *Lexington* (Kentucky) *Herald* entitled "Caudill Program Not for Appalachia"—confined to small newspapers such as the *Washington County* (Kentucky) *News,* which reported that "some pretty far-out ideas" had been advanced by CAD and that some "lank-haired youths once known . . . as beatniks" had been seen at the Abingdon meeting.

Ebersole and Caudill attempted to gain the support of both the Appalachian Regional Commission and the Interior Department but were not successful. ARC's States Regional Representative John Whisman (who had helped divert both ARA and ARC from public power) and Executive Director Ralph Widner were polite but cool when Ebersole and Lewis Smith explained CAD's objectives to them in late January. Interior Secretary Udall also offered no support or encouragement. Ebersole wrote to Udall in March, urging him to seize Interior's opportunity to develop a public power system in Appalachia, implement a land ethic, and help "ease the colonialism" of corporate hegemony. He received no reply. At a subsequent meeting Udall would agree only to a possible strip-mining reclamation effort by the Soil Conservation Service.

Except for Secretary Wilbur Cohen of HEW, whose wife was active in CAD's fundraising efforts, none of the many federal officials who were approached could be persuaded to endorse or provide funds for the CAD program of public power development. Only a few supporters could be found in Congress: Senator Mundt of South Dakota, sponsor of legislation on balanced economic development; Kentucky's Senator John Sherman Cooper, who liked the new town plan; Montana's Senator Lee Metcalf, an opponent of private utilities; and West Virginia Representative Ken Hechler, a strong critic of coal's domination of central Appalachia.[18]

The Demise of CAD

Throughout the fall of 1966 and much of the following winter, Gordon Ebersole, joined at times by Caudill, Smith, and others, trod the streets and corridors of Washington, seeking support for the Congress for Appalachian Development. But substantial financial support never materialized. Those who liked the idea were not in a position to help; those who were either could not or would not become involved. While Ebersole was in Washington, Harry Caudill was making speeches about CAD all over the Appalachian region. In April he told the faculty and students of the University of Tennessee Graduate School, "We in the Congress for Appalachian Development believe that it is time Appalachia should catch up with . . . other peoples of the globe who have had the guts and the brains to run out the colonialists and set themselves free."[19]

Good will abounded, but tangible support could not be found. Large foundations were unresponsive. In October 1966 Caudill wrote to the Ford Foundation's Paul Ylvisaker, whose success with the foundation's "gray areas" program had made him a leading consultant to Sargent Shriver during the drafting of the Economic Opportunity Act of 1964. Two months later, the foundation declined to pursue the matter further. Neither Jay Rockefeller, a rising West Virginia politician, nor millionaire industrialist Milton Shapp (who had rather hesitantly accepted a position on the CAD board) would agree to support CAD financially. In May, UAW economist Leo Goodman encouraged Caudill to believe that the Citizen's Crusade Against Poverty (funded by the UAW and the Ford Foundation) might contribute as much as $100,000 to CAD. But the grant never materialized. The American Public Power Association claimed to be unable to provide funds. A letter to hundreds of individuals who had expressed interest in CAD netted less than $100 in contributions.

Lacking financial backing, CAD was virtually limping along only four months after its founding. Ebersole was serving as executive secretary without salary and paying rent and other expenses for CAD's Washington office out of his pocket. Most CAD correspondence was handwritten, since there was no money to hire a secretary; Caudill's wife was typing minutes and other records. Other CAD board members were too busy with full-time jobs to offer much help. CAD was caught in its own cycle of poverty: lacking staff and funds, and operating without the full energies of anyone but Ebersole, it could not mount a successful fundraising or lobbying effort.

By early July, CAD's organizers were demoralized. "Not a dime has been contributed to our cause," Caudill wrote to Ebersole, "and it is now apparent . . . that none will be forthcoming. . . . Contact after contact has lauded our goals . . . but, like so many of the phonies who run modern America, they are unwilling to move . . . into active struggle for reform." As late as August 1967 Ebersole was still trying to raise money, but CAD was doomed. The Washington office was soon closed, and except for a brief partial revival in connection with the Blue Ridge power controversy in 1970, CAD ceased to exist in late 1967, only a year after the first meeting in Bristol.[20]

The Lessons of CAD:
Dollars and Galluses

The Congress for Appalachian Development failed because it could not generate either money or broad popular support. But why was the money not forthcoming? And why did grassroots support not develop?

At least four factors accounted for CAD's cycle of poverty. The first was that liberals were profligate with their good will and stingy with their money. CAD's files bulged with letters approving its aims, but its coffers remained empty. The second factor was that the federal government could not be persuaded to fund an effort that questioned the assumptions of the free enterprise system, especially as they were represented by coal companies and private utilities in Appalachia. What it had already declined to do through both the Area Redevelopment Administration and the Appalachian Regional Commission, it would not agree to do through CAD two years later. No federal department or agency (Interior, the Corps of Engineers, ARC, the Bureau of Land Reclamation) would touch CAD.

If these two factors help explain why private and public money from outside the region was not available, another perhaps accounted for the lack of funds from closer to home: CAD was too often identified with TVA and the Appalachian Volunteers. Once CAD was tied to TVA, as it was in a number of Harry Caudill's early articles and speeches, it could not be separated from it, even after the TVA analogy was dropped by most CAD people themselves. Ben Franklin's *New York Times* article (the most frequently reprinted of all) made the connection, as did most other newspaper coverage of CAD's activities.

Association with the AVs was apparently also a liability. AV Director Milton Ogle was on the CAD board, and for a time CAD received funds through the AVs while awaiting its own tax-exempt clearance. A letter from Ebersole to the vice-president of a Pikeville, Kentucky, bank requesting a donation for CAD elicited a polite but firm refusal which hinted vaguely that CAD might be connected with the AVs.[21] The AVs at the time were charged with spreading sedition in coal-rich Pike County.

Grassroots support for CAD inside the region failed to develop partly because of the confusing and fragmenting multiplicity of the organization's aims. The core idea had been to establish PUDs in Appalachia. That would have been a difficult enough task in itself if initial efforts had been concentrated upon forming *one* successful PUD, say in Harry Caudill's own Letcher County, Kentucky, or in Summers County, West Virginia, where the publicly owned Bluestone Dam stood ready to have generators installed while the Appalachian Power Company was attempting to turn more of the New River to private development.[22] But eventually PUDs became only one goal among many: general tax reform, a severance tax on coal, mine-mouth power, new towns, and so on. Although the goals were conceptually and practically related, it was impossible either to pursue all of them on limited resources or to communicate their interrelatedness with sufficient force and clarity to gain public understanding and support.

Among the more important reasons for CAD's failure to develop grassroots support (and financial backing), however, was that until quite late it was strictly a "top-down" effort. The PUDs of the Pacific Northwest had been formed by farmers through their Grange, but the PUD idea was "laid on" Appalachian people from above. The Congress for Appalachian Development came much closer to being the "holding company" Lloyd Davis called for at the Bristol meeting than the "one-gallus" organization Tom Gish and others said was necessary.

A late effort to generate grassroots support for CAD took the form of plans for an Appalachian People's Congress—an outdoor meeting of perhaps several thousand people to be held in the summer of 1967. Its organizers hoped it would be a combination political rally, tent meeting, activities fair, and folk celebration where people could meet each other, sing and dance, air their grievances, and perhaps form working coalitions to push CAD's program of democratic resource development. But the People's Congress was never held.

The Congress had been originally suggested by board members Richard Austin, Don West, Milton Ogle, and Myles Horton to counter CAD's "top-down" orientation. "The boldness of [CAD's] plan for the region," Horton wrote to West in early February,

> is not matched by the conventional organizational form. . . . The heady new wine has been put in old bottles. . . . If CAD continues to spend time perfecting the Plan, leaving the broadening of the organization . . . to chance, the end result is predictable. CAD will end up with a technically perfect plan and the opposition will end up with the people and power. [The] energies and creativity and un-academic wisdom of the heretofore unheard-from must be given top priority. . . . Those people who live at the branch-heads and across swinging bridges are correctly suspicious of programs that have been worked out for them.[23]

Even after it was agreed that a Congress should be held, there was no consensus on whose ideas should predominate. Ebersole envisioned a meeting with "speakers of outstanding experience," but Austin wanted the experts in the background. Caudill wanted to "put our ideas before the people," but West urged that the ideas of the people themselves be listened to first.[24] Without resolving the issue, plans were laid to hold a three- to four-day Congress for perhaps five thousand people during the summer of 1967. The budget was $65,000, and a planning meeting was set for mid-May.

The Knoxville planning meeting drew a number of new proponents of the "one-gallus" position, including five representatives of the AVs, Guy Carawan from Highlander Center, two participants from Chicago's JOIN community organization in the Uptown Appalachian ghetto, and one from the Raleigh County, West Virginia, CAP recently taken over by the AVs. Others were from more conservative organizations such as the North Carolina Fund, the Council of the Southern Mountains, and the Citizens Crusade Against Poverty. Six came from local community organizations.

The outcome of the meeting, like the impulse that produced it, was schizophrenic. The group agreed that it "did not include sufficient representation from indigenous community action and regional groups" to issue a "valid call" for the Congress, and therefore decided to submit the idea to local and state groups, which could then issue a call if they were so inclined. Nevertheless, an advisory committee was set up to coordinate planning for the Congress, and Austin left Knoxville convinced that it would be held in August at Henderson Settlement School in Frakes, Kentucky. The Council of the Southern Mountains offered an issue of *Mountain Life and Work* for publicity purposes, and the AVs were understood to have promised planning money and staff support. Austin said CAD would continue to play "a significant, but back-seat role."

By late June, the AVs' Tom Rhodenbaugh was making arrangements for using the Frakes site. But the AVs' involvement in the anti–strip-mining conflict in eastern Kentucky and West Virginia was growing more intense, and within a few weeks they decided that a regional People's Congress was not a good idea. By early July, Rhodenbaugh reported that some local people felt that their concerns did not cross state lines and that the AVs could not do all that was required to make the Congress a success. He suggested statewide meetings as an alternative, and (without notifying anyone in CAD) discontinued planning.[25]

Thus although Harry Caudill's "Operation Bootstrap" article had envisioned CAD as a people's movement in the sense that important resources were to be returned to public ownership and used for the common good, CAD never became a people's movement in the political and organizational sense. But there were gains, nevertheless. Public power was discussed freshly for the first time since the late 1930s, and a model for public power development more attractive than TVA was introduced.[26] The severance tax advocated by CAD was later enacted in two Appalachian states. The Appalachian Power Company was blocked in its attempt to build another private power project on the New River.[27] The failure of the Appalachian Regional Commission to consider basic economic and political realities in its development strategy was brought to public attention. And public control and allocation of primary resources moved nearer to the top of the agenda among those seeking alternative development strategies for the region.

Notes

1. An account of Caudill's involvement in regional issues may be found in David G. McCullough, "The Lonely War of a Good Angry Man," *American Heritage*, XXI (December 1969), 97–113. The following account of his work with Ebersole is based on the files of the Congress for Appalachian Development made available to me by Mr. Ebersole and on interviews with Richard Austin, William Blizzard, Robb Burlage, Harry Caudill, Gordon Ebersole, Ed Fraley, Thomas Gish, Myles Horton, Paul Kaufman, Milton Ogle, Thomas Rhodenbaugh, and Don West. A brief account of Ebersole's background appears in the *Congressional Record,* June 8, 1973, p. 4541.

2. Morris L. Cooke, *Report of the Giant Power Survey Board to the General Assembly of the Commonwealth of Pennsylvania* (Harrisburg, Pa.: Telegraph Printing, 1925). Private utilities considered the report so threatening that their representatives reportedly checked out copies from some libraries and destroyed them.

3. See William M. Greene, *Rufus Woods' Magnificent Pipe Dream* (Washington, D.C.: U.S. Department of the Interior, n.d.).

4. See Lee Metcalf and Vic Reinemer, *Overcharge* (New York: David McKay, 1967), pp. 72, 228. Even after rejuvenation following the Eisenhower years, the commission was smaller in 1965 than it had been in 1949.

5. Harry Caudill, *Night Comes to the Cumberlands: A Biography of a Depressed Area* (Boston: Atlantic–Little, Brown, 1963), p. 367.

6. See *Louisville Courier-Journal*, September 1, 1963; Harry Caudill, "Appalachia: The Path from Disaster," *The Nation*, CXCVIII (March 9, 1964), 240; and *idem*, "The Permanent Poor: The Lesson of Eastern Kentucky," *Atlantic Monthly*, CCXIII (June 1964), 49–53.

7. Ebersole to Caudill, February 24, 1964.

8. My account of the development of the PUD model is based upon Ted F. Berry, "The PUD Story: History of a Phenomenal Grass Roots Movement in the State of Washington," *Grange News*, December 19, 1952; John B. Dawson, "Legal Aspects and Historic Background of Public Power," undated mimeo report from the legal firm of Wood, King, and Dawson; *Louisville Courier-Journal and Times Magazine*, March 5, 1967, pp. 7 ff.; Vincent Hovanec's article in the *Wall Street Journal*, August 25, 1967; *National Power Survey: A Report by the Federal Power Commission* (Washington, D.C.: Government Printing Office, 1965); and the files of the Congress for Appalachian Development.

9. See Metcalf and Reinemer, *Overcharge*, p. 11, and Thomas Brom and Edward Kirshner, "Buying Power: Towards a Public Utility Network," *Ramparts*, October 1974, pp. 1–6.

10. *Louisville Courier-Journal*, March 20, 1974, p. B-1. The Federal Office of Revenue Sharing refused to consider the utility-generated local funds in

computing the city's share of revenue-sharing money. The ruling put all cities with municipal power systems at a competitive disadvantage.

11. Caudill, "A New Plan for a Southern Mountain Authority," *Appalachian Review*, I (Summer 1966), 6–11, and "An 'Operation Bootstrap' for Eastern Kentucky," *Appalachian South*, I (Spring–Summer 1966), 16–18. See also Caudill's remarks on CAD and the colonial status of eastern Kentucky in "Appalachia: The Dismal Land," in Jeremy Larner and Irving Howe (eds.), *Poverty: Views from the Left* (New York: William Morrow, 1970), pp. 264–73; Harry Caudill, *A Darkness at Dawn: Appalachian Kentucky and The Future* (Lexington: University Press of Kentucky, 1976); and Gordon Ebersole, "Appalachia: Potential . . . with a View," *Mountain Life and Work (MLW)*, XLII (Winter 1966), 10–12.

12. See an article by John Fetterman in the *Louisville Courier-Journal*, March 5, 1967, p. 5, and National Committee for the Defense of Political Prisoners, *Harlan Miners Speak* (New York: Harcourt, 1932), pp. 123 ff. The involvement of mountaineers in the Gastonia, Marion, and Elizabethton textile strikes is recounted in Tom Tippett's *When Southern Labor Stirs* (New York: Jonathan Cape and Harrison Smith, 1931).

13. See *Appalachian South*, I (Fall–Winter 1965), 39.

14. Minutes of meeting, Harry Lasker Library, Highlander Center. A brief account of the meeting appears in *Appalachian South*, I (Fall–Winter 1966), 42. See also Bill Blizzard, "West Virginia Wonderland," *Appalachian South*, I (Spring–Summer 1966), 9–16; Paul Kaufman, "Wistfulginia: A Fable with a Sad Ending," *Appalachian South*, II (Spring–Summer 1967), 24–25; and Lewis G. Smith, "New Towns from Mountaintops," *Appalachian Review*, II (Winter 1968), 20–23. Caudill commented on Smith's plan in "An Appalachian Switzerland," *Appalachian South*, II (Spring–Summer 1967), 7–8.

15. Minutes of October 15 meeting, and William Blizzard, "Dawn Over Appalachia," *Charleston Gazette-Mail State Magazine*, November 6, 1966. Those on the steering committee were Austin, Blizzard, Caudill, Davis, Ebersole, Fraley, Gish, Kaufman, Ogle, and West.

16. See John Fetterman, "A Bold Idea for a New Appalachia," *Louisville Courier-Journal and Times Magazine*, March 5, 1967, pp. 6–10, reprinted in David S. Walls and John B. Stephenson (eds.), *Appalachia in the Sixties: Decade of Reawakening* (Lexington: University Press of Kentucky, 1972), pp. 232 ff. Woodrow R. Clevinger reported in "Southern Appalachian Highlanders in Western Washington," *Pacific Northwest Quarterly*, XXXIII (1942), 3–25, that fifteen thousand western Washington mountaineers were "immigrants or Washington-born children of immigrants from Appalachia."

17. Quotation from *News-Sentinel*, January 24, 1967. See reports in the *Herald-Virginian*, January 26, 1967; the *Washington Post*, February 16, 1967; and the *Mountain Eagle*, January 26, 1967. Thomas F. Stafford had written a long and informative article on PUDs in the *Charleston Gazette-Mail*, January 8, 1967. The *National Observer* carried a piece on CAD by John Fetterman on March 27, 1967. The *Charleston Gazette* reprinted the Ben Franklin article on March 26, and the *Courier-Journal* on March 27. The *Wall Street Journal* article, by Vincent Hovanec, did not appear until August 25. Mine-mouth power generation became an important plank in the CAD platform for Ap-

palachia. Instead of shipping coal by railroad hundreds of miles to generating plants, the idea was to build plants adjacent to the mines and transmit the power to distant load centers ("shipping coal by wire"). The possible benefits of mine-mouth power for eastern Kentucky were hinted at as early as 1932 by Melvin P. Levy in an essay in *Harlan Miners Speak*, p. 26.

18. Metcalf inserted one of Fetterman's articles on CAD into the *Congressional Record* on March 27, 1967. Harry Caudill and Lewis Smith testified as CAD members at congressional hearings on Senator Mundt's Balanced Economic Development legislation in the summer of 1967.

19. Harry Caudill, "Education for a New Appalachia," April 20, 1967 (mimeo). Caudill also spoke at the West Virginia University Institute for Labor Studies, before the National Advisory Commission on Rural Poverty, to law students at the University of Kentucky (whom he urged to draft a model PUD bill), and elsewhere.

20. Caudill quotation from letter of July 7, 1967.

21. Letter from John M. Yost to Ebersole, August 11, 1967.

22. In March 1966, several months before CAD was formed, the Federal Power Commission denied the Appalachian Power Company's request to install generators in Bluestone on the grounds that the facility had been authorized by Congress for public development. There was some discussion of proposing public development of Bluestone at the October 15, 1966, CAD board meeting, but no subsequent action—except arranging for an informal, preliminary study—was taken.

23. Horton to West, February 1, 1967. An expanded version of Horton's remarks was published in *Appalachian South*, II (Spring–Summer 1967), 15. In the same issue, other commentators agreed with Horton's analysis.

24. Minutes of CAD board meeting, March 25, 1967, at Hinton, West Virginia. My account of planning for the Congress is based on CAD files; an unpublished paper by Richard Austin dated October 10, 1967; documents in the Highlander Center library; and interviews with Austin, West, Ogle, Ebersole, and Horton.

25. Memo of July 2, 1967, Berea College Library. The West Virginia AVs actually helped to organize a statewide congress in August, which crystallized local efforts leading to the formation of the Fair Elections Committee and the Political Action League. It is doubtful whether the AVs could have organized a regional congress had they chosen to. They were working in only two states (Kentucky and West Virginia), and there was little coordination between their staffs even in those two.

26. See, for example, a renewed discussion of PUDs in *The Elements*, No. 4 (January 1975), pp. 1 ff.

27. For an account of CAD's involvement in the controversy over the New River power project in 1970, see David E. Whisnant, "A Case Study in Appalachian Development," *New South*, XXVIII (Spring 1973), 34–43.

CHAPTER 9

Paradoxes of Insurgency: Revolt Against the Planners in the Kentucky River Area Development District

[What] I cannot understand is why the American people which has been drilled from the beginning in the necessity . . . of the individual and his point of view, does not now realize how complete is the collapse of that idea as a working social formula. . . . .

As it is now, we have gotten no further than the right of the most cunning and strong among us to aggrandize [our]selves, leaving the rest of us . . . to subsist on what is left. . . . .

Americans should mentally follow individualism to its ultimate conclusion, for society is not and cannot be a jungle. It should be . . . an escape from this drastic individualism which, for some, means all, and for the many, little or nothing. . . . .

[It] is really not complete individualism for anybody that we need or want or can endure even, but a limited form of individualism which will guarantee to all, insofar as possible, the right, if there is such a right, to life, liberty, and the pursuit of happiness, and also an equitable share of the economic results of any such organization as the presence and harmony of numerous individuals presupposes and compels.

Theodore Dreiser, *Harlan Miners Speak* (1932)

LETCHER COUNTY, KENTUCKY, is a relatively small area in which most of the Appalachian region's social, economic, and political problems can be seen, like the topography of the county itself, in high relief.

In July and August 1972, hundreds of angry citizens in Letcher County, one of the eight counties of the ARC's Kentucky River Area Development District (KRADD), gathered at a series of heated public meetings to oppose the district's comprehensive plan for the county. When the dust had settled, the county fiscal court had abolished both the plan and the KRADD-backed planning commission, the executive director of KRADD had resigned, and the Democratic county judge who had originally supported the plan had been defeated in his bid for re-election.[1]

The controversy raised most of the critical issues involved in planning for Appalachia: the value assumptions and cultural biases of planners; the politics of planning and zoning; the dynamics of citizen involvement in planning; the dangers and possibilities of regionalism and "creative federalism"; and the actual impact of planning, growth, and development on people's lives. It also revealed, as few recent events have, the extent to which Appalachian people—although exploited for generations by mainstream society—paradoxically share many of the social and political values of mainstream America that produced the exploitation, and thus are stymied in their need to imagine and create new lives, social forms, and institutions for themselves and their children. It was as if the ghostly echo of Dreiser's voice still rang through Letcher County forty years after Bloody Harlan.

Letcher County: What You Have to Work With

> Letcher County was formed in 1842, and since that time we have survived six wars and eleven depressions. . . . Through all those troublesome times, our county system was adequate to meet our needs. . . . Now the planners tell us our county system can no longer meet our needs—that we need plans made by development districts.
>
> Willard Gilliam, Chairman,
> Committee to Save Letcher County[2]

By the time it was established and named for the then Governor of Kentucky in 1842 the area of Letcher County (in which a year later vacant land could be bought by mail order for two and a half cents an acre) had already known several decades of settlement and abuse. Following the first permanent settler around 1795, commercial fur traders moved in about 1804. When fur trading ceased to be profitable, entrepreneurs turned to timber cutting in the vast virgin forests of poplar and hardwoods. After the Civil War, large lumber companies began floating their valuable cuttings, bought for almost nothing, down the North Fork of the Kentucky River to Frankfort.

Two decades later timber was becoming scarce, but the county's rich coal resources, contained in multiple seams up to seven feet thick lying fifty to a thousand feet above the narrow valley floor, were being mapped by northern corporations. In a report to the American Missionary Association in 1909, H. Paul Douglas graphically sketched the implications of the beginnings of that process:

[The] old mountain life is fast passing. We went a three days' horseback ride . . . until we came at nightfall to the cabin of Old

Man Jackson on the border of Letcher County. . . . He has a four-room cabin with three great stone chimneys, and there with his strong sons and daughters he dwells in self-sufficiency. His farm and pasture furnish food; his wool, clothing. The loom stands on the back porch, and the family . . . are chiefly clad in homespun. We slept under many thicknesses of homespun blankets, in a room where rings of pumpkins were drying on spikes stuck between the stones of the great fireplace. . . . I thought that of this spot at least I would be safe for fifty years in telling the old story of the mountaineer. . . . Yet, within three months, I read [that] "The Blank & Blank Company of Indiana will spend a million dollars in Letcher County in the coming year. It will build thirty miles of railroad and open nineteen coke ovens." And why? Because the Lord sent a freshet which ran under Old Man Jackson's kitchen and laid bare a bed of coal. . . . Therefore, where never in all the world had the shadow of one human habitation fallen upon another, a narrow valley will be crammed with crowded miners' huts. [And] Old Man Jackson's sons, who have never been in bondage to any man, . . . will toil underground.[3]

Actually, twenty years before Douglas wrote, Consolidation, Elkhorn, South-East and other companies were already buying coal rights in Letcher County for a tiny fraction of their value. After the arrival of the railroad in 1911, the coal boom peaked rapidly, with companies throwing up coal camps all over the county named for the companies themselves (Seco = South-East Coal Company) or their executives (Jenkins, Haymond, McRoberts, Fleming). The population of Letcher County jumped from 10,500 in 1910 to nearly 25,000 a decade later. During the three decades after 1910, it quadrupled before peaking at approximately 40,500 in 1940.[4]

The social and political costs of such convulsive change were nearly incalculable. Besides carting off billions of dollars worth of lumber and coal on which they paid no taxes, corporations changed the basic social structure, gained control of county politics, and in effect turned the whole county to their own private uses. When a combination of periodic declines in the coal market and the development of automated mining techniques after World War II reduced the companies' needs for human labor (mining employment dropped 31 percent between 1950 and 1970), many coal camps became ghost towns almost overnight. Seco was a home of sorts to 644 people in 1950; only 88 remained in 1970. Letcher County as a whole lost nearly half its total population between 1940 and 1970.

At the time of the KRADD controversy in 1972, unemployment

ran around 10 percent; per capita income was about one-half the U.S. average; 30 percent of the family incomes were below the poverty level; 16 percent of the population was on welfare, and there were only about fifty manufacturing jobs in the entire county. The demand for jobs was so great that when the U.S. Shoe Corporation announced in 1969 that it would locate a plant in the county that would provide 400 jobs, more than 5,000 people showed up to apply. Although offered a free site, utilities, and other inducements, the company eventually located elsewhere. Farming, which once provided a livelihood for many, did so no longer; in 1969, only eighty-three farms remained of the more than six hundred that had existed a decade earlier.

Even automated deep mining had given way increasingly to fast, cheap (if social costs are discounted) strip-mining, which required an even smaller labor force and compounded environmental problems. One man working in an automated deep mine could produce about 2,000 tons of coal in a year; on a strip-auger operation he could produce about 5,000, using methods and equipment that were almost primitive in their simplicity. Thus strip-mining output in the county rose from 62,000 tons in 1950 to more than 3 million tons in 1970. More than 8,000 acres of land had been stripped, and it seemed likely that by 1990 the figure would rise to 60,000 (almost one-third of the total land area). At current levels of use, the county's 6,500 million tons of coal reserves were expected to last 300 to 600 years.[5]

Thus one could hardly expect to find a county in which the effects of past abuse, present conditions, and the probability of continued exploitation in the future would make rational, humane planning seem more essential. The land itself was being ruined by strip-mining; well-paid jobs were few; health care and educational facilities were poor; the tax structure was regressive; and heavy out-migration of the work force had left a high percentage of the very young, the old, and the disabled.

Paradoxically, Letcher County for a decade or more had been in the forefront of planning in eastern Kentucky. Caudill's *Night Comes to the Cumberlands* had ended with a plan for a "Southern Mountain Authority." Tom Gish, chairman of Whitesburg's town planning commission, described as early as 1964 how his town had benefited from planning and participating in federal aid programs, which brought a new court house, a sewer system, residential zoning and development, a county library, a shopping center, and other less tangible benefits. Asked to explain how such events had been brought to pass, Gish said the most effective means had been the Whitesburg Planning and Zoning Commission.[6]

How did it happen, then, in view of the apparently urgent need for planned improvement and the county's background of experience with planning, that KRADD's *Comprehensive Plan* evoked such tumult? Why was there such bitter invective, with each side calling the other "Communists" and the resigned KRADD director calling the leader of the opposition "a nut, and a tool," his followers "stupid, selfish, uninformed, and some of them deliberate damned liars," and editor Gish "a damned agitator"?[7]

Part of the answer was that there was a lot of money to be made, quickly and easily, from coal and (increasingly) oil. Although for the many a century of unfettered entrepreneurial exploitation had left the county a poverty-stricken wasteland, for the fortunate few it was like being in California in 1849. Oil production doubled (to 226,000 barrels) between 1968 and 1971 as the large oil companies moved in, frequently through their coal company subsidiaries. And coal prices were to rise steadily during the next several years.

Ultimately as important as money in shaping the controversy, however, was that each side adopted a doctrinaire position only partially in accord with the complexities of the situation. The planners naively disregarded the potential of supposedly liberal planning approaches to be co-opted and used repressively in a county dominated almost totally by the coal industry. Their opponents declined (as Dreiser had lamented) to "follow individualism to its ultimate conclusion" and realize "how complete is the collapse of that idea as a working social formula."

The *Comprehensive Plan* and the Planning Process

The *Comprehensive Plan* was written by William Kingsbury, a planner for R. W. Booker and Associates of Lexington, under a HUD planning grant administered by KRADD.[8] Work began on the plan in mid-1971 and was completed about a year later. Kingsbury worked fairly closely with the Fleming, Jenkins, Neon, and Letcher County Planning Commission (LCPC). In fact his plan for the most part merely repeated recommendations the LCPC had already adopted without controversy in 1971: creating jobs through industrial diversification, improving public facilities and services, and zoning. The *Comprehensive Plan* went beyond the LCPC's recommendations only in its so-called initial housing element, based on a "windshield survey" of housing in the county.[9]

In some respects, then, the plan was a more or less "standard" document whose chief effect might merely have been, as was claimed by its backers, that the county would become eligible for much-needed federal funds. But the plan had substantive defects that were not only serious in themselves but were magnified by an almost total failure to involve the county's people in the planning process.

Most of the substantive defects derived from the bland assumption that the "dominant position of the coal industry in Letcher County has existed since the 1920s . . . and it appears that the industry will continue to hold this position in the future." Although at one level the statement merely acknowledged political and economic realities in the county, it also rationalized declining to recommend changes from the status quo. Taken as the starting point for planning, it meant that coal was and would be king and that people would have to get along as best they could.

Thus strip-mining was mentioned, but in a way not likely to offend mining interests ("Stripmining can . . . make land unsuitable for future utilization"). Gingerly acknowledging the social costs of strip-mining, the plan said, "It would not appear unfair that [the] cost [of new water supplies and land reclamation] be calculated in the price of coal, and that these practices be so regulated that the ill effects of stripmining are stopped."

Some language apparently had been made intentionally ambiguous. The statement that residential areas "should be free from the influence and possible encroachment of incompatible land uses" (p. 61) could be (and was by some people in the county) taken to mean that people would be permitted to live only where there was no coal. Although the plan also said, "Mining should take place only where it will not have a detrimental effect on other land uses" (p. 62), considerable discretionary latitude lay between the two statements. And in Letcher County, discretionary questions are usually resolved in favor of coal. The plan repeatedly either said or implied, in fact, that it might be necessary to move people's homes, but when it pointed out that "it would appear highly desirable to relocate the [coal] tipple in Mayking," it added that such an outcome "appears unlikely."

"If stripmining is to continue," the plan concluded, omitting the county's citizens as a party to the discussion, "the miner [read, mine operator], government and developer will have to work together to make this . . . land use plan a reality" (p. 75). The problem in eastern Kentucky was, however, that the government had a habit of working more cooperatively with mine operators than with private citizens. One highly visible and dangerous result of such cooperation had been the cavalier building of illegal slag dams for the impoundment of mine waste water all over the Appalachian coal fields. Thirteen such dams were in Letcher County, but none was mentioned in the *Comprehensive Plan*.[10]

besides failing to take into account the political and economic influence of the coal industry, the plan was based upon assumptions biased in favor of middle- and upper-class values and of urban areas. "As in most rural areas," it said, "people believe that they should be allowed to use their land as they see fit" (p. 47). Whether such attitudes were in fact more characteristic of rural than city people, or of poor than rich, was left unasked.

Similarly, the plan argued that land-use planning is "conducive to . . . the efficiency of private enterprise." But in Letcher County strip-mining and auger mining, the most visible examples of unfettered private enterprise, were inefficient even by the narrowest of definitions, for each renders more coal irrecoverable than it produces and entails high social costs not computed in the cost of production.

In sum, then, the *Comprehensive Plan* turned out to be conventional and uninspired in its approach to planning, laced with uncritical assumptions, and limited by a simplistic technocratic rationality. Laissez-faire economic arrangements, conventional bureaucratic structures, and middle-class "facilities and services" were assumed to be absolute necessities for a civilized social order. None of the alternative development ideas that had been widely discussed during the last fifteen years (for example, on housing, land use, transportation, energy production and use, community planning) figured even marginally in the plan.

The plan was in any case bound to create conflict, because it was not prepared in consultation with the community. Whether the citizens of Letcher County in fact had an opportunity to help prepare the plan is a matter of dispute. Opponents of the plan said they had no opportunity; backers said they had it but did not use it.

The R. W. Booker and Associates contract itself merely specified, "*After the final printed [plan is] available* a public meeting will be conducted . . . to stimulate local interest in the [plan] and the planning process" (emphasis added). The planner himself never came closer to most of the county's people than scrutinizing their houses through an automobile windshield, and even that inspection was carried out mostly by hired assistants. Indeed, it is doubtful that "participation" would have altered the plan significantly. The models and assumptions around which the "planning process" was built were by their nature inhospitable to any suggestions that might have arisen from community participation.

On July 18, 1972, the Letcher County Planning Commission approved the *Comprehensive Plan* and transmitted it to the fiscal court for adoption. In the ensuing weeks, reaction to the plan fanned into flame most of the latent fears, grievances, resentments, and factionalisms that were smoldering in Letcher County.

The Committee to Save Letcher County

> The people of Appalachia are no more and no less stupid, no more and no less intelligent, than people anywhere else. They can and will spot a phony, be it a phony individual or a phony program. . . . Once the facts are laid before a mountain man, once he understands a program or an issue, he almost invariably makes a proper decision.
>
> Thomas Gish, editor,
> *Mountain Eagle*

> Gilliam shines on one side. Gilliam's like the moon, you know. As he revolves he is dark on one side, and that way you can't figure Gilliam out.
>
> Joe Begley,
> Blackey, Kentucky
> March, 1974[11]

Opposition formed as soon as the *Comprehensive Plan* was introduced at the required public hearing on July 18, 1972. Planner William Kingsbury was questioned pointedly: Why were copies of the plan not available for public inspection? Who benefits if local people have their land condemned for federal tourist complexes? Is there any use to plan, with the county being destroyed by strip-mining? Kingsbury's suggestion that people "sit down with the coal operators and say we have to live together" allayed no fears. Noting the plan's estimate that 60,000 acres of the county would be stripped by 1990, Columbus Sexton of Sandlick said that "we'll be lucky to have 60,000 acres left by the time the strippers are done."[12]

As details of the plan continued to leak out, opposition intensified. On July 22 two hundred people gathered in a tense meeting at the Mayking school. Spokesman Willard Gilliam declared: "This [plan] could be the first step in enslaving you." Fred Back of Mayking said, "I built my home and use my land to suit me, and that's the way it's going to stay." Residents of Eolia (on the far side of Pine Mountain, where the plan suggested the creation of a tourist area) were strongly opposed. County Judge Robert Collins tried to get permission for KRADD director Holliday to explain the plan but was voted down and challenged to reply to reports that he had recently bought land in the Eolia area. The following night at a meeting in the circuit courtroom in Whitesburg, a protesting group of three hundred people overflowed into the halls. Voicing a theme that was to become increasingly important, William Ison of Eolia said, "I can't see anything in this plan . . . except communism, one hundred percent." Phil Bentley of Mayking urged the crowd to take control over their own lives, and plans were made for citizens to attend the next meeting of the fiscal court en masse, wearing black armbands and patches signifying "doom for Letcher County" and suicide for any public official who approved of the plan.

Two days later five hundred people showed up at a meeting of the fiscal court and presented 1,300 signatures on a petition demanding that the plan be rejected. Faced with such opposition, and forced to admit that few people (including the county commissioners) had detailed knowledge of the plan, Letcher County Planning Commission chairman Alvin Webb withdrew it. At the court's next meeting, Webb formally submitted the plan but recommended that it be rejected. The court did so, and then for good measure abolished the Commission itself. The meeting had not been announced, so the crowd was smaller than it might have been, but those who attended made sure their sentiments were clearly understood. Willie Lamb of the McRoberts community drew cheers with his statement: "When we first went . . . to the cities, they called us hillbillies. Now they want to move us off the hills. If we're satisfied being hillbillies, why don't they leave us alone?" The meeting ended with the singing of "Cabin on the Hill":

> Oh, I'd like to wander back
> To the cabin on the hill;
> Beneath the shadow of the trees
> I'd like to linger still.

For all its surface simplicity, Willie Lamb's remark was a complicated response to what was correctly perceived as a complex threat. Those who crowded into the courtroom were not ignorant of the history of the lumbermen and coal operators in Letcher County. They had lost jobs because the mines closed or automated, and had lost children when the only new jobs available were in distant cities. They had witnessed a succession of liberal social programs that had turned out to be either worthless or harmful. The only tangible security left to many was a house and perhaps a small plot of land. Thus they could not bring themselves to approve a plan that might even potentially compromise their freedom to hold and use their property.

As with so much else in Letcher County, the "Cabin on the Hill" meeting was a response to circumstances not unique to Appalachia. It merely exhibited in high relief not only the general (and in this case fairly abstract) dilemma of balancing individual human rights against the common good but also the more immediate problem of personal survival in an essentially hostile social system. One implicit message of the meeting was that, in such a system, liberal planning assumptions are not valid. "They've welfared us and studied us and stripped us," said a man at one of the opposition meetings. "Now they want to move us."[13]

Opposition did not cease when the plan was voted down. By the time of the decisive fiscal court meeting, Willard Gilliam (an employee of the Department of Economic Security) had formed the Committee to Save Letcher County. Meetings were being held in several communities, and there was talk of moving into KRADD's seven other counties. Within a few days, the initially rather diffuse opposition (housing, zoning, strip-mining, tourism, and other issues were mentioned) focused on the issue of planning itself and on several narrower concerns typified by an excerpt from the plan published on the front page of the *Mountain Eagle:*

> The limited land available for development in Letcher County requires [that] space needed for various land uses be carefully calculated. In addition, there is a need for the rearrangement of space within the county. *For example, many houses should be moved off a hillside or out of the hollow into an area where urban services can be provided.*[14]

The *Eagle* dubbed the plan the "land-use move-'em-out plan," and Gilliam chose the term "rusticide" ("the killing of rural areas") to denote the "gradual, systematic, relentless destruction of our customs, traditions, our mode of living, our civil rights, the right to retain and use our land as we see fit, under the law, and the right of local people to rule themselves."

The plan's arguments for relocation were that some land being used for residential purposes was subject to slides or flooding, some dwellings were too close together, and others were too sparsely scattered up the hollows to provide "urban services" (water and sewer lines). To the planners, and perhaps to most urban dwellers, such arguments appeared both sensible and benign. But to rural residents of the county they were ominous; prior events had suggested the existence of a general strategy of depopulating the region. One of the earliest reports on the region done during the Appalachian decade of the 1960s argued that there was a "low percentage [of people] in metropolitan areas" compared to the rest of the nation.[15] The subsequent growth center strategy and highway program of the Appalachian Regional Commission were calculated to change that pattern.

Relocating portions of the Appalachian population was not a wholly alien idea, however. Indeed, Letcher County's Harry Caudill wrote in 1963:

> A physical resettlement of much of the [Cumberland] plateau's
> human resources is . . . essential to a modernization of the re-
> gion. . . . Lonesome houses and shacks have been pushed onto
> mountain benches and into remote coves. [It] is time for an
> enlightened society to devote [the land] to a, valuable use in
> keeping with its capacities.

Two years later, in an article on the Appalachian Regional Commission, he resumed, "No valid justification for living on rough and
isolated creeks exists at the present time. By every reasonable standard
the people would be far better off living in towns, where the amenities
of life could be supplied at bearable costs."[16]

As Caudill and others came to suspect that an admitted need for
relocation in some instances was being used by the Commission and
other agencies to justify a general policy of depopulation, their views
changed. In an interview in 1966 (only one year after the Commission
was established), federal Cochairman John Sweeney said Commission
policy was to "ignore the pockets of poverty . . . scattered in inacces-
sible hollows all over the area [and build] roads so that [people]
can . . . commute to new jobs in or near the cities," which in turn
would "radiate some of their prosperity into the impoverished darker
reaches of the region."[17] Tom Gish, perhaps skeptical of the evangelical flavor of Sweeney's metaphor, replied a few months later that
the "new line [is] move or starve. [The] new Tough Guy solution is
to eliminate the people from the mountains."[18]

In 1968, Caudill reported that a cochairman of the Commission
visited him and, when asked what the Commission's aim was, responded bluntly, "To move people out of the mountains." Executive
Director Ralph Widner spoke upon occasion of a "residual maintenance population," and his successor Alvin Arnett speculated about
giving over some parts of the region to the mining of coal while
"bringing miners in, treating them like a work crew on a train." Why
should people "have to live that kind of life," he asked an interviewer,
adding that "there are places [in the region] now that I would write
off as acceptable places to live." Asked if he envisioned wholesale
exporting of people from the region, he said, "We're not talking
anything like that *at this stage.*" By August 1972, Caudill had concluded
that "depopulation is a part of ARC's scheme, not because it will
benefit people but because it will clear the land for a new round of
exploitation by the absentee companies."[19]

Thus people in Letcher County had substantial justification for
feeling that, regardless of how benign the *Comprehensive Plan* seemed
to others, someone intended to move them forcibly—out of the hollows in any case, and perhaps out of the mountains as well. Tom Gish

put it even more bluntly: "Make no mistake about it. The [Appalachian Regional Commission] is planning genocide in the mountains. . . . No mountain residents, no mountaineers, no mountain poverty, no problems."[20]

As opposition to the plan formed, it had some promise not only of providing an effective critique of a badly flawed local plan and regional development strategy but also of generating a creative discussion of the county's problems and alternatives, and perhaps even of forming the nucleus of a populist political organization. In its best moments, the controversy turned people's attention toward fundamental consitutional questions. At a November 1972 meeting of the Committee to Save Letcher County, 150 people heard Williard Gilliam read from the Declaration of Independence: "We hold these truths to be self-evident. . . . That to secure these rights, governments are instituted among men, deriving their just power from the consent of the governed; that whenever any form of government becomes destructive to these ends, it is the right of the people to alter or abolish it." Comparing development district bureaucrats to the agents of King George, Gilliam continued to read the subsequent charges that the King "has erected a multitude of new offices, and has sent hither swarms of officers to harass our people and eat out their substance."

Practically, the Committee accomplished a good deal. It served notice that autocratic planning would not be tolerated in Letcher County. It generated petitions to return to a more accountable magisterial system of county government, placed the question on the ballot, and persuaded voters to approve it. And it defeated a plan that, however potentially useful in some respects, had sinister possibilities.

And yet, in the final analysis, the uprising fell short of its promise. It foundered on the limitations of its own ideology, the domination of the county (especially jobs and public opinion) by the coal companies, the internecine rivalries of local politics, and the heritage of red-baiting in eastern Kentucky.

County Politics and Communist Plans

> The conservationists who demand that strip-miners do a better job of [reclaiming] what they tear up are stupid idiots, socialists, and commies who don't know what they are talking about. I think it is our bounden duty to knock them down and subject them to the ridicule they deserve.
>
> James Riley, vice-president,
> Consolidation Coal Company
> September 1970

We are spending billions of dollars yearly to fight communism
overseas. But it looks like we are fighting it in the pasture when
really it is right here in the barn.

Relon Hampton,
Jeremiah, Kentucky
March 1973[21]

On January 4, 1973, Willard Gilliam announced his candidacy for
the office of county judge, bringing to the surface a previously submerged factor in the planning controversy. Gilliam said he had "no
political ambitions" and was entering the race only to "resist the planners." It was a disingenuous position; to some extent, the planning
controversy was, at least among its leaders, an intraparty power struggle among Letcher County Democrats.

Prior to the planning controversy, one faction of the party supported incumbent county judge Robert Collins, and the other James
Caudill, his predecessor in office (1962–69). Shortly before the *Comprehensive Plan* was submitted to the fiscal court, the county Democratic convention (controlled by the Collins faction) denied any seats
to the Caudill faction in the forthcoming state convention. The slate
chosen, moreover, was heavily weighted with delegates tied directly
to either KRADD (four of sixteen delegates) or the county planning
commission, whose chairman, Alvin Webb, was close to Collins and
had himself been a candidate for county judge in 1965. Willard Gilliam was allied with the Caudill faction, having served as judge pro
tem in the Caudill administration.

Another complicating factor—marginally connected to county
Democratic politics and directly related to the informal politics of
KRADD policies—was press coverage in the *Mountain Eagle*. Editor
Tom Gish's service on the KRADD board several years earlier had
convinced him that the agency (especially under the leadership of
Malcom Holliday) did more harm than good. Some evidence there-
fore suggests that when the planning controversy arose, Gish may
have seen it as an opportunity to help get rid of Holliday and permanently curb KRADD's power. Gish also appears to have been closer
to the progressive Caudill faction of the Democratic party than to
Collins's conservative faction. Caudill had been on the board of the
nonprofit Eastern Kentucky Housing Development Corporation
(EKHDC) run by Mrs. Gish, and a laudatory editorial in the *Mountain
Eagle* had followed his retirement from office. KRADD's Holliday,
for his part, had opposed EKHDC's attempts to get funding for its
experimental housing program.[22]

However it is to be explained, the *Mountain Eagle's* treatment of
Gilliam was more positive than appears warranted in retrospect. In
early September 1972 Gilliam quit his job with the state Department

of Economic Security, charging that he had been harassed because of his opposition to the KRADD's plan. In an editorial Gish asked:

> How much is your freedom worth? Well, it's worth your job, Willard Gilliam learned this week. . . . Gilliam learned that you can't be a state employee . . . and exercise your constitutional right of free speech—not if in so doing you are critical of land use plans and planners [and] the Kentucky River Area Development District.

Gish concluded that the "fact that those behind the plan would use such extreme pressure upon Gilliam . . . demonstrates that the [plan's] threat to mountain people was every bit as real as Gilliam stated."

Possibly. There is evidence that telephone calls may have been made from both KRADD and Judge Collins's office to Gilliam's superiors in Frankfort and that Department of Economic Security investigators came to Whitesburg to inquire about his activities. But it is not self-evident that Gilliam was harassed primarily because he opposed the plan. He was also opposing Robert Collins, whose political future was threatened by controversy over any policy (including the formulation of the plan) that he had supported and who as incumbent judge could and reportedly did use his political influence both in Frankfort and in Hazard (headquarters of KRADD, on whose board he served as county judge) to help silence his opponents, regardless of the issue.

The *Mountain Eagle* also did not point out the reactionary aspects of Gilliam's position. As a result, principled opposition to exploitative plans and planners became very nearly submerged by red-baiting, which had been a consistent feature of eastern Kentucky politics for forty years. So easily does the charge of communism spring forth in eastern Kentucky that when Fleming resident Ralph Smith spoke out against strip-mining in 1972, he felt it necessary to defend himself in advance. "People of the coal counties," he said, "I am not a communist, but I am a natural-born coal camp boy who is against the destruction of our land because I love it."[23]

Repeatedly, Gilliam and other opponents of the plan called it "un-American" and associated it with communism. "In Russia they have their five-year plans," he said. "In this country we have development districts. These are two different roads to the same destination." Later he added that the planners were using "the method used by socialistic and communistic governments." In letter after letter to the *Mountain Eagle*, and in meeting after meeting, others joined Gilliam in castigating the "socialistic" and "communistic" planners and their efforts "to collectivize us."[24] Nor was the tactic used solely by one side. Asked to explain Gilliam's possible motives, ex-judge Collins said he was "a damn Communist."

The most immediate beneficiary of these tactics was the Letcher County Republican party. In the Democratic primary, Collins defeated Caudill (2,571–2,334). Gilliam polled only 784 votes out of more than 5,000 cast, failing to carry even his home precinct of Mayking. Although Democrats outnumbered Republicans in the county three to one, Collins lost to Estill Blair in November (4,720–3,805), and the county acquired its first Republican judge in twenty-five years.

For the people of Letcher County to see the *Comprehensive Plan* as "Communist" was in one sense simply ludicrous—a product of incomplete analysis, bad leadership, and possibly cynical manipulation by vested interests, which had decades of experience in raising the charge of communism to silence their opponents. But the *core* of the response (a perception of antidemocratic methods and possibly repressive intent) was legitimate. Indeed, one of the most persistent features of Letcher County history had been that its people were moved about at the behest of a succession of public and private planners and social strategists.[25]

What were ultimately at issue in the Letcher County plan were class bias, cultural condescension, and the potential co-optation of the plan by the coal industry. None of those features was unique to planning in Letcher County. Class bias was a prominent feature of domestic "urban renewal" planning in the 1960s, which frequently demolished poor neighborhoods to make way for luxury high-rise buildings and expressways. Cultural condescension has surfaced regularly when colonial powers have planned the lives of their conquered subjects: India and Latin America in the nineteenth century, for example, and Southeast Asia in the twentieth.

At the end of the nineteenth century, to take a remote but nevertheless instructive example, the United States took over the Philippines as a possession after suppressing a popular independence movement led by Emilio Aguinaldo. An American architect, Daniel Burnham, noted for his design of the "imperial white city" at the 1893 World's Fair, was commissioned to redesign the capital city of Manila. Rejecting the design vocabulary implicit in native architecture and community organization, he chose an axial street plan because he reasoned that "every section of the city should look with deference toward the symbol of the nation's power."[26] "Sometime in the future, when the Filipino finally settles down to . . . things artistic," observed the authoritiative *Architectural Record,* making explicit the political and cultural implications of the design, we may look for the creation of an indigenous architecture expressive of the country and its people. Until then little can reasonably be expected from a race without deep artistic tradition or scientific knowledge. In the meantime, the . . . improvements executed by [the U.S.] Government will stand as worthy examples, setting a high standard from which . . . native architects can derive abundant inspiration.[27]

Such explicit rhetoric of cultural condescension and political repression is relatively rare among architects and planners, who usually speak of "balance," "unity," "efficient land use," and (in Letcher County) "the provision of urban services." Political repression and cultural condescension may nevertheless flow, as Robert Goodman has suggested, from the work of those who adhere to "the conventions of a repressive social structure . . . biased against the people [the] plans are supposed to serve." Even if the intent is benign, the functional result may be "culturally acceptable rationalizations for projects whose form and use have already been determined" by their usefulness to vested interests.[28]

In Letcher County, the principal vested interests were, of course, in the coal industry. Full details of coal company involvement in the planning controversy may never be known, but some evidence indicates that it was not uninvolved in either the controversy itself or the related Democratic party battle.

Mining and Planning: A No-Win Situation

> The proposals contained herein . . . are presently subject to changes based on private, rather than public decisions. . . . As matters now stand, . . . decisions regarding the [KRADD] area's economic and social future development rest almost totally with the owners of . . . sub-surface [i.e., coal, oil, gas] rights. This is . . . a policy inherent in the present legal status.
>
> *Land Use Plan for Kentucky River Area*
> *Development District* (1973)

Immediately after his resignation from the Department of Economic Security, Willard Gilliam became a salaried "advance man" for Crawford Engineering Company, which served mining companies. His responsibilities included researching mineral deeds and acquiring strip-mining agreements from property owners. On the eve of the November 1972 general election, he revealed his sympathy for the industry by declaring that "in rural areas industry should be allowed to choose its own location. With all the constraints already on in-dustry," he said, "we don't want to add another." Later he said he was "not defending" strip-mining but nevertheless maintained that reports of environmental damage were "played up out of proportion," that the broad form deed was perfectly valid, and that reclamation was easier in the mountains than on level land. "To me what [strip-mining] amounts to [is that] they've just sort of shifted the mountain over a few feet," Gilliam said. "You still have the same thing you had before they went in, minus the coal."[29]

The unmistakable smell of coal dust hangs over the planning en-terprise in eastern Kentucky, and especially in Letcher County, where strip-mining and the consequent control of the county by coal com-panies is virtually complete. Connections between coal, politics, and planning pile upon one another in wearying profusion. According to some reports, R. W. Booker and Associates may have acquired the Letcher County planning contract partly because of Booker vice-pres-ident Hubert Hall's personal relationship with Judge Robert Collins. Hall, who had come to Booker from the L & N (Louisville and Nash-ville) Railroad, later went to work for Harry Laviers's South-East Coal Company. The chairman of the Letcher County Democratic party, under Collins's control during the planning controversy, was a public relations man for McCulloch Consolidated Coal Company, the largest mining company in the county. After Collins left office, he began to mine his own coal leases. Percy Elkins, a KRADD official who admitted having made a telephone call to Frankfort concerning Gilliam, was a protégé of Collins and was chosen as a delegate to the 1972 state Democratic convention.[30]

During the KRADD controversy, there were two theories about coal companies and planning. One was that the companies wanted planning and zoning so portions of the country could be set aside for stripping without the encumbrance of adjacent residential develop-ment. Many opponents of the plan held this belief, which gained plausibility from the connections between coal and county politics. A counterargument held, however, that strip-mining could be con-trolled only through zoning, for which a comprehensive plan was a prerequisite.

Recent developments in neighboring Knott County gave credence to the counterargument. After massive citizen protests, the Knott County fiscal court had passed an ordinance declaring strip-mining to be a "public nuisance and against the public policy" of the county. The Knott County action was not beyond challenge (the state attorney general denied that counties could regulate strip-mining under Ken-tucky's 1968 strip-mining statute, but an opinion predating the Knott County case said that counties could regulate strip-mining through zoning), but there was a consensus among the KRADD staff and the Letcher County Planning Commission that zoning was the only possible way to control strip-mining.[31]

But neither argument was finally better than the other, because the coal companies in fact stood to win in either case. If there were no planning and zoning, they could continue to operate as before. Otherwise, they could dominate the planning process, as was apparent in the assumptions and content of the *Comprehensive Plan.* For the people of the county, it was a classic no-win situation, reminiscent of that on the eve of the Civil War, when the State of Kentucky struggled to remain neutral while being squeezed between secessionists and Unionists. "No matter which party wins," said one observer, "we lose."[32]

The LDD as Planning Model: Building on the Sand

The KRADD planning controversy contradicted most of the arguments that had been used to support the local development district (LDD) concept and suggested that LDDs might create more problems than they solved. The issue, finally, was not the circumscribed jurisdictional boundaries and minimal bargaining power of small counties, originally cited to justify creating multicounty LDDs, but the fundamental maldistribution of economic and political power in the Appalachian region. KRADD both reflected and extended that maldistribution.

The Kentucky River Area Development District, created in 1969 by the merger of two four-county districts, covers more than 2,500 square miles (an area half the size of Massachusetts and twice as large as Delaware). It plans for more than a hundred thousand people. Its governing board is made up of the eight county judges, mayors of the county seat towns, and other "citizen members" selected by the judges. No one is elected directly to the board by the District's voters, and there is therefore no way to ensure that the views of ordinary citizens will be represented.[33]

During the early days of the LDDs in eastern Kentucky, there was an organized effort by Community Action agencies and others to gain a proportional voice for the poor on governing boards. It was defeated by the Kentucky Program Development Office (KPDO) and Governor Louie D. Nunn, who insisted that "an adequate voice for the poor is built into the concept of the . . . districts." When Director Frank Groschelle of KPDO interpreted the governor's statement to be satisfied by the appointment of one poor person and one poverty worker to boards that averaged forty members, an angry, foot-stomping crowd of more than a thousand poor people assembled in the auditorium of Saint Mary's School in Covington, Kentucky, to protest. But their protest was unavailing.[34]

For several years the LDDs' lack of accountability was of small consequence; cities and counties could and did simply bypass them in their dealings with state and federal agencies. But with the advent of the so-called A-95 Project Notification and Review System, the situation changed. What LDDs had not been able to generate by virtue of broad popular support, they gained when they were designated by the governor as A-95 clearinghouses: control over the expenditure of virtually all federal funds within their boundaries. Such control was intended to be exercised only in the pursuit of soundness of planning, lack of overlap and waste, minimal environmental impact, and similar laudable objectives. But because LDDs were subject to political control and other external pressures, other considerations quickly entered.[35]

An early instance of bias in KRADD's policies was its handling of the so-called Special Impact Program (SIP) established by the Title I-D amendment to the Economic Opportunity Act. Apparently as a result of a visit by Senator Robert Kennedy in late 1968, OEO's four-county LKLP area in eastern Kentucky was designated to receive $1.4 million in SIP funds, which were to be spent so as to produce a "special impact" in a concentrated area, and were intended to involve local community people in economic development enterprises that they themselves designed and controlled. Although OEO's local LKLP CAP agency would have appeared to be the logical organization to administer the funds, they came instead (via the Agriculture Department and the Farmer's Home Administration) to KRADD.[36]

An early applicant for SIP funds was Pat Gish's Eastern Kentucky Housing Development Corporation (EKHDC), formed to use local materials and unskilled labor to build homes for low-income residents. The homes (described in a detailed proposal to KRADD) were imaginatively designed for maximum economy (using modular, prefabricated construction), suitability for the local environment, and adaptability to the customary ways of life of local people. EKHDC's proposal also included broader community development aims consistent with the intent of Title I-D, including ownership of the corporation by its own workers within five years. The proposal was a natural for SIP funds and would undoubtedly have been funded had the SIP money been administered by the LKLP CAP, which had in fact handled the original OEO funding for EKHDC in 1967.

KRADD, however, denied the EKHDC request in favor of a proposal from Tandy Industries, a private, profit-making builder of prefabricated houses from Tulsa. Tandy's "proposal" to KRADD consisted of a hastily edited document originally prepared for a project on an Indian reservation; it had none of the desirable features of the EKHDC proposal. By any standard, it was a conventional commercial venture. Yet after a long sequence of apparently irregular administrative procedures involving actions and decisions contrary to the letter and intent of the SIP legislation and influenced by personal and political considerations, KRADD approved the Tandy proposal and agreed to "acquire land, develop a site, and construct a building [to be] leased . . . by Tandy at . . . a dollar a year."[37]

The Westinghouse Learning Corporation study concluded that eastern-Kentucky people were not well served by KRADD's handling of the SIP funds (more than $250,000 was given to a mining supply company to help expand its operations, for example), that personal and political considerations figured prominently in the decision-making process, that KRADD's allocation of SIP money was counterproductive and contrary to the legislative mandate, and that KRADD consistently demonstrated a "lack of faith in the ability of the people of eastern Kentucky to direct and run their own affairs and to successfully launch their own economic enterprises."

Other examples of KRADD's political bias and catering to vested interests regularly came to light. In 1971, when anti–strip-mining activity in the eight-county area was at its highest level ever, KRADD agreed only reluctantly and after considerable vacillation to hold hearings on the issue. The hearing was opposed by board member Charles Beach, who the next year helped get KRADD support for a Corps of Engineers dam at Booneville, opposed unanimously by local residents but favored by merchants downstream at Beattyville, who wanted flood protection. Beach was a banker from Beattyville.[38]

When the KRADD bylaws were changed in 1972 to allow "major industries of the area" to place representatives on the board, both the Kentucky Coal Association and the Hazard Coal Operators Association nominated William B. Sturgill (possibly the wealthiest strip-mine operator in eastern Kentucky and an important TVA supplier) for the position. Sturgill was appointed by KRADD director Malcolm Holliday. The coal industry was already represented on the board by Louis Quick, an engineer for Beth-Elkhorn, who had been appointed once to represent the "professions" and once to represent "civic groups." There were no representatives of working miners or conservation groups.

The influence of the coal industry in KRADD's A-95 reviews was apparent in the unfavorable review given in early 1973 to the Ap-

palachian Research and Defense Fund's request for OEO money to
continue its advocacy legal work on behalf of welfare recipients,
anti–strip-mining groups, and black-lung claimants. A few months
later, however, KRADD submitted its own request for $78,000 to the
Appalachian Regional Commission to do a complete aerial mapping
of the district, which some observers suspected was instigated by coal
operators. KRADD insisted that the project involved only innocuous
general land-use mapping, but the specifications called for the mapping of all mined areas and sites of mineral deposits (coal, oil, gas,
limestone). Despite local opposition, ARC approved KRADD's request.[39]

Beyond LDD Politics: A Final Paradox

To an uninformed observer, the landscape of Letcher County
looks like the result of irrational, random, unplanned development.
Paradoxically, however, the condition of much of the county is the
result of coldly rational planning. Where there was coal, mines were
mapped and opened; where mines were opened, towns were built.[40]
The towns were located and planned for efficiency and economy in
sheltering workers and providing social services: food, clothing, education, medical care, fuel, tools, even funerals. The coal industry
sought to derive maximum public relations value from some of the
best planned towns, and indeed some of them initially offered better
houses and more conveniences than could generally be had elsewhere.[41]

The town of Jenkins, in the upper end of Letcher County, was
built by Consolidation Coal Company in 1911 and named for George
C. Jenkins, one of the company's directors from Baltimore. It was
one of the many such towns built when the railroad reached the
county and the great Hazard field was opened. The company constructed its own sawmills, planing mills, drying kilns, and brick factories on the site. Besides the necessary houses for officials and
workers (a total of 1,600 dwellings), there was a complete water, sewer,
and garbage system; a school that offered both day and night classes;
a library; a recreational lake and park with clubhouse; a department
store; a hospital; an electricity-generating plant; and several churches.
An article in the industry publication *Coal Age* for 1923 conveyed the
pride that Consolidation officials felt in building such a showcase:

Jenkins . . . is a town of real beauty. . . . The main street . . . is concreted and separated from the sidewalks by plots of grass [which] the people . . . are prohibited from tramping down. . . . The homes of the officials have all modern conveniences, and the miners' dwellings have as many improvements as have been found practicable. Most . . . are plastered [and] fifty per cent . . . are provided with sinks. [The] houses are painted white, [and] the color scheme of the trimmings is varied by interchanging four dark colors. Every four or five years the houses are repainted. . . . Prizes are offered for the best vegetable gardens, the prettiest flower gardens and the most attractive places. . . . The company plows all lots and furnishes manure; it also supplies trees, vines and shrubbery to those who ask for them, at a cost just great enough to check wanton requests for this favor.[42]

But the personal and social costs of obtaining such "advantages" were high. Every aspect of life had to conform to the plan, which was used to increase control and reinforce class divisions (Italian stone masons were brought in to work on managers' houses in Jenkins). Miners, once they moved into the towns, found their lives under the complete control of the company. They lived in company houses, went to company churches and schools, saw the company doctor when they were ill, were usually required to shop at the company store, and frequently could have house guests only with company permssion. Union organizers found company towns almost impossible to crack; miners who joined unions were at the mercy of bosses and company police.[43]

How completely the plans were thought out was indicated by a 1914 U.S. Bureau of Mines manual on the building of mining towns. Families should be provided with garden plots, it said, because they

> . . . furnish a pleasurable and profitable way of engaging the miner's unoccupied time. . . . Raising a garden means the investment of labor in the premises on the part of the tenant, and in the absence of individual ownership creates an added attachment to the place which tends to offset the temptation of packing up and following vague rumors about steadier work, higher wages, [and] thicker seams.[44]

Thus people who before the coming of the coal companies and their planned towns were too scattered and independent for anyone to control, afterward were crowded close together under conditions that increased their dependency year by year.

But as the plans of the coal industry changed with changing markets and technologies, the camps fell into disrepair and eventually were sold. Jenkins was sold in 1947, when Consol changed its mind about the wisdom of owning the town it had planned and built. Soon it closed the nearby mines of McRoberts and Fleming, and not quite a decade later it sold its entire holdings in the county, leaving the upper end of the county to the next corporate planner, Bethlehem Steel. Meanwhile the Jenkins-McRoberts area population dropped from 9,500 in 1940 to 3,600 in 1970.

Bethlehem's plan for the county included strip-mining, and within a few years it had become the primary participant in stripping the 8,000 acres (3 million tons a year) that KRADD's *Comprehensive Plan* reported. Bethlehem's stripping brought heavy destruction to the same hollows (such as Millstone) where OEO and LKLP were using government money to plan and wage a "war on poverty." Bethlehem engineer Louis Quick in time was appointed to the KRADD board, where he served when the board rejected OEO-funded EKHDC's plan to build (in an abandoned coal company building in Neon) pre-fabricated homes to replace many of those in other abandoned and dilapidated mining camps.

Thus it is not difficult to see why Letcher Countians, whose parents had moved in as a result of one plan and whose neighbors and children had moved out as the result of another, suspected that yet another sinister plan was in the works during the summer of 1972. They had seen plans come and go, and change to meet the changing needs of those for whom they were primarily made in the first place. There was little reason to suppose that the plan put forth by KRADD and the Fleming, Neon, Jenkins, and Letcher County Planning Commission would be any different.

And yet, although sober reflection is seldom possible in the heat of battle, it is nonetheless unfortunate that Letcher Countians did not pause to consider the limits of mainstream assumptions and values. Paradoxically, the county's residents were surrounded by visible evidence of those limits: the coal camps created by the late-nineteenth-century exponents of individualism and free enterprise, and the strip-mined hollows of their late-twentieth-century corporate and ideological heirs.

Unfortunately, Willard Gilliam and his supporters chose to base most of their opposition to the plan on conventional notions of individualism and free enterprise. "If I want to dig me a hole in those wonderful mountains out there," said a man from Eolia at one protest meeting, "it's my right."[45] It could have been (and probably was) said by George C. Jenkins as he gazed upon the hundred thousand acres of coal lands Consol bought in Letcher County in 1911.

Thus Willard Gilliam must be seen not as a villain but as an unwitting prisoner of a bankrupt ideology, attempting from a position of acute vulnerability to protect the few elements of security afforded him by an inequitable political and social system. Almost plaintively, and apparently with a sense of deep betrayal, he invoked the promise of America: "Over the years," he said in a letter to the *Eagle* in February, 1973, "many immigrants have looked to America as a land of opportunity in which one could own his own home and piece of land. The KRADD planners . . . are making the fulfillment of this dream more difficult . . . by their unrealistic plans." But it is ironic that Gilliam and his supporters called the plan un-American, because in most respects it was American to the core. Its image of individual fulfillment and public order was urban and suburban middle America, with sanitized single-family homes clustered on manicured lawns and provided with "urban services."

Indeed, it was by focusing on that image that the planners masked deeper structural problems. And by raising the specter of communism, the plan's opponents sidestepped a thoughtful analysis of both the plan itself and the possibility of moving toward a new and humane balance of individual rights and the common good.

Notes

1. Research for this chapter was supported in part by a grant from the Southern Investigative Research Project of the Southern Regional Council, Inc. Views expressed here are, of course, my own.

2. *Mountain Eagle*, November 9, 1972, p. 21.

3. H. Paul Douglas, *Christian Reconstruction in the South* (Boston: Pilgrim Press, 1909), pp. 339–40.

4. For a more extended account of this process, see Harry Caudill, *Night Comes to the Cumberlands* (Boston: Atlantic–Little, Brown, 1963), pp. 97–103. McRoberts was named for Samuel McRoberts, vice-president of the City National Bank of New York and a director of Consolidation Coal Company. Data on population changes taken from *Comprehensive Plan and Initial Housing Element, Letcher County, Kentucky* (Lexington, Ky.: R. W. Booker and Associates, 1972), referred to hereinafter as *Comprehensive Plan*.

5. Data from *Comprehensive Plan*, pp. 19, 65. See Caudill, *Night Comes to Cumberlands*, pp. 305 ff., and *idem, My Land Is Dying* (New York: E. P. Dutton, 1971).

6. Thomas Gish, "What a Town Can Do—and How," *Mountain Life and Work (MLW)*, XL (Fall 1964), 25–31.

7. Quotations from taped interview with former KRADD Director Malcolm Holliday, February 4, 1974. Tom Gish bought the *Mountain Eagle* in the mid-1950s and built it into the most influential weekly in the region

through superb (and frequently courageous) reporting and consistent in-depth analysis of important local and regional issues. In 1974 he received the University of Arizona's John Peter Zenger Award for contributions to freedom of the press.

8. HUD Project KY P-88. The contract was executed shortly after July 22, 1971. Eight eastern Kentucky counties make up KRADD: Letcher, Knott, Leslie, Perry, Breathitt, Owsley, Lee, and Wolfe. Earlier, the first four counties (OEO's LKLP counties) had constituted one LDD, and the latter four another.

9. *Comprehensive Plan*, pp. 43–58. The survey found 29 percent of the houses in the county dilapidated ("not economically feasible to repair") and 38 percent deteriorating (requiring major repair).

10. The *Interim Report: Emergency Investigations of Coal-mine Waste Embankments* (Washington, D.C.: U.S. Department of the Interior, 1972) listed Letcher County site numbers 103, 104, 104A, 107, 107A, 108, 110, 110A, 110B, 120, R-5-A, R-5-C, and X-34. The first five were classified as having "obvious deficiencies." Articles and photographs of some of the sites appeared in the *Mountain Eagle* on March 2, April 27, and June 8, 1972, during R. W. Booker's preparation of the *Comprehensive Plan*.

11. Gish, "What a Town Can Do—and How," pp. 34–35, and taped interview, respectively.

12. This paragraph and the subsequent discussion of the controversy are based on a series of reports, articles, and editorials from the *Mountain Eagle* during the period following July 18, 1972, and on interviews with Mary Ann Adams, Joe Begley, Percy Elkins, Willard Gilliam, Pat Gish, Tom Gish, Malcolm Holliday, William Kingsbury, and Alvin Webb. I am grateful for their cooperation but must of course accept sole responsibility for all interpretations set forth here.

13. *Louisville Courier-Journal*, August 13, 1972, p. E-1.

14. Emphasis added. Backers of the plan argued that moving people "out of the hollows" was not emphasized in the text. But a close reading (esp. pp. 34, 37, 45, 47, 63, and 68) does not bear out their contention. The plan said that some residential areas "should be cleared and the citizens relocated" (p. 71).

15. *The Appalachian Region* (Annapolis: Maryland Department of Economic Development, 1960), p. 8.

16. Caudill, *Night Comes to Cumberlands*, p. 384, and "Misdeal in Appalachia," *Atlantic Monthly*, CCXV (June 1965), 46.

17. *U.S. News and World Report*, LIX (September 27, 1965), 68–70.

18. *Mountain Eagle*, June 30, 1966, p. 2. Compare a similar conclusion by the *Nashville Tennessean's* Nat Caldwell in *MLW*, XLIV (July 1968), 22.

19. *West Virginia Hillbilly*, June 22, 1968; *People's Appalachia*, I (August–September 1970), 19; and *Mountain Eagle*, June 29, 1972, p. 1 (emphasis added), and August 24, 1972, p. 2, respectively.

20. Tom Gish, "The Homogenized, All-American Model American," *MLW*, XLIX (May 1973), 14.

21. Quoted from *MLW*, XLVII (July–August 1971), p. 5, and *Mountain Eagle*, March 15, 1973, p. 2, respectively.

22. David Hawpe, "Report Criticizing Impact Administration Rejected," *Louisville Courier-Journal*, May 29, 1970. Holliday's criticisms of the EKHDC were repudiated by the KRADD board. For further discussion of KRADD's response to the EKHDC housing plan, see below.

23. *Ibid.*, May 8, 1969, p. 4, and April 20, 1972, p. 2, respectively. An early source of red-baiting was the mine wars in Harlan and Bell Counties in the 1930s, sparked by the organizing drive of the Communist-backed National Miners Union.

24. See a letter to the *Mountain Eagle*, September 27, 1973, p. 2. Not even Gish himself was completely immune from making such arguments. Commenting on the Kentucky Infant and Pre-School Program (KIP), Gish said, "It is no secret that the KIP program is patterned after the Russian system of child-rearing which was developed to destroy the traditional rugged character of the Russian peasant." See Gish, "Homogenized, All-American," p. 14. The KIP program may have deserved Gish's criticism, but its presumed origins or analogues were not germane.

25. Five years before the KRADD controversy, Letcher County people had organized effective opposition to the Corps of Engineers' Kingdom Come Dam, which would have displaced many families. See *Mountain Eagle*, September 28 and October 5–19, 1967, and February 27, 1969.

26. Daniel Burnham, *Report on the Improvement of Manila* (Chicago, 1905), cited in Robert Goodman, *After the Planners* (New York: Simon & Schuster, 1971), p. 101.

27. A. N. Rebori, "The Works of [United States Consulting Architect] William E. Parsons in the Philippine Islands," *Architectural Record*, XL (May 1917), p. 434, cited in Goodman, *After the Planners*, p. 102. See also Michael T. Klare, "The Architecture of Imperial America," *Science and Society*, XXXIII (Summer–Fall 1969), 280–83.

28. Goodman, *After the Planners*, pp. 12 ff.

29. *Mountain Eagle*, November 9, 1972, p. 3, and taped interview, February 4, 1974.

30. In fairness to Collins, it should be pointed out that in 1970 he led a campaign to get a severance tax enacted, which would have been of great benefit to the county. See *Mountain Eagle*, February 26 and October 15, 1970. Such a tax was enacted in 1974.

31. Letter of Attorney General Robert Matthews (citing KRS 100 and 147), February 17, 1966. See *Opinions of the Attorney General of Kentucky for the Period January 1, 1968—December 31, 1971* (Cleveland: Banks-Baldwin Law Publishing Co., 1972), pp. 679–80, 782–83; *New York Times*, June 8, 1970, p. 21; and *Mountain Eagle*, May 7, June 11 and 18, and August 27, 1970.

32. Gary L. Williams, "Lincoln's Neutral Allies: The Case of the Kentucky Unionists," *South Atlantic Quarterly*, LXXIII (Winter 1974), 70.

33. Counties have the same number of representatives regardless of their size or population. Perry County has seven times the population of Wolfe, and Letcher has about one-third of the District's total. The argument of KRADD officials that representativeness is assured by the presence of elected judges and mayors on the board is not persuasive. Frank Groschelle of the Kentucky Program Development Office said in 1969 that the state law es-

tablishing LDDs required citizen representatives to be elected to the board. See *MLW*, XLV (February 1969), 4–8. If there ever was such a law, there is no evidence it was enforced.

34. See Hollis West, "CAA Directors Dissent," *MLW*, XLV (February 1969), 8–9, and Groschelle's "The Guidelines" in XLV (February 1969), 4–8. For other commentary on the unrepresentative boards, see Donald N. Rothblatt, *Regional Planning: The Appalachian Experience* (Lexington, Mass.; D. C. Heath, 1971), p. 156; *New York Times* reporter Ben Franklin's article in the *Mountain Eagle*, April 9, 1970, p. 3; and a *Louisville Courier-Journal* editorial, April 30, 1972.

35. Deference to special interests dated back to KRADD's predecessor, the Upper Kentucky River Development Council. Tom Gish noted as early as 1964 that proposals from local citizens met with embarrassed silence from the board members, who preferred to consult with each other and local "leaders." See *Mountain Eagle*, November 26, 1964, p. 2. When representatives of the Appalachian Committee for Full Employment (the "Roving Pickets") attempted to present a proposal in 1964, they were refused permission, even though they represented hundreds of unemployed miners from the district. See Everette Tharpe, "Appalachian Committee for Full Employment," *Appalachian South*, I (Summer 1965), 45.

36. OEO commissioned the Westinghouse Learning Corporation to study the use of SIP funds in 1969. The following discussion is based on Martha Grosse, *Report on the 1968 Kentucky Special Impact Program* (New York: Westinghouse Learning Corporation, 1970). KRADD contested the findings of the report, which led to a freeze on the funds. *Louisville Courier-Journal*, May 24, 1970.

37. Grosse, *Report*, p. 22. Exact details of the agreement are not known, as KRADD would not allow the Westinghouse Learning Corporation analyst to examine the contract. A full discussion of the Tandy decision may be found in *ibid.*, pp. 21–76. At the time of the original Tandy request, the state FHA administrator (who handled the SIP funds in Kentucky) was a Democrat not on good terms with KRADD's Republican director Holliday. A month after a Republican FHA administrator was appointed in June 1969, KRADD approved the Tandy project *(Mountain Eagle*, May 28, 1970, p. 1).

38. See *Mountain Eagle*, March 4, 1971, p. 1, and *Louisville Courier-Journal*, July 19, 1972, p. 4, respectively. Beach was at one time chairman of the KRADD board.

39. On the ARDF review, see *Mountain Eagle*, February 1, 1973, pp. 1, 14, and *Louisville Courier-Journal*, June 8, 1973, p. 6. On the mapping proposal, see *Mountain Eagle*, September 6 and 20 and November 29, 1973.

40. KRADD's *Comprehensive Plan* noted (p. 43) that "the large concentrations of poor housing are found in the former coal camps where houses were built quickly on small lots."

41. See, for example, Edward W. Parker, "Workmen's Houses in the Anthracite Regions," National Planning Association *Proceedings*, V (1916), 54–66; Thomas F. Downing, "Where to Build Mining Towns and What to Build," West Virginia Coal Mining Institute *Proceedings* (1923), pp. 41–51; H. O. Zimmerman, "Modernization of Living Conditions in a Coal Mining

Town," Kentucky Mining Institute *Proceedings,* I (1940), 23–30; and a series of articles in *Coal Age:* III (1911–12), 38–41 and 211–14; V (1914), 936–39; VI (1914), 739–41; XI (1917), 1045–48; XII (1917), 717–20; XX (1921), 532–36; and December 1944, pp. 86–93.

42. Alphonse F. Brosky, "Building a Town for a Mountain Community," *Coal Age,* XXIII (April 5, 1923), 560–63. Photographs published with the article indicate that Brosky's description is reliable. Portions of my discussion of Jenkins are drawn from Elizabeth Dramcyzk, *The History of Jenkins, Kentucky* (Jenkins, Ky.: Jenkins Area Jaycees, 1973).

43. Running parallel to the industry's laudatory articles on coal towns was persistent criticism in the public media. See Arthur Gleason, "Company Owned Americans," *The Nation,* CX (1920), 794–95; Helen G. Norton, "Feudalism in West Virginia," *The Nation,* CXXXIII (1931), 154–55; Jennie Lee, "Kentucky Through English Eyes," *Living Age,* 342 (1932), 184–85; Bruce Crawford, "Piney Ridge, Virginia," *Virginia Quarterly Review,* VIII (1932), 371–84; Helen Hall, "Miners Must Eat," *Atlantic Monthly,* CLII (1933), 153–62; and Adelaide Walker, "Living Conditions in the Coal Fields," in *Harlan Miners Speak,* pp. 83 ff.

44. Joseph H. White, *Houses for Mining Towns.* U.S. Bureau of Mines Bulletin No. 87 (Washington, D.C.: Government Printing Office, 1914), pp. 48–49.

45. *Mountain Eagle,* August 10, 1972, p. 1.

CHAPTER 10

Conclusion: Cultural Values and Regional Development

> We wake and find ourselves on a stair; there are stairs below us,
> which we seem to have ascended; there are stairs above us, many
> a one, which go upward and out of sight. . . .
>   Dream delivers us to dream, and there is no end to illusion. Life
> is a train of moods, like a string of beads, and as we pass through
> them they prove to be many-colored lenses which paint the world
> their own hue, and each shows only what lies in its focus.
>   Ralph W. Emerson, "Experience" (1844)

EMERSON'S "MANY-COLORED LENSES" image reminds us that our views
of reality are at last inescapably personal. At the outset I told how my
own set of lenses and "train of moods"—or stages of personal growth,
as a modern psychologist would have it—shaped my understanding
of the particular reality I set out to comprehend and describe.

But views of reality are colored by more than merely *personal*
"moods." We also see the world through the *collective* lens of culture.
Most of us recognize that as a general principle, of course, but the
importance of the principle in this particular context I perceived only
gradually.

Initially I was compelled by two apparently disconnected clusters
of images. In one cluster there was hillbilly music, dance, and material
culture—string bands and gospel singers, square dancers and clog-
gers, houses and barns, fences and chimneys, fireplaces and split-
bottomed chairs. Some of those images came immediately from my
own experience: a fiddler and a banjo picker in the neighborhood,
the square dance team in our county high school, several thousand
acres of mountain land to wander over behind our house. Others
came indirectly: visits to my grandfather's Rutherford County, North
Carolina, farm at 'lassy makin' time; hillbilly music on the "Carolina
Farm Hour" every day at noon: WSM's "Grand Ole Opry" on Saturday night; and—when the weather was right—WWVA from Wheeling.

In the other cluster there were wasted and polluted streams; smog
heavy in the valley and washing up the mountainsides; other kids'

daddies who had to work "three to 'lebm" or graveyard; busloads of workers from Sunburst and Shelton Laurel, Big Ivy and Barnardsville, rolling into the textile mill parking lot where I sold papers before daylight.

For a long while after I began to write, the clusters remained separate, the cultural cluster usually in the background. The "developmental" cluster claimed most of my attention as I read legislative hearings, planning documents, and consultants' studies, and struggled with the vocabulary and technical concepts of planners. But connections urged themselves upon me.

Church missionaries and settlement school workers most often turned out to have seen mountain people as their experience *disposed* them to, and to have "helped" as they were led by their own cultural lights. Beneath the vast technological superstructure of TVA I perceived a substructure of cultural values and assumptions that controlled the agency more surely than the geomorphology of the Tennessee River valley itself. The infrastructure planners of ARA and ARC—like their missionary and New Deal predecessors—could at last be understood better in cultural than in theoretical or technical terms. Like rotors in TVA's generators, they were whirled between twin poles of culture.

One pole was their own deeply imbedded mainstream culture—a conflicted amalgam of authoritarianism and libertarianism, individualism and paternalism, elitism and populism, nostalgia and futurism, self-help and social responsibility. The other was the ancient, tattered but treasured hand-me-down fabric of untenable cultural assumptions and judgments about mountain people. The "Appalachia" they sought to develop was, to some extent, an Appalachia created in their own minds—a mythic Appalachia, as Henry Shapiro's *Appalachia on Our Mind* has recently shown, held to as a cultural talisman by the rest of America.

As a variety of organic connections between culture and regional development continued to emerge, I at length concluded that *regional development must finally be understood as cultural drama rather than technocratic enterprise.* It is an arena in which the dynamics of conflict are set at the deepest spiritual, psychic, and cultural levels. Conflicts over the technical details of development theory and practice are at most secondary; they are the shadows on the walls of Plato's cave.

Cultural values and assumptions turn out to have controlled the development process in Appalachia in an astonishing number of its aspects. Of profoundest importance is the fact that the cultural values and predispositions shared by most planners and development agency bureaucrats have set the narrowest of limits upon their imagination; constricted the boundaries of their tolerance for social, economic, and political alternatives; and marked off the little that seemed to them "reasonable" or "sensible" from the much that did not. Thus the planning and development process turned out over and over again to be culturally narcissistic rather than *imaginative* and progressive.

In sum, the cultural drama of development as I have come to understand it is made up of four related aspects: (1) Development strategy is controlled by the cultural "set" of the developers themselves. (2) The dominance of that "set" renders the strategy insensitive to the cultural values of the "target population" (to use the contemporary phrase). (3) That insensitivity predisposes development programs to be culturally destructive. (4) Among those who plan and control development, a feigned reverence for and understanding of the affected culture is used as a cover for the essentially autocratic agendas of the developers.

These dimensions of the cultural drama, which emerged progressively throughout the foregoing case studies, were crystallized for me—bodied forth with great power, clarity, and poignance—by a historical analogue drawn from Scotland two centuries ago.

"Improving" the Highlanders

·Nearly every romantic statement ever concocted to explain Appalachian people—from John Fox, Jr., to CBS's "Sixty Minutes"—has told wistfully of their proud Scotch-Irish forebears. Like many serious students of the region, I learned to discount such statements as essentially beside the point, whatever their historical basis or lack of it. But in John Prebble's *The Highland Clearances* (1963), I discovered levels of significance previously undreamt of in that romantic philosophy.[1]

The clearances in the Scottish Highlands were of course part of a larger process of enclosure that had been under way in Europe since about the twelfth century. In England the process was facilitated after 1688 by the landlords' ability to obtain private enclosure acts from Parliament. My own interest in that particular historical instance of enclosure stems from its pertinence to certain aspects of Appalachian experience, but the phenomenon bears as well upon the experience of many economically, politically, and culturally marginal groups displaced by a variety of processes commonly assumed to constitute "progress."[2]

The Battle of Culloden in 1746 was a critical turning point for an entire social and cultural order in the Scottish Highlands. The Highland lairds had long stood at the apex of a feudal pyramid that extended downward through their tacksmen and subtenants to a broad base of landless cotters. The leaseless tenantry of the great mass of landless highlanders had continued unbroken for many generations, so long as tenants heeded their lairds' call to arms. But after Culloden, the lairds found themselves landlords rather than warlords, and their tenants became a liability rather than an asset. No matter that their tenants were deeply attached to the land, which, as Prebble says, they had peopled from time immemorial with "talking stones, snow-giants, and mythical warriors of mountain granite." No matter that the social order rested upon a texture of unspoken but vital understandings between people. No matter that tenants had no alternatives. The Highland people had to go because they had become an economic burden.

The lairds, however, had an alternative or two. The news among them by the late eighteenth century was that there was money to be made from sheep. Sir John Lockhart-Ross introduced the black-faced Lintons in County Ross in 1762, on lands leased to a lowland grazier. His displaced tenants, recognizing the threat, shot sheep at night, drove them into the lochs, and terrorized the shepherds. But with the introduction a few years later of the great Cheviots—sturdier hybrids from the English-Scottish border—the tide began to shove the Highlanders relentlessly before it.

Ironically, Cheviots had first been brought north by Sir John Sinclair, a laird who wanted to better the lot of his tenants. Sinclair planned to train them to be shepherds so as to keep them on the land, to encourage them to pool their resources and build their own flocks, to control the pace of change and moderate its effects. But Sinclair's humane concern and belief in the essential dignity and worth of his tenants was not shared widely by his peers.

Though Highlanders themselves, most of the lairds had consciously stripped themselves of the cultural markers that bound them to their tenants. They cast off Gaelic as a barbarous tongue, affected luxurious life-styles, and encouraged their daughters to marry southerners. Many became absentee landlords. As their mounting debts demanded that their estates turn generous profits, it came to a choice between Cheviots and people. Having dissociated themselves from the people made it easier to choose Cheviots.

The lairds rationalized their self-interested economic policy of land clearance as an enlightened policy of "Improvement." Improvement became the century's crusade, Prebble says, and the greatest of the Improvers was the Duke of Sutherland. Officially he was known as the Most Noble George Granville Levenson-Gower, second Marquess of Stafford, third Earl Gower and Viscount Trentham, fourth Lord Gower of Stittenham in Yorkshire. But he was in fact, as Prebble notes, "coal and wool joined by a stately hyphen." He had inherited his father's estates in Stafford and Shropshire as well as the vast fortune of his uncle, "the canal-cutting Duke of Bridgewater." His wife's dowry included two-thirds of the shire of Sutherland, a 1,735-square-mile piece of the Highlands inhabited by 25,000 people. The story of the Duke of Sutherland's "improvements" must stand here for those of most of the Highland lairds.

To pursue his agenda of Improvement, Sutherland employed James Loch as commissioner. Loch moved relentlessly. Writs of removal were prepared by the thousands. And though upon occasion the officers serving the writs were met by angry Highlanders who stoned them, stripped them of their clothes, overturned their carriages, and burned the writs, the clearances continued. People were given an hour's notice to clear out and salvage what they could. Houses and barns were pulled down and burned, furniture and crops destroyed, and stock scattered. Old people, children, and the sick died by the scores; the healthier ones took refuge in caves or holes scooped in the ground, eating scraps scavenged from the countryside. During the Strathnaver clearances of 1814, Highlander Donald Macleod climbed a hill one night and counted 250 buildings burning, and towns burning in a line stretching ten miles. Two thousand people had been turned out of Kildonan parish alone. Notified that people were starving that winter, Sutherland's wife, Lady Stafford, wrote to a friend that "Scotch people are of happier constitutions, and do not fatten like the larger breed of animals."

When the fires died down, the land was turned over to Lowland sheep herders and their flocks of Cheviots. The whole was called Improvement, the rationale for which James Loch expounded in 1820 in a treatise Prebble says became the "great apologia of the Improvers" for the rest of the century. His purpose, Loch explained, was

> . . . to render this mountainous district contributory as far as it was possible to the general wealth and industry of the country, and in the manner most suitable to its situation and peculiar circumstances. To convert the former population of these districts to industrious and regular habits and to enable them to bring to market a very considerable surplus quantity of provisions for the supply of the large towns in the southern parts of the land, or for the purpose of exportation. [This is] a wise and generous policy and well calculated to increase the happiness of the individuals who were the objects of this change and to benefit those to whom these extensive domains belonged.

Loch's policy was disastrous for the Highlanders. Tens of thousands emigrated to Canada. Further devastated by the cholera epidemic of 1832, the harvest failure of 1836, and the potato blight of 1846, the Highland population was effectively destroyed within about two or three generations. Those who did not emigrate were forced into the fish-packing plants of Sutherland and the slums of Glasgow.

For the Duke of Sutherland and his like, the results of Improvement were rather better. Wool production and prices climbed steadily. Rental and sale prices for Highland estates increased five- to tenfold in five years. Two hundred thousand head of sheep grazed on Sutherland's lands, producing 415,000 pounds of wool a year. His income was £300,000 a year. Loch's book proudly detailed the herrings barreled and fleece sheared, the roads, bridges, and harbors built.

To justify their policies with respect to the Highlanders, Loch and others first stigmatized the displaced people as animals, primitives, or barbarians and then claimed that Improvement would have a civilizing effect upon them. "Ignorant and credulous people," Loch called them. Dr. John McCullough, a prestigious Fellow of the Royal Society, viewed the burned towns of Sutherland as "the former hamlets of [an] idle and useless population." Of the people's attachment to the land he wrote in 1824:

> The attachment of the wretched creatures in question was a habit . . . of indolence and inexperience, the attachment of an animal. [They] were children, unable to judge for themselves. . . . As children, it was the duty of their superiors to judge for them, and to compel them for their own advantage.

Sir George MacKenzie, another great Improver, reflected that, having been "compelled for their own advantage," the Highland people "will yet find themselves happier and more comfortable in the capacity of servants to the substantial tenantry than in their present situation." Prebble says the ministers, for the most part,

> . . . chose the side of the landlords, who built them new manses, made carriage roads to their doors, and [granted them] a few acres of sheep pasturage. In return the churchmen gave God's authority to Improvement, and threatened the more truculent of the evicted with damnation.

Thus a self-serving economic policy was transmuted into a divinely ordained social and moral obligation. No one, Prebble notes, asked the Highlanders what they wanted:

> Suspicious of improvements that announced themselves in writs

of eviction, the Highlanders . . . may have desired to live as they had always lived, to do without roads, bridges, wheeled vehicles and the religion of their lairds; to wear the bonnet or cotton cap, neck-cloth and coarse plaid, to operate illicit stills, to sing the psalms in Gaelic and to believe in the Evil Eye. Their way of life, their apparent indifference to the stimulating rewards of industry, were the despair of the Improvers.

With a final touch of irony, the Improvers created two organizations calculated to both hasten their program and moderate some of its worrisome side-effects: an association to stimulate emigration and an Association for the Suppression of Sheep Stealing. Fittingly, the penalty for sheep stealing was transportation.

From this analogue (a final aspect of which I will shortly relate) I extract a structural paradigm of Improvement that can serve as a remarkably close analogue to regional development. The paradigm can be quickly stated: The Improvers' agenda arose out of a reassessment of their self-interest following unanticipated economic changes. Improvement was tailored to serve their newly assessed self-interest. It required for its moral justification the systemic denigration of a captive population, and for its success the systematic removal and subjugation of that population. The population understood the agenda beneath the pious rhetoric and attempted to resist, but was unable to do so. As the inhumane results of the policy became manifest, the policy itself was justified by appeal to the national interest and other safely abstract and transcendent values. Its end was nevertheless the destruction of an entire social and economic order and of the cultural values that gave it life.

Development and Improvement

The analogue illuminates many aspects of the foregoing case studies. It is particularly helpful, for example, in understanding the cultural biases and impacts of the two largest and most powerful development agencies ever to operate in the Appalachian region: the Tennessee Valley Authority and the Appalachian Regional Commission.

TVA and ARC arose, of course, out of vastly different political circumstances. They are structured very differently as agencies and in many respects have markedly different histories, as the case studies have shown. But with respect to the intersection between development policy and cultural assumptions, values, and impact, they can usefully be considered together.

In both cases, the advent of the agency—like that of the lairds' agenda of Improvement—followed upon large-scale economic and social crisis: the Depression for TVA and the end of the postwar economic boom for ARC. It was considered in the national interest to "do something" about both the Tennessee Valley and Appalachia. In the valley in the 1930s, the national interest was interpreted as requiring harnessing the river system and producing large volumes of fertilizer and electric power. In the region in the 1960s, the need was defined as reducing the cost of welfare, reallocating a work force displaced by automation of the coal industry, and eliminating the embarrassing anomaly of a "depressed area" within a theoretically egalitarian political and economic system.

Like the Improvers, TVA and ARC planners employed a formal rhetoric that was liberal, humane, and progressive. Roosevelt promised that TVA would "touch and give life to all forms of human concerns"; Lilienthal saw "democracy on the march"; and Harcourt Morgan (I will come to Arthur Morgan later) spoke of "our common mooring." And indeed, Lilienthal's dominant metaphor of the "seamless web" foreshadowed later progressive concepts of systems analysis, holistic planning, and environmental ethics. While ARC's rhetoric was less elevated and its concepts less sophisticated, the agency was nevertheless projected as an enlightened and progressive boon to the region. Much of the 1964 planning document of the President's Appalachian Regional Commission could indeed have been written by James Loch two hundred years earlier.

Both TVA and ARC were initially justified not only by reference to the benefits of their development programs, however, but also through a systematic denigration of what we have lately learned to call their "target populations." The people must first be shown to be desperately in need of help and helpless, as they were in TVA's 1940s movie "The Valley of the Tennessee," produced cooperatively with the Office of War Information.

Through the manipulation of a system of images that could well engage the analytical talents of Erving Goffman, Edward T. Hall, and Claude Lévi-Strauss, TVA is projected as the savior of a barren land and a ruined and spiritless people. Arrayed in shapeless granny dresses and bib-front overalls, steel-rimmed spectacles on their noses, hillbillies peer suspiciously around corners of tumbledown houses. Postures are slack, chests sunken, hands jammed into pockets; looks are down and away; expressions range from puzzled frowns to wide-eyed stares; movements are furtively and fearfully *away from.* These are technological primitives who start like a deer at the sound of dynamite or the rumbling of a bulldozer. By contrast, TVA men are erect; their gazes are focused, analytical and direct; their movements measured, sure, and *toward*. They comprehend the system and command the technology, as their fingers knowingly trace charts, blueprints, and scale models. Their hands run bulldozers and swing crane booms against the sky, and their feet guide them nimbly along the high steel. The oppositions are clear: timidity versus courage; fear versus confidence; dead past versus open future; ignorance versus intelligence; passivity versus aggressiveness; befuddlement versus comprehension. At one level, what are presented are not an impersonal government agency and its "target population" but statements about the viability of two cultures.

Although ARC rarely attempts TVA-like excursions into poetry, the characterization of the culture of mountain people implicit in its development policies nevertheless agrees with TVA's. ARC has collected, disseminated, and thereby given new credibility to much of the romantic misinformation about mountaineers of the past hundred years. It has compared them uncritically with the mainstream and used the whole to rationalize a development policy tailored to serve vested corporate interests. Its dominant thesis about the culture of mountain people has been a sort of implied corollary of a "legacy of [economic] neglect": Whatever is there is no more than the cultural analogue of economic backwardness. In ARC's view, people in the "hinterlands" lack entrepreneurial ability, vision, and booster hustle. ARC's infrequent explicitly cultural statements embrace the old romanticism: Mountaineers are quaint cultural anachronisms, insulated by pride from the realities of modern life. It is as if ARC oscillates between two stereotypic images of Appalachian culture. One is drawn in black and white by Al Capp; the other is photographed in living color by *National Geographic*.

As analyzed by both agencies, the few positive qualities of Appalachian culture are both borrowed from the mainstream and essentially dormant in Appalachian people. The *system* has the virtues; *people* are admirable to the extent that the system's consensus virtues become immanent in them. Thus the inquisitive, scampering, tow-headed children in TVA's film are not the biological and cultural offspring of bib-front overalls and granny dresses, but clones of the "frontier spirit." ARC, on the other hand, has not even peopled its developmental sets with token tow-headed clones. The serviceable cultural traits are all located outside in the thoroughbred mainstream and must be transfused into the Appalachian bloodstream, or bred into its depleted gene pool.

It comes as no surprise, then, that the two agencies have not treated indigenous culture as a vital consideration in development policy. One important cultural dimension of ARC's strategy can be simply stated: It has written off culturally as well as economically most portions of the region outside its growth centers. People in, the "hinterlands" must exchange their culture and lifeways for growth center sewers, roads, and factory jobs. ARC does not consider it worthwhile to compute the cultural cost of the exchange, because the acquired mainstream culture is assumed to be much more desirable than whatever it replaced. To ARC, economic infrastructure is all; culture is at best a peripheral consideration, a secondary effect, a "result."

Through a policy reminiscent of Sir George MacKenzie's observation that Highlanders would "find themselves happier and more comfortable in the capacity of servants to the substantial tenantry," ARC has littered the region with vocational schools tailored to the explicit programs of the substantial corporate tenantry. It has built the Duke of Sutherland's coal haul roads and bridges. It has paid millions to politically, ethically, and culturally blinkered consultants to compile shelves of James Loch's self-justifying statistics. Low-wage, nonunion plants turning out shirts, underwear, socks, shoes, electronic subassemblies, and housetrailers have swept down ARC's "development highways" and moved through the region like a flock of Cheviots, feeding upon the lush tax breaks and free industrial sites rationalized by ARC's development rhetoric. The coal operators—those modern-day Highland lairds who discount the pious rhetoric of development because they know that its deep structures are theirs—continue to behave as they always have. In the noncoal areas, ARC-induced corporate tourism development blankets the landscape with condominiums, ski slopes and golf courses, A-frame subdivisions, and hillbilly theme parks. And ARC-designed "hospitality training programs" in the vo-tech schools groom highland boys and girls as maids and waiters for the tourist industry.

In recent decades, TVA's mode of operation at the boundary between culture and development has not differed greatly from ARC's, even though the development strategies are markedly different. One of TVA's favorite images is that of lovingly moving, before flooding a new reservoir, a fire that had burned for a hundred years on the hearth of an elderly mountain woman's cabin. TVA's sensitivity to cultural concerns since 1938 has nevertheless not gone much beyond conducting archeological salvage operations at reservoir sites. The agency's disregard for cultural values was especially evident in its handling of the Watauga Dam, Land Between the Lakes, and Tellico removals. Their recent Upper French Broad tributary area development plan was defeated·by local citizens partly because of its disregard for cultural values.

TVA's first five years, however, present a more complex story. I choose 1938 because that was the year President Roosevelt removed TVA's first chairman, Arthur Morgan, after his public feud with David Lilienthal. The Morgan-Lilienthal feud has previously been analyzed as a personality conflict, a dispute over electric power policy, and an example of political infighting within an agency.[3] And indeed it was to some degree all of those things. But it may also be understood partly as a profound disagreement over the role of cultural considerations in development policy.

For all his liberal rhetoric about seamless webs and grassroots democracy, Lilienthal was essentially a technocrat and an infrastructure developer who believed that if the valley developed a diversified industrial and commercial economy, all else would fall into place. He was moreover a cultural elitist who delighted in watching his son learn to play the cello but remarked rather cynically in his journal after naming four new dams on the Hiwassee River that TVA had "called on a few dead Indian chiefs to make up one or two of the lot. We have found that slapping Indian or historical names on dams before they are born is a good way to keep down agitation for naming them after some politician . . . and, besides, it is a nice gesture to the ghosts of the Indians." Lilienthal disparaged the explicitly social and cultural concerns of Chairman Morgan as "basket-making" and "social engineering." As chairman of TVA, Morgan wrote about the social dimensions of development policy; Lilienthal wrote mainly about electric-power policy. Lilienthal basically believed in and trusted free enterprise; he argued that, like rivers, engineers and technocrats have no politics; his democratic faith was apparently unencumbered by the complexities of class structure; he seems to have believed sincerely that in all areas whatsoever, TVA knew best.

Although Arthur Morgan was in some respects an impractical dreamer and idealist, he was also a morally aware and socially concerned engineer who insisted that human, social, and cultural values were primary rather than secondary or peripheral policy considerations. The evidence suggests that whatever operational (rather than merely rhetorical) concern for social and cultural values TVA ever had at the highest policy levels appears to have come from him, and to have gone into eclipse when he was removed as Chairman in 1938.

One historiographical result of Morgan's feud with Lilienthal is that references to Morgan are quite sparse in most of the official books on TVA.[4] It is nevertheless relatively easy to document Morgan's lonely campaign to make TVA recognize social, ethical, and cultural values in many policy areas: land acquisition, dam construction, population relocation, reforestation, agriculture, town planning, housing, education, and health care.[5]

Morgan himself uses the image of moving the elderly woman's

fire, but not to idealize TVA's sensitivity. Instead he takes it as an opportunity to comment on the human tragedy of relocation. His voice is almost the antithesis of James Loch's when he says there has been "almost no recognition of the fact that tens of thousands of cases of land sales to the government involved an important and often tragic human experience."[6] There was, Morgan insisted, a need for "radical change in the process of acquiring public land." Morgan's approach to providing decent housing for dam construction crews in the planned town of Norris combined a Thoreauvian philosophy with a labor theory of value. "In carrying out our housing program," Morgan wrote,

> I thought we might be able to determine how expensive a house would be socially justified for a competent workman. One way of arriving at an estimate was by asking "What part of a man's working life would be used in building an adequate house?" [We also] undertook to determine what part of the cost of the lumber we used represented actual human labor, and we made similar estimates of the labor cost of the equipment used in producing the lumber. We did the same for the other materials used in building the houses.

Throughout his writing, Morgan held social, cultural, and ethical values uppermost. Indeed, it might be successfully argued (as in some respects Philip Selznick has already) that both Morgan himself and his philosophy of development were purged from TVA partly because to pursue such a philosophy would have entailed costs unacceptable to the entrenched interests with whom TVA for political and ideological reasons increasingly chose to work—even before it was forced to do so by the advent of World War II and the cold war. TVA abandoned the visions and agendas of George Norris and Arthur Morgan, and threw in with James Loch and the lairds of the valley and beyond.

The Uses of Cultural Nostalgia

I return to my analogue. While the Duke of Sutherland was eager to have done with the burdensome Highlanders themselves, he and his peers took unto themselves the more picturesque trappings of a romanticized version of Highland culture. They found their models in Sir Walter Scott, who Prebble notes "took the Highlander out of his environment, disinfected him, [and] dressed him in romance."

A dramatic exemplar of the process was Alistair Ranaldson Macdonnell, heir to the Macdonnell estate in Glengarry. Macdonnell's parents removed twenty thousand Highland tenants from their estate and transported them to Canada. Alistair himself became a romantic antiquarian who dressed in tartan and went accompanied always by bard and piper. Even while continuing to evict tenants, he helped to organize the Society of True Highlanders "in support of the Dress, Language, Music and Characteristics of our illustrious and ancient race." At his death, four Highlanders with flaming torches bore his lead and wood coffin; 150 members of the Society had a funeral feast lighted by candles set in the white skulls of stags he had killed.

Instead of being viewed as mere eccentrics, Ranaldson and his like themselves became role models and style setters. Lord Brougham introduced tartan trousers to London, where they became the rage. John and Charles Stuart aped Highland dress and wrote the fraudulent *Vestiarium Scoticum*, a treatise on the tartan based on three ancient manuscripts no one ever saw. As the style caught on in London, Prebble says, the Highlands themselves became "Britain's Alps, a stage for romanticism and healthy sport." Renting out sportsmen's shooting rights on their estates gave the lairds an important new source of income. The English baronet William Ward bought the estate of Glengarry itself and resurrected the spirit of Alistair Ranaldson Macdonnell. He wore the kilt and tartan and staged Highland games for his friends, including plowing matches among the few tenants who remained between the sheep walks.

The ironies of the Highland clearances are so abundant and so instructive that I cannot resist relating a final one. When at last the ladies of the Highland lairds found their consciences aroused, it was occasioned not by the clearances but by slavery in America. Accustomed to the best in clothing, furniture, and ideas, they invited no lesser personage than Harriet Beecher Stowe herself to confer with them about this moral outrage. Miss Stowe stayed at Sutherland's Stafford House, where her son was provided with a plaid of the Sutherland tartan and she herself received a copy of James Loch's treatise on Improvement. Hearing that Miss Stowe was preparing to write something about the clearances, Donald Ross, the fiercest critic of Loch and the lairds, wrote to her bluntly:

> [You are] ill-prepared to write anything worthy of being read regarding the clearances and the cruelties to which the Highland people are subjected. . . . You are shown all the glory and grandeur of the Ducal residence. You are brought to see extensive gardens, aviaries, pleasure groves, waterfalls and all that is beautiful and attractive, and you are occasionally treated to a

drive . . . through rich farms and beautiful corn fields and to finish all you are asked to be present at an exhibition of stockings, plaids, winceys, and tartans made up by poor females from a distant part of the country. But you have not visited Strathnaver, you have not penetrated into Kildonan, . . . you have not seen the ruins of hundreds and hundreds of houses of the burnt-out tenants.

I suspect that Miss Stowe harkened not unto Donald Ross, for her account of the visit to Stafford House appeared under the romantic title *Sunny Memories,* together with her observations upon the Louvre, Alpine glaciers, and Saint Bernards. She herself judged Improvement to be "an almost sublime instance of the benevolent employment of superior wealth and power in shortening the struggles of advancing civilization, and elevating in a few years a whole community to a point of education and material prosperity, which, unassisted, they might never have obtained."[7]

I suggest finally that the institutionalized, policy-related romanticizing of culture intentionally destroyed in its originally viable form by contemporary regional developers is no less dramatic than it was among the Improvers.

I cite ARC first because its policies have been more pointed, cynical, and self-serving than TVA's—and are consequently less difficult to analyze. The essential facts as I see them are: (1) ARC has been at bottom oblivious to cultural values and the cultural implications of its own development policy. (2) The central policies and programs of ARC's infrastructure approach to development—development highways, growth centers and trickle-down, tourism promotion, the rationalizing of private entrepreneurial development, and the importation of third-rate industries—have had an adverse effect upon the serviceable cultural values of the region. (3) ARC has ultimately projected a romanticized image of Appalachian culture that is at variance with the facts of the region's cultural past and present, and has used that image as a cover for its culturally destructive development policies.

The most potent evidence is available in ARC's tourism-development programs, already examined in the foregoing case study. But three other bits of evidence are worth scrutiny: ARC's public-relations magazine, *Appalachia;* its "Appalachia Sounding" road show; and its *Appalachian Ways* cultural guidebook.

One searches *Appalachia* in vain for a serious analytical article on the complexities of the region's cultural history or its connections with ARC's own development policies. The magazine is indeed a veritable mine of ignorance, misconception, and misinformation on the subject of Appalachian culture. Its view of the culture is more compatible with that of the local-color writers of the 1870s than with that of even modestly sophisticated folklorists, anthropologists, and cultural historians of the 1970s.

A few examples must stand for many: An October 1971 article on Appalachian pottery was devoted entirely to art-pottery designer-craftsman Charles Counts, who is a fine potter but whose work has almost nothing to do with traditional pottery in the region. A September 1972 article on the Morris brothers' music festival called "Maple on the Hill," actually a nineteenth-century parlor song, a "ballad which typically celebrates the natural beauty of the West Virginia hills." The same article described clogging as a "bouncy, energetic, foot-stomping dance practiced gleefully by hill folks." Frequent articles (such as two published December 1972 and October 1973) have celebrated and promoted the writings of arch-romanticizer of Appalachian culture Jesse Stuart. An April 1974 article reported approvingly that the organizers of Morris Harvey College's Appalachian festival had brought in Richard "John Boy" Thomas and Earl Hamner from TV's "The Waltons" to expatiate upon Appalachian people and culture and had presented them with gold medallions and thousand-dollar honoraria. An article on the "mountain heritage exhibit" at Huntington Galleries (June 1975) demonstrated once again the historical irony of the West Virginia state motto, "Mountaineers are always free."

ARC presented its cultural road show, "Appalachia Sounding," as a "dramatic portrayal of the essence of the Appalachian character and experience . . . meant to represent the life of a mountain everyman."[8] The Appalachian Everymen, it turns out, were hired through a New York theatrical agency, and the show's two main themes are straight out of the most romantic and confused of the nineteenth-century local colorists: "mountain people's insistence on personal independence and their opposition to change." The show, which could have been produced by the Society of True Highlanders, pleased ARC's executive director, Harry Teter. It was, he said, a "delightful way to spend an evening being reminded of what life in the Appalachian mountains over the past two hundred years has really been."

Appalachian Ways, which so far as I know is the only extensive piece of work on the region's culture ever produced by ARC, was constructed more out of the intra-agency politics of ARC than any even moderately sophisticated analysis of the region's culture.[9] In his Foreword, Executive Director Teter virtually rewrote the ARC's history so as to rationalize its goals and policies in cultural terms.

Coedited by William Shamblin, who previously assisted in ARC's communications-satellite misadventure, *Appalachian Ways* presents sixteen pages of *National Geographic*–style color photos, twenty-six sketches of Appalachian cultural figures (chosen in pairs from each of the states in ARC's thirteen-state Appalachia, like the lucky beasts who trooped two by two on board Noah's ark), four tourist-map guides to cultural sites, and a superficial cultural essay on each of the thirteen states (trimmed by the protocol-conscious editors so that each runs precisely four pages). The closest the book comes to cultural analysis is a comfortingly romantic and circumspect 2,800-word essay by Wilma Dykeman and James Stokely. "There's a great deal 'still here' in Appalachia," they tell us:

> It is to be found in mountains not yet disturbed by stripmines, unique with scenic splendor and treasures of feather, fur, and fin; in forests like living cathedrals, pungent with the scent of balsam and woods-moss, not yet despoiled with "tourist attractions" [despite ARC's best efforts, one must observe]; streams and lakes not yet despoiled by burdens of waste but clear, cold, abundant in this land of generous rainfall. Above all, the people are "still here."

After reading *Appalachian Ways*, Harry Teter said, "you will understand why, in Appalachia, the hand that runs the computer . . . can enthrall you with a banjo tune. . . . It is a place where the past walks softly with the future."

The message reaches us across the waters, across the centuries from the Society of True Highlanders: We can have our Cheviots and our plowing matches, our clogging and our shirt factories, our strip-mines and picturesque Amish farmers. Although Teter asserts that *Appalachian Ways* is a "tribute to Appalachia, where traditional American values still flourish," a more sober analysis of the flourishing of values within both ARC's Appalachia and ARC itself would perhaps be that some do and some don't.

The situation within TVA during the Arthur Morgan years was more complicated, because TVA is a conceptually and administratively more complex agency because of philosophical and policy differences between Morgan and the other two directors, and ultimately because of tensions and contradictions within Morgan himself. Specifically, Morgan's notions of culture and culture change, though more sensitive and progressive than Lilienthal's, were flawed by elitism and romanticism. Some of the contradictions may be glimpsed in Morgan's comments on the planned town of Norris, which TVA built in the 1930s and which remains its most elaborate attempt at culturally sensitive social planning.

From his apprentice days on engineering and construction projects, when the boss told him, "All right, get you a blanket and a woman and come along," Morgan had been aware of the general lack of concern for the personal and social needs of construction crews. As head of the Morgan Engineering Company working on the Miami (Ohio) Conservancy District project and other large-scale engineering undertakings, he had tried to meet some of those needs. His efforts were an early and progressive example of internalizing some of the social costs of engineering projects. What he learned came with him to TVA.

At some levels, Norris was a successful experiment. Its overall environmental design and the design and construction of houses, the library, churches, and shops received thoughtful attention. Educational, cultural, and social programs for children, adults, and families were created. Forty years after the fact, Norris is still an impressive village.

And yet culturally Norris was a confused experiment. As an engineer Morgan was far ahead of his time, but as a cultural analyst he was very much a creature of his era. Like the early Church and secular missionaries in the mountains, like Eleanor Roosevelt at Arthurdale, he simultaneously romanticized and condescended to his subjects, respected their creative coping with marginality, despised their deviance, and urged them toward respectability. Because there had been "few cultural relationships" in mountain homes, Morgan remarked ambiguously, mountain people needed to "learn the arts of living" as they moved from "their early cabin homes . . . to their new cottage homes." Like many other romantic social reformers, Morgan wanted to teach handicraft work and strengthen the nuclear family. Because "in crafts work . . . a man and his wife could do something together," he said, he envisioned the Norris craft shop as a "family-building place as well as a product-building place."

Contributing to Morgan's euphemistic statement that "there is nothing like participation in interesting and productive activities to reduce the occurrence of undesirable types of action" were not only his legitimate distaste for the "woman and a blanket" suggestion of his youth but also his own residue of Victorian mores. "We have . . . a clean-cut lot of fellows" at Norris, Morgan said, calling up images of scores of successfully reformed Ragged Dicks and Mark the Match Boys.

I draw two tentative conclusions from this glimpse of Morgan and the Norris experiment: (1) Progressive and enlightened as he was in some areas, Morgan had serious lacks as a cultural analyst and policy-maker. (2) Whatever those lacks, Morgan's policies and experiments defined the outer boundary for TVA's essays into cultural matters. Although the past forty years have seen TVA make great strides in some areas of power-generation technology, it became a cultural paraplegic in 1938. Any doubts of this may be set aside by examining TVA's record at Watauga (the 1940s), Land Between the Lakes (1950s), Tellico (1960s), the Upper French Broad (1970s), and elsewhere.[10]

Epilogue: "Let Sheep Defend You"

With respect to the response of Appalachian people to the development process, the Highland clearances analogue needs qualification. Appalachian people were quite unlike Scottish Highlanders in that large numbers of them—voluntarily or forcibly—had entered urban and industrial environments a quarter to a half century before the advent of the first official public development programs. The region had never had the rigidly feudal social structure of the Scottish Highlands, and its people had never possessed so homogeneous a culture. Continual migratory activity, mass education, and (later) mass communications had left them at best bicultural and had rendered many of their core values indistinguishable from those of most of American society.

Because Appalachian people are and are not part of the mainstream, many of their quarrels with it have been lovers' quarrels. Their history of interaction with it reflects both principled resistance and opportunistic collaboration. They have, therefore, neither the emotional luxury nor the historical warrant to consider themselves *simply* victims of destructive public policies, although they have indeed been that on many occasions.

The lesson of the analogue and of the foregoing case studies for Appalachian people (indeed, for all who have been on the receiving end of the development process) is thus rather subtle and complex. As I see it, it is: (1) Development agendas are inevitably and by nature multilayered. Generally only the top layer is addressed in the formal rhetoric and exposed to public view. Like that of a modern supertanker, most of the bulk is below the surface. (2) The layering is created and defined by the cultural, class, and power differentials between those who prepare the agendas and those for whom they are prepared. (3) The agendas cannot be understood, resisted, or transformed without understanding the relationships among the layers. (4) Simple resistance is not sufficient. To go creatively beyond resistance requires not only the cherishing and affirmation of one's own cultural values but also an act of detachment and distancing *from* them that will free the imagination.

We will ultimately get only the kind of development allowed by our level of cultural sensitivity, sanctioned by our values, demanded by our ethics. Until the cultural identity, values, and rights of our multicultural citizenry become one of the centrally controlling parameters of development strategies, we are likely to repeat the callous hypocrisy of the lairds and the bumbling ineffectiveness of Appalachian development history.

Prebble says that at the beginning of the Crimean War, a century after Culloden, England turned again to the Scottish Highlands for recruits. Highland men came in protest to recruiting meetings, and not one soldier could be raised in Sutherland. The message from the few men remaining there was: "We have no country to fight for. You robbed us of our country and gave it to the sheep. Therefore, since you have preferred sheep to men, let sheep defend you!"

The exploitation of the Highlands during the next hundred years, Prebble notes,

> . . . was within the . . . pattern of colonial development—new economies introduced for the great wealth of the few, and the unproductive obstacle of a native population removed or reduced. In the beginning the men who imposed the change were of the same blood, tongue and family as the people. They used the advantages given them by the old society to profit from the new, but in the end they were gone with their clans.
>
> The Lowlander has inherited the hills, and the tartan is a shroud.

Our challenges in the immediate future are more likely to be political, cultural, and environmental than military. But if we continue systematically to destroy the social and cultural fabric of the United States in the service of economic development—or whatever other high-minded rhetoric—we will get our shroud nevertheless.

Notes

1. The following account is based on John Prebble, *The Highland Clearances* (London: Secker & Warburg, 1963).

2. See Harriett Bradley, *The Enclosures in England: An Economic Reconstruction* (1918; reprint, New York: AMS Press, 1968), and G. E. Mingay, *Enclosure and the Small Farmer in the Age of the Industrial Revolution* (London: Macmillan, 1968).

3. See Thomas K. McCraw, *Morgan vs. Lilienthal: The Feud Within the TVA* (Chicago: Loyola University Press, 1970).

4. In addition to Lilienthal's *TVA: Democracy on the March* (1944; reprint, Chicago: Quadrangle, 1966), see Gordon Clapp, *The TVA: An Approach to the Development of a Region* (Chicago: University of Chicago Press, 1955), and Marguerite Owen, *The Tennessee Valley Authority* (New York: Praeger, 1973).

5. See, for example, Philip Selznick, *TVA and the Grass Roots* (Berkeley: University of California Press, 1949) and the following articles by Arthur E. Morgan: "Log of the TVA," in *Survey Graphic,* January 1934 through April 1936; "The TVA Ideals and Program," *National Municipal Review,* XXIII (November 1934), 576 ff.; "The Social Methods of the TVA," *Journal of Educational Sociology,* VIII (January 1935), 262–65; "Sociology in the TVA," *American Sociological Review,* II (April 1937), 157–65; and *The Making of the TVA* (1974), from which the quotations that follow are taken.

6. W. T. Hunt's *Report of Relocation and Removal of Families from Reservoirs in the Tennessee Valley* (typescript report, TVA Library, Knoxville, Tenn., 1953) lists 14,728 families removed during TVA's first twenty years.

7. Harriet Beecher Stowe, *Sunny Memories of Foreign Lands,* 2 vols. (New York: J. C. Derby, 1854), I, 313.

8. *Appalachia,* IX (February 1976), 33.

9. Jill Durrance and William Shamblin (eds.), *Appalachian Ways: A Guide to the Historic Mountain Heart of the East* (Washington, D.C.: Appalachian Regional Commission, 1976).

10. On Land Between the Lakes, for example, see John Egerton, *The Americanization of Dixie: The Southernization of America* (New York: Harper's Magazine Press, 1974).

Selected References

Archives and Personal Papers

Campbell, John C. Papers. Southern Historical Collection. Wilson Library, University of North Carolina at Chapel Hill.

Congress for Appalachian Development. Files. Archives of Appalachia. Sherrod Library, East Tennessee State University.

Ebersole, Gordon K. Papers. Archives of Appalachia. Sherrod Library, East Tennessee State University.

Grout Family Papers. Duke University Manuscript Collection. Perkins Library, Duke University.

Taylor, Alva W. Papers. Disciples of Christ Historical Society, Nashville, Tennessee.

Newspapers and Journals

Appalachian Lookout
Asheville [N.C.] *Citizen*
Asheville [N.C.] *Times*
Baltimore Sun
Charleston [W.Va.] *Gazette*
Charleston [W.Va.] *Gazette-Mail*
Chattanooga [Tenn.] *Times*
Christian Science Monitor
Columbus [Ohio] *Citizen-Journal*
Durham [N.C.] *Morning Herald*
Knoxville [Tenn.] *News-Sentinel*
Louisville [Ky.] *Courier-Journal*
Louisville [Ky.] *Times*
Middlesboro [Ky.] *Daily News*
Mountain Eagle [Whitesburg, Ky.]
New York Times
Richmond [Va.] *Times-Dispatch*
Wall Street Journal
Washington Evening Star
Washington Post
Washington Star-News
West Virginia Hillbilly
Winston-Salem [N.C.] *Journal-Sentinel*

Interviews

Mary Ann Adams
Douglas Arnett
Richard Austin
Joe Begley
Gary Bickell
William Blizzard
James Branscome
Denis Brubaker
A. T. Brust
Robb Burlage
Harry Caudill
Michael Clark
Gene Conti
Steve Daugherty
Edith Easterling
Gordon Ebersole
Percy Elkins
J. D. Foust
Ed Fraley
Willard Gilliam
Pat Gish
Thomas Gish
Gene S. Graham
Aelred J. Gray
Malcolm Holliday
Myles Horton
Sam Howie
Loyal Jones
Paul Kaufman
Gibbs Kinderman
William Kingsbury
Sue Kobak
Charles Maggard
Alan McSurely
Flem Messer
Eric Metzner
Joseph Mulloy
Milton Ogle
Ann Pollard
Thomas Rhodenbaugh
David Walls
Alvin Webb
Don West
Sam White
Harry Wiersema, Sr.
Douglas Yarrow

Books and Articles

Adams, Frank. *Unearthing Seeds of Fire: The Idea of Highlander.* Winston-Salem, N.C.: John F. Blair, 1975.

Ansley, Fran, and Brenda Bell. "Davidson-Wilder, 1932: Strikes in the Coal Camps." *Southern Exposure* 1 (Winter 1974): 113-33.

Appalachian People's History Book. Louisville: Southern Conference Education Fund, n.d.

Appalachian Regional Commission. *The Appalachian Experiment, 1965-1970.* Washington, D.C.: Appalachian Regional Commission, 1971.

————. *Capitalizing on New Development Opportunities Along the Baltimore-Cincinnati Appalachian Development Highway.* Washington, D.C.: Appalachian Regional Commission, 1968.

————. *The Scope of Primary Care and Emergency Medical Services.* Appalachian Regional Commission, ca. April 1974. Mimeo.

————. *State and Regional Development Plans in Appalachia, 1968.* Washington, D.C.: Appalachian Regional Commission, 1969.

————. *The Status of Secondary Vocational Education in Appalachia.* Washington, D.C.: Appalachian Regional Commission, 1968.

Appalachian Volunteers. "Evaluation Report of the Appalachian Volunteers in Eastern Kentucky, June 24 to July 3, 1968." 1 August 1968. Mimeo.

Area Redevelopment Administration. *Conceptual Report on Middle Island Creek Development for Pumped-Storage Power and Large-Scale Recreation for Pleasants, Tyler, and Doddridge Counties, West Virginia.* Part I. Washington, D.C.: Area Redevelopment Administration, 1963.

————. *Opportunities for Economic Development in Doddridge County.* Washington, D.C.: Area Redevelopment Administration, 1963.

————. *Opportunities for Economic Growth in . . . Breathitt, Lee, Owsley, and Wolfe Counties.* Washington, D.C.: Area Redevelopment Administration, 1964.

————. *Recreation and Tourism Development Through Federal Programs.* Washington D.C.: Area Redevelopment Administration, 1965.

Axelrod, Jim, ed. *Growin' Up Country.* Clintwood, Va.: Council of the Southern Mountains, 1973.

Ayer, Perley F. "Along Came Jones." *Mountain Life and Work* 34 (Summer 1958): 33-35.

————. *Seeking a People Partnership.* Berea: Council of the Southern Mountains, 1969.

Barnes, John. "A Case Study of the Mingo County Economic Opportunity Commission: The Use of Title II of the Economic Opportunity Act of 1964 in a Rural County in West Virginia." Ph.D. diss., University of Pennsylvania, 1970.

Becker, Joseph M. *In Aid of the Unemployed.* Baltimore: Johns Hopkins University Press, 1965.

Beers, Howard. "The Changing Highlands." *Mountain Life and Work* 34 (Fall 1958): 5-7.

Berle, Adolph, Jr., and Gardiner C. Means. *The Modern Corporation and Private Property.* Revised edition. New York: Harcourt, Brace and World, 1968.

Berry, Ted F. "The PUD Story: History of a Phenomenal Grass Roots Movement in the State of Washington." *Grange News,* 19 December 1952.

Blaustein, Arthur I., ed. *Man Against Poverty: World War III.* New York: Random House, 1968.

Blizzard, William. "West Virginia Wonderland." *Appalachian South* 1 (Fall-Winter 1966): 9-16.

Booker, R. W. and Associates. *Comprehensive Plan and Initial Housing Element, Letcher County, Kentucky.* Lexington, Ky.: R. W. Booker and Associates, 1972.

Bradley, Harriett. *The Enclosures in England: An Economic Reconstruction.* 1918. Reprint. New York: AMS Press, 1968.

Britnell, Jim. "The Buffalo Creek Flood: A Demonstration Health Program Responds to an Emergency." *Appalachia*, July-August 1972, 1-7.

Brodsky, Alphonse F. "Building a Town for a Mountain Community." *Coal Age*, 5 April 1923, 560-63.

Brom, Thomas, and Edward Kirshner. "Buying Power: Towards a Public Utility Network." *Ramparts*, October 1974, 1-6.

Caldwell, Morris G. "The Adjustments of Mountain Families in an Urban Environment." *Social Forces* 16 (1938): 389-95.

Caldwell, Nat, and Gene S. Graham. "The Strange Romance Between John L. Lewis and Cyrus Eaton." *Harper's*, December 1961, 25-32.

Cameron, Gordon. *Regional Economic Development: The Federal Role.* Baltimore: Resources for the Future, 1970.

Campbell, John C. *The Southern Highlander and His Homeland.* 1921. Reprint. Lexington: University Press of Kentucky, 1969.

Campbell, Olive Dame. *Southern Mountain Schools Maintained by Denominational and Independent Agencies.* Revised edition. New York: Russell Sage Foundation, 1929.

Carnathan, Ralph D. "Experiment in Regional Federalism: Implementation of the Appalachian Regional Development Act of 1965 in Georgia, North Carolina, and Tennessee." Ph.D. diss., University of Tennessee, 1973.

Carrit, G. "American Students and Kentucky Gunmen." *New Statesman and Nation*, 28 May 1932, 703-4.

Carter, Luther J. "Appalachian Program: A Mechanism for a National Growth Policy?" *Science*, 3 July 1970, 32-35.

Caudill, Harry. "Appalachia: The Path from Disaster." *Nation*, 9 March 1964, 239-41.

———. "An Appalachian Switzerland." *Appalachian South* 2 (Spring-Summer 1967): 7-8.

———. "Corporate Fiefdom, Poverty and the Dole in Appalachia." *Commonweal*, 24 January 1969, 523-25.

———. *A Darkness at Dawn: Appalachian Kentucky and the Future.* Lexington: University Press of Kentucky, 1976.

———. "Education for a New Appalachia." 20 April 1967. Mimeo.

———. "Misdeal in Appalachia." *Atlantic Monthly*, June 1965, 43-47.

———. *My Land is Dying.* New York: E. P. Dutton, 1971.

———. "A New Plan for a Southern Mountain Authority." *Appalachian Review* 1 (Summer 1966): 6-11.

———. *Night Comes to the Cumberlands: A Biography of a Depressed Area.* Boston: Little, Brown, 1963.

———. "An 'Operation Bootstrap' for Eastern Kentucky." *Appalachian South* 1 (Spring-Summer 1966): 16-18.

―――. "The Permanent Poor: The Lesson of Eastern Kentucky." *Atlantic Monthly*, June 1964, 49-53.

Centaur Management Consultants. *Evaluation of Impact of Tourism/Recreation Projects for Economic Development Administration.* Washington, D.C.: Centaur Management Consultants, 1973.

―――. *Tourism Policy Study for Appalachia.* Washington, D.C.: Centaur Management Consultants, 1975.

Childs, Marquis. *Sweden: The Middle Way.* Revised edition. New Haven: Yale University Press, 1947.

Citizens' Commission to Investigate the Buffalo Creek Disaster. *Disaster on Buffalo Creek: A Citizen's Report on Criminal Negligence in a West Virginia Mining Community.* Charleston, W.Va.: Citizens' Commission to Investigate the Buffalo Creek Disaster, n.d.

Clapp, Gordon R. *The TVA: An Approach to the Development of a Region.* Chicago: University of Chicago Press, 1955.

Clevinger, Woodrow R. "Southern Appalachian Highlanders in Western Washington." *Pacific Northwest Quarterly* 33 (1942): 3-25.

Coady, Moses M. *Masters of Their Own Destiny: The Story of the Antigonish Movement of Adult Education through Economic Cooperation.* 4th edition; New York: Harper, 1939.

Coles, Robert. "A Fashionable Kind of Slander." *Atlantic Monthly*, November 1970, 53-55.

Coles, Robert, and Joseph Brenner. "American Youth in a Social Struggle (II): The Appalachian Volunteers." *American Journal of Orthopsychiatry* 38 (January 1968): 31-46.

Comptroller General of the United States. *The Effects of Federal Expenditures on the Economy of Johnson County, Kentucky.* Washington, D.C.: Government Printing Office, 1972.

―――. *Review of Selected Activities of Regional Commissions.* Washington, D.C.: Government Printing Office, 1974.

Conn, Philip. "Appalachian Volunteers (AV): An Experiment in Community Development." Thesis, The Hague, 1966.

Conner, Pick. "Cannon Builds an Industry." *Mountain Life and Work* 43 (Spring 1967): 17-19.

Cooke, Morris L. *Report of the Giant Power Survey Board to the General Assembly of the Commonwealth of Pennsylvania.* Harrisburg, Pa.: Telegraph Printing, 1925.

Council of the Southern Mountains. "Final Report from the Council of the Southern Mountains to the Ford Foundation on the Appalachian Project." 22 July 1967. Mimeo.

Cowart, Andrew J. "Antipoverty Expenditures in the American States." *Midwest Journal of Political Science* 13 (May 1969): 219-36.

Crawford, Bruce. "Piney Ridge, Virginia." *Virginia Quarterly Review* 8 (1932): 371-84.

Daniel, Walter M. *Should We Have More TVAs?* New York: H. W. Wilson, 1950.

Danielson, David A. "The First Years of the Appalachian Health Program." Appalachian Regional Commission, Washington, D.C., 1970. Mimeo.

Davidson, Donald. "Political Regionalism and Administrative Regionalism." *Annals of the American Academy of Political and Social Science* 207 (January 1940): 138-43.

Delaplaine, John W., and Edward D. Hollander. "Federal Spending for Human

Resources Helps the Growth Rate in Depressed Areas." *Growth and Change* 1.1 (January 1970): 28-33.

Derthick, Martha. *Between State and Nation: Regional Organizations in the United States.* Washington D.C.: Brookings Institution, 1974.

Disciples of Christ Historical Society. *Alva W. Taylor: A Register of His Papers in the Disciples of Christ Historical Society.* Nashville: Disciples of Christ Historical Society, 1964.

Dix, Keith. "Appalachia: Third World Pillage?" *People's Appalachia*, August-September 1970, 9-13.

Donovan, John C. *The Politics of Poverty.* New York: Pegasus, 1967.

Douglas, H. Paul. *Christian Reconstruction in the South.* Boston: Pilgrim Press, 1909.

Downing, Thomas F. "Where to Build Mining Towns and What to Build." *Proceedings* of the West Virginia Coal Mining Institute (1923): 41-51.

Dramcyzk, Elizabeth. *The History of Jenkins, Kentucky.* Jenkins, Ky.: Jenkins Area Jaycees, 1973.

Droze, Wilmon Henry. *High Dams and Slack Waters: TVA Rebuilds a River.* Baton Rouge: Louisiana State University Press, 1965.

Durrance, Jill, and William Shamblin, eds. *Appalachian Ways: A Guide to the Historic Mountain Heart of the East.* Washington, D.C.: Appalachian Regional Commission, 1976.

Duscha, James. "The Depressed Areas: Two Years After." *Progressive*, September 1963, 29-32.

Dutton, William S. *Stay On, Stranger.* New York: Farrar, Straus and Young, 1954.

East Tennessee Energy Group. *Consumer's Bill of Rights.* Knoxville: East Tennessee Energy Group, 1975.

Eastern Kentucky Regional Planning Commission. *Program 60: A Decade of Action for Progress in Eastern Kentucky.* Hazard: Eastern Kentucky Regional Planning Commission, 1960.

Ebersole, Gordon. "Appalachia: Potential . . . With a View." *Mountain Life and Work* 42 (Winter 1966): 10-12.

Egerton, John. *The Americanization of Dixie: The Southernization of America.* New York: Harper's Magazine Press, 1974.

Environmental Protection Agency. *EPA Alkali Scrubbing Test Facility: Advanced Program, First Progress Report.* Washington, D.C.: Environmental Protection Agency, 1975.

Erikson, Kai T. *Everything in Its Path.* New York: Simon and Schuster, 1976.

Fanon, Frantz. *The Wretched of the Earth.* 1963. Reprint. New York: Random House, 1968.

Fantus Corporation. *Report No. 3: . . . The Apparel Industry.* Washington, D.C.: Appalachian Regional Commission, 1966.

———. *Report No. 4: . . . Summary and Recommendations.* Washington, D.C.: Appalachian Regional Commission, 1966.

———. *Research Report No. 6: Industrial Location Research Studies: The Chlor-Alkali Industry.* Washington, D.C.: Appalachian Regional Commission, 1966.

———. *Research Report No. 11: . . . The Mobile Home and Special Purpose Vehicle Industries.* Washington, D.C.: Appalachian Regional Commission, 1966.

———. *Research Report No. 13: . . . Highway Transportation and Economic Development.* Washington, D.C.: Appalachian Regional Commission, 1966.

————. *Research Report No. 14: . . . Recreational Potential in the Appalachian Highlands: A Market Analysis*. Washington, D.C.: Appalachian Regional Commission, 1971.

Federal Power Commission. *National Power Survey: A Report by the Federal Power Commission*. Washington D.C.: Government Printing Office, 1965.

Ferman, Louis A. *Poverty in America*. Ann Arbor: University of Michigan Press, 1968.

Fetterman, John. *Stinking Creek: The Portrait of a Small Mountain Community in Appalachia*. 1967. Reprint. New York: E. P. Dutton, 1970.

Finer, Herman. *The TVA: Lessons for International Application*. New York: Da Capo Press, 1972.

Finkle, Jason L. *The President Makes a Decision: A Study of Dixon-Yates*. Ann Arbor: University of Michigan Institute of Public Administration, 1960.

Ford, Thomas W., ed. *The Southern Appalachian Region: A Survey*. Lexington: University Press of Kentucky, 1962.

Fox, Daniel. "The Unalienated Intellectuals: The Background of Community Action." *Mountain Life and Work* 42 (Spring 1966): 12-15.

Frost, William G. *For the Mountains: An Autobiography*. New York: Fleming H. Revell, 1937.

————. "Our Contemporary Ancestors in the Southern Mountains." *Atlantic Monthly*, March 1899, 311-19.

Fuller, John G. *We Almost Lost Detroit*. New York: Reader's Digest Press, 1975.

Fuller, Stephen S. "The Appalachian Experiment: Growth or Development." Ph.D. diss., Cornell University, 1969.

Furman, Lucy. *Quare Women: A Story of the Kentucky Mountains*. Boston: Atlantic Monthly Press, 1923.

Gish, Thomas. "The Homogenized, All-American Model American." *Mountain Life and Work* 49 (May 1973): 14-16.

————. "What a Town Can Do—and How." *Mountain Life and Work* 40 (Fall 1964): 25-36.

Gitlin, Todd, and Nanci Hollander. *Uptown: Poor Whites in Chicago*. New York: Harper, 1970.

Gleason, Arthur. "Company Owned Americans." *Nation*, 12 June 1920, 794-95.

Glenn, John M. "John C. Campbell and the Conference." *Mountain Life and Work* 13 (July 1937): 8-11.

Good, Paul. "Kentucky's Coal Beds of Sedition." *Nation*, 4 September 1967, 166-69.

Goodman, Robert. *After the Planners*. New York: Simon and Schuster, 1971.

Goodman, Walter. "The Senate v. Alan and Margaret McSurely." *New York Times Magazine*, 10 January 1971, 28-29.

Gordon, Margaret, ed. *Poverty in America*. San Francisco: Chandler, 1970.

Grafton, Joan. "Relief Liquidated: March 1936." *Mountain Life and Work* 13 (April 1937): 1-8.

Gray, Aelred J. "The Maturing of a Planned New Town: Norris, Tennessee." *The Tennessee Planner* 32 (1974): 1-25.

Green, Archie. *Only a Miner*. Urbana: University of Illinois Press, 1972.

Green, Edith. "Who Should Administer the War on Poverty?" *American County Government* 33.1 (January 1968): 8-10.

Greene, William M. *Rufus Woods' Magnificent Pipe Dream*. Washington, D.C.: U.S. Department of the Interior, n.d.

Grosse, Martha. *Report on the 1968 Kentucky Special Impact Program.* New York: Westinghouse Learning Corporation, 1970.

Guild, Elizabeth. "Summary Descriptive Report: Hot Springs Health Program." School of Public Health, University of North Carolina, 1974. Mimeo.

Hale, Carl W., and Joe Walters. "Appalachian Regional Development and the Distribution of Highway Benefits." *Growth and Change* 5.1 (January 1974): 3-11.

Hall, Helen. "Miners Must Eat." *Atlantic Monthly,* August 1933, 153-62.

Hansen, Niles M. *A Review of the Appalachian Regional Commission Program.* Austin: University of Texas Press, 1969.

Harrington, Michael. "The Politics of Poverty." *Dissent* 12 (Autumn 1965): 412-30.

Hicks, George L. "The War on Poverty: A Southern Appalachian Case." *Journal of the Steward Anthropological Society* 3 (Spring 1972): 155-69.

Hobday, Victor C. *Sparks at the Grass Roots: Municipal Distribution of TVA Electricity in Tennessee.* Knoxville: University of Tennessee Press, 1969.

Hoffman, Richard L. "Community Action: Innovative and Coordinative Strategies in the War on Poverty." Ph.D. diss., University of North Carolina, 1969.

Horton, Billy D. "The Appalachian Volunteers: A Case Study in Community Organization and Conflict." Master's thesis, University of Kentucky, 1971.

Horton, Myles. "Highlander Folk School." *Mountain Life and Work* 17 (Spring 1941): 15-16.

————. "Myles Horton on CAD." *Appalachian South* 2 (Spring-Summer 1967): 15.

Hubbard, Preston J. *Origins of the TVA: The Muscle Shoals Controversy, 1920-1932.* Nashville: Vanderbilt University Press, 1961.

Hume, Brit. *Death and the Mines: Rebellion and Murder in the UMW.* New York: Grossman Publishers, 1971.

Hunt, W. T. *Report of Relocation and Removal of Families from Reservoirs in the Tennessee Valley.* TVA Library, Knoxville, Tenn., 1953. Typescript.

Jackson, Bruce. "In the Valley of the Shadows: Kentucky." *Transaction* 8 (June 1971): 28-38.

Johnson, Linda, and Sue Kobak. "Government Sponsored Grassroots Organizing." 1973. Typescript.

Jones, Loyal. "1970's CSM." *Mountain Life and Work* 46 (January 1970): 7-11, 15-17.

Kafoglis, Madelyn L. "The Economics of the Community Action Program." *Tennessee Survey of Business* 3 (December 1967): 1-11.

Kane, Harnett T. *Miracle in the Mountains.* New York: Doubleday, 1956.

Kaufman, Paul. "Wistfulginia: A Fable with a Sad Ending." *Appalachian South* 2 (Spring-Summer 1967): 24-25.

Kendrick, James. "Communities Gain Stature by Progressive Programs." *Mountain Life and Work* 41 (Winter 1965): 22-23.

Keniston, Kenneth. *Young Radicals: Notes on Committed Youth.* New York: Harcourt, Brace and World, 1968.

[Kentucky] Bureau of Outdoor Recreation. *Tourism and Recreation Potential, Middle Island Creek.* Frankfort: Bureau of Outdoor Recreation, 1963.

Keun, Odette. *A Foreigner Looks at the TVA.* New York: Longmans, Green, 1937.

Kinderman, Gibbs. "Appalachian Volunteers will Expand Activities in 1965." *Mountain Life and Work* 21 (Spring 1965): 25.

King, Judson R. *The Conservation Fight: From Theodore Roosevelt to the Tennessee Valley Authority*. Washington, D.C.: Public Affairs Press, 1959.

Klare, Michael T. "The Architecture of Imperial America." *Science and Society* 33 (Summer-Fall 1969): 257-84.

Kohn, Lucille. "Pioneer Youth and the Labor Movement." *Labor Age*, November 1932, 20.

———. "Solidarity in Kanawha Valley." *Labor Age*, September 1931, 11-12.

———. "There Are Classes in the West Virginia Hills." *Labor Age*, September 1932, 11.

Langlois, Lucille. "The Cost and Prevention of Coal Workers' Pneumoconiosis." Appalachian Regional Commission, Washington, D.C., 1971. Mimeo.

Larner, Jeremy, and Irving Howe, eds. *Poverty: Views from the Left*. New York: William Morrow, 1968.

Lash, Joseph P. "Students in Kentucky." *New Republic*, 20 April 1932, 267-69.

Lens, Sidney. "Shriver's Limited War." *Commonweal*, 1 July 1966, 412-14.

Levitan, Sar. *Federal Aid to Depressed Areas: An Evaluation of the Area Redevelopment Administration*. Baltimore: Johns Hopkins University Press, 1964.

———. *The Great Society's Poor Law*. Baltimore: Johns Hopkins University Press, 1969.

Leybourne, G. G. "Urban Adjustment of Migrants from Southern Appalachia [to Cincinnati]." *Social Forces* 16 (1937): 238-46.

Lilienthal, David E. *The Journals of David E. Lilienthal*. New York: Harper and Row, 1964.

——— *TVA: Democracy on the March*. 1944. Reprint. Chicago: Quadrangle, 1966.

Litton Industries. *A Preliminary Analysis for an Economic Development Plan*. Washington, D.C.: Litton Industries, 1965.

Lovins, Amory B. "The Case Against the Breeder Reactor." *Bulletin of the Atomic Scientists*, March 1973, 29-35.

MacDonald, Lois. "Mountaineers in Mill Villages." *Mountain Life and Work* 4 (January 1929): 3-7.

Manuel, Ernest H. "The Appalachian Development Highway Program in Perspective." Appalachian Regional Commission, Washington, D.C., 1971. Mimeo.

Marris, Peter, and Martin Rein. *Dilemmas of Social Reform: Poverty and Community Action in the United States*. Chicago: Aldine Publishing, 1973.

Martin, Roscoe C., ed. *TVA: The First Twenty Years*. University, Ala., and Knoxville: University of Alabama Press and University of Tennessee Press, 1956.

Maryland Department of Economic Development. *The Appalachian Region*. Annapolis: Maryland Department of Economic Development, 1960.

Mason, Gene L. "Stripping Kentucky: The 'Subversive' Poor." *Nation*, 30 December 1968, 721-24.

Maurer, Maurer, and Calvin F. Senning. "Billy Mitchell, the Air Service and the Mingo War." *Airpower Historian* 12 (April 1965): 37-43.

McClure, James G. K., Jr. "Ten Years of the Farmer's Federation." *Mountain Life and Work* 6 (April 1931): 23-25.

McCraw, Thomas K. *Morgan vs. Lilienthal: The Feud Within the TVA*. Chicago: Loyola University Press, 1970.

———. *TVA and the Power Fight, 1933-1939*. New York: J. B. Lippincott, 1971.

McCullough, David G. "The Lonely War of a Good Angry Man." *American Heritage*, December 1969, 97-113.

McGoldrick, Joseph D. "College Students and Kentucky Miners." *American Scholar* 1 (1932): 363-65.

McSurely, Alan. "How to Create Instant Socialism: Ace Organizer Confesses." *Progressive Labor*, August 1969, 32-35.

————. "A New Political Union." 17 January 1967. Typescript.

McVey, Jack E. "Eastern Kentucky Cardiopulmonary Diagnostic Program." Report to Appalachian Regional Commission, Washington, D.C., 1973. Mimeo.

Metcalfe, Lee, and Vic Reinemer. *Overcharge*. New York: David McKay, 1967.

Miles, Emma Bell. *The Spirit of the Mountains*. 1905. Reprint. Knoxville: University of Tennessee Press, 1975.

Miller, S. M., and Pamela Roby. *The Future of Inequality*. New York: Basic Books, 1970.

Mills, C. Wright. *Power, Politics and People: The Collected Essays of C. Wright Mills.* Edited by Irving L. Horowitz. New York: Oxford University Press, 1963.

Mingay, G. E. *Enclosure and the Small Farmer in the Age of the Industrial Revolution.* London: Macmillan, 1968.

Morgan, Arthur E. "Log of the TVA." Series in *Survey Graphic*, January 1934 through April 1936.

————. *The Making of the TVA*. Buffalo: Prometheus Books, 1974.

————. "The Social Methods of the Tennessee Valley Authority." *Journal of Educational Sociology* 8 (January 1935): 262-65.

————. "Sociology in the TVA." *American Sociological Review* 2 (April 1937): 157-65.

————. "The TVA Ideals and Program." *National Municipal Review* 23 (November 1934): 576-80.

Morgan, Lucy. *Gift from the Hills*. Indianapolis: Bobbs-Merrill, 1958.

Moynihan, Daniel P. *Maximum Feasible Misunderstanding*. New York: Free Press, 1969.

————. "The Professionalization of Reform." *Public Interest* 1 (Fall 1965): 6-16.

————. "What Is 'Community Action'?" *Public Interest* 5 (Fall 1966): 3-8.

Mulloy, Joseph. "The Appalachia Story." *Bill of Rights Journal* 2 (December 1969): 31-32.

Munn, Robert F. "The Development of Strip Mining in Southern Appalachia." *Appalachian Journal* 3 (Autumn 1975): 87-93.

————. *Stripmining: An Annotated Bibliography*. Morgantown: West Virginia University Library, 1973.

Munro, John M. "Planning the Appalachian Development Highway System: Some Critical Questions." *Land Economics* 45 (May 1969): 149-61.

Nathan, Robert R., and Associates. *Research Report No. 2: Recreation as an Industry.* Washington, D.C.: Appalachian Regional Commission, 1966.

National Committee for the Defense of Political Prisoners. *Harlan Miners Speak: Report on Terrorism in the Kentucky Coal Fields*. New York: Harcourt, Brace, 1932.

Newman, Monroe. *Political Economy of Appalachia: A Case Study in Regional Integration.* Lexington, Mass.: D. C. Heath, 1972.

North Carolina Public Interest Research Group. *The Impact of Recreational Development in the North Carolina Mountains*. Durham, N.C.: North Carolina Public Interest Research Group, 1975.

Norton, Helen G. "Feudalism in West Virginia." *Nation*, 12 August 1931, 154-55.

Oberdorfer, Don. "The Proliferating Appalachias." *Reporter*, 9 September 1965, 22-27.

Office of Economic Opportunity. *A Nation Aroused: 1st Annual Report of the Office of Economic Opportunity.* Washington, D.C.: Office of Economic Opportunity, 1965.

————. *Poverty Program Information.* Washington, D.C.: Office of Economic Opportunity, 1966.

Owen, Marguerite. *The Tennessee Valley Authority.* New York: Praeger Publishers, 1973.

Parker, Edward W. "Workmen's Houses in the Anthracite Regions." *Proceedings* of the National Planning Association 5 (1916): 54-66.

Peden, Katherine G., and Associates. *An Enterprise Development Program for Appalachia.* Louisville: Katherine G. Peden and Associates, 1974.

Perry, Huey. *"They'll Cut Off Your Project": A Mingo County Chronicle.* New York: Praeger Publishers, 1972.

Peterson, Bill. *Coaltown Revisited.* Chicago: Regnery, 1972.

Piven, Frances Fox, and Richard Cloward. *Regulating the Poor: The Functions of Public Welfare.* New York: Vintage, 1971.

Pope, Liston. *Millhands and Preachers.* New Haven: Yale University Press, 1942.

Powers, Richard. "The Vocational Education Program in Appalachia from Fiscal 1966 Through Fiscal 1969: An Appraisal." Appalachian Regional Commission, Washington, D.C., 1971. Mimeo.

Prebble, John. *The Highland Clearances.* London: Secker and Warburg, 1963.

President's Appalachian Regional Commission. *Appalachia: A Report by the President's Appalachian Regional Commission, 1964.* Washington, D.C.: Government Printing Office, 1964.

Pritchett, C. Herman. *The Tennessee Valley Authority: A Study in Public Administration.* Chapel Hill: University of North Carolina Press, 1943.

Ridgeway, James. *The Last Play: The Struggle to Monopolize the World's Energy Resources.* New York: E. P. Dutton, 1973.

————. "Sedition in Kentucky." *New Republic*, 2 September 1967, 10-11.

Ross, Malcolm. *Machine Age in the Hills.* New York: Macmillan, 1933.

Rothblatt, Donald N. *Regional Planning: The Appalachian Experience.* Lexington, Mass.: D. C. Heath, 1971.

Sale, Kirkpatrick. *SDS.* New York: Random House, 1973.

Schnapper, M. B., ed. *New Frontiers of the Kennedy Administration: The Texts of the Task Force Reports Prepared for the President.* Washington, D.C.: Public Affairs Press, 1961.

Seaman, Richard Morgan. "An Analysis of Federative Patterns in Social Organization with a Field Study of the Council of Southern Mountain Workers." Ph.D. diss., Northwestern University, 1947.

Seligman, Ben B., ed. *Poverty as a Public Issue.* New York: Free Press, 1965.

Selznick, Philip. *TVA and the Grass Roots: A Study in the Sociology of Formal Organization.* Berkeley: University of California Press, 1949.

Semple, Ellen Churchill. "The Anglo-Saxons of the Kentucky Mountains: A Study in Anthropogeography." *Geographical Journal* 18 (1901): 588-623.

Shapiro, Henry D. *Appalachia on Our Mind: The Southern Mountains and Mountaineers in the American Consciousness, 1870-1920.* Chapel Hill: University of North Carolina Press, 1978.

————. "A Strange Land and a Peculiar People: The Discovery of Appalachia, 1870-1920." Ph.D. diss., Rutgers University, 1967.

Shellhammer, Kenneth. "Growth Center Strategy as Applied to Depressed Areas in Advanced Countries: The Case of Appalachia." Ph.D. diss., University of Colorado, 1972.

Sinclair, Hamish. "Hazard, Ky.: Committee for Miners." *Studies on the Left* 5 (Summer 1965): 87-107.

————. "Hazard, Ky.: Document of the Struggle." *Radical America* 2 (January-February 1968): 1-24.

Smathers, Mike. "Notes of a Native Son." *Mountain Life and Work* 49 (February 1973): 19-22.

Smith, Ellsworth M. "Cooperatives—The Hope and Unknown of the Southern Highlands." *Mountain Life and Work* 15 (July 1939): 14-19.

Solie, Richard. "Employment Effects of Retraining the Unemployed." *Industrial and Labor Relations Review* 21 (January 1968): 210-25.

Solow, Herbert. "Modern Education." *Nation*, 27 April 1932.

Stern, Gerald M. *The Buffalo Creek Disaster*. New York: Vintage, 1977.

Stowe, Harriet Beecher. *Sunny Memories of Foreign Lands*. 2 vols. New York: J. C. Derby, 1854.

Street, Paul. "Community Action in a Appalachian County: Slower but Surer?" *Welfare in Review* 8.6 (November-December 1970): 1-8.

Sundquist, James L. *Making Federalism Work*. Washington D.C.: Brookings Institution, 1969.

————. *Politics and Policy: The Eisenhower, Kennedy and Johnson Years*. Washington, D.C.: Brookings Institution, 1968.

————, ed. *On Fighting Poverty: Perspectives from Experience*. New York: Basic Books, 1969.

Sutton, Willis A., Jr. "Differential Perceptions of Impact of a Rural Anti-Poverty Campaign." *Social Science Quarterly* 50 (December 1969): 657-67.

Taylor, Alva. "Sub-marginal Standards of Living in the Southern Mountains." *Mountain Life and Work* 14 (July 1938): 12-14.

Tennessee Valley Authority. *Development of the Water Resources on the French Broad River Basin in North Carolina*. Knoxville: Tennessee Valley Authority, 1966.

Terkel, Studs. *Working*. New York: Pantheon Books, 1974.

Tippett, Tom. *When Southern Labor Stirs*. New York: Jonathan Cape and Harrison Smith, 1931.

University of Kentucky Research Foundation. *Community Action in Appalachia: An Appraisal of the War on Poverty in a Rural Setting in Southeastern Kentucky*. 3 vols. Lexington: University of Kentucky Research Foundation, 1968.

U.S. Congress. House. Committee on Banking and Currency. *Hearings Before a Subcommittee of the Committee on Banking and Currency on Bills to Establish an Effective Program to Alleviate Conditions of . . . Unemployment and Underemployment in Certain Economically Depressed Areas*. 87th Cong., 1st sess., 1961.

————. *Hearings Before a Subcommittee of the Committee on Banking and Currency . . . on S. 1163, a Bill to Amend Certain Provisions of the Area Redevelopment Act*. 88th Cong., 1st sess., 1963.

————. *Hearings Before the House Committee on Banking and Currency on H.R. 4569.* 87th Cong., 1st sess., 1961.

U.S. Congress. House. Committee on Education and Labor. *Hearings Before the Subcommittee on Economic Development of the Committee on Public Works and Transportation . . . to Extend the Appalachian Regional Development Act of 1965.* 94th Cong., 1st sess., 1975.

————. *Hearings Before the Subcommittee on the War on Poverty of the Committee on Education and Labor . . . on H.R. 10440: A Bill to Mobilize the Human and Financial Resources of the Nation to Combat Poverty in the United States.* 88th Cong., 2d sess., 1964.

U.S. Congress. Senate. Committee on Labor and Public Welfare. *Economic Opportunity Act of 1964: Report No. 1218.* 88th Cong., 2d sess., 1964.

————. *Examining the War on Poverty: Staff and Consultant Reports Prepared for the Subcommittee on Employment . . . of the Committee on Labor and Public Welfare, United States Senate.* 90th Cong., 1st sess., 1967.

————. *Hearings Before the Select Committee on Poverty of the Committee on Labor and Public Welfare . . . on S. 2642.* 88th Cong., 2d sess., 1964.

U.S. Congress. Senate. Committee on Public Works. *Hearings Before the Committee on Public Works, U.S. Senate . . . on S. 3.* 89th Cong., 1st sess., 1965.

————. *Hearings Before the Subcommittee on Economic Development of the Committee on Public Works {on} Extension of the Appalachian Regional Development Act.* 94th Cong., 1st sess., 1975.

————. *Hearings Before the Subcommittee on Economic Development of the Committee on Public Works . . . on S. 3381.* 92nd Cong., 2d sess., 1972.

U.S. Department of Agriculture. *Economic and Social Problems and Conditions of the Southern Appalachians.* Washington, D.C.: U.S. Department of Agriculture, 1935.

————. *The Relation of the Southern Appalachian Mountains to the Development of Water Power.* Forestry Circular 144. Washington D.C.: Government Printing Office, 1908.

U.S. Department of Labor. *Training for Jobs in Redevelopment Areas.* Washington, D.C.: U.S. Department of Labor, 1962.

U.S. Department of the Interior. *Interim Report: Emergency Investigations of Coal-mine Waste Embankments.* Washington, D.C.: U.S. Department of the Interior, 1972.

Vance, Rupert B. "How Much Better Will the Better World Be?" *Mountain Life and Work* 41 (Fall 1965): 25-27.

Vecsey, George. *One Sunset a Week: The Story of a Coal Miner.* New York: Saturday Review Press, 1974.

Votaw, Albert N. "The Hillbillies Invade Chicago." *Harper's*, February 1958, 64-67.

Walinsky, Adam. "Keeping the Poor in Their Place: Notes on the Importance of Being One-Up." *New Republic*, 4 July 1964, 15-18.

Walls, David S., and John B. Stephenson, eds. *Appalachia in the Sixties: Decade of Reawakening.* Lexington: University Press of Kentucky, 1972.

Warbasse, James B. *Cooperative Democracy.* New York: Harper and Row, 1942.

Waxman, Chaim I., ed. *Poverty: Power and Politics.* New York: Grosset and Dunlap, 1968.

West Virginia University Human Resources Institute. *An Evaluation of the Impact of the Community Action Program upon Poverty Conditions in McDowell County.* Morgantown: West Virginia University Human Resources Institute, 1969.

Westvaco Corporation. *1973 Annual Report: Westvaco on the Move.* New York: Westvaco Corporation, 1974.

Wharton, May Cravath. *Doctor Woman of the Cumberlands*. Pleasant Hill, Tenn.: Uplands, 1953.

Whisnant, David E. "Career and Calling: A Personal Record and Tentative Suggestion," *Soundings* 53 (Summer 1970): 111-23.

————. "A Case Study in Appalachian Development." *New South* 28 (Spring 1973): 34-43.

————. "Ethnicity and the Recovery of Regional Identity in Appalachia." *Soundings* 56 (Spring 1973): 124-38.

————. "Finding New Models for Appalachian Development," *New South* 25 (Fall 1970): 70-77. Reprinted in *Appalachia: Its People, Heritage and Problems,* ed. Frank S. Riddel (Dubuque: Kendall-Hunt, 1974).

————. "The Folk Hero and Appalachian Struggle History." *New South* 28 (Fall 1973): 30-47.

White, Joseph H. *Houses for Mining Towns*. U.S Bureau of Mines Bulletin No. 87. Washington, D.C.: Government Printing Office, 1914.

Williams, Gary. "Lincoln's Neutral Allies: The Case of the Kentucky Unionists." *South Atlantic Quarterly* 73 (Winter 1974): 70-84.

Williams, Nancy Sue. *An Early History of Mingo County*. Williamson, W.Va.: Williamson Printing, 1960.

Windmiller, Marshall. *The Peace Corps and Pax Americana*. Washington, D.C.: Public Affairs Press, 1970.

Zimmerman, H. O. "Modernization of Living Conditions in a Coal Mining Town." *Proceedings* of the Kentucky Mining Institute 1 (1940): 23-30.

Index